The Helping Relationship Sourcebook

The Helping Relationship Sourcebook

Edited by

DONALD L. AVILA
ARTHUR W. COMBS
WILLIAM W. PURKEY

University of Florida

ALLYN AND BACON, INC.   BOSTON

Contents

v

III/ *The Helping Process*

Preface

The search for personal fulfillment and satisfying relationships with others has been a never-ending quest for human beings. Its achievement in our time has become at once more possible and more precarious than ever. On the one hand, science has provided us with the means to fill our physical needs in a fashion never dreamed of previously and, in doing so, has released us to turn our energies to higher considerations. On the other hand, we find ourselves in jeopardy as the great human and social problems we have created threaten to overwhelm us. Troubled people everywhere are searching deeply within themselves for personal meaning and exploring relationships with others for solutions as never before. To aid in this search, the established professions of medicine, law, teaching, and the clergy are being asked to expand their traditional services and responsibilities. In their quest for purpose, peace, and fulfillment, men have created new helping professions expressly designed to assist persons, singly or in groups, to find more effective and satisfying ways of living with themselves and others.

Based upon the life sciences of biology, psychology, sociology, and anthropology, a whole new constellation of professions has come into being, each designed to aid in the greater fulfillment of human hopes and longing. Among those more recently developed helping professions are psychiatry, psychology, social work, and their myriad branches and practical applications. Some names of these helpers, like *counselor, psychotherapist, psychiatrist, probation officer, child psychologist, social worker,* and *psychiatric nurse* are household words. A host of other specialists, like crisis teachers, human development specialists, encounter group leaders, rehabilitation counselors, and labor-management arbitrators are less well known to the man in the street. There will be many more whose nature we cannot discern as yet because the need for helping persons becomes ever greater as population expands and society becomes more complex. It is to the potential members of these professions and to those people already engaged in helping relationships that this book is directed.

In the earliest forms of the helping professions, it was generally believed that what helped the client, student, or patient was what the helper did or said. As a consequence, helpers conceived of their tasks as "diagnosing and treating," "teaching the facts," "giving advice," or exerting some overt or covert form of direction. This might be applied gently, as in persuasion or blandishment; loudly, as in exhortation and demand; even physically, as in the use of force and punishment. With such a view the training of helpers was primarily directed toward teaching proper techniques or methods.

With further study and experience, it has become apparent that the specific acts or behavior employed by the helper are far less important to the helping process than the nature of the relationships established between helper and helpee. The processes of helping, we now understand, are much more than mechanical questions of input and output. They are complex human encounters—personal interrelationships which determine the meaning of whatever content or technique the helper attempts to employ.

The success of the helping professions is dependent upon change in personal meaning. But the dynamics of communication involve much more than what is said or done in a given setting. They are affected by many additional factors among which might be, Who said it? When? Under what conditions? With what tone of voice, attitude, stance, and personality characteristics? Techniques and information are important to the helping process, to be sure, but the relationships in which they are used are crucial. For this reason, training programs in the helping professions devote much time to the study of relationships; and the nature and dynamics of the helping encounter have become primary topics of psychological research.

Sufficient evidence has now been collected from this research to support the belief that the relationships required for most of the helping professions are highly similar. This is not surprising, since all of these professions are in actuality forms of learning and therefore depend upon a common psychology. The basic goal of the helping professions is learning new and more effective ways of perceiving the self and one's relationships with the world in which he must live. Whatever we discover about the proper conditions for bringing about this end must, therefore, have wide applicability to all of the helping professions. In this volume, the editors have attempted to collect those papers of broad relevance to all of the helping professions, which seem to shed most light upon the nature and dynamics of the helping relationship.

A second reason for creating this collection is the belief that the serious student in the helping professions should be exposed to original sources in his field. So many survey texts are now available that it is possible for a student, even at the graduate level, to obtain a degree in one of the professions without ever having had this experience. This is a pity. No matter how well an interpretation of a man's work has been done by someone else, there is something special to be gained from hearing it "from the horse's mouth." It is not always easy, however, to search out original documents and there is need to make them more readily available. The editors believe that the papers included here are among the most important and pertinent articles currently at hand for the helping professions. By publishing them in this form they hope to make them more readily available to their own students and to others in the helping professions.

The editors have recently completed a companion work, *Helping Relationships: Basic Concepts for the Helping Professions* (Allyn and Bacon, Inc., 1971). Many of the papers used in the development of the principles and practices espoused in that book are included in this one. They are presented in this form to provide the student with a useful complement—by introducing him to some of the original work upon which the above volume is based, and by affording an opportunity to delve much deeper into some of the ideas presented there.

The Helping Relationship Sourcebook is divided into four parts. Part I deals with some essential aspects of a helping relationship and identifies the groups of people to whom the book is directed. Part II focuses on some of the philosophic, theoretical, and scientific aspects of the helping relationship. Part III examines the helping process and the persons doing the helping. Part IV deals with the person being helped and his potential for growth.

This selection is not meant to be exhaustive. Too many excellent writers have written too extensively to hope for that in a single volume. Instead, this collection represents a sample of what, in the editors' opinions, are some of the best and most pertinent articles currently available. The papers chosen are primarily representative of modern humanistic orientations in psychological thought. This bias is due in part to the personal commitments of the editors who lean toward that persuasion. It is also a consequence of the fact that much of humanistic psychology is designed expressly for understanding the problems of the human condition and so speaks more often and more directly to questions of concern to the helping professions. In selecting these papers the editors sought to achieve impact and relevance rather than touch on all aspects of the helping relationship or give proper credit to all of the many fine behavioral scientists who have contributed to a better understanding of the helping professions.

The editors are indebted to Mr. and Mrs. Robert Spangler for their invaluable assistance in the preparation of the manuscript. To those authors whose work is represented here, the editors express their deepest appreciation—first, for producing their fine articles, and second, for permitting us to reproduce them.

DLA
AWC
WWP

The Helping Relationship Sourcebook

I

The Professional Helper

It is fitting that Carl Rogers' "The Characteristics of a Helping Relationship" should open this book. This paper is rapidly becoming a classic. In it Dr. Rogers first used the term "helping relationship," a term that has since spread widely among all kinds of workers engaged in helping processes. He describes the helping relationship as the crucial vehicle by which helping processes are carried out. Out of his research and lifelong experience with counseling and psychotherapy he sets forth the dynamics of helping relationships with such clarity that many other workers have been inspired to explore these important questions since the publication of this article.

Part I explores the questions, "What are the characteristics of those helping relationships which seem to make a difference," and "Who are the people charged by society with the responsibility of 'helping'?" It is tempting to answer the questions of who are the helpers and what are their characteristics either by being too general (the characteristic of the helper is sensitivity) or by being too specific (workers in the helping relationship are ministers, physicians, psychiatrists, nurses, psychologists, teachers, and counselors). Fortunately, a number of researchers and serious students have begun to turn attention to the above questions and bit by bit we are acquiring more accurate and useful descriptions of the nature and dynamics of helping processes. The two articles presented in Part I are most helpful toward that end.

Dr. Rogers discusses the nature of the relationship whereas Dr. Arkoff, author of the second paper, speaks of the kinds of professional workers who engage in helping relationships. Some of these, like the clergy and physicians, are very old professions. Others, like psychiatry,

1

social work, counseling and psychology, are much newer applications of the helping relationship. Though each of these professions is designed to deal with its special area of competence for helping, large areas of overlap in philosophy and function are clearly apparent in the varied professions described by Dr. Arkoff.

The Characteristics of a Helping Relationship

Carl R. Rogers

I have long had the strong conviction—some might say it was an obsession—that the therapeutic relationship is only a special instance of interpersonal relationships in general, and that the same lawfulness governs all such relationships. This was the theme I chose to work out for myself when I was asked to give an address to the convention of the American Personnel and Guidance Association at St. Louis, in 1958.

Evident in this paper is the dichotomy between the objective and the subjective which has been such an important part of my experience during recent years. I find it very difficult to give a paper which is either wholly objective or wholly subjective. I like to bring the two worlds into close juxtaposition, even if I cannot fully reconcile them.

My interest in psychotherapy has brought about in me an interest in every kind of helping relationship. By this term I mean a relationship in which at least one of the parties has the intent of promoting the growth, development, maturity, improved functioning, improved coping with life

Reprinted from *Personnel and Guidance Journal*, 1958, **37**, 6–16, by permission of the author and the American Personnel and Guidance Association.

of the other. The other, in this sense, may be one individual or a group. To put it in another way, a helping relationship might be defined as one in which one of the participants intends that there should come about, in one or both parties, more appreciation of, more expression of, more functional use of the latent inner resources of the individual.

Now it is obvious that such a definition covers a wide range of relationships which usually are intended to facilitate growth. It would certainly include the relationship between mother and child, father and child. It would include the relationship between the physician and his patient. The relationship between teacher and pupil would often come under this definition, though some teachers would not have the promotion of growth as their intent. It includes almost all counselor-client relationships, whether we are speaking of educational counseling, vocational counseling, or personal counseling. In this last-mentioned area it would include the wide range of relationships between the psychotherapist and the hospitalized psychotic, the therapist and the troubled or neurotic individual, and the relationship between the therapist and the increasing number of so-called "normal" individuals who enter therapy to improve their own functioning or accelerate their personal growth.

These are largely one-to-one relationships. But we should also think of the large number of individual-group interactions which are intended as helping relationships. Some administrators intend that their relationship to their staff groups shall be of the sort which promotes growth, though other administrators would not have this purpose. The interaction between the group therapy leader and his group belongs here. So does the relationship of the community consultant to a community group. Increasingly the interaction between the industrial consultant and a management group is intended as a helping relationship. Perhaps this listing will point up the fact that a great many of the relationships in which we and others are involved fall within this category of interactions in which there is the purpose of promoting development and more mature and adequate functioning.

THE QUESTION

But what are the characteristics of those relationships which *do* help, which do facilitate growth? And at the other end of the scale is it possible to discern those characteristics which make a relationship unhelpful, even though it was the sincere intent to promote growth and development? It is to these questions, particularly the first, that I would like to take you with me over some of the paths I have explored, and to tell you where I am, as of now, in my thinking on these issues.

THE ANSWERS GIVEN BY RESEARCH

It is natural to ask first of all whether there is any empirical research which would give us an objective answer to these questions. There has not been a large amount of research in this area as yet, but what there is, is stimulating and suggestive. I cannot report all of it but I would like to make a somewhat extensive sampling of the studies which have been done and state very briefly some of the findings. In so doing, oversimplification is necessary, and I am quite aware that I am not doing full justice to the researches I am mentioning, but it may give you the feeling that factual advances are being made and pique your curiosity enough to examine the studies themselves, if you have not already done so.

STUDIES OF ATTITUDES

Most of the studies throw light on the attitudes on the part of the helping person which make a relationship growth-promoting or growth-inhibiting. Let us look at some of these.

A careful study of parent-child relationships made some years ago by Baldwin [1] and others at the Fels Institute contains interesting evidence. Of the various clusters of parental attitudes toward children, the "acceptant-democratic" seemed most growth-facilitating. Children of these parents with their warm and equalitarian attitudes showed an accelerated intellectual development (an increasing I.Q.), more originality, more emotional security and control, less excitability than children from other types of homes. Though somewhat slow initially in social development, they were, by the time they reached school age, popular, friendly, nonaggressive leaders.

Where parents' attitudes are classed as "actively rejectant" the children show a slightly decelerated intellectual development, relatively poor use of the abilities they do possess, and some lack of originality. They are emotionally unstable, rebellious, aggressive, and quarrelsome. The

---

1. Baldwin, A. L., Kalhorn, J., & Breese, F. H. Patterns of parent behavior. *Psychological Monographs*, 1945, **58**, 1–75.

children of parents with other attitude syndromes tend in various respects to fall in between these extremes.

I am sure that these findings do not surprise us as related to child development. I would like to suggest that they probably apply to other relationships as well, and that the counselor or physician or administrator who is warmly emotional and expressive, respectful of the individuality of himself and of the other, and who exhibits a non-possessive caring, probably facilitates self-realization much as does a parent with these attitudes.

Let me turn to another careful study in a very different area. Whitehorn and Betz [2] investigated the degree of success achieved by young resident physicians in working with schizophrenic patients on a psychiatric ward. They chose for special study the seven who had been outstandingly helpful, and seven whose patients had shown the least degree of improvement. Each group had treated about fifty patients. The investigators examined all the available evidence to discover in what ways the A group (the successful group) differed from the B group. Several significant differences were found. The physicians in the A group tended to see the schizophrenic in terms of the personal meaning which various behaviors had to the patient, rather than seeing him as a case history or a descriptive diagnosis. They also tended to work toward goals which were oriented to the personality of the patient, rather than such goals as reducing the symptoms or curing the disease. It was found that the helpful physicians, in their day by day interaction primarily made use of active personal participation—a person-to-person relationship. They made less use of procedures which could be classed as "passive permissive." They were even less likely to use such procedures as interpretation, instruction or advice, or emphasis upon the practical care of the patient. Finally, they were much more likely than the B group to develop a relationship in which the patient felt trust and confidence in the physician.

Although the authors cautiously emphasize that these findings relate only to the treatment of schizophrenics, I am inclined to disagree. I suspect that similar facts would be found in a research study of almost any class of helping relationship.

Another interesting study focuses upon the way in which the person

2. Betz, B. J., & Whitehorn, J. C. The relationship of the therapist to the outcome of therapy in schizophrenia. *Psychiatric Research Reports #5*. Research *Techniques in Schizophrenia* (Washington, D. C., American Psychiatric Association, 1956), pp. 89–117. See also, A study of psychotherapeutic relationships between physicians and schizophrenic patients. *American Journal of Psychiatry*, 1954, **III**, 321–331.

being helped perceives the relationship. Heine [3] studied individuals who had gone for psychotherapeutic help to psychoanalytic, client-centered, and Adlerian therapists. Regardless of the type of therapy, these clients report similar changes in themselves. But it is their perception of the relationship which is of particular interest to us here. When asked what accounted for the changes which had occurred, they expressed some differing explanations, depending on the orientation of the therapist. But their agreement on the major elements they had found helpful was even more significant. They indicated that these attitudinal elements in the relationship accounted for the changes which had taken place in themselves: the trust they had felt in the therapist; being understood by the therapist; the feeling of independence they had had in making choices and decisions. The therapist procedure which they had found most helpful was that the therapist clarified and openly stated feelings which the client had been approaching hazily and hesitantly.

There was also a high degree of agreement among these clients, regardless of the orientation of their therapists, as to what elements had been unhelpful in the relationship. Such therapist attitudes as lack of interest, remoteness or distance, and an over-degree of sympathy, were perceived as unhelpful. As to procedures, they had found it unhelpful when therapists had given direct specific advice regarding decisions or had emphasized past history rather than present problems. Guiding suggestions mildly given were perceived in an intermediate range—neither clearly helpful nor unhelpful.

Fiedler, in a much quoted study,[4] found that expert therapists of differing orientations formed similar relationships with their clients. Less well known are the elements which characterized these relationships, differentiating them from the relationships formed by less expert therapists. These elements are: an ability to understand the client's meanings and feelings; a sensitivity to the client's attitudes; a warm interest without any emotional over-involvement.

A study by Quinn [5] throws light on what is involved in understanding

3. Heine, R. W. A comparison of patients' reports on psychotherapeutic experience with psychoanalytic, nondirective, and Adlerian therapists. Unpublished doctoral dissertation, University of Chicago, 1950.

4. Fiedler, F. E. Quantitative studies on the role of therapists' feelings toward their patients. In O. H. Mowrer (Ed.), *Psychotherapy: Theory and research.* New York: Ronald Press, 1953, Chap. 12.

5. Quinn, R. D. Psychotherapists' expressions as an index to the quality of early therapeutic relationships. Unpublished doctoral dissertation, University of Chicago, 1950.

the client's meanings and feelings. His study is surprising in that it shows that "understanding" of the client's meanings is essentially an attitude of *desiring* to understand. Quinn presented his judges only with recorded therapist statements taken from interviews. The raters had no knowledge of what the therapist was responding to or how the client reacted to his response. Yet it was found that the degree of understanding could be judged about as well from this material as from listening to the response in context. This seems rather conclusive evidence that it is an attitude of wanting to understand which is communicated.

As to the emotional quality of the relationship, Seeman [6] found that success in psychotherapy is closely associated with a strong and growing mutual liking and respect between client and therapist.

An interesting study by Dittes [7] indicates how delicate this relationship is. Using a physiological measure, the psychogalvanic reflex, to measure the anxious or threatened or alerted reactions of the client, Dittes correlated the deviations on this measure with judges' ratings of the degree of warm acceptance and permissiveness on the part of the therapist. It was found that whenever the therapist's attitudes changed even slightly in the direction of a lesser degree of acceptance, the number of abrupt GSR deviations significantly increased. Evidently when the relationship is experienced as less acceptant the organism organizes against threat, even at the physiological level.

Without trying fully to integrate the findings from these various studies, it can at least be noted that a few things stand out. One is the fact that it is the attitudes and feelings of the therapist, rather than his theoretical orientation, which is important. His procedures and techniques are less important than his attitudes. It is also worth noting that it is the way in which his attitudes and procedures are perceived which makes a difference to the client, and that it is this perception which is crucial.

"MANUFACTURED" RELATIONSHIPS

Let me turn to research of a very different sort, some of which you may find rather abhorrent, but which nevertheless has a bearing upon the

---

6. Seeman, J. Counselor judgments of therapeutic process and outcome. In C. R. Rogers and R. F. Dymond (Eds.), *Psychotherapy and personality change.* Chicago: University of Chicago Press, 1954, Chap. 7.

7. Dittes, J. E. Galvanic skin response as a measure of patient's reaction to therapist's permissiveness. *Journal of Abnormal and Social Psychology,* 1957, 55, 295–303.

nature of a facilitating relationship. These studies have to do with what we might think of as manufactured relationships.

Verplanck,[8] Greenspoon [9] and others have shown that operant conditioning of verbal behavior is possible in a relationship. Very briefly, if the experimenter says "Mhm," or "Good," or nods his head after certain types of words or statements, those classes of words tend to increase because of being reinforced. It has been shown that by using such procedures one can bring about increases in such diverse verbal categories as plural nouns, hostile words, statements of opinion. The person is completely unaware that he is being influenced in any way by these reinforcers. The implication is that by such selective reinforcement we could bring it about that the other person in the relationship would be using whatever kinds of words and making whatever kinds of statements we had decided to reinforce.

Following still further the principles of operant conditioning as developed by Skinner and his group, Lindsley [10] has shown that a chronic schizophrenic can be placed in a "helping relationship" with a machine. The machine, somewhat like a vending machine, can be set to reward a variety of types of behaviors. Initially it simply rewards—with candy, a cigarette, or the display of a picture—the lever-pressing behavior of the patient. But it is possible to set it so that many pulls on the lever may supply a hungry kitten—visible in a separate enclosure—with a drop of milk. In this case the satisfaction is an altruistic one. Plans are being developed to reward similar social or altruistic behavior directed toward another patient, placed in the next room. The only limit to the kind of behavior which might be rewarded lies in the degree of mechanical ingenuity of the experimenter.

Lindsley reports that in some patients there has been marked clinical improvement. Personally I cannot help but be impressed by the description of one patient who had gone from a deteriorated chronic state to being given free grounds privileges, this change being quite clearly associated with his interaction with the machine. Then the experimenter

8. Verplanck, W. S. The control of the content of conversation: Reinforcement of statements of opinion. *Journal of Abnormal and Social Psychology,* 1955, **51,** pp. 668–676.

9. Greenspoon, J. The reinforcing effect of two spoken sounds on the frequency of two responses. *American Journal of Psychology,* 1955, **68,** 409–416.

10. Lindsley, O. R. Operant conditioning methods applied to research in chronic schizophrenia. *Psychiatric Research Reports #5. Research Techniques in Schizophrenia* (Washington, D. C.: American Psychiatric Association, 1956), pp. 118–153.

decided to study experimental extinction, which, put in more personal terms, means that no matter how many thousands of times the lever was pressed, no reward of any kind was forthcoming. The patient gradually regressed, grew untidy, uncommunicative, and his grounds privilege had to be revoked. This (to me) pathetic incident would seem to indicate that even in a relationship to a machine, trustworthiness is important if the relationship is to be helpful.

Still another interesting study of a manufactured relationship is being carried on by Harlow and his associates,[11] this time with monkeys. Infant monkeys, removed from their mothers almost immediately after birth, are, in one phase of the experiment, presented with two objects. One might be termed the "hard mother," a sloping cylinder of wire netting with a nipple from which the baby may feed. The other is a "soft mother," a similar cylinder made of foam rubber and terry cloth. Even when an infant gets all his food from the "hard mother" he clearly and increasingly prefers the "soft mother." Motion pictures show that he definitely "relates" to this object, playing with it, enjoying it, finding security in clinging to it when strange objects are near, and using that security as a home base for venturing into the frightening world. Of the many interesting and challenging implications of this study, one seems reasonably clear. It is that no amount of direct food reward can take the place of certain perceived qualities which the infant appears to need and desire.

Two Recent Studies

Let me close this wide-ranging—and perhaps perplexing—sampling of research studies with an account of two very recent investigations. The first is an experiment conducted by Ends and Page.[12] Working with hardened chronic hospitalized alcoholics who had been committed to a state hospital for sixty days, they tried three different methods of group psychotherapy. The method which they believed would be most effective was therapy based on a two-factor theory of learning; a client-centered approach was expected to be second; a psychoanalytically oriented approach was expected to be least efficient. Their results showed that the

11. Harlow, H. F. The nature of love. *American Psychologist,* 1958, **13**, 673–685.

12. Ends, E. J., & Page, C. W. A study of three types of group psychotherapy with hospitalized male inebriates. *Quarterly Journal on the Study of Alcohol,* 1957, **18**, 263–277.

therapy based upon a learning theory approach was not only not helpful, but was somewhat deleterious. The outcomes were worse than those in the control group which had no therapy. The analytically oriented therapy produced some positive gain, and the client-centered group therapy was associated with the greatest amount of positive change. Follow-up data, extending over one and one-half years, confirmed the in-hospital findings, with the lasting improvement being greatest in the client-centered approach, next in the analytic, next in the control group, and least in those handled by a learning theory approach.

As I have puzzled over this study, unusual in that the approach to which the authors were committed proved *least* effective, I find a clue, I believe, in the description of the therapy based on learning theory.[13] Essentially it consisted (a) of pointing out and labeling the behaviors which had proved unsatisfying, (b) of exploring objectively with the client the reasons behind these behaviors, and (c) of establishing through re-education more effective problem-solving habits. But in all of this interaction the aim, as they formulated it, was to be impersonal. The therapist "permits as little of his own personality to intrude as is humanly possible." The "therapist stresses personal anonymity in his activities, i.e., he must studiously avoid impressing the patient with his own (therapist's) individual personality characteristics." To me this seems the most likely clue to the failure of this approach, as I try to interpret the facts in the light of the other research studies. To withhold one's self as a person and to deal with the other person as an object does not have a high probability of being helpful.

The final study I wish to report is one just being completed by Halkides.[14] She started from a theoretical formulation of mine regarding the necessary and sufficient conditions for therapeutic change.[15] She hypothesized that there would be a significant relationship between the extent of constructive personality change in the client and four counselor variables: (a) the degree of empathic understanding of the client manifested by the counselor; (b) the degree of positive affective attitude (unconditional positive regard) manifested by the counselor toward the cli-

13. Page, C. W., & Ends, E. J. A review and synthesis of the literature suggesting a psychotherapeutic technique based on two-factor learning theory. Unpublished manuscript, loaned to the writer.

14. Halkides, G. An experimental study of four conditions necessary for therapeutic change. Unpublished doctoral dissertation, University of Chicago, 1958.

15. Rogers, C. R. The necessary and sufficient conditions of psycho-therapeutic personality change. *Journal of Consulting Psychology*, 1957, **21**, 95–103.

ent; (c) the extent to which the counselor is genuine, his words matching his own internal feeling; and (d) the extent to which the counselor's response matches the client's expression in the intensity of affective expression.

To investigate these hypotheses she first selected, by multiple objective criteria, a group of ten cases which could be classed as "most successful" and a group of ten "least successful" cases. She then took an early and late recorded interview from each of these cases. On a random basis she picked nine client-counselor interaction units—a client statement and a counselor response—from each of these interviews. She thus had nine early interactions and nine later interactions from each case. This gave her several hundred units which were now placed in random order. The units from an early interview of an unsuccessful case might be followed by the units from a late interview of a successful case, etc.

Three judges, who did not know the cases of their degree of success, or the source of any given unit, now listened to this material four different times. They rated each unit on a seven point scale, first as to the degree of empathy, second as to the counselor's positive attitude toward the client, third as to the counselor's congruence or genuineness, and fourth as to the degree to which the counselor's response matched the emotional intensity of the client's expression.

I think all of us who knew of the study regarded it as a very bold venture. Could judges listening to single units of interaction possibly make any reliable rating of such subtle qualities as I have mentioned? And even if suitable reliability could be obtained, could eighteen counselor-client interchanges from each case—a minute sampling of the hundreds or thousands of such interchanges which occurred in each case—possibly bear any relationship to the therapeutic outcome? The chance seemed slim.

The findings are surprising. It proved possible to achieve high reliability between the judges, most of the inter-judge correlations being in the 0.80's or 0.90's, except on the last variable. It was found that a high degree of empathic understanding was significantly associated, at a .001 level, with the more successful cases. A high degree of unconditional positive regard was likewise associated with the more successful cases, at the .001 level. Even the rating of the counselor's genuineness or congruence—the extent to which his words matched his feelings—was associated with the successful outcome of the case, and again at the .001 level of significance. Only in the investigation of the matching intensity of affective expression were the results equivocal.

It is of interest too that high ratings of these variables were not associated more significantly with units from later interviews than with units from early interviews. This means that the counselor's attitudes were quite constant throughout the interviews. If he was highly empathic, he tended to be so from first to last. If he was lacking in genuineness, this tended to be true of both early and late interviews.

As with any study, this investigation has its limitations. It is concerned with a certain type of helping relationship, psychotherapy. It investigated only four variables thought to be significant. Perhaps there are many others. Nevertheless it represents a significant advance in the study of helping relationships. Let me try to state the findings in the simplest possible fashion. It seems to indicate that the quality of the counselor's interaction with a client can be satisfactorily judged on the basis of a very small sampling of his behavior. It also means that if the counselor is congruent or transparent, so that his words are in line with his feelings rather than the two being discrepant; if the counselor likes the client, unconditionally; and if the counselor understands the essential feelings of the client as they seem to the client—then there is a strong probability that this will be an effective helping relationship.

SOME COMMENTS

These then are some of the studies which throw at least a measure of light on the nature of the helping relationship. They have investigated different facets of the problem. They have approached it from very different theoretical contexts. They have used different methods. They are not directly comparable. Yet they seem to me to point to several statements which may be made with some assurance. It seems clear that relationships which are helpful have different characteristics from relationships which are unhelpful. These differential characteristics have to do primarily with the attitudes of the helping person on the one hand and with the perception of the relationship by the "helpee" on the other. It is equally clear that the studies thus far made do not give us any final answers as to what is a helping relationship, nor how it is to be formed.

How Can I Create a Helping Relationship?

I believe each of us working in the field of human relationships has a similar problem in knowing how to use such research knowledge. We cannot slavishly follow such findings in a mechanical way or we destroy the personal qualities which these very studies show to be valuable. It seems to me that we have to use these studies, testing them against our own experience and forming new and further personal hypotheses to use and test in our own further personal relationships.

So rather than try to tell you how you should use the findings I have presented I should like to tell you the kind of questions which these studies and my own clinical experience raise for me, and some of the tentative and changing hypotheses which guide my behavior as I enter into what I hope may be helping relationships, whether with students, staff, family, or clients. Let me list a number of these questions and considerations.

1/ Can I *be* in some way which will be perceived by the other persons as trustworthy, as dependable or consistent in some deep sense? Both research and experience indicate that this is very important, and over the years I have found what I believe are deeper and better ways of answering this question. I used to feel that if I fulfilled all the outer conditions of trustworthiness—keeping appointments, respecting the confidential nature of the interviews, etc.—and if I acted consistently the same during the interviews, then this condition would be fulfilled. But experience drove home the fact that to act consistently acceptant, for example, if in fact I was feeling annoyed or skeptical or some other non-acceptant feeling, was certain in the long run to be perceived as inconsistent or untrustworthy. I have come to recognize that being trustworthy does not demand that I be rigidly consistent but that I be dependably real. The term "congruent" is one I have used to describe the way I would like to be. By this I mean that whatever feeling or attitude I am experiencing would be matched by my awareness of that attitude. When this is true, then I am a unified or integrated person in that moment, and hence I can *be* whatever I deeply *am*. This is a reality which I find others experience as dependable.

2/ A very closely related question is this: Can I be expressive enough as a person that what I am will be communicated unambiguously? I believe that most of my failures to achieve a helping relationship can be traced to unsatisfactory answers to these two questions. When I am experiencing an attitude of annoyance toward another person but am unaware of it, then my communication contains contradictory messages. My words are giving one message, but I am also in subtle ways communicating the annoyance I feel and this confuses the other person and makes him distrustful, though he too may be unaware of what is causing the difficulty. When as a parent or a therapist or a teacher or an administrator I fail to listen to what is going on in me, fail because of my own defensiveness to sense my own feelings, then this kind of failure seems to result. It has made it seem to me that the most basic learning for anyone who hopes to establish any kind of helping relationship is that it is safe to be transparently real. If in a given relationship I am reasonably congruent, if no feelings relevant to the relationship are hidden either to me or the other person, then I can be almost sure that the relationship will be a helpful one.

One way of putting this which may seem strange to you is that if I can form a helping relationship to myself—if I can be sensitively aware of and acceptant toward my own feelings—then the likelihood is great that I can form a helping relationship toward another.

Now, acceptantly to be what I am, in this sense, and to permit this to show through to the other person, is the most difficult task I know and one I never fully achieve. But to realize that this *is* my task has been most rewarding because it has helped me to find what has gone wrong with interpersonal relationships which have become snarled and to put them on a constructive track again. It has meant that if I am to facilitate the personal growth of others in relation to me, then I must grow, and while this is often painful it is also enriching.

3/ A third question is: Can I let myself experience positive attitudes toward this other person—attitudes of warmth, caring, liking, interest, respect? It is not easy. I find in myself, and feel that I often see in others, a certain amount of fear of these feelings. We are afraid that if we let ourselves freely experience these positive feelings toward another we may be trapped by them. They may lead to demands on us or we may be disappointed in our trust, and these outcomes we fear. So as a reaction we tend to build up distance between ourselves and others—aloofness, a "professional" attitude, an impersonal relationship.

I feel quite strongly that one of the important reasons for the professionalization of every field is that it helps to keep this distance. In the clinical areas we develop elaborate diagnostic formulations, seeing the person as an object. In teaching and in administration we develop all kinds of evaluative procedures, so that again the person is perceived as an object. In these ways, I believe, we can keep ourselves from experiencing the caring which would exist if we recognized the relationship as one between two persons. It is a real achievement when we can learn, even in certain relationships or at certain times in those relationships, that it is safe to care, that it is safe to relate to the other as a person for whom we have positive feelings.

4/ Another question the importance of which I have learned in my own experience is: Can I be strong enough as a person to be separate from the other? Can I be a sturdy respecter of my own feelings, my own needs, as well as his? Can I own and, if need be, express my own feelings as something belonging to me and separate from his feelings? Am I strong enough in my own separateness that I will not be downcast by his depression, frightened by his fear, nor engulfed by his dependency? Is my inner self hardy enough to realize that I am not destroyed by his anger, taken over by his need for dependence, nor enslaved by his love, but that I exist separate from him with feelings and rights of my own? When I can freely feel this strength of being a separate person, then I find that I can let myself go much more deeply in understanding and accepting him because I am not fearful of losing myself.

5/ The next question is closely related. Am I secure enough within myself to permit him his separateness? Can I permit him to be what he is—honest or deceitful, infantile or adult, despairing or over-confident? Can I give him the freedom to be? Or do I feel that he should follow my advice, or remain somewhat dependent on me, or mold himself after me? In this connection I think of the interesting small study by Farson [16] which found that the less well adjusted and less competent counselor tends to induce conformity to himself, to have clients who model themselves after him. On the other hand, the better adjusted and more competent counselor can interact with a client through many interviews without interfering with the freedom of the client to develop a personality quite separate from that of his therapist. I should prefer to be in this latter class, whether as parent or supervisor or counselor.

6/ Another question I ask myself is: Can I let myself enter fully into the world of his feelings and personal meanings and see these as he does? Can I step into his private world so completely that I lose all desire to evaluate or judge it? Can I enter it so sensitively that I can move about in it freely, without trampling on meanings which are precious to him? Can I sense it so accurately that I can catch not only the meanings of his experience which are obvious to him, but those meanings which are only implicit, which he sees only dimly or as confusion? Can I extend this

16. Farson, R. E. Introjection in the psychotherapeutic relationship. Unpublished doctoral dissertation, University of Chicago, 1955.

understanding without limit? I think of the client who said, "Whenever I find someone who understands a *part* of me at the time, then it never fails that a point is reached where I know they're *not* understanding me again . . . What I've looked for so hard is for someone to understand."

For myself I find it easier to feel this kind of understanding, and to communicate it, to individual clients than to students in a class or staff members in a group in which I am involved. There is a strong temptation to set students "straight," or to point out to a staff member the errors in his thinking. Yet when I can permit myself to understand in these situations, it is mutually rewarding. And with clients in therapy, I am often impressed with the fact that even a minimal amount of empathic understanding—a bumbling and faulty attempt to catch the confused complexity of the client's meaning—is helpful, though there is no doubt that it is most helpful when I can see and formulate clearly the meanings in his experiencing which for him have been unclear and tangled.

7/ Still another issue is whether I can be acceptant of each facet of this other person which he presents to me. Can I receive him as he is? Can I communicate this attitude? Or can I only receive him conditionally, acceptant of some aspects of his feelings and silently or openly disapproving of other aspects? It has been my experience that when my attitude is conditional, then he cannot change or grow in those respects in which I cannot fully receive him. And when—afterward and sometimes too late—I try to discover why I have been unable to accept him in every respect, I usually discover that it is because I have been frightened or threatened in myself by some aspect of his feeling. If I am to be more helpful, then I must myself grow and accept myself in these respects.

8/ A very practical issue is raised by the question: Can I act with sufficient sensitivity in the relationship that my behavior will not be perceived as a threat? The work we are beginning to do in studying the physiological concomitants of psychotherapy confirms the research by Dittes in indicating how easily individuals are threatened at a physiological level. The psychogalvanic reflex—the measure of skin conductance—takes a sharp dip when the therapist responds with some word which is just a little stronger than the client's feeling. And to a phrase such as, "My you *do* look upset," the needle swings almost off the paper. My desire to avoid even such minor threats is not due to a hypersensitivity about my client. It is simply due to the conviction based on experience that if I can free him as completely as possible from external threat, then he can begin to experience and to deal with the internal feelings and conflicts which he finds threatening within himself.

9/ A specific aspect of the preceding question but an important one is: Can I free him from the threat of external evaluation? In almost every phase of our lives—at home, at school, at work—we find ourselves under the rewards and punishments of external judgments. "That's good"; "that's naughty." "That's worth an A"; "that's a failure." "That's good counseling"; "that's poor counseling." Such judgments are a part of our lives from infancy to old age. I believe they have a certain social usefulness to institutions and organizations such as schools and professions. Like everyone else I find myself all too often making such evaluations. But, in my experience, they do not make for personal growth and hence I do not believe that they are a part of a helping relationship. Curiously enough a positive evaluation is as threatening in the long run as a negative one, since to inform someone that he is good implies that you also have the right to tell him he is bad. So I have come to feel that the more I can keep a relationship free of judgment and evaluation, the more this will permit the other person to reach the point where he recognizes that the locus of evaluation, the center of responsibility, lies within himself. The meaning and value of his experience is in the last analysis something which is up to him, and no amount of external judgment can alter this. So I should like to work toward a relationship in which I am not, even in my own feelings, evaluating him. This I believe can set him free to be a self-responsible person.

10/ One last question: Can I meet this other individual as a person who is in process of *becoming,* or will I be bound by his past and by my past? If, in my encounter with him, I am dealing with him as an immature child, an ignorant student, a neurotic personality, or a psychopath, each of these concepts of mine limits what he can be in the relationship. Martin Buber, the existentialist philosopher of the University of Jerusalem, has a phrase, "confirming the other," which has had meaning for me. He says "Confirming means . . . accepting the whole potentiality of the other. . . . I can recognize in him, know in him, the person he has been . . . *created* to become. . . . I confirm him in myself, and then in him, in relation to this potentiality that . . . can now be developed, can evolve." [17] If I accept the other person as something

---

17. Buber, M., & Rogers, C. Transcription of dialogue held April 18, 1957, Ann Arbor, Mich. Unpublished manuscript.

fixed, already diagnosed and classified, already shaped by his past, then I am doing my part to confirm this limited hypothesis. If I accept him as a process of becoming, then I am doing what I can to confirm or make real his potentialities.

It is at this point that I see Verplanck, Lindsley, and Skinner, working in operant conditioning, coming together with Buber, the philosopher or mystic. At least they come together in principle, in an odd way. If I see a relationship as only an opportunity to reinforce certain types of words or opinions in the other, then I tend to confirm him as an object— a basically mechanical, manipulable object. And if I see this as his potentiality, he tends to act in ways which support this hypothesis. If, on the other hand, I see a relationship as an opportunity to "reinforce" *all* that he is, the person that he is with all his extent potentialities, then he tends to act in ways which support *his* hypothesis. I have then—to use Buber's term—confirmed him as a living person, capable of creative inner development. Personally I prefer this second type of hypothesis.

CONCLUSION

In the early portion of this paper I reviewed some of the contributions which research is making to our knowledge *about* relationships. Endeavoring to keep that knowledge in mind I then took up the kind of questions which arise from an inner and subjective point of view as I enter, as a person, into relationships. If I could, in myself, answer all the questions I have raised in the affirmative, then I believe that any relationships in which I was involved would be helping relationships, would involve growth. But I cannot give a positive answer to most of these questions. I can only work in the direction of the positive answer.

This has raised in my mind the strong suspicion that the optimal helping relationship is the kind of relationship created by a person who is psychologically mature. Or to put it in another way, the degree to which I can create relationships which facilitate the growth of others as separate persons is a measure of the growth I have achieved in myself. In some respects this is a disturbing thought, but it is also a promising or challenging one. It would indicate that if I am interested in creating helping relationships I have a fascinating lifetime job ahead of me, stretching and developing my potentialities in the direction of growth.

Some Workers in Improvement

Abe Arkoff

Where do people go for help? Some of us may keep our problems pretty much to ourselves. (This may be one of our problems.) Some of us turn to relatives or friends for support and assistance. Sometimes, however, our problems are such that further help is necessary.

Where do people go for *professional* help? Of the 2,460 adults interviewed in a national survey, 345 reported that they had sought such help for a personal problem. Clergymen were most frequently consulted; they were turned to in 42 percent of the cases. Doctors were second, with 29 percent of the cases, and psychiatrists and psychologists were third, with 18 percent (Gurin, Veroff, & Feld, 1960) (see Table 1).

Generally speaking, there is a serious shortage of manpower in mental health professions. More workers need to be trained. Workers who are available need to be better distributed and utilized (Albee, 1959).

Many professions play roles in the improvement of adjustment and mental health. This section will describe the professions whose activities seem most central. And it will note the increasingly important part played by volunteers.

THE MINISTER

Ministers are an important source of help for personal problems. Many people report that in times of stress they turn to prayer (McCann, 1962). It is not surprising that in times of stress they turn to their minister as well.

From the standpoint of numbers alone, ministers are an important mental health resource. It has been estimated that there are 350,000 ordained clergymen in the United States, the majority of whom serve parishes and congregations. There are more clergymen than all other mental health personnel combined, and they are found in many communities where no other personnel are available (Adler, 1965; McCann, 1962).

TABLE 1   Where do people go for help? Of the 2,460 people interviewed in a national survey, 345 had sought professional help for a personal problem. Below are the sources of help and the percentage of time each source was sought. Since some respondents gave more than one response, the total comes to more than 100 percent. *

Source of Help	Percent
Clergyman	42
Doctor	29
Psychiatrist (or psychologist): private practitioner or not ascertained whether private or institutional	12
Psychiatrist (or psychologist) in clinic, hospital, other agency; mental hospital	6
Marriage counselor; marriage clinic	3
Other private practitioners or social agencies for handling psychological problems	10
Social service agencies for handling nonpsychological problems (e.g., financial problems)	3
Lawyer	6
Other	11

* From *Americans View Their Mental Health* by G. Gurin, J. Veroff and S. Feld, Basic Books, Inc., Publishers, New York, 1960. P. 307.

In addition to their availability, there are a number of other reasons why ministers are sought out for help. The troubled parishioner may already have a close relationship with his minister, and it is easier on that account to seek assistance. In going to a minister, the troubled person has less need to identify a problem as "mental." There are no intake procedures, no waiting lists, and no charge for services (Adler, 1965; McCann, 1962).

Ministers vary considerably in the amount of pastoral counseling they do. In a survey made of a random sample of 100 Protestant clergymen, it was found that an average of two or three hours per week was spent in counseling. In this sample, 7 percent of the ministers counseled from ten to twenty-two hours per week, 33 percent from two to nine hours per week, and 60 percent counseled less than two hours per week. As a group, the ministers who counseled more had more training in psychology and counseling (Nameche, 1958).

Seven categories of problems dominated the counseling activity. Marriage and family problems and concern with psychological distress were most common. Then, in order of frequency, were problems of youth behavior, illness and aging, alcoholism, religious and spiritual questions, and occupation. Actually, religious concerns made up only a small percentage of the problems (Nameche, 1958).

In order to help ministers in their mental health functions, many theological training programs include courses in psychology and counseling. Special programs in clinical pastoral education have been offered for theological students and clergymen seeking further training. These programs range from short-term academic courses to intensive training in a clinic, hospital, or some other mental health setting.

How ministers help persons with psychological problems is succinctly set forth in the following paragraphs:

> Ministers are in a key position to intervene constructively in incipient difficulties, and many are skillful in being able to respond to a parishioner's demands, expectations and emotional turmoil in a manner that is corrective rather than disjunctive. Clergy enable many parishioners to gain relief by ventilating strong feelings, by unburdening themselves of guilt-laden thoughts and tension-producing conflicts, and by revealing socially unacceptable actions. The minister's acceptance and support is meaningful especially since he represents the authority of God and the church. He is often the one who can be most supportive as he brings the individual in need closer to the strengths inherent in religious practices, such as prayer, sacraments, etc.
>
> The clergyman may be an accepting listener. He may also take an active part in redirecting the parishioner's attention to pertinent issues, such as clarifying thoughts and feelings and supporting constructive steps in problem-solving. Providing emotional support, clarifying the difference between the reality of a situation and the counselee's special perception of that reality, and referral for more specialized treatment are all approaches that ministers may take in endeavoring to help parishioners to resume healthy functioning (Adler, 1965; pp. 66–67).

THE PHYSICIAN

As in the case of ministers, one reason that people turn to their physician for help with personal problems is that a relationship already exists. Furthermore, in time of stress, a person may not know for sure whether his problem is physical or otherwise, and it seems logical to consult a medical doctor. Moreover, seeing him is less formidable and threatening than going to a psychiatrist, psychologist, or some other specialist.

The family doctor can play a vital role in the prevention and alleviation of maladjustment and mental illness. He frequently is in contact with the family during its trying periods, as for example, following the birth of a mentally defective child, during a serious illness, and in time of death. Beyond his medical skill itself, the doctor's counsel and support can bolster the family's ability to bear up in its critical moments (Caplan, 1961).

A knowledge of psychology and psychiatry is essential for all physicians (Lief & Lief, 1963; Rosenbaum, 1963). In recent decades, there has been an increasing amount of psychiatric instruction in medical schools (Levine & Lederer, 1959). There is also an increasing number of postgraduate courses to keep general practitioners and other doctors abreast of latest developments in psychiatry and mental health.

Some physicians are well convinced of the value of psychiatric techniques. They make use of these techniques within the limit of their competence, and they make referral to other mental health personnel. Other physicians, however, are neither comfortable with nor convinced of the value of such approaches. They may minimize, ignore, or even ridicule psychological factors (Lief & Lief, 1963).

Early help or early referral by a physician may be the crucial factor in preventing the later hospitalization of a patient. As programs in community mental health grow, the physician will have an even more vital role to play. He will be increasingly called upon to participate in patient aftercare and other mental health programs (Lief & Lief, 1963).

Here is an example of the treatment of a troubled person by a physician. With the consultation of a psychiatrist, the medical resident who was not psychiatrically trained himself was able to be of help. The patient was a married woman, twenty-three years old, who entered the hospital with severe headaches, persistent hypertension (high blood pressure), and attacks of abdominal pain. She was a very dependent person, and, unable to accept the role of wife and mother, she and her children lived with her parents.

> The current illness had started when her younger brother had returned from the Army and she had been forced to move from her mother's house into her own apartment to make room for him at her parents' home. From this situation, which was a repetition of the original traumatic experience (the birth of her younger brother), she developed intense hostility toward

her mother and her siblings who were still living at home. These unexpressed feelings appeared to be associated with the severe attacks of headache and abdominal pain for which she was hospitalized.

After formulation of the psychodynamics in a conference with the psychiatric consultant, a therapeutic plan was proposed which was directed at meeting her frustrated dependency needs. This included occasional contacts with the psychiatric consultant, offers of material giving when indicated, and continued contacts with the medical resident. However, her presenting symptoms in combination with hypertension and severe spasm of the retinal arterioles aroused considerable anxiety in the medical resident who was following the case. The physician's anxiety was manifested by repetitive physical and laboratory examinations and frequent consultations. This affected the patient in two ways: first, it gave the symptoms attention-getting value, and second, it augmented the patient's anxiety, with a resulting increase in symptoms.

The psychiatric consultant continually reassured the medical resident that the patient was being handled properly, and, after a few months, the resident became more secure in dealing with her because he recognized that the symptoms were not evidence of malignant hypertension but that they recurred in direct relation to emotional and environmental problems. As a result of this knowledge, each time the patient suffered an exacerbation of symptoms the physician immediately inquired into her current life situation, with special emphasis on immediate difficulties with her husband, children, siblings, or mother. The patient was allowed to talk freely about such problems, and temporal relationships to the development of symptoms were discussed. This discussion, plus a rapid physical check-up, served to relieve both the patient's and physician's anxiety. With such therapy there was a remarkable diminution in both the frequency and severity of the "attacks." Although the blood pressure was unchanged, the patient became symptom-free and matured considerably, functioning more adequately as a mother and wife. When there was trouble she and her doctor had little difficulty in quickly discovering the precipitating factors (Rosenbaum, 1963, pp. 508–509).

THE PSYCHIATRIST

Physicians who specialize in the diagnosis and treatment of mental illness and adjustment problems are called *psychiatrists*. Some psychiatrists —a relatively small number compared with psychologists—are engaged in research. It has been estimated that there are about thirteen thousand physicians who devote themselves to the full-time practice of psychiatry (Blain, 1959).

In order to become a psychiatrist, a person must first complete a premedical and medical program, obtain the M.D. degree (doctor of medicine), and serve a medical internship. Then, generally speaking, he takes a psychiatric residency in which he receives additional course work and supervised experience, possibly in a variety of inpatient and outpatient settings.

Since the psychiatrist is first of all a physician, he is trained in the medical treatment of disease. He is qualified to employ such somatotherapies as shock treatment and drugs, and he is able to prescribe programs of hospitalization for his patients. Psychiatrists are also trained in psychotherapy.

In a recent study of psychiatrists in a Midwestern metropolitan community, it was found that the predominant pattern of treatment involved the use of drugs and shock treatment along with brief psychotherapy which was characterized by direct suggestions and persuasion. Their practice was primarily private and involved adult patients whose problems were of intermediate severity. Physical examinations or neurological examinations were not ordinarily performed (Malmquist, 1964).

Psychiatrists are found in a variety of settings. Many are in private practice. Many are on the staffs of clinics, hospitals, and other mental health facilities. Some psychiatrists serve as consultants to various mental health agencies, such as the juvenile court and family services. Commonly, a psychiatrist combines a number of different activities in his professional practice.

Psychiatric treatment takes so many forms and occurs in so many different settings that it would be impossible for any one case history to be considered representative. The following case, treated by a psychiatrist, involved a serious problem and was treated with both electroshock and psychotherapy:

This forty-nine-year-old married woman was referred to the psychiatrist by her own local physician. He had attempted for several weeks to deal with her complaints but had found that his therapy was not producing any improvement. The patient complained of a general loss of interest in her family and her friends. She said that she was becoming increasingly irritable and frequently suffered from crying spells. In addition to this she had a number of vague physical complaints for which no organic basis had been found by her local physician. She often suffered from headaches, constipation, and a general feeling of lassitude and weakness.

Upon questioning it developed that the patient's inability to sleep was a particularly bothersome symptom, and that much of her depression occurred during the early morning hours after a sleepless night. She had, on many occasions, entertained thoughts of suicide but had, at least at the time she was referred, not acted upon any of them. She felt that she was of no further use to her husband or to her two grown children, who had married and moved away. She was concerned about her general physical condition and also about her attractiveness, feeling that both were below par. She was no longer interested in pursuing the many social duties and obligations which she had in the past indulged in. She had resigned from most of the organizations to which she had previously belonged. She found herself no longer interested in her husband nor in his work. She could not even talk to him for any length of time without becoming irritable and critical of him. She was bitter about the fact that her married children visited her with decreasing frequency and yet, when pressed, made it evident that she treated them in an uncordial manner whenever they did come to see her.

This patient's past history revealed that she had always been a rigid person with perfectionistic, meticulous standards. She had led a life which appeared on the surface to have been full, yet which contained no deep emotional values. She had had many friends, but none of them had been close or warm to her. She had always been an ambitious person striving for higher goals many of which she now felt she had never attained. She had spent a great deal of time and interest in her home and yet had chronically been displeased with the results. Although she initially attempted to paint her earlier life as having been satisfactory, happy, and contented, it soon became evident that she had never achieved any measure of pleasurable living. She had been a chronically worrisome person concerned about everything in the life of her husband, her children, and herself. She watched over her family and had carried this tendency to the point of domination.

When this woman found herself in the menopause and realized that she was beginning to grow older, she became increasingly bitter about not having attained many of her goals. She resented the fact that her children no longer paid her the attention which they had previously done. She resented the fact that her husband no longer found her as important as she thought he should. She began complaining of her physical symptoms, initially, and then made increased demands upon her husband and her children. She bitterly resented the fact that they did not respond as she wished to these excessive demands. As the situation continued she became increasingly depressed.

Three interviews, using a psychotherapeutic technique, did not result in any improvement and it was impossible to establish a useful relationship with this patient. Therefore, electroshock was recommended and the patient received a total of eight treatments. After approximately five she began to improve and by the end of eight her improvement had reached a more healthy pattern so that she was able to continue her psychotherapeutic interviews. Attempts were then made to help her re-establish her social activities and her interest in her children and grandchildren. She was also helped to understand how her previous life had been constricted, rigid, and lacking in joy. She was encouraged to make a more flexible adjustment and to appreciate the meaning and value of family and of friends. She gradually began to accept herself more thoroughly and to seek the companionship of others. She was seen in fifteen interviews over a period of several months. Her improvement was marked after electroshock and remained stabilized. After a follow-up of approximately four years, she suffered no relapse, as might well have occurred if she had not had the electroshock or had she had this treatment alone without any follow-up psychotherapy.[1]

THE PSYCHOANALYST

Physicians who are trained to treat adjustment problems through the use of psychoanalytic methods are called *psychoanalysts*. Individuals planning to be psychoanalysts ordinarily must complete their medical program, including a year of internship and a year of psychiatric training before beginning their specialized training. (There are a few psychoanalysts who do not have medical degrees, and these are referred to as *lay* analysts in distinction to the majority who are identified as *medical* analysts.)

After completing his medical and psychiatric training, the prospective psychoanalyst must himself be psychoanalyzed. When this process is successfully accomplished, he is assigned several cases to psychoanalyze under close supervision. During this time he will also be taking various courses at a psychoanalytic institute. With the completion of his own analysis, his supervised analyses of others, and his course work, he becomes a fully qualified psychoanalyst. There are only about one thousand psychoanalysts in the United States.

In its classical form, psychoanalysis is an intensive, extensive, and expensive process. The patient may meet with his analyst an hour each day four or five days a week for perhaps a year or more. Analyses have gone on for three or four years or even longer periods. There are, however, some newer and briefer forms of psychoanalysis.

Today many psychotherapists make use of psychoanalytic concepts and techniques. Therefore, the therapeutic differences between a psychoanalyst (especially one using a modified approach) and a psychiatrist or psychologist (especially one who is psychoanalytically oriented) is not so great.

Psychoanalysis is not an easy process to describe. Most of us have some conception or misconception of psychoanalysis from seeing it por-

---

1. Reprinted by permission from English, O. Spurgeon, & Finch, Stuart M. *Introduction to psychiatry.* New York: W. W. Norton, 1957, pp. 406–408.

trayed or caricatured in motion pictures, television, novels, plays, cartoons, and dozens of jokes. Many people have the mistaken notion that to go to any psychiatrist or psychologist is to be psychoanalyzed.

The key method of psychoanalysis is free association. Other important aspects are resistance and interpretation, transference and countertransference, and abreaction, insight, and working through. Each of these is discussed in this description of psychoanalytic process:

Let me describe what psychoanalysis is actually like. The analyst usually begins by getting something of the personal biography of the patient, after the manner of a social worker's case history. The patient sits up and talks as he would to any physician. The analyst may have better interviewing methods, but there is little that is distinctive about the early sessions. There may be several sessions before the patient takes to the couch, before the typical free association method is used. Then the patient is taught to follow, as well as he is able, *the basic rule:* to say everything that enters his mind, without selection. This is much harder than it sounds, even for patients who are eager to co-operate with the analyst. As Fenichel puts it, "Even the patient who tries to adhere to the basic rule fails to tell many things because he considers them too unimportant, too stupid, too indiscreet, and so on. There are many who never learn to apply the basic rule because their fear of losing control is too great, and before they can give expression to anything they must examine it to see exactly what it is." . . . In fact, the whole lifetime has been spent learning to be tactful, to achieve self-control, to avoid outbursts of emotion, to do what is proper rather than what is impulsive. This all has to be unlearned for successful free association.

What free association aims at is the bringing to awareness of impulses and thoughts of which the person is not aware. Because these impulses are active, but out of awareness, they are called unconscious. It is necessary to break through resistances in order to bring them to awareness. The role of the psychoanalyst is, essentially, to help the patient break down these resistances, so that he may face his disguised motives and hidden thoughts frankly, and then come to grips in realistic manner with whatever problems or conflicts are then brought into view.

The activity of the analyst is directed skillfully at this task of helping the patient eliminate resistances. He does this in part by pointing out to the patient the consequences of his resistances: the times of silence when his mind seems to go blank, forgetting what he intended to say, perhaps forgetting to show up at an appointment, drifting into superficial associations, or giving glib interpretations of his own. The analyst not only calls attention to signs of resistance, but he also interprets the patient's associations in such a way as to facilitate further associations.

Fenichel defines interpretation as "helping something unconscious to become conscious by naming it at the moment it is striving to break through." . . . If this is accepted, then the first interpretations are necessarily fairly "shallow" ones, the "deeper" interpretations waiting until the patient is ready for them.

The deeper interpretations are the ones we often think of in characterizing psychoanalysis, but very much of the time in an actual psychoanalysis is spent in rather matter-of-fact discussion of attitudes toward other people and toward oneself as they show themselves in daily life, without recourse to universal symbols, references to libidinal stages, and so on. Not all psychoanalysts agree on just how interpretations should be made, or when they should be made, and it is my guess that those who think they do agree may actually behave quite differently when conducting analyses of their patients. This is one reason why it is difficult to study psychoanalytic therapy, and a reason, also, why there are so many schisms within psychoanalytic societies.

Another aspect of the psychoanalytic therapy goes by the name of "transference." Transference refers to the tendency for the patient to make of the analyst an object of his motivational or emotional attachments. It is too simple to say that the patient falls in love with the analyst. Sometimes he makes of the analyst a loved parent, sometimes a hated parent; sometimes the analyst substitutes for a brother or sister, or for the boss at the office. The patient unconsciously assigns roles to the analyst of the important people in the patient's own life. Part of the task of the analyst is to handle the transference. The word "handle" is easily spoken, but this handling of the transference is said to be the most difficult part of the analyst's art.

The psychoanalytic interview is a social one, an interpersonal one, with two people involved. The analyst is a person, too, and he reacts to the adoration and abuse of the patient he is analyzing. He is a good analyst to the extent that he understands himself well enough so that he preserves his role in the analytic situation, and does not himself become involved, as his patient is, in what is called counter-transference, that is, using the patient as an outlet for his own emotions. If the patient's exploits become the occasion for the analyst's fantasy life, then the analyst gets preoccupied with his own free associations and cannot listen attentively to his patient. The discipline of learning to listen, and only to listen, is considered by Frieda Fromm-Reichman . . . to be the essence of the analyst's problem. . . .

Very often there is within the midst of psychoanalysis a state in which the patient is more disturbed than he was before entering treatment. Those unfriendly to psychoanalysis occasionally use this as an indication of its therapeutic ineffectiveness. . . . Two comments can be made here. First, what appears to others to be disturbance may not be "neurotic" at all. Some individuals are excessively kind to other people, at great cost to themselves. If they suddenly express their feelings more openly, they may become less pleasant to live with or to work with, because they can no longer be exploited. The troublesome child may be a healthier child than the child who is too "good." If a person changes, new social adjustments are required, and some that were in equilibrium now get out of focus. This is the first observation regarding apparent disturbance in the midst of analysis. The second comment is that the disturbance in the midst of analysis may be a genuinely neurotic one, an aggravation of the typical transference. That is, the substitution of the analyst for other figures emotionally important to the patient may produce an emotional crisis, in which the patient actually acts more irrationally than before treatment. If this crisis is well handled, the patient emerges the better for it. Although some analysts believe that such crises are inevitable in an analysis, other analysts attempt to ward them off by such devices as less frequent therapeutic sessions when transference problems become too hard to handle. . . . In any case, the fact that an aggravated transference neurosis may occur does not invalidate the therapeutic usefulness of psychoanalytic technique.

Three words often crop up in discussion of what is taking place as the patient improves. These are "abreaction," "insight," and "working through." "Abreaction" refers to a living again of an earlier emotion, in a kind of emotional catharsis—literally getting some of the dammed-up emotion out of the system. The therapeutic need is that described by the poet:

> Home they brought her warrior dead.
> She nor wept nor uttered cry.
> All her maidens watching said:
> "She must weep or she will die."
>
> —TENNYSON, *The Princess*

"Insight" refers to seeing clearly what motives are at work, what the nature of the problem is, so that instinctual conflicts, as psychoanalysts call them, are recognized for what they are. Insight is not limited to the recovery of dramatic incidents in early childhood that were later repressed. Sometimes such insights do occur, and sometimes they are associated with relief of symptoms. But neither a single flood of emotion in abreaction nor a single occasion of surprised insight relieves the patient of his symptoms. He requires, instead, the process of "working through," that is, facing again and again the same old conflicts and finding himself reacting in the same old ways to them, until eventually the slow processes of reeducation manifest themselves and he reacts more nearly in accordance with the objective demands of the situation and less in accordance with distortions that his private needs create.

It is chiefly because the process of working through takes so long that psychoanalysis takes so long. The psychoanalyst often has the basic insights into the patient's problems quite early in treatment, but the patient is unready for them and could not understand the analyst if he were to insist upon confronting him with these interpretations. I have sometimes likened an analysis to the process of learning to play the piano. It is not enough to know what a good performance is and to wish to give one. The process has to be learned. The learner may know all about musical notation and may have manual skill and musical appreciation. But there is no short cut. Even with a good teacher the lessons must continue week after week before the player can achieve the kind of spontaneous performance he wishes to achieve. We do not begrudge this time, because we believe that the end is worth it. What the analyst is attempting to do is far more complex than what the piano teacher is attempting to do. The skilled management of a life is more difficult than the skilled management of a keyboard.[2]

THE NURSE

Many workers serve as nurses in medical and psychiatric facilities. The largest percentage of these workers do not have full professional status but nevertheless perform a vital function in providing care, companionship, and social activity. These workers include the practical nurse, the ward attendant, and the psychiatric technician.

To have full status as a nurse, a person usually completes a three-year program at a training hospital (after which she is awarded a diploma) or a four-year or five-year college program (after which she is awarded a bachelor of science degree). Then she takes a state board examination and is registered to practice.

Every nurse receives some psychiatric training, but some complete an advanced program of education and training and are called *psychiatric nurses*. Such nurses work in hospitals and in a variety of outpatient services. The role and function of the psychiatric nurse varies widely from setting to setting.

Some of the work roles filled by the psychiatric nurse include mother figure, manager, teacher, socializing agent, and counselor or psychotherapeutic agent (Peplau, 1959). As a mother, the nurse may care for the patient's physical needs—bathing, dressing, and feeding him—or for his psychological needs—providing protection, support, discipline, and guidance. As a manager, the nurse arranges the patient's physical and social environment to facilitate improvement. As a teacher, the nurse orients the patient to the programs of the facility and provides him with information about health and hygiene. As a socializing agent, the nurse helps the patient develop and perfect social skills and the ability to relate to others. As a therapist, the nurse may provide service similar to that of a psychiatrist, or her work may be complimentary or supplementary to that of a psychiatrist (Miller & Sabshin, 1963).

2. From Hilgard, E. R. Experimental approaches to psychoanalysis. In E. Pumpian-Mindlin (Ed.), *Psychoanalysis as science.* New York: Basic Books, pp. 25–29. Copyright © 1952 by California Institute of Technology, Basic Books, Inc., Publishers, New York.

THE OCCUPATIONAL THERAPIST

An *occupational therapist* is a person who is trained to help people recover from illness through constructive activity—through being "occupied" in meaningful ways. Occupational therapy has been called "curing by doing." Through involvement in various creative, educational, physical, and recreational activities, the person is able to regain strength and skill as well as confidence and a sense of worth.

Occupational therapists work with people of all ages and with various kinds of illnesses and handicaps. For example, these therapists work with retarded and cerebral palsied children and help them learn to help themselves. Such therapists also work with adults who have been disabled by polio, stroke, or injury and help them recover or learn to live with their handicap.

Occupational therapists work in many different settings including general and mental hospitals, mental health clinics and centers, schools and workshops for handicapped or disabled children and adults, correctional institutions, homes for the aged, and so on. To become qualified as a worker in this area, a person first completes a four-year undergraduate program leading to the bachelor of science degree. Then, in order to qualify for professional registration, he must complete a clinical internship of nine or ten months.

All the occupational therapist's work is bound up with mental health since it involves helping people adjust to themselves and their environment. In addition to this, the occupational therapist plays a central role in the rehabilitation of the mentally ill.

Here are several brief illustrations of occupational therapy. For each of these hospitalized patients, the activity which was utilized allowed a meaningful contact with the therapist and a meaningful approach to improvement.

Karen, an 18-year-old girl, had been hospitalized for five years. She was a mute, autistic girl who spent most of her time sitting on the floor in the corner of the dayroom picking at her skin and twisting her hair. She was inaccessible to interview psychotherapy, and medication did not appreciably change her behavior.

The occupational therapist then began to make contact with this girl through food. Over a period of several weeks, she was given candy, chewing gum, soda, and milk. As she began to respond to this feeding, Karen was able to leave the ward with the occupational therapist and help to cook simple food for them to eat together. Ultimately the patient was able to talk during these experiences and later began to speak to her doctor when he would give her food and also in the dining room while she was eating. As the eating and cooking experiences continued in occupational therapy Karen began to assume more responsibility for both the planning and the cooking and was able to reach out to patients and staff by making candy and cookies for the ward. She was able to work with her psychotherapist and assisted in the hospital diet kitchen until her discharge.

Mrs. T. S., a 32-year-old woman, had been admitted to the hospital because of increased anger, which she could no longer control, hyperactivity, and suspiciousness. She had become completely overwhelmed by the demands of her two small children and was no longer able to care for them. Psychiatric interviews indicated that this patient had very strong dependency needs which were anxiety-provoking for her and which she denied to the extent that she was unable to form any really close relationship and ultimately became unable to give, even to her children. She was an aloof, critical, controlling, and hostile woman.

In occupational therapy it was suggested that she make a piece of jewelry for herself. Since the occupational therapist was unfamiliar with the particular craft process, it was arranged for them to work together from a book of instructions. Mrs. S. would read the directions aloud to the therapist, and they worked in this manner until the project was completed.

Emphasis on the activity and learning process made it possible for this patient to work with another person with much less feeling of threat, and the use of the book of instructions provided a sense of both safe distance and control, which was necessary at this time. The success of their shared experience made it possible for the patient to feel more secure in this relationship and to begin to accept a more dependent relationship.[3]

THE PSYCHOLOGIST

Psychologists of varying descriptions work in the field of mental health. There are, to cite some of the most common designations, school psychologists, consulting psychologists, counseling psychologists, and clinical psychologists. Regardless of their different designations and the somewhat different settings in which they may be found, there is considerable overlap both in their training and in the techniques they employ to evaluate and help the persons with whom they deal.

The clinical psychologist occupies a very central position in the men-

3. Reprinted by permission from Fidler, G. S., & Fidler, J. W. *Occupational therapy*. New York: Macmillan, 1963, pp. 88 and 90. Copyright © 1963, The Macmillan Company.

tal health field. He is a psychologist who has received special training in the assessment and correction of adjustment problems. He is also specially trained in doing research in this area of psychology.

Most clinical psychologists have the Ph.D. degree (doctor of philosophy). In order to become a clinical psychologist, a person usually majors in psychology or some related science as an undergraduate. He then enters into three or more years of graduate study in psychology. He is also generally required to complete a one-year internship in a clinic or hospital, and some psychologists take further postdoctoral training.

Unlike most other persons in mental health fields, clinical psychologists receive considerable training in psychological testing, and they are frequently called to assist in diagnosis and evaluation. Clinical psychologists are trained in psychotherapy; however, they are not medical doctors and do not perform somatotherapies. Clinical psychologists also receive intensive training in research, and much of the exploration in the field of mental health is carried on by them or with their assistance.

Like psychiatrists, with whom their work has considerable overlap, clinical psychologists are found in a number of different settings. Many work in clinics and hospitals. Many others work in colleges and universities where they may teach, counsel students, and do research. Psychologists are frequently members of the staffs of correctional and educational agencies. Many psychologists are in private practice, but ordinarily this is in addition to other assignments.

In the material which follows, two psychologists tell of their professional careers:

A Psychologist in a Child Guidance Clinic

One of the easiest things in the world is to look back and "misperceive" one's own motives. That is precisely what most persons probably do when asked how they "got into" the occupational field in which they find themselves in adult life. Nevertheless, I shall try.

Since I came from a minority group background with a feeling for the oppressed and from a childhood which constantly emphasized in discussion and practice the importance of people, it would not be unexpected that my interest should turn to medicine. But, fortunately or unfortunately, I was destined for bitter disillusionment when as a premed junior in college I was called into the office of one of my science professors to be told that in his opinion, and in spite of the fact that I had "satisfactory" grades, I was not the "type" to become a physician and I ought to change majors immediately. Without this man's recommendation my chances for medical school were minimal. Another of my professors suggested that I try the business department, but here I was told that it was too late to start the program and that no one could take any business courses without the prerequisite full year introductory course in that field. As a possible help to me in my dilemma it was suggested that I take a battery of psychological tests. I shall never forget my interview giving me the "results" of these tests (and my confused, forced indecision certainly made me a ripe target for psychological instruments) and the summary statement of the person in charge of the testing, "Frankly, R., I don't see how you can succeed at anything."

This "advice" did several things: first, it made me angry; secondly, it increased my need for personal and academic support and for acceptance by someone; thirdly, it raised a big question in my mind regarding the efficacy of psychological tests. The anger made me work harder for grades and recognition than I ever had before; the need for support and confidence in myself and a statement by the speech professor suggesting confidence in me led me to take further courses in public speaking; the doubts about psychological tests remained as a gnawing problem to emerge at a later date.

Successful completion of college took me on to graduate school majoring in speech and with a growing interest in speech correction, in which I obtained a master's degree. Meanwhile interest in psychology was increasing, both in its application to speech correction and to other kinds of personal problems, especially those which involved communication and the understanding or acceptance of people's feelings. When World War II came, I was assigned to clinical work in an army hospital on the basis of my graduate courses in psychology. After the war, the GI bill gave me a financial opportunity I had never had before to continue studying for a Ph.D.

My advanced work was not altogether the usual clinical training, being modified in the direction of its application to children's problems. This was largely a result of the support, interest, and thinking of another professor who stressed the importance of giving every child a "good start." In addition, it had been suggested, and accepted by me, that *child* clinical psychology was almost an open door for activity where it was unnecessary to cross swords with any other profession. When children are concerned, there is much less tendency to become jealous over professional proprieties.

Seldom have I regretted emerging, occupationally, as whatever I am. The work has not always been "satisfying" but the learning is continual. My interest in teaching has remained. Nearly every term I teach an evening course at a nearby state college. Undoubtedly, my choice of what I should teach—psychological diagnosis and psychological testing—has been influenced by my own unfortunate experience with psychological tests. The diagnostic interest remains and finds its outlet both in my regular work as a psychologist in a child clinic and also in private diagnostic work. My interest in the welfare of people finds its major satisfaction in therapeutic endeavor—in collaboration with other disciplines and the resources of the community—with children and their parents.

Thus, I now find myself leading the "full life" of diagnostic and therapeutic work in a child clinic, carrying on diagnostic work with both children and adults in private practice, teaching university extension courses in psychological diagnosis and testing, and having a growing interest in community interaction and cooperation in the field of mental health.[4]

A CLINICIAN IN A LARGE GOVERNMENT HOSPITAL

My professional life at present is busy and varied. Besides working full-time for a government hospital, I teach at a medical school and have a private practice. The working hours in a week often total sixty, but I do not consider myself overworked—in fact, I consider myself fortunate to lead an interesting and stimulating life. What do I do at the hospital? As a supervisory psychologist, I work with psychology trainees in their testing and treatment activities. The ward I am assigned to has been experimenting with a night-hospital program for those patients still hospitalized but who work in the community during the day, and I have been made administrator of that program. Our ward has over 100 patients in a group therapy program—I am responsible for assigning patients to groups and arranging for supervisory conferences with hospital consultants on problems which arise in group handling. I am occasionally called on to lecture on the nature of mental illness to groups of hospital workers who are either regularly employed or are receiving training. My position with the government offers opportunities in testing, treatment, administration, training, lecturing, and carrying on research.

My duties in the medical school at present consist of lecturing to junior students once a week on the forms of mental illness and on personality theory. These duties have varied from time to time. I have worked in the out-patient psychiatric clinic and have assisted in departmental research projects. I find time for these activities during the day because my night-hospital duties require me to work at the hospital one evening a week.

The remainder of my working hours I devote to private practice of individual and group therapy. My patients come to me by referral from physicians and psychiatrists or from finding my name in the classified pages of the telephone book. Those whose condition is too serious for me to work with I refer to psychiatrists in the neighborhood. My approach is analytically oriented and I attempt to set therapeutic goals which can be reached in one or two years.

Whence came my interest in psychology—and, specifically, clinical psychology? This is a difficult question to answer. I have always felt curiosity about people. At one time, in high school and while an undergraduate, this expressed itself as an interest in literature (I suppose for its portrayal of human experience in behavior and feeling) and this led me to consider

4. Reprinted by permission from Sundberg, Norman D., & Tyler, Leona E. *Clinical psychology.* New York: Appleton-Century Crofts, 1962, pp. 453–454. Copyright © 1962 by Meredith Publishing Co. (Appleton-Century Crofts is a division of Meredith Publishing Co.).

seriously the career of teaching in English or the Humanities. However, during my sophomore and junior years, courses in psychology awakened my interest in the origins of human behavior, which has continued unabated ever since.

One of the reasons I find clinical psychology exciting is the fact that the final answers are not in. There are many basic questions in the areas of intelligence, perception, personality development, group dynamics, etc., etc. Thus I feel I am part of an expeditionary force on the outer frontier of human knowledge, and that I may be fortunate to be on the scene to share the thrill of discovery of what exists in the inner world of the mind. Clinical psychology is probably too unobstructed for those who feel secure only when they deal with closed systems—so I recommend it only to those who are challenged, not confused, by uncertainty.[5]

THE SOCIAL WORKER

Like psychologists, social workers in many different placements are concerned with the problem of mental health and illness. The situations with which social workers deal—poverty, unemployment, inadequate housing, broken homes, maladjusted individuals and families, illness, handicap, antisocial behavior and so forth—are of central importance to mental health.

Social workers generally are employed with public and private agencies which carry out programs designed to improve the social welfare and mental health of certain individuals or groups of individuals. There are, for example, public assistance services, child and family services, medical care and health services, and mental health and psychiatric services.

Many social workers have only a bachelor's degree, but employment or advancement beyond an elementary level in certain placements is limited to those who have done graduate work. In order to achieve full professional status as a social worker, a person ordinarily majors in sociology, psychology, or some other social science in her undergraduate work (we say "her" because most social workers are women although increasing numbers of men are coming into the profession). Then she enters into a two-year graduate program at a school of social work. This program leads to the master of social work degree (M.S.W.). Some schools, however, award a certificate of proficiency upon completion of a

5. Reprinted by permission from Sundberg, Norman D., & Tyler, Leona E. *Clinical psychology*. New York: Appleton-Century Crofts, 1962, p. 452. Copyright © 1962 by Meredith Publishing Co. (Appleton-Century Crofts is a division of Meredith Publishing Co.)

one-year graduate program, and a few schools have doctoral programs leading to a doctor of philosophy degree (Ph.D.) or a doctor of social work degree (D.S.W.).

Some social workers, called "caseworkers," deal directly with individuals and families. They may help a person to deal with his environment and at the same time try to change the environment (or find a new environment) to better fit or accommodate the person. Case workers frequently work with a whole family, attempting to strengthen relationships in it, improve its medical and financial health, and its position in the community. Whether called casework or psychotherapy, the activities of a social worker in helping a maladjusted person or marriage pair or whole family have a good deal in common with the procedures used by psychiatrists and psychologists.

Other social workers, called "group workers," employ group experiences to benefit both the individual and the larger society. Such workers may serve youth groups or participate in senior citizen programs. They may provide group services in correctional institutions, public housing projects, clinics, hospitals, and other mental health facilities.

A few social workers, called "community organization workers," work to improve the social welfare facilities of the entire community. They help the community identify its needs and work to fill these needs. They seek to coordinate and expand existing services and to involve a broad spectrum of professional people and lay people in programs of the community.

The following case illustrates the work of the social caseworker. The woman identified below as "Mrs. M" was a neglectful mother and homemaker. However, with the help and encouragement of the worker, she was able to deal more effectively with her problems.

The M family was referred to the agency because the children were chronically malnourished, poorly clothed, and generally neglected. Their home was badly deteriorated. Several windows were broken and both the interior and exterior of the house were very dirty. The father, aged forty, was an illiterate, alcoholic manual laborer who did not work steadily. The mother, aged thirty-three, was a poor housekeeper, and obese. They had been married for sixteen years. Most members of the community considered them "hopeless" and thought the mother uninterested in her children. The four children, who ranged in age from eight to fifteen years, were said to be mentally retarded and attended special classes at school.

During her first visit with Mrs. M, after spelling out the agency's concern for the children, the worker told Mrs. M that she was there to help her deal with her problems. Mrs. M responded by saying her husband was

Presentation: *The broad spectrum of adjustment-related activities per-formed by social workers can be seen in this description of the principal areas of practice.*

Public assistance workers are employed largely by State and local gov-ernment agencies on public welfare programs which extend financial assistance to needy persons such as the disabled, blind, or aged; unem-ployed persons; and dependent children. Their duties include determin-ing their clients' needs and whether they are eligible for financial as-sistance; strengthening family ties; helping clients to become self-suffi-cient; explaining pertinent laws and requirements; and providing or ar-ranging for other needed social services.

Family service workers in private agencies are primarily concerned with providing counseling services to families and individuals. They seek to strengthen family life, by improving interpersonal relationships, and to establish satisfactory relations between the family and the community.

Child welfare workers in government and voluntary agencies deal with the problems of children. They may find foster homes or institute legal action for the protection of neglected or mistreated children, arrange for homemaker service during the illness of a mother, arrange for adoptions or placements in specialized institutions, counsel youthful delinquents, or advise parents on their children's problems.

School social workers or "visiting teachers" employed by school sys-tems also help troubled children, including those who are excessively shy, aggressive, or withdrawn; failing in school subjects for no apparent rea-son; hungry or ill; or truants. Workers consult with parents, teachers, principals, doctors, truant officers, and other interested people. They frequently refer a child to other social work agencies in the community for help.

Medical social workers employed by hospitals, clinics, health agencies, rehabilitation centers, and public welfare agencies work directly with patients and their families, helping them meet problems accompanying illness, recovery, and rehabilitation. Usually these workers function as part of a medical team composed of doctors, nurses, and therapists.

Psychiatric social workers attend patients in mental hospitals or clinics. In clinical teams, composed of psychiatrists, psychologists, and other professional personnel, these workers help patients and their families to understand the nature of the illness, enlist the patients' aid in using the various kinds of help available, and guide the patients in their social adjustment to their homes and communities. In some organizations med-ical and psychiatric social workers are grouped together as "clinical social workers." Psychiatric social workers also participate in commu-nity mental health programs concerned with the prevention of mental illness and with the readjustment of mental patients to normal home and community living.

Social workers in rehabilitation services assist emotionally or physically disabled persons in adjusting to the demands of everyday living. As part of a rehabilitation team, which usually includes physical or occupational therapists, these social workers serve as a link with the community while patients are in the hospital and later help them adjust to home and community life.

Probation and parole officers and other correctional workers, who are employed primarily by Federal, State, county, and city governments, assist probationers, parolees, and juvenile offenders in their readjustment to society. They make investigations and submit reports to the courts concerning the activities of their clients. They also counsel their clients and may help them find jobs; keep a close watch on their clients' conduct; and direct them to other services in the community when possible. In addition, they frequently arrange for child placements or adoptions, provide marriage counseling, and collect court-ordered payments for support of families and children.

Social group workers are employed by a multitude of agencies—settlements and community centers; youth-serving groups; public housing developments; correctional institutions; resident and day centers for children, adolescents, or elderly people; and general and psychiatric clinics and hospitals. Group workers help individuals to develop their personalities and find satisfaction in life through group experiences in educational, recreational, or other activities. They may plan or direct group activities; or recruit, train, and supervise volunteer workers. Many administer departments and agencies which provide social group services.

Community organization workers plan welfare, health, and recreation services for the community; coordinate existing social services; develop volunteer leadership; and assist in fund raising for community social welfare activities. Usually these workers are employed by community chests, welfare councils, religious federations, health associations and federations, agencies which combine community planning and direct service, and by other professional groups in social work and related fields. Unlike other areas of social work, this field employs men in the majority. (Occupation Outlook Handbook, 1963–1964, pp. 258–259.)

---

her problem: because he drank so much, she did not have enough money to buy food; he kept most of his wages for himself and gave her only $10 or $15 a week. She also resented her mother-in-law's criticism of her way of rearing the children. She discussed the children's poor clothing and the fact that other children made fun of them. The family was in danger of being evicted, and Mrs. M said she hoped she could find a job to help pay the arrears of rent and the electricity and water bills. The worker told Mrs. M that she would visit her every week to help her straighten out her affairs.

During the next month Mrs. M was depressed. She complained about feeling ill and hopeless. She continued to discuss the reality problems facing the family, but she did not think the situation could ever be improved. The worker learned that Mrs. M's parents had brought her up strictly and that she had had very few friends as a child. She thought of herself as "not very bright" and she had married soon after quitting school in the tenth grade.

The worker encouraged Mrs. M to visit the school to discuss her children's problems with the teachers and praised her when she did so. She accompanied Mrs. M when she applied for emergency relief, and also took her shopping.

Some time later, Mrs. M found the strength necessary to make a court complaint against her husband for nonsupport, for the first time. The judge put him on probation and ordered him to give his wife most of his earnings. The worker continued to accompany Mrs. M when she went shopping and also helped her to make economical choices. Although Mrs. M doubted her ability to handle money, the worker helped her assume responsibility in this sphere.

In the tenth interview, the worker reported that Mrs. M was in a "fairly cheerful state." In the twelfth interview, she was in a happy mood. She said that the children were not fighting so much as they had previously, perhaps because they were no longer hungry. She also reported that her husband's behavior was much improved.

After four months of encouragement and warm support, the caseworker noted that Mrs. M had wallpapered one room and was planning to buy curtains and that the broken windows had all been replaced. Mrs. M was losing weight under the care of a physician. She purchased several new dresses for herself and was beginning to care more for her appearance. She also was learning how to wash and care for her children's hair. Mrs. M continued receiving supplementary financial assistance (Jacobucci, 1965, pp. 224–225).

OTHER SOCIAL SCIENTISTS

As mental health concerns go beyond narrow medical conceptions and emphasis shifts from the person to the person-in-the-environments, social scientists of many disciplines play greater and greater roles in mental health. Sociologists and cultural anthropologists have a good deal to tell us about societies and how they may be altered to achieve mental health goals. The terms "applied anthropology" and "applied sociology" as well as "clinical anthropology" and "clinical sociology" designate these areas of concern.

Applied sociologists have played key roles in the reshaping of large metropolitan areas. They have helped plan, conduct, and evaluate programs concerning juvenile delinquency and crime. They have helped improve educational and occupational conditions. They have participated in the renewal of old neighborhoods and the construction of new and better ones (Miller, 1965).

Anthropologists, sociologists and psychologists alike have provided important insights concerning the social and cultural factors in mental illness. Today there is considerable overlap in the research and applied activities of these groups of scientists. Other social scientists, such as economists, historians, and political scientists, are making contributions in this area.

THE COUNSELOR

In mental health, the terms "counseling" and "psychotherapy" are sometimes used interchangeably. However, counseling is more likely to be reserved for assistance that has to do with educational, vocational, or less severe personal problems, while psychotherapy characterizes assistance with problems of an intermediate or serious nature.

Many different workers are called counselors or provide counseling service of one kind or another. Some persons not in the field of mental health use this title, for example, life insurance counselors. Since the title "counselor" is not restricted by law, anyone can use this designation or similar ones, such as "marriage counselor," "personal problems counselor," and "family counselor." Therefore, it is necessary to use care in finding professional assistance.

The project dedicated to training lay persons as "mental health counselors" and "mental health aides" has already been mentioned. Below— briefly noted—are the activities of the psychological counselor, the rehabilitation counselor, and the school counselor.

THE PSYCHOLOGICAL COUNSELOR

Psychological counselors or counseling psychologists render some of the same kinds of assistance that clinical psychologists do. Counselors are generally more experienced in educational and vocational guidance than clinical psychologists and less experienced in dealing with personal problems of greater severity.

Counselors of this kind are found at various community agencies, clinics, and hospitals. Colleges and universities frequently have counseling centers or clinics where counseling and clinical psychologists are available to assist students with educational, vocational, and personal problems.

A master's degree (M.A.) or doctor's degree (Ph.D.) in psychology is the usual preparation for this kind of counseling. Like graduate programs in clinical psychology, counseling curricula include courses in evaluation, diagnosis, and counseling or psychotherapy.

THE REHABILITATION COUNSELOR

Rehabilitation counselors assist handicapped and disabled persons in obtaining suitable employment. These counselors may work with one kind or a variety of clients, including the deaf or blind, the mentally ill or retarded, the physically handicapped, alcoholics, and others. This work is done in close cooperation with physicians, psychiatrists, psychologists, and other professional persons who are involved in their cases as well as with actual and prospective employers.

The counselor's task includes evaluating the disabled person to determine the kind of work he can do, placing him, and helping him adjust in this placement. The counselor needs considerable ability to relate to others. He also needs considerable patience and persistence.

Some rehabilitation counselors have the master's degree (M.A.) earned in rehabilitation counseling programs or in related curricula in psychology, social work, or education. Some are graduates of doctoral programs in counseling or clinical psychology. Others have a bachelor's degree (B.A.) in addition to various kinds of work and training experience.

THE SCHOOL COUNSELOR

School counselors provide counseling service for pupils in elementary and secondary schools. They also help modify school environments so that they become more suitable climates for learning.

School counselors help pupils directly; they also act as consultants, offering advice and suggestions to teachers and parents. Counselors help evaluate the interest and abilities of pupils and assist them in the selection of courses and in making employment or college plans. Counselors also arrange programs which supply the students with educational and vocational information.

School counselors generally are from teaching ranks. In fact, many of them teach or perform other duties in addition to their counseling activities. Most states issue certificates to school counselors if they have had a certain amount of experience and graduate work. Many school counselors have a master's degree.

THE VOLUNTEER

The problems of mental health and illness are being brought more and more into the community. And, as it should be, the community is being brought more and more into the problems of mental health and illness. The layman is being increasingly involved in this area as a volunteer worker and as a member of various organizations involved in mental health activities.

Local chapters of nationwide groups, such as the National Association for Mental Health, perform important tasks in the community. These organizations work to inform and arouse the community concerning the problems of mental health. They also attempt to ensure that proper facilities are available in the community for the evaluation, correction, and prevention of various kinds of problems.

Lay volunteers contribute their talents and energies in many different mental health settings. Their contributions provide an important addition to staff services. In mental hospitals, for example, these volunteers teach courses, crafts, and skills of various sorts. They also help conduct the recreational programs.

Lay volunteers may provide important sources of social stimulation and support for inpatients and outpatients. Some outpatient centers sponsor club and social activities involving both patients and volunteers, and some hospitals have established visitor or companion programs.

One interesting hospital companion program has involved college students and chronically ill mental patients. A program is set up in which each student is assigned a patient whom he then visits weekly throughout the academic year. Each student also participates in weekly meetings of the volunteers which are conducted by a member of the hospital staff. The program provides an important social relationship for the patients, many of whom have little contact with the outside world, and at the same time, helps the student achieve new insights into mental health and illness (Holzberg & Knapp, 1965; Holzberg, Whiting, & Lowy, 1964).

A pioneer volunteer program was initiated in 1954 at Metropolitan State Hospital by students at Harvard College and Radcliffe College. Since that time more than two thousand students have participated in the program. A variety of projects have been undertaken for both children and adult patients. Some of the projects have been group or ward activities and others have involved two-person (student-patient) relationships. Students working on the wards keep a diary or journal of their activities. Here are some excerpts from a diary of volunteer work and progress on an adult ward (E-3) during one school year:

10/9: Six of us altogether; we spent two hours in E-3 talking with the patients. Organized an art class which proved to be great success with many of the patients, who wish it to be continued. We asked to take patients to the courtyard, but were not allowed to because the male patients were already using it.

10/16: Five people out tonight; two took some patients bowling, and rest stayed on ward playing bingo, singing, doing jigsaw puzzles, drawing and talking. It would be hard to be too enthusiastic about the responsiveness on E-3 this evening, the patients greeted us eagerly and participated with remarkable interest and gusto in all activities.

The supervisor of the ward expressed delight at the success of this evening's work, and praised the activities. Especially pleasing to her (and to us) was the responsiveness of one who laughed and talked with enthusiasm for the first time in many months.

The only complaint was that we should come out earlier.

Next week one girl is going to bring equipment to give haircuts and another will bring her guitar.

We all enjoyed ourselves tonight, and many patients came up to us afterwards and told us that they had had a good time.

10/30: Seven people out tonight; activities included piano and singing, checkers, puzzles, horse shoes, beanbags, and talking.

Sometimes in E-3 we can see the silhouettes of men from D-3 pressed against the door, as though they wanted to have a feeling of association or participation with our activity. So we decided to open the door, and see if they really were amenable to joining us for games, talking and other pastimes. As it happens, they weren't amenable last night. I think, though, they might be if we try a few more times.

11/10: Attended a group meeting with the resident doctor and the E-3 attendants. Both the other volunteers and myself participated actively in the discussions, all our comments were well received.

12/4: First time out after two week lapse for exams. Enthusiastic reception, with several breakthroughs to formerly uncommunicative or inactive patients.

12/18: Excellent results with lipstick applications and the lipstick to keep as a bingo prize. Established communication with a patient who has never spoken to us before; she accepted a lipstick application from another patient and seemed pleased at the compliments she drew.

2/26: I spoke to a group of patients tonight and asked them what they thought of the idea of putting on some sort of play. They seemed genuinely interested and made their own suggestions as to what kind of play they wanted—opinion ran high for a comedy, especially a light musical comedy.

Some of our volunteers came from Emerson College; they will approach the Theater Arts Dept. there for help in getting scripts.

3/17: Today we had our St. Patrick's Day party. It was highly successful. It was held on E-3, and all adjoining wards; the patients organized much of the party and this added greatly to its success.

This spreading of the volunteers into D-3 has done much for the male patients. Also, several of the women on E-3 who were at the party, commented on the dismal, drab appearance of the male ward and expressed a desire to help the men improve their surroundings. I think it might be a good project for us to paint and decorate the men's side.

3/19: We've gotten permission from Dr. McLaughlin to take girls onto C-3 and D-3 (male wards for the very sick patients) in the evenings, and the blessing of Mrs. Holmes to do sewing and crafts projects for the improvement of E-3 curtains, wastebaskets, and so forth.

Taking the women from E-3 onto the male wards for dancing is a joy to watch. This advance onto men's wards is of incalculable importance.

3/21: On E-3 we've started for the first time to aim directly at group dynamics—group activities that are united, and require patient interaction. It was not particularly easy tonight, for many of our "best" patients were at a party, elsewhere. But we did make a hard try at charades. The game was tough; the patients slow to catch on. Enthusiasm was only spotty. But the important point to note is that patients who at the onset withdrew from the group, and who refused flatly to participate, did ultimately take part—at first hesitantly, then more willing—in the game.

4/23: Banjo playing was highly successful last week. First part of the evening was used for the play-reading. Only three patients participated—the others claiming poor eyesight, etc., but they did quite well.

For the first time all year, Diana, the Greek-speaking patient stopped talking to herself and came over—completely voluntarily to sit with the group.[6]

---

6. Umbarger, C. C., Dalsimer, J. S., Morrison, A. P., & Breggin, P. R. *College students in a mental hospital.* New York: Grune & Stratton, 1962, pp. 26–28. By permission.

SUMMARY

New ideas concerning mental illness and new approaches in dealing with it have been reflected in treatment facilities. Mental hospitals have undergone three main changes. First, they have moved from being primarily custodial institutions toward being more therapeutic ones. Second, they have moved from relative isolation to a place in the community. Third, they have taken an increasing responsibility for changing the community to facilitate the recovery of troubled persons.

Partial-hospitalization programs—in effect, semihospitals—have been established for persons who need less than around-the-clock care but more than one or two or three hours a week of outpatient service. These programs include the day hospital, the night hospital, and the weekend hospital.

A number of other residential facilities have been established for persons who do not require intensive care. The residential or halfway house provides a home for persons who are not ready to become full members of their families or communities. The foster home, or family care program, provides a home for a person within a private family.

Other facilities include the sheltered workshop and the social club. The former is a resource for training people who have been disabled by injury or illness. The latter is an organization established for individuals who share common adjustment problems.

A new and promising facility is the community mental health center. Such centers are planned to provide a complete and coordinated program of services within a community. These centers would provide help for people of all ages and with all kinds of mental illness and adjustment problems.

Among the most important workers concerned with improving adjustment are ministers. There are more clergymen than all other mental health personnel combined, and they are frequently consulted by members of their congregation in times of trouble.

Physicians also play an important role in this area. People frequently turn to their family doctor in times of stress, and he can play a vital role in the prevention and alleviation of maladjustment and mental illness.

Psychiatrists are physicians who specialize in the diagnosis and treatment of mental illness and adjustment problems. Psychiatric treatment takes many different forms and occurs in many different settings. Some psychiatrists are in private practice; others are on the staffs of clinics, hospitals, and other mental health facilities.

Psychoanalysts, generally speaking, are physicians who have been trained to treat adjustment problems through the use of psychoanalytic methods. In its classical form, psychoanalysis is an intensive, extensive, and expensive process. There are, however, some newer and briefer forms of psychoanalysis.

Many workers serve as nurses in medical and psychiatric facilities. There are, for example, the practical nurse, the ward attendant, and the psychiatric technician. Psychiatric nurses combine both nursing and psychiatric training. Such nurses work in hospitals and in a variety of outpatient services.

An occupational therapist is a person who is trained to help people recover from illness through constructive activities, that is, through being occupied in meaningful ways. Occupational therapists work with people of all ages and with various kinds of illnesses and handicaps. By involving the person in creative, educational, physical, and recreational activities, the therapist helps him regain strength and skill as well as confidence and a sense of worth.

Psychologists of varying descriptions work in the field of mental health. The clinical psychologist occupies a very central position. He is trained in evaluating and changing behavior. He also is responsible for a good deal of research that is done in mental health and illness.

Social workers provide a wide range of services in mental illness. Some social workers, called caseworkers, deal directly with individuals and families. Others, called group workers, employ group experiences to benefit both the individual and the larger society. A few social workers, called organizational community workers, work to improve the social welfare facilities of the entire community.

In addition to these workers, many other people play a part in improvement processes. These include sociologists, anthropologists, and other social scientists, counselors of various kinds, and last but not least, lay volunteers.

Adler, M. D. An analysis of role conflicts of the clergy in mental health work. *Journal of Pastoral Care,* 1965, **19**(2), 65–75.

Albee, G. W. *Mental health manpower trends.* New York: Basic Books, 1959.

Barton, W. E. Introduction. In R. M. Glasscote, D. S. Saunders, H. M. Forstenzer, & A. R. Foley, *The community mental health center.*

Washington, D.C.: Joint Information Service of the American Psychiatric Association and the National Association for Mental Health, 1964, pp. xiii–xvi.

Blain, D. The organization of psychiatry in the United States. In S. Arieti (Ed.), *American handbook of psychiatry*. New York: Basic Books, 1959, Vol. 2, pp. 1960–1982.

Caplan, G. *An approach to community mental health*. New York: Grune & Stratton, 1961.

English, O. S., & Finch, S. M. *Introduction to psychiatry* (2nd ed.) New York: W. W. Norton, 1957.

Fidler, G. S., & Fidler, J. W. *Occupational therapy*. New York: Macmillan, 1963.

Glasscote, R., Sanders, D., Forstenzer, H. M., & Foley, A. R. *The community mental health center*. Washington, D.C.: Joint Information Service of the American Psychiatric Association and the National Association for Mental Health, 1964.

Greenblatt, M., & Levinson, D. Mental hospitals. In B. B. Wolman (Ed.), *Handbook of clinical psychology*. New York: McGraw-Hill, 1965, pp. 1343–1359.

Gurin, G., Veroff, J., & Feld, S. *Americans view their mental health*. New York: Basic Books, 1960.

Hilgard, E. R. Experimental approaches to psychoanalysis. In E. Pumpian-Mindlin (Ed.), *Psychoanalysis as science*. New York: Basic Books, 1952, pp. 3–45.

Holzberg, J. D., & Knapp, R. H. The social interaction of college students and chronically ill mental patients. *American Journal of Orthopsychiatry*, 1965, **35**(3), 487–492.

Holzberg, J. D., Whiting, H. S., & Lowy, D. G. Chronic patients and a college companion program. *Mental Hospital*, 1964, **15**(3), 152–158.

Jacobucci, L. Casework treatment of the neglectful mother. *Social Casework*, 1965, **46**(4), 221–226.

Kramer, B. M. *Day hospital*. New York: Grune & Stratton, 1962.

Levine, M., & Lederer, H. D. Teaching of psychiatry in medical schools. In S. Arieti (Ed.), *American handbook of psychiatry*. New York: Basic Books, 1959, Vol. 2, pp. 1923–1934.

Lief, V. F., & Lief, N. R. The general practitioner and psychiatric problems. In H. I. Lief, V. F. Lief, & N. R. Lief (Eds.), *The psychological basis of medical practice*. New York: Hoeber-Harper, 1963, pp. 485–500.

McCann, R. V. *The churches and mental health*. New York: Basic Books, 1962.

Malmquist, C. P. Psychiatry in a Midwestern metropolitan community. *Mental Hygiene*, 1964, **48**, 55–65.

Miller, A. A., & Sabshin, M. Psychotherapy in psychiatric hospitals. *Archives of General Psychiatry*, 1963, **9**, 53–63.

Miller, S. M. Prospects: The applied sociology of the center-city. In A. W. Gouldner & S. M. Miller (Eds.), *Applied sociology*. New York: Free Press, 1965, pp. 441–456.

Moll, A. E. Psychiatric night treatment unit in a general hospital. *American Journal of Psychiatry*, 1957, **113**, 722–727.

Nameche, G. F. Pastoral counseling in Protestant churches. Part I. The minister as counselor. Unpublished manuscript, 1958. Cited by R. V. McCann, *The churches and mental health*. New York: Basic Books, 1962, pp. 76–80.

Occupational outlook handbook. U.S. Department of Labor, 1963–1964.

Olshansky, S. The transitional sheltered workshop: A survey. *Journal of Social Issues*, 1960, **16**(2), 33–39.

Padula, H. Foster homes for the mentally ill. *Mental Hygiene*, 1964, **48**, 366–371.

Peplau, H. E. Principles of psychiatric nursing. In S. Arieti (Ed.), *American handbook of psychiatry*. New York: Basic Books, 1959, Vol. 2, pp. 1840–1856.

Robinson, R., DeMarche, D. F., & Wagle, M. K. *Community resources in mental health*. New York: Basic Books, 1960.

Rosenbaum, M. Treatment of psychosomatic disorders. In H. I. Lief, V. F. Lief, & N. R. Lief (Eds.), *The psychological basis of medical practice*. New York: Hoeber-Harper, 1963, pp. 501–509.

Rothwell, N. D., & Doniger, J. Halfway house and mental hospital: Some comparisons. *Psychiatry*, 1963, **26**, 281–288.

Sundberg, N. D., & Tyler, L. E. *Clinical psychology*. New York: Appleton-Century-Crofts, 1962.

Umbarger, C. C., Dalsimer, J. S., Morrison, A. P., & Breggin, P. R. *College students in a mental hospital*. New York: Grune & Stratton, 1962.

Vernallis, F. F., & Reinert, R. E. The weekend hospital. *Mental Hospitals*, May, 1963, pp. 254–258.

Wechsler, H. The expatient organization: A survey. *Journal of Social Issues*, 1960. **16**(2), 47–53. (a)

Wechsler, H. Halfway houses for former mental patients: A survey. *Journal of Social Issues*, 1960, **16**(2), 20–26. (b)

II

The Psychological Bases
for Helping

Psychology and its related specialities provide theoretical and philosophical models useful to the professional helper in organizing his understanding of behavior. Psychology can provide him especially with partial answers to the difficult questions involved in predicting and controlling human behavior, the nature of human motivation, the processes basic to human learning, and the influence of human perception—all concepts of great importance in determining the direction and dynamics of helping processes. Because the beliefs of helpers about the nature of behavior have inevitable effects on practice, it is important that helpers acquire the most accurate and useful concepts about people and behavior available in our time.

In this section "Two Models of Man" are described by William Hitt and further discussed in a famous debate between Carl Rogers and B. F. Skinner. Casting his lot with the humanists, Dr. Combs, in his article, "Some Basic Concepts in Perceptual Psychology," explains that a perceptual approach is especially valuable to helpers, and particularly pertinent to the problems with which the helper must deal. This emphasis on a perceptual orientation is echoed by Dr. Snygg in his article, "A Cognitive Field Theory of Learning." Since the goal of helping is learning new ways to see the self and its relationships to the world, the helper's beliefs about the nature of learning are crucial. Dr. Snygg reviews the contributions of various learning theories, opts for a concept of learning as a process of perception, and points out advantages of such a view for solving practical problems in teaching and learning.

Taking a different perspective on the subject, Drs. Avila and Purkey attempt to show how humanistic and behavioristic positions can be integrated into a single theoretical model. This is especially helpful in view of the fact that these two frames of reference are frequently seen as antagonistic.

The influence of perception in everyday affairs is illustrated by three provocative articles: Ittelson's "The Involuntary Bet," Marshall's "The Evidence," and White's "Misperception and the Vietnam War." Each of these papers describes practical implications of approaching problems of human behavior from a perceptual point of view. They show how understanding events from the viewpoint of the behaver can improve our comprehension, while failure to see from the other fellow's position can destroy communication and confound our best efforts to deal with human problems.

The purposive character of human behavior is stressed in the final three articles which face the central issues of human life goals, human values, and the meaning of personal wholeness. Here Kelley, Snygg, and Buhler stress the importance of goals in determining the direction of human striving and the central role of personal goals for the creation of limited helping relationships or the building of whole societies salutary for human existence.

Two Models of Man

William D. Hitt

A symposium sponsored by the Division of Philosophical Psychology of the American Psychological Association clearly pointed up the cleavage in contemporary theoretical and philosophical psychology. The sympo-

Reprinted from *American Psychologist,* 1969, **24,** 651–658, by permission of the author and the American Psychological Association.

sium was held at Rice University to mark the inception of the Division of Philosophical Psychology as a new division of the APA. Participants included Sigmund Koch, R. B. MacLeod, B. F. Skinner, Carl R. Rogers, Norman Malcolm, and Michael Scriven. The presentations and associated discussions were organized in the book: *Behaviorism and Phenomenology: Contrasting Bases for Modern Psychology* (Edited by T. W. Wann, 1964).

THE ARGUMENT

As indicated in the title of the book, the main argument of the symposium dealt with phenomenology versus behaviorism. This argument also could be described as one between existential psychology and behavioristic psychology. The presentations dealt with two distinct models of man and the scientific methodology associated with each model. The discussions following each presentation may be described as aggressive, hostile, and rather emotional; they would suggest that there is little likelihood of a reconciliation between the two schools of thought represented at the symposium.

To illustrate the nature of the argument, some of the statements made by the participants are presented below.

In Support of Behaviorism

● Skinner (1964):

An adequate science of behavior must consider events taking place within the skin of the organism, not as physiological mediators of behavior, but as part of behavior itself. It can deal with these events without assuming that they have any special nature or must be known in any special way. . . . Public and private events have the same kinds of physical dimensions [p. 84].

● Malcolm (1964):

Behaviorism is right in insisting that there must be some sort of conceptual tie between the language of mental phenomena and outward circumstances and behavior. If there were not, we could not understand other people, nor could we understand ourselves [p. 152].

ATTACKS ON BEHAVIORISM

● Koch (1964):

Behaviorism has been given a hearing for fifty years. I think this generous. I shall urge that it is essentially a role-playing position which has outlived whatever usefulness its role might once have had [p. 6].

● Rogers (1964):

It is quite unfortunate that we have permitted the world of psychological science to be narrowed to behavior observed, sounds emitted, marks scratched on paper, and the like [p. 118].

IN SUPPORT OF PHENOMENOLOGY

● MacLeod (1964):

I am . . . insisting that what, in the old, prescientific days, we used to call "consciousness" still can and should be studied. Whether or not this kind of study may be called a science depends on our definition of the term. To be a scientist, in my opinion, is to have boundless curiosity tempered by discipline [p. 71].

● Rogers (1964):

The inner world of the individual appears to have more significant influence upon his behavior than does the external environmental stimulus [p. 125].

ATTACKS ON PHENOMENOLOGY

● Malcolm (1964):

I believe that Wittgenstein has proved this line of thinking (introspectionism) to be disastrous. It leads to the conclusion that we do not and cannot understand each other's psychological language, which is a form of solipsism [1] [p. 148].

● Skinner (1964):

Mentalistic or psychic explanations of human behavior almost certainly originated in primitive animism [p. 79]. . . . I am a radical behaviorist simply in the sense that I find no place in the formulation for anything which is mental [p. 106].

1. Solipsism is defined as the theory that only the self exists, or can be proven to exist.

This appears to be the heart of the argument:

The behaviorist views man as a passive organism governed by external stimuli. Man can be manipulated through proper control of these stimuli. Moreover, the laws that govern man are essentially the same as the laws that govern all natural phenomena of the world; hence, it is assumed that the scientific method used by the physical scientist is equally appropriate to the study of man.

The phenomenologist views man as the *source* of acts; he is free to choose in each situation. The essence of man is *inside* of man; he is controlled by his own consciousness. The most appropriate methodology for the study of man is phenomenology, which begins with the world of experience.

These two models of man have been proposed and discussed for many years by philosophers and psychologists alike. Versions of these models may be seen in the contrasting views of Locke and Leibnitz (see Allport, 1955), Marx and Kierkegaard, Wittgenstein and Sartre, and, currently, Skinner and Rogers. Were he living today, William James probably would characterize Locke, Marx, Wittgenstein, and Skinner as "tough-minded," while Leibnitz, Kierkegaard, Sartre, and Rogers would be viewed as "tender-minded." Traditionally, the argument has been one model versus the other. It essentially has been a black-and-white argument.

The purpose of this article is to analyze the argument between the behaviorist and the phenomenologist. This analysis is carried out by presenting and discussing two different models of man.

CONTRASTING VIEWS OF MAN

The two models of man are presented in terms of these contrasting views:

1. Man can be described meaningfully in terms of his behavior; or man can be described meaningfully in terms of his consciousness.
2. Man is predictable; or man is unpredictable.
3. Man is an information transmitter; or man is an information generator.
4. Man lives in an objective world; or man lives in a subjective world.
5. Man is a rational being; or man is an arational being.
6. One man is like other men; or each man is unique.

7. Man can be described meaningfully in absolute terms; or man can be described meaningfully in relative terms.
8. Human characteristics can be investigated independently of one another; or man must be studied as a whole.
9. Man is a reality; or man is a potentiality.
10. Man is knowable in scientific terms; or man is more than we can ever know about him.

Each of these attributes is discussed below.

SUPPORT FOR BOTH MODELS

The evidence offered below in support of each of the two models of man is both empirical and analytical. Perhaps some of the evidence is intuitive, but it at least seems logical to the author of this article.

MAN CAN BE DESCRIBED MEANINGFULLY IN TERMS OF HIS BEHAVIOR; OR MAN CAN BE DESCRIBED MEANINGFULLY IN TERMS OF HIS CONSCIOUSNESS

According to John B. Watson, the founder of American behaviorism, the behavior of man and animals was the only proper study for psychology. Watson strongly advocated that

> Psychology is to be the science, not of consciousness, but of behavior. . . . It is to cover both human and animal behavior, the simpler animal behavior being indeed more fundamental than the more complex behavior of man. . . . It is to rely wholly on objective data, introspection being discarded [Woodworth & Sheehan, 1964, p. 113].

Behaviorism has had an interesting, and indeed productive, development since the time of Watson's original manifesto. Tolman, Hull, and a number of other psychologists have been important figures in this development. Today, Skinner is the leading behaviorist in the field of psychology. Skinner (1957) deals with both overt and covert behavior; for example, he states that "thought is simply *behavior*—verbal or nonverbal, covert or overt [p. 449]."

As a counterargument to placing all emphasis on behavior, Karl Jaspers, an existential psychologist and philosopher, points up the importance of consciousness or self-awareness. According to Jaspers

(1963), consciousness has four formal characteristics: (*a*) the feeling of activity—an awareness of being active; (*b*) an awareness of unity; (*c*) awareness of identity; and (*d*) awareness of the self as distinct from an outer world and all that is not the self (p. 121). Jaspers (1957) stresses that "Man not only exists but knows that he exists [p. 4]."

It is apparent from this argument that psychologists over the years have been dealing with two different aspects of man—on the one hand, his actions, and on the other, his self-awareness. It seems reasonable that man could be described in terms of either his behavior *or* his consciousness or both. Indeed, behavior is more accessible to scientific treatment, but the systematic study of consciousness might well give the psychologist additional understanding of man.

MAN IS PREDICTABLE; OR MAN IS UNPREDICTABLE

Understanding, prediction, and control are considered to be the three objectives of science. Prediction and control are sometimes viewed as evidence of the scientist's understanding of the phenomenon under study. The objective of prediction rests on the assumption of determinism, the doctrine that all events have sufficient causes. Psychological science has traditionally accepted the objective of predicting human behavior and the associated doctrine of determinism.

Indeed, there have been some notable successes in predicting human behavior. Recent predictions of the number of fatalities resulting from automobile accidents on a given weekend, for example, have been within 5–10% of the actual fatalities. College administrators can predict fairly accurately the number of dropouts between the freshman and sophomore years. Further, a psychometrician can readily predict with a high degree of accuracy the distribution of scores resulting from an achievement test administered to a large sample of high school students. As another example, the mean reaction time to an auditory stimulus can be predicted rather accurately for a large group of subjects. All of these examples lend support to the doctrine of determinism.

There also have been some notable failures in attempts to predict human behavior. For example, the therapist has had little success in predicting the effectiveness of a given form of therapy applied to a given patient. Similarly, the guidance counselor has had relatively little success in predicting the occupation to be chosen by individual high school students. Such failures in predicting human behavior sometimes prompt one to question the basic assumption of determinism.

To illustrate the complexity associated with predicting the behavior of man—as contrasted with that of other complex systems—consider the following illustration. Suppose that a research psychologist has made a detailed study of a given human subject. He now tells the subject that he predicts that he will choose Alternative A rather than Alternative B under such and such conditions at some future point in time. Now, with this limited amount of information, what do you predict the subject will do?

The evidence suggests that there is support for both sides of this issue. It is difficult to argue with the deterministic doctrine that there are sufficient causes for human actions. Yet these causes may be unknown to either the observer or the subject himself. Thus, we must conclude that man is both predictable and unpredictable.

MAN IS AN INFORMATION TRANSMITTER; OR MAN IS AN INFORMATION GENERATOR

The information theorists and cyberneticists have formulated a model of man as an information transmitter. W. Ross Ashby (1961), the cyberneticist, has proposed a basic postulate that says that man is just as intelligent as the amount of information fed into him.

> Intelligence, whether of man or machine, is absolutely bounded. And what we can build into our machine is similarly bounded. The amount of intelligence we can get into a machine is absolutely bounded by the quantity of information that is put into it. We can get out of a machine as much intelligence as we like, if and only if we insure that at least the corresponding quantity of information gets into it [p. 280].

Ashby believes that we could be much more scientific in our study of man if we would accept this basic postulate and give up the idea that man, in some mysterious manner, generates or creates new information over and above that which is fed into him.

The information-transmitting model of man is indeed very compelling. It promises considerable rigor and precision; it is compatible with both empiricism and stimulus-response theory; and it allows the behavioral scientist to build on past accomplishments in the fields of cybernetics, systems science, and mechanics.

But, alas, man does not want to be hemmed in by the information-transmitting model. Man asks questions that were never before asked; he identifies problems that were never before mentioned; he generates new ideas and theories; he formulates new courses of action; and he even formulates new models of man. Now to say that all of these human activities are merely a regrouping or recombining of existing elements is an oversimplification, a trivialization of human activity. Further, the assumption that all information has actually been in existence but hidden since the days of prehistoric man is not intuitively satisfying.

Considering the evidence in support of man both as an information transmitter and as an information generator, would it be reasonable to view man as both a *dependent* variable and an *independent* variable?

Man Lives in an Objective World; or Man Lives in a Subjective World

Man lives in an objective world. This is the world of facts and data. This is a reliable world; we agree that this or that event actually occurred. This is a tangible world; we agree that this or that object is actually present. This is the general world that is common to all.

But man also lives in a subjective world. This is the individual's private world. The individual's feelings, emotions, and perceptions are very personal; he attempts to describe them in words but feels that he can never do complete justice to them.

In making this comparison between the objective world and subjective world, it is important to distinguish between two types of knowledge. We can know *about* something, or we can personally *experience* something. These two forms of knowledge are not the same.

We conclude that man is both object and subject. He is visible and tangible to others, yet he is that which thinks, feels, and perceives. The world looks at man, and he looks out at the world.

Are both the objective world and the subjective world available to the methods of science? Empiricism in general and the experimental method in particular can be applied to the objective world; phenomenology can be applied to the subjective world. In his efforts to understand man, perhaps the psychologist should attempt to understand both worlds.

Man Is a Rational Being; or Man Is an Arational Being

Man is sometimes referred to as a rational animal. He is intelligent; he exercises reason; he uses logic; and he argues from a scientific standpoint. Indeed, man is considered by man to be the *only* rational animal.

An individual's action or behavior, of course, is sometimes considered irrational. This is the opposite of rational. The irrational person defies the laws of reason; he contradicts that which is considered rational by some particular community of people.

But man also is arational. This characteristic transcends the rational–irrational continuum; it essentially constitutes another dimension of man's life. As an example of man being arational in his life, he makes a total commitment for a way of life. This commitment may be for a given faith, a religion, a philosophy, a vocation, or something else. It may be that any analysis of this decision would reveal that it was neither rational nor irrational—it merely was.

Man's actions are guided by both empirical knowledge and value judgment. Empirical knowledge belongs to the rational world, whereas value judgment often belongs to the arational world. According to Jaspers (1967): "An empirical science cannot teach anybody what he ought to do, but only what he can do to reach his ends by statable means [p. 60]."

To achieve greater understanding of man, it would seem essential that the psychologist investigate man's arational world as well as his rational world.

One Man Is Like Other Men; or Each Man Is Unique

A major goal of science is to develop general laws to describe, explain, and predict phenomena of the world. These laws are frequently based upon the study of one sample of objects or events and are then expected to be valid for a different sample of objects or events. It then follows that a major goal of psychology is to formulate general laws of man. In fact, without the possibility of developing general laws of human behavior, can psychology even be considered a science?

There is a considerable amount of evidence to support the possibility of developing general laws of human behavior. For example, the results of the reaction-time experiments have held up very well over the decades. Moreover, the many conditioning experiments conducted over the past several decades—either classical or operant—certainly suggest that man is governed by general laws applicable to all. Further, the cultural anthropologist and social psychologist have clearly pointed up the similarity of people in a given culture, suggesting that they might be taken from the same mold.

On the other hand, there is considerable evidence to support the concept of individual uniqueness. For example, there are thousands of possible gene combinations and thousands of different environmental determinants, all of which bring about millions of different personalities. Further, it is apparent that no two people ever live in exactly the same environment. As someone once said about two brothers living in the same house, with the same parents, and with the same diet: "Only one of the boys has an older brother." Then, too, we might reflect on a statement made by William James (1925): "An unlearned carpenter of my acquaintance once said in my hearing: 'There is very little difference between one man and another; but what little there is, *is very important'* [pp. 242–243]."

Our conclusion from this brief analysis is that the evidence appears to support both models of man: (*a*) that he is governed by general laws that apply to all of mankind, and (*b*) that each individual is unique in a nontrivial way.

MAN CAN BE DESCRIBED MEANINGFULLY IN ABSOLUTE TERMS; OR MAN CAN BE DESCRIBED MEANINGFULLY IN RELATIVE TERMS

If we believe that man can be described in absolute terms, we view such descriptions as being free from restriction or limitation. They are independent of arbitrary standards. Contrariwise, if we believe that man can be described in relative terms, we see him as existing or having his specific nature only by relation to something else. His actions are not absolute or independent.

If the concept of absoluteness is supported, we must accept the idea of general laws for all of mankind, and we also must accept the related idea that man is governed by irrefutable natural laws. On the other hand, if the concept of relativism is supported, we probably can have no general laws of man; we must realize that everything is contingent upon something else; and we can be certain of nothing.

It would appear that there is evidence to support the concept of absoluteness in psychology. The basic psychophysical laws, for example, might be characterized as irrefutable natural laws. Similarly, the basic laws of conditioning seem to be free from restriction or limitation. This evidence might lead us to conclude that man can be described in absolute terms.

But before we can become smug with this false sense of security, the relativist poses some challenging questions. For example: What is considered intelligent behavior? What is normal behavior? What is an aggressive personality? What is an overachiever? At best, it would seem that we could answer such questions only in relative terms. The answers would be contingent on some set of arbitrary standards.

What can we conclude? Perhaps man can be described meaningfully in either absolute terms or relative terms, depending on what aspect of man is being described.

HUMAN CHARACTERISTICS CAN BE INVESTIGATED INDEPENDENTLY OF ONE ANOTHER; OR MUST BE STUDIED AS A WHOLE

The question here is: Can man be understood by analyzing each attribute independently of the rest, or must man be studied as a whole in order to be understood? Another way of phrasing the question is: Can we take an additive approach to the study of man, or is a holistic or Gestalt approach required?

There is some evidence to support an additive approach to the study of man. Consider the following areas of research: psychophysics, physiological psychology, motor skills, classical and operant conditioning, and sensation. All of these areas have produced useful results from experimentation involving the manipulation of a single independent variable and measuring the concomitant effects on a single dependent variable. Useful results have been produced by investigating a single characteristic independently of other characteristics.

Other areas of research, however, point up the value of a holistic point of view. Research in the area of perception, for example, has demonstrated the effect of individual motivation on perception. Similarly, studies of human learning have shown the great importance of motivation and intelligence on learning behavior. Further, as one more example, research in the area of psychotherapy has revealed that the relation between the personality of the therapist and that of the patient has a significant influence on the effectiveness of the therapy. All of these examples illustrate the importance of the interactions and interdependencies of the many variables operating in any given situation.

Support for a holistic view of man is seen in the works of Polanyi and Tielhard de Chardin, to mention only two. Polanyi (1963) gives this example: "Take a watch to pieces and examine, however carefully, its separate parts in turn, and you will never come across the principles by which a watch keeps time [p. 47]." Tielhard de Chardin (1961) says:

In its construction, it is true, every organism is always and inevitably reducible into its component parts. But it by no means follows that the sum of the parts is the same as the whole, or that, in the whole, some specifically new value may not emerge [p. 110].

What can be concluded from this discussion? First, it would seem that a detailed analysis of man is essential for a systematic understanding. Yet, synthesis also is required in order to understand the many interactions and interdependencies. We can conclude that the most effective strategy for the behavioral scientist might be that used by the systems analyst—a working back and forth between analysis and synthesis.

MAN IS A REALITY; OR MAN IS A POTENTIALITY

Is man a reality? If so, he exists as fact; he is actual; he has objective existence. Or is man a potentiality? If so, he represents possibility rather than actuality; he is capable of being or becoming. The question here is: Can we study man as an actually existing entity—as we would study any other complex system—or must we view man as a completely dynamic entity, one that is constantly emerging or becoming?

There is support for the view of man as an actuality. The numerous results from the many years of research in the area of experimental psychology, for example, suggest that man is definable and measurable, and is capable of being investigated as an actually existing complex system. Further, the many current studies in the area of cybernetics, which point up similarities between man and machine, lend credence to the concept of man as an existing system.

There also is evidence to support the view of man as a potentiality. For example, case studies have revealed that long-term criminals have experienced religious conversions and then completely changed their way of life. Further, complete personality transformations have resulted from psychoanalysis and electroshock therapy. Indeed, man is changeable, and any given individual can become something quite different from what he was in the past.

Maslow (1961) has stressed the importance of human potentiality:

I think it fair to say that no theory of psychology will ever be complete that does not centrally incorporate the concept that man has his future within him, dynamically active at this present moment [p. 59].

What can we conclude? Only that man is both a reality and a potentiality. He represents objective existence, yet he can move toward any one of many different future states that are essentially unpredictable.

Man Is Knowable in Scientific Terms;
or Man Is More Than We Can Ever Know about Him

This final issue is basic to the entire study of man, and is closely tied to all the previous issues discussed. Is man knowable in scientific terms, or is man more than we can ever know about him?

There are many centuries of evidence to support the idea that man is scientifically knowable. Aristotle, for example, applied the same logic to his study of man as he did to other phenomena in the world. Further, volumes of data resulting from psychological experiments since the time of Wundt's founding of the first experimental psychology laboratory in 1879 indicate that man is scientifically knowable. Then, too, the many laboratory experiments and field studies recently conducted by the different disciplines included in the behavioral and social sciences certainly suggest that man is scientifically knowable.

Yet, there also is support for the idea that man is more than we can ever know about him. Man has continued to transcend himself over the past million or so years, as demonstrated by the theory of evolution. Further, on logical grounds, it can be demonstrated that man becomes something different every time he gains new knowledge about himself, which would suggest that man is truly an "open system."

It is apparent that we know very little about man. William James (1956) says: "Our science is a drop, our ignorance a sea [p. 54]." Erich Fromm (1956) believes that "Even if we knew a thousand times more of ourselves, we would never reach bottom [p. 31]."

What can we conclude? We must conclude that man is scientifically knowable—at least to a point. Yet there is no evidence to support the idea that man is—or ever will be—*completely* knowable.

CONCLUSIONS

This paper has presented two models of man:

The behavioristic model. Man can be described meaningfully in terms of his behavior; he is predictable; he is an information transmitter; he lives in an objective world; he is rational; he has traits in common with other men; he may be described in absolute terms; his characteristics can be studied independently of one another; he is a reality; and he is knowable in scientific terms.

The phenomenological model. Man can be described meaningfully in terms of his consciousness; he is unpredictable; he is an information generator; he lives in a subjective world; he is arational; he is unique alongside millions of other unique personalities; he can be described in relative terms; he must be studied in a holistic manner; he is a potentiality; and he is more than we can ever know about him.

This analysis of behaviorism and phenomenology leads to these conclusions:

1. The acceptance of either the behavioristic model or a phenomenological model has important implications in the everyday world. The choice of one versus the other could greatly influence human activities (either behavior or awareness) in such areas as education, psychiatry, theology, behavioral science, law, politics, marketing, advertising, and even parenthood. Thus, this ongoing debate is not just an academic exercise.

2. There appears to be truth in both views of man. The evidence that has been presented lends credence to both the behavioristic model and the phenomenological model. Indeed, it would be premature for psychology to accept either model as the final model.

3. A given behavioral scientist may find that both models are useful, depending upon the problem under study. The phenomenological model, for example, might be quite appropriate for the investigation of the creative process in scientists. On the other hand, the behavioristic model might be very useful in the study of environmental factors that motivate a given population of subjects to behave in a certain manner.

4. Finally, we must conclude that the behaviorist and the phenomenologist should listen to each other. Both, as scientists, should be willing to listen to opposing points of view. Each should endeavor to understand what the other is trying to say. It would appear that a dialogue is in order.

Allport, G. W. *Becoming: Basic considerations for a psychology of personality.* New Haven: Yale University Press, 1955.

Ashby, W. R. What is an intelligent machine? *Proceedings of the Western Joint Computer Conference,* 1961, **19,** 275–280.

de Chardin, P. T. *The phenomenon of man.* New York: Harper & Row, 1961 (Harper Torchback Edition).

Fromm, E. *The art of loving.* New York: Harper & Row, 1956.

James, W. *The will to believe and other essays on popular philosophy.* New York: Dover, 1956 (Orig. publ. 1896).

James, W. The individual and society. In *The philosophy of William James.* New York: Modern Library, 1925 (Orig. publ. 1897).

Jaspers, K. *Man in the modern age.* New York: Doubleday, 1957 (Orig. publ. in Germany, 1931).

Jaspers, K. *General psychopathology.* Manchester, England: Manchester University Press, 1963. (Publ. in U.S.A. by University of Chicago Press.)

Jaspers, K. *Philosophy is for everyman.* New York: Harcourt, Brace & World, 1967.

Koch, S. Psychology and emerging conceptions of knowledge as unitary. In T. W. Wann (Ed.), *Behaviorism and phenomenology: Contrasting bases for modern psychology.* Chicago: University of Chicago Press, 1964.

MacLeod, R. B. Phenomenology: A challenge to experimental psychology. In T. W. Wann (Ed.), *Behaviorism and phenomenology: Contrasting bases for modern psychology.* Chicago: University of Chicago Press, 1964.

Malcolm, N. Behaviorism as a philosophy of psychology. In T. W. Wann (Ed.), *Behaviorism and phenomenology: Contrasting bases for modern psychology.* Chicago: University of Chicago Press, 1964.

Maslow, A. H. Existential psychology—What's in it for us? In R. May (Ed.), *Existential psychology.* New York: Random House. 1961.

Polanyi, M. *The study of man.* Chicago: University of Chicago Press, 1963 (First Phoenix Edition).

Rogers, C. R. Toward a science of the person. In T. W. Wann (Ed.), *Behaviorism and phenomenology: Contrasting bases for modern psychology.* Chicago: University of Chicago Press, 1964.

Skinner, B. F. *Verbal behavior.* New York: Appleton-Century-Crofts, 1957.

Skinner, B. F. Behaviorism at fifty. In T. W. Wann (Ed.), *Behaviorism and phenomenology: Contrasting bases for modern psychology.* Chicago: University of Chicago Press, 1964.

Wann, T. W. (Ed.) *Behaviorism and phenomenology: Contrasting bases for modern psychology.* Chicago: University of Chicago Press, 1964.

Woodworth, R. S., & Sheehan, M. R. *Contemporary schools of psychology.* New York: Ronald Press, 1964.

Some Issues Concerning the Control of Human Behavior

Carl R. Rogers/B. F. Skinner

I [SKINNER]

Science is steadily increasing our power to influence, change, mold—in a word, control—human behavior. It has extended our "understanding" (whatever that may be) so that we deal more successfully with people in nonscientific ways, but it has also identified conditions or variables which can be used to predict and control behavior in a new, and increasingly rigorous, technology. The broad disciplines of government and economics offer examples of this, but there is special cogency in those contributions of anthropology, sociology, and psychology which deal with individual behavior. Carl Rogers has listed some of the achievements to date in a recent paper (1). Those of his examples which show or imply the control of the single organism are primarily due, as we should expect, to psychology. It is the experimental study of behavior which carries us beyond awkward or inaccessible "principles," "factors," and so on, to variables which can be directly manipulated.

It is also, and for more or less the same reasons, the conception of human behavior emerging from an experimental analysis which most directly challenges traditional views. Psychologists themselves often do not seem to be aware of how far they have moved in this direction. But the change is not passing unnoticed by others. Until only recently it was customary to deny the possibility of a rigorous science of human behavior by arguing, either that a lawful science was impossible because man was a free agent, or that merely statistical predictions would always leave room

Reprinted from *Science*, 1956, **124** (3231), 1057–1066, by permission of the authors and publisher.

for personal freedom. But those who used to take this line have become most vociferous in expressing their alarm at the way these obstacles are being surmounted.

Now, the control of human behavior has always been unpopular. Any undisguised effort to control usually arouses emotional reactions. We hesitate to admit, even to ourselves, that we are engaged in control, and we may refuse to control, even when this would be helpful, for fear of criticism. Those who have explicitly avowed an interest in control have been roughly treated by history. Machiavelli is the great prototype. As Macaulay said of him, "Out of his surname they coined an epithet for a knave and out of his Christian name a synonym for the devil." There were obvious reasons. The control that Machiavelli analyzed and recommended, like most political control, used techniques that were aversive to the controllee. The threats and punishments of the bully, like those of the government operating on the same plan, are not designed—whatever their success—to endear themselves to those who are controlled. Even when the techniques themselves are not aversive, control is usually exercised for the selfish purposes of the controller and, hence, has indirectly punishing effects upon others.

Man's natural inclination to revolt against selfish control has been exploited to good purpose in what we call the philosophy and literature of democracy. The doctrine of the rights of man has been effective in arousing individuals to concerted action against governmental and religious tyranny. The literature which has had this effect has greatly extended the number of terms in our language which express reactions to the control of men. But the ubiquity and ease of expression of this attitude spells trouble for any science which may give birth to a powerful technology of behavior. Intelligent men and women, dominated by the humanistic philosophy of the past two centuries, cannot view with equanimity what Andrew Hacker has called "the specter of predictable man" (2). Even the statistical or actuarial prediction of human events, such as the number of fatalities to be expected on a holiday weekend, strikes many people as uncanny and evil, while the prediction and control of individual behavior is regarded as little less than the work of the devil. I am not so much concerned here with the political or economic consequences for psychology, although research following certain channels may well suffer harmful effects. We ourselves, as intelligent men and women, and as exponents of Western thought, share these attitudes. They have already interfered with the free exercise of a scientific analysis, and their influence threatens to assume more serious proportions.

Three broad areas of human behavior supply good examples. The first of these—*personal control*—may be taken to include person-to-person relationships in the family, among friends, in social and work groups, and in counseling and psychotherapy. Other fields are *education* and *government*. A few examples from each will show how nonscientific preconceptions are affecting our current thinking about human behavior.

PERSONAL CONTROL

People living together in groups come to control one another with a technique which is not inappropriately called "ethical." When an individual behaves in a fashion acceptable to the group, he receives admiration, approval, affection, and many other reinforcements which increase the likelihood that he will continue to behave in that fashion. When his behavior is not acceptable, he is criticized, censured, blamed, or otherwise punished. In the first case the group calls him "good"; in the second, "bad." This practice is so thoroughly ingrained in our culture that we often fail to see that it is a technique of control. Yet we are almost always engaged in such control, even though the reinforcements and punishments are often subtle.

The practice of admiration is an important part of a culture, because behavior which is otherwise inclined to be weak can be set up and maintained with its help. The individual is especially likely to be praised, admired, or loved when he acts for the group in the face of great danger, for example, or sacrifices himself or his possessions, or submits to prolonged hardship, or suffers martyrdom. These actions are not admirable in any absolute sense, but they require admiration if they are to be strong. Similarly, we admire people who behave in original or exceptional ways, not because such behavior is itself admirable, but because we do not know how to encourage original or exceptional behavior in any other way. The group acclaims independent, unaided behavior in part because it is easier to reinforce than to help.

As long as this technique of control is misunderstood, we cannot judge correctly an environment in which there is less need for heroism, hardship, or independent action. We are likely to argue that such an environment is itself less admirable or produces less admirable people. In the old days, for example, young scholars often lived in undesirable quarters, ate unappetizing or inadequate food, performed unprofitable tasks for a living or to pay for necessary books and materials or publication. Older scholars and other members of the group offered compensating reinforcement in the form of approval and admiration for these sacrifices. When the modern graduate student receives a generous scholarship, enjoys good living conditions, and has his research and publication subsidized, the grounds for evaluation seem to be pulled from under us. Such a student no longer *needs* admiration to carry him over a series of obstacles (no matter how much he may need it for other reasons), and, in missing certain familiar objects of admiration, we are likely to conclude that such *conditions* are less admirable. Obstacles to scholarly work may serve as a useful measure of motivation—and we may go wrong unless some substitute is found—but we can scarcely defend a deliberate harassment of the student for this purpose. The productivity of any set of conditions can be evaluated only when we have freed ourselves of the attitudes which have been generated in us as members of an ethical group.

A similar difficulty arises from our use of punishment in the form of censure or blame. The concept of responsibility and the related concepts of foreknowledge and choice are used to justify techniques of control using punishment. Was So-and-So aware of the probable consequences of his action, and was the action deliberate? If so, we are justified in punishing him. But what does this mean? It appears to be a question concerning the efficacy of the contingent relations between behavior and punishing consequences. We punish behavior because it is objectionable to us or the group, but in a minor refinement of rather recent origin we have come to withhold punishment when it cannot be expected to have any effect. If the objectionable consequences of an act were accidental and not likely to occur again, there is no point in punishing. We say that the individual was not "aware of the consequences of his action" or that the consequences were not "intentional." If the action could not have been avoided—if the individual "had no choice"—punishment is also withheld, as it is if the individual is incapable of being changed by punishment because he is of "unsound mind." In all these cases—different as they are—the individual is held "not responsible" and goes unpunished.

Just as we say that it is "not fair" to punish a man for something he could not help doing, so we call it "unfair" when one is rewarded beyond his due or for something he could not help doing. In other words, we also object to wasting *reinforcers* where they are not needed or will do no good. We make the same point with the words *just* and *right*. Thus we have no right to punish the irresponsible, and a man has no right to reinforcers he does not earn or deserve. But concepts of choice, responsibility, justice, and so on, provide a most inadequate analysis of efficient reinforcing and punishing contingencies because they carry a heavy semantic cargo of a quite different sort, which obscures any attempt to clarify controlling practices or to improve techniques. In particular, they fail to prepare us for techniques based on other than aversive techniques of control. Most people would object to forcing prisoners to serve as subjects of dangerous medical experiments, but few object when they are induced to serve by the offer of return privileges—even when the reinforcing effect of these privileges has been created by forcible deprivation. In the traditional scheme the right to refuse guarantees the individual against coercion or an unfair bargain. But to what extent *can* a prisoner refuse under such circumstances?

We need not go so far afield to make the point. We can observe our own attitude toward personal freedom in the way we resent any interference with what we want to do. Suppose we want to buy a car of a particular sort. Then we may object, for example, if our wife urges us to buy a less expensive model and to put the difference into a new refrigerator. Or we may resent it if our neighbor questions our need for such a car or our ability to pay for it. We would certainly resent it if it were illegal to buy such a car (remember Prohibition); and if we find we cannot actually afford it, we may resent governmental control of the price through tariffs and taxes. We resent it if we discover that we cannot get the car because the manufacturer is holding the model in deliberately short supply in order to push a model we do not want. In all this we assert our democratic right to buy the car of our choice. We are well prepared to do so and to resent any restriction on our freedom.

But why do we not ask *why* it is the car of our choice and resent the forces which made it so? Perhaps our favorite toy as a child was a car, of a very different model, but nevertheless bearing the name of the car we now want. Perhaps our favorite TV program is sponsored by the manufacturer of that car. Perhaps we have seen pictures of many beautiful or prestigeful persons driving it—in pleasant or glamorous places. Perhaps the car has been designed with respect to our motivational patterns: the device on the hood is a phallic symbol; or the horsepower has been stepped up to please our competitive spirit in enabling us to pass other cars swiftly (or, as the advertisements say, "safely"). The concept of freedom that has emerged as part of the cultural practice of our group makes little or no provision for recognizing or dealing with these kinds of control. Concepts like "responsibility" and "rights" are scarcely applicable. We are prepared to deal with coercive measures but we have no traditional recourse with respect to other measures which in the long run (and especially with the help of science) may be much more powerful and dangerous.

EDUCATION

The techniques of education were once frankly aversive. The teacher was usually older and stronger than his pupils and was able to "make them learn." This meant that they were not actually taught but were surrounded by a threatening world from which they could escape only by learning. Usually they were left to their own resources in discovering how to do so. Claude Coleman has published a grimly amusing reminder of these older practices (*3*). He tells of a schoolteacher who published a careful account of his services during 51 years of teaching, during which he administered: ". . . 911,527 blows with a cane; 124,010 with a rod; 20,989 with a ruler; 136,715 with the hand; 10,295 over the mouth; 7,905 boxes on the ear; [and] 1,115,800 slaps on the head. . . ."

Progressive education was a humanitarian effort to substitute positive reinforcement for such aversive measures, but in the search for useful human values in the classroom it has never fully replaced the variables it abandoned. Viewed as a branch of behavioral technology, education remains relatively inefficient. We supplement it, and rationalize it, by admiring the pupil who learns *for himself;* and we often attribute the learning process, or knowledge itself, to something *inside* the individual. We admire behavior which seems to have inner sources. Thus we admire one who *recites* a poem more than one who simply *reads* it. We admire one who *knows* the answer more than one who *knows where to look it up.* We admire the *writer* rather than the *reader.* We admire the arithmetician who can do a problem in his head rather than with a slide rule or calculating machine, or in "original" ways rather than by a strict application of rules. In general we feel that any aid or "crutch"—except those aids to which we are now thoroughly accustomed—reduces the credit due. In Plato's *Phaedus,* Thamus, the king, attacks the invention of the alphabet on similar grounds! He is afraid "it will produce forgetfulness in the minds of those who learn to use it, because they will not practice their memories. . . ." In other words, he holds it more admirable to remember than to use a memorandum. He also objects that pupils "will read many things without instruction . . . [and] will therefore seem to know many things when they are for the most part ignorant." In the same vein we are today sometimes contemptuous of book learning, but, as educators, we can scarcely afford to adopt this view without reservation.

By admiring the student for knowledge and blaming him for ignorance, we escape some of the responsibility of teaching him. We resist any analysis of the educational process which threatens the notion of inner wisdom or questions the contention that the fault of ignorance lies with the student. More powerful techniques which bring about the same changes in behavior by manipulating *external* variables are decried as brainwashing or thought control. We are quite unprepared to judge *effective* educational measures. As long as only a few pupils learn much of what is taught, we do not worry about uniformity or regimentation. We do not fear the feeble technique; but we should view with dismay a system under which every student learned everything listed in a syllabus— although such a condition is far from unthinkable. Similarly, we do not fear a system which is so defective that the student must *work* for an education; but we are loath to give credit for anything learned without effort—although this could well be taken as an ideal result—and we flatly refuse to give credit if the student already knows what a school teaches.

A world in which people are wise and good without trying, without "having to be," without "choosing to be," could conceivably be a far better world for everyone. In such a world we should not have to "give anyone credit"—we should not need to admire anyone—for being wise and good. From our present point of view we cannot believe that such a world would be admirable. We do not even permit ourselves to imagine what it would be like.

GOVERNMENT

Government has always been the special field of aversive control. The state is frequently defined in terms of the power to punish, and jurisprudence leans heavily upon the associated notion of personal responsibility. Yet it is becoming increasingly difficult to reconcile current practice and theory with these earlier views. In criminology, for example, there is a strong tendency to drop the notion of responsibility in favor of some such alternative as capacity or controllability. But no matter how strongly the facts, or even practical expedience, support such a change, it is difficult to make the change in a legal system designed on a different plan. When governments resort to other techniques (for example, positive reinforcement), the concept of responsibility is no longer relevant and the theory of government is no longer applicable.

The conflict is illustrated by two decisions of the Supreme Court in the 1930's which dealt with, and disagreed on, the definition of control or coercion (*4*, p. 233). The Agricultural Adjustment Act proposed that the Secretary of Agriculture make "rental or benefit payments" to those farmers who agreed to reduce production. The government agreed that the Act would be unconstitutional if the farmer had been *compelled* to reduce production but was not, since he was merely *invited* to do so. Justice Roberts (*4*) expressed the contrary majority view of the court that "The power to confer or withhold unlimited benefits is the power to coerce or destroy." This recognition of positive reinforcement was withdrawn a few years later in another case in which Justice Cardozo (*4*, p. 244) wrote "To hold that motive or temptation is equivalent to coercion is to plunge the law in endless difficulties." We may agree with him, without implying that the proposition is therefore wrong. Sooner or later the law must be prepared to deal with all possible techniques of governmental control.

The uneasiness with which we view government (in the broadest possible sense) when it does not use punishment is shown by the reception of my utopian novel, *Walden Two* (*4a*). This was essentially a proposal to apply a behavioral technology to the construction of a workable, effective, and productive pattern of government. It was greeted with wrathful violence. *Life* magazine called it "a travesty on the good life," and "a menace . . . a triumph of mortmain or the dead hand not envisaged since the days of Sparta . . . a slur upon a name, a corruption of an impulse." Joseph Wood Krutch devoted a substantial part of his book, *The Measure of Man* (*5*), to attacking my views and those of the protagonist, Frazier, in the same vein, and Morris Viteles has recently criticized the book in a similar manner in *Science* (*6*). Perhaps the reaction is best expressed in a quotation from *The Quest of Utopia* by Negley and Patrick (*7*):

"Halfway through this contemporary utopia, the reader may feel sure, as we did, that this is a beautifully ironic satire on what has been called 'behavioral engineering.' The longer one stays in this better world of the psychologist, however, the plainer it becomes that the inspiration is not satiric, but messianic. This is indeed the behaviorally engineered society, and while it was to be expected that sooner or later the principle of psychological conditioning would be made the basis of a serious construction of utopia—Brown anticipated it in *Limanora*—yet not even the effective satire of Huxley is adequate preparation for the shocking horror of the idea when positively presented. Of all the dictatorships espoused by utopists, this is the most profound, and incipient dictators might well find in this utopia a guidebook of political practice."

One would scarcely guess that the authors are talking about a world in which there is food, clothing, and shelter for all, where everyone chooses his own work and works on the average only 4 hours a day, where music and the arts flourish, where personal relationships develop under the most favorable circumstances, where education prepares every child for the social and intellectual life which lies before him, where— in short—people are truly happy, secure, productive, creative, and forward-looking. What is wrong with it? Only one thing: someone "planned it that way." If these critics had come upon a society in some remote corner of the world which boasted similar advantages, they would undoubtedly have hailed it as providing a pattern we all might well follow —provided that it was clearly the result of a natural process of cultural evolution. Any evidence that intelligence had been used in arriving at this version of the good life would, in their eyes, be a serious flaw. No matter if the planner of *Walden Two* diverts none of the proceeds of the community to his own use, no matter if he has no current control or is, indeed, unknown to most of the other members of the community (he planned that, too), somewhere back of it all he occupies the position of prime mover. And this, to the child of the democratic tradition, spoils it all.

The dangers inherent in the control of human behavior are very real. The possibility of the misuse of scientific knowledge must always be faced. We cannot escape by denying the power of a science of behavior or arresting its development. It is no help to cling to familiar philosophies of human behavior simply because they are more reassuring. As I have pointed out elsewhere (8), the new techniques emerging from a science of behavior must be subject to the explicit countercontrol which has already been applied to earlier and cruder forms. Brute force and deception, for example, are now fairly generally suppressed by ethical practices and by explicit governmental and religious agencies. A similar countercontrol of scientific knowledge in the interests of the group is a feasible and promising possibility. Although we cannot say how devious the course of its evolution may be, a cultural pattern of control and countercontrol will presumably emerge which will be most widely supported because it is most widely reinforcing.

If we cannot foresee all the details of this (as we obviously cannot), it is important to remember that this is true of the critics of science as well. The dire consequences of new techniques of control, the hidden menace in original cultural designs—these need some proof. It is only another example of my present point that the need for proof is so often overlooked. Man has got himself into some pretty fixes, and it is easy to believe that he will do so again. But there is a more optimistic possibility. The slow growth of the methods of science, now for the first time being applied to human affairs, *may* mean a new and exciting phase of human life to which historical analogies will not apply and in which earlier political slogans will not be appropriate. If we are to use the knowledge that a science of behavior is now making available with any hope of success, we must look at human nature as it is brought into focus through the methods of science rather than as it has been presented to us in a series of historical accidents.

If the advent of a powerful science of behavior causes trouble, it will not be because science itself is inimical to human welfare but because older conceptions have not yielded easily or gracefully. We expect resistance to new techniques of control from those who have heavy investments in the old, but we have no reason to help them preserve a series of principles that are not ends in themselves but rather outmoded means to an end. What is needed is a new conception of human behavior which is compatible with the implications of a scientific analysis. All men control and are controlled. The question of government in the broadest possible sense is not how freedom is to be preserved but what kinds of control are to be used and to what ends. Control must be analyzed and considered in its proper proportions. No one, I am sure, wishes to develop new master-slave relationships or bend the will of the people to despotic rulers in new ways. These are patterns of control appropriate to a world without science. They may well be the first to go when the experimental analysis of behavior comes into its own in the design of cultural practices.

II [ROGERS]

There are, I believe, a number of matters in connection with this important topic on which the authors of this article, and probably a large majority of psychologists, are in agreement. These matters then are not issues as far as we are concerned, and I should like to mention them briefly in order to put them to one side.

POINTS OF AGREEMENT

I am sure we agree that men—as individuals and as societies—have always endeavored to understand, predict, influence, and control human behavior—their own behavior and that of others.

I believe we agree that the behavioral sciences are making and will continue to make increasingly rapid progress in the understanding of behavior, and that as a consequence the capacity to predict and to control behavior is developing with equal rapidity.

I believe we agree that to deny these advances, or to claim that man's behavior cannot be a field of science, is unrealistic. Even though this is not an issue for us, we should recognize that many intelligent men still hold strongly to the view that the actions of men are free in some sense such that scientific knowledge of man's behavior is impossible. Thus Reinhold Niebuhr, the noted theologian, heaps scorn on the concept of psychology as a science of man's behavior and even says, "In any event, no scientific investigation of past behavior can become the basis of predictions of future behavior" (9). So, while this is not an issue for psychologists, we should at least notice in passing that it is an issue for many people.

I believe we are in agreement that the tremendous potential power of a science which permits the prediction and control of behavior may be misused, and that the possibility of such misuse constitutes a serious threat.

Consequently Skinner and I are in agreement that the whole question of the scientific control of human behavior is a matter with which psychologists and the general public should concern themselves. As Robert Oppenheimer told the American Psychological Association last year (10) the problems that psychologists will pose for society by their growing ability to control behavior will be much more grave than the problems posed by the ability of physicists to control the reactions of matter. I am not sure whether psychologists generally recognize this. My impression is that by and large they hold a laissez-faire attitude. Obviously Skinner and I do not hold this laissez-faire view, or we would not have written this article.

POINTS AT ISSUE

With these several points of basic and important agreement, are there then any issues that remain on which there are differences? I believe there are. They can be stated very briefly: Who will be controlled? Who will exercise control? What type of control will be exercised? Most important of all, toward what end or what purpose, or in the pursuit of what value, will control be exercised?

It is on questions of this sort that there exist ambiguities, misunderstandings, and probably deep differences. These differences exist among psychologists, among members of the general public in this country, and among various world cultures. Without any hope of achieving a final resolution of these questions, we can, I believe, put these issues in clearer form.

SOME MEANINGS

To avoid ambiguity and faulty communication, I would like to clarify the meanings of some of the terms we are using.

Behavioral science is a term that might be defined from several angles but in the context of this discussion it refers primarily to knowledge that the existence of certain describable conditions in the human being and/or in his environment is followed by certain describable consequences in his actions.

Prediction means the prior identification of behaviors which then occur. Because it is important in some things I wish to say later, I would point out that one may predict a highly specific behavior, such as an eye blink, or one may predict a class of behaviors. One might correctly predict "avoidant behavior," for example, without being able to specify whether the individual will run away or simply close his eyes.

The word *control* is a very slippery one, which can be used with any one of several meanings. I would like to specify three that seem most important for our present purposes. *Control* may mean: (i) The setting of conditions by B for A, A having no voice in the matter, such that certain predictable behaviors then occur in A. I refer to this as external control. (ii) The setting of conditions by B for A, A giving some degree of consent to these conditions, such that certain predictable behaviors then occur in A. I refer to this as the influence of B on A. (iii) The setting of conditions by A such that certain predictable behaviors then occur in himself. I refer to this as internal control. It will be noted that Skinner lumps together the first two meanings, external control and influence, under the concept of control. I find this confusing.

USUAL CONCEPT OF CONTROL OF HUMAN BEHAVIOR

With the underbrush thus cleared away (I hope), let us review very briefly the various elements that are involved in the usual concept of the control of human behavior as mediated by the behavioral sciences. I am drawing here on the previous writings of Skinner, on his present statements, on the writings of others who have considered in either friendly or antagonistic fashion the meanings that would be involved in such control. I have not excluded the science fiction writers, as reported recently by Vandenburg (*11*), since they often show an awareness of the issues involved, even though the methods described are as yet fictional. These then are the elements that seem common to these different concepts of the application of science to human behavior.

1) There must first be some sort of decision about goals. Usually desirable goals are assumed, but sometimes, as in George Orwell's book *1984,* the goal that is selected is an aggrandizement of individual power with which most of us would disagree. In a recent paper Skinner suggests that one possible set of goals to be assigned to the behavioral technology is this: "Let men be happy, informed, skillful, well-behaved and productive" (*12*). In the first draft of his part of this article, which he was kind enough to show me, he did not mention such definite goals as these, but desired "improved" educational practices, "wiser" use of knowledge in government, and the like. In the final version of his article he avoids even these value-laden terms, and his implicit goal is the very general one that scientific control of behavior is desirable, because it would perhaps bring "a far better world for everyone."

Thus the first step in thinking about the control of human behavior is the choice of goals, whether specific or general. It is necessary to come to terms in some way with the issue, "For what purpose?"

2) A second element is that, whether the end selected is highly specific or is a very general one such as wanting "a better world," we proceed by the methods of science to discover the means to these ends. We continue through further experimentation and investigation to discover more effective means. The method of science is self-correcting in thus arriving at increasingly effective ways of achieving the purpose we have in mind.

3) The third aspect of such control is that as the conditions or methods are discovered by which to reach the goal, some person or some group establishes these conditions and uses these methods, having in one way or another obtained the power to do so.

4) The fourth element is the exposure of individuals to the prescribed

conditions, and this leads, with a high degree of probability, to behavior which is in line with the goals desired. Individuals are now happy, if that has been the goal, or well-behaved, or submissive, or whatever it has been decided to make them.

5) The fifth element is that if the process I have described is put in motion then there is a continuing social organization which will continue to produce the types of behavior that have been valued.

SOME FLAWS

Are there any flaws in this way of viewing the control of human behavior? I believe there are. In fact the only element in this description with which I find myself in agreement is the second. It seems to me quite incontrovertibly true that the scientific method is an excellent way to discover the means by which to achieve our goals. Beyond that, I feel many sharp differences, which I will try to spell out.

I believe that in Skinner's presentation here and in his previous writings, there is a serious underestimation of the problem of power. To hope that the power which is being made available by the behavioral sciences will be exercised by the scientists, or by a benevolent group, seems to me a hope little supported by either recent or distant history. It seems far more likely that behavioral scientists, holding their present attitudes, will be in the position of the German rocket scientists specializing in guided missiles. First they worked devotedly for Hitler to destroy the U.S.S.R. and the United States. Now, depending on who captured them, they work devotedly for the U.S.S.R. in the interest of destroying the United States, or devotedly for the United States in the interest of destroying the U.S.S.R. If behavioral scientists are concerned solely with advancing their science, it seems most probable that they will serve the purposes of whatever individual or group has the power.

But the major flaw I see in this review of what is involved in the scientific control of human behavior is the denial, misunderstanding, or gross underestimation of the place of ends, goals or values in their relationship to science. This error (as it seems to me) has so many implications that I would like to devote some space to it.

ENDS AND VALUES IN RELATION TO SCIENCE

In sharp contradiction to some views that have been advanced, I would like to propose a two-pronged thesis: (i) In any scientific endeavor— whether "pure" or applied science—there is a prior subjective choice of the purpose or value which that scientific work is perceived as serving. (ii) This subjective value choice which brings the scientific endeavor into being must always lie outside of that endeavor and can never become a part of the science involved in that endeavor.

Let me illustrate the first point from Skinner himself. It is clear that in his earlier writing (*12*) it is recognized that a prior value choice is necessary, and it is specified as the goal that men are to become happy, well-behaved, productive, and so on. I am pleased that Skinner has retreated from the goals he then chose, because to me they seem to be stultifying values. I can only feel that he was choosing these goals for others, not for himself. I would hate to see Skinner become "well-behaved," as that term would be defined for him by behavioral scientists. His recent article in the *American Psychologist* (*13*) shows that he certainly does not want to be "productive" as that value is defined by most psychologists. And the most awful fate I can imagine for him would be to have him constantly "happy." It is the fact that he is very unhappy about many things which makes me prize him.

In the first draft of his part of this article, he also included such prior value choices, saying for example, "We must decide how we are to use the knowledge which a science of human behavior is now making available." Now he has dropped all mention of such choices, and if I understand him correctly, he believes that science can proceed without them. He has suggested this view in another recent paper, stating that "We must continue to experiment in cultural design . . . testing the consequences as we go. Eventually the practices which make for the greatest biological and psychological strength of the group will presumably survive" (*8*, p. 549).

I would point out, however, that to choose to experiment is a value choice. Even to move in the direction of perfectly random experimentation is a value choice. To test the consequences of an experiment is possible only if we have first made a subjective choice of a criterion value. And implicit in his statement is a valuing of biological and psychological strength. So even when trying to avoid such choice, it seems inescapable that a prior subjective value choice is necessary for any scientific endeavor, or for any application of scientific knowledge.

I wish to make it clear that I am not saying that values cannot be included as a subject of science. It is not true that science deals only with certain classes of "facts" and that these classes do not include values. It is a bit more complex than that, as a simple illustration or two may make clear.

If I value knowledge of the "three R's" as a goal of education, the methods of science can give me increasingly accurate information on how this goal may be achieved. If I value problem-solving ability as a goal of education, the scientific method can give me the same kind of help.

Now, if I wish to determine whether problem-solving ability is "better" than knowledge of the three R's, then scientific method can also study those two values but *only*—and this is very important—in terms of some other value which I have subjectively chosen. I may value college success. Then I can determine whether problem-solving ability or knowledge of the three R's is most closely associated with that value. I may value personal integration or vocational success or responsible citizenship. I can determine whether problem-solving ability or knowledge of the three R's is "better" for achieving any one of these values. But the value or purpose that gives meaning to a particular scientific endeavor must always lie outside of that endeavor.

Although our concern in this symposium is largely with applied science, what I have been saying seems equally true of so-called "pure" science. In pure science the usual prior subjective value choice is the discovery of truth. But this is a subjective choice, and science can never say whether it is the best choice, save in the light of some other value. Geneticists in the U.S.S.R., for example, had to make a subjective choice of whether it was better to pursue truth or to discover facts which upheld a governmental dogma. Which choice is "better"? We could make a scientific investigation of those alternatives but only in the light of some other subjectively chosen value. If, for example, we value the survival of a culture, then we could begin to investigate with the methods of science the question of whether pursuit of truth or support of governmental dogma is most closely associated with cultural survival.

My point then is that any endeavor in science, pure or applied, is carried on in the pursuit of a purpose or value that is subjectively chosen by persons. It is important that this choice be made explicit, since the particular value which is being sought can never be tested or evaluated, confirmed or denied, by the scientific endeavor to which it gives birth. The initial purpose or value always and necessarily lies outside the scope of the scientific effort which it sets in motion.

Among other things this means that if we choose some particular goal or series of goals for human beings and then set out on a large scale to control human behavior to the end of achieving those goals, we are locked in the rigidity of our initial choice, because such a scientific endeavor can never transcend itself to select new goals. Only subjective human persons can do that. Thus if we chose as our goal the state of happiness for human beings (a goal deservedly ridiculed by Aldous Huxley in *Brave New World*), and if we involved all of society in a successful scientific program by which people became happy, we would be locked in a colossal rigidity in which no one would be free to question this goal, because our scientific operations could not transcend themselves to question their guiding purposes. And without laboring this point, I would remark that colossal rigidity, whether in dinosaurs or dictatorships, has a very poor record of revolutionary survival.

If, however, a part of our scheme is to set free some "planners" who do not have to be happy, who are not controlled, and who are therefore free to choose other values, this has several meanings. It means that the purpose we have chosen as our goal is not a sufficient and a satisfying one for human beings but must be supplemented. It also means that if it is necessary to set up an elite group which is free, then this shows all too clearly that the great majority are only the slaves—no matter by what high-sounding name we call them—of those who select the goals.

Perhaps, however, the thought is that a continuing scientific endeavor will evolve its own goals; that the initial findings will alter the directions, and subsequent findings will alter them still further, and that science somehow develops its own purpose. Although he does not clearly say so, this appears to be the pattern Skinner has in mind. It is surely a reasonable description, but it overlooks one element in this continuing development, which is that subjective personal choice enters in at every point at which the direction changes. The findings of a science, the results of an experiment, do not and never can tell us what next scientific purpose to pursue. Even in the purest of science, the scientist must decide what the findings mean and must subjectively choose what next step will be most profitable in the pursuit of his purpose. And if we are speaking of the application of scientific knowledge, then it is distressingly clear that the increasing scientific knowledge of the structure of the atom carries with it no necessary choice as to the purpose to which this knowledge will be put. This is a subjective personal choice which must be made by many individuals.

Thus I return to the proposition with which I began this section of my remarks—and which I now repeat in different words. Science has its meaning as the objective pursuit of a purpose which has been subjectively chosen by a person or persons. This purpose or value can never be investigated by the particular scientific experiment or investigation to which it has given birth and meaning. Consequently, any discussion of the control of human beings by the behavioral sciences must first and most deeply concern itself with the subjectively chosen purposes which such an application of science is intended to implement.

Is the Situation Hopeless?

The thoughtful reader may recognize that, although my remarks up to this point have introduced some modifications in the conception of the processes by which human behavior will be controlled, these remarks may have made such control seem, if anything, even more inevitable. We might sum it up this way: Behavioral science is clearly moving forward; the increasing power for control which it gives will be held by someone or some group; such an individual or group will surely choose the values or goals to be achieved; and most of us will then be increasingly controlled by means so subtle that we will not even be aware of them as controls. Thus, whether a council of wise psychologists (if this is not a contradiction in terms), or a Stalin, or a Big Brother has the power, and whether the goal is happiness, or productivity, or resolution of the Oedipus complex, or submission, or love of Big Brother, we will inevitably find ourselves moving toward the chosen goal and probably thinking that we ourselves desire it. Thus, if this line of reasoning is correct, it appears that some form of *Walden Two* or of *1984* (and at a deep philosophic level they seem indistinguishable) is coming. The fact that it would surely arrive piecemeal, rather than all at once, does not greatly change the fundamental issues. In any event, as Skinner has indicated in his writings, we would then look back upon the concepts of human freedom, the capacity for choice, the responsibility for choice, and the worth of the human individual as historical curiosities which once existed by cultural accident as values in a prescientific civilization.

I believe that any person observant of trends must regard something like the foregoing sequence as a real possibility. It is not simply a fantasy. Something of that sort may even be the most likely future. But is it an inevitable future? I want to devote the remainder of my remarks to an alternative possibility.

Alternative Set of Values

Suppose we start with a set of ends, values, purposes, quite different from the type of goals we have been considering. Suppose we do this quite openly, setting them forth as a possible value choice to be accepted or rejected. Suppose we select a set of values that focuses on fluid elements of process rather than static attributes. We might then value: man as a process of becoming, as a process of achieving worth and dignity through the development of his potentialities; the individual human being as a self-actualizing process, moving on to more challenging and enriching experiences; the process by which the individual creatively adapts to an ever-new and changing world; the process by which knowledge transcends itself, as, for example, the theory of relativity transcended Newtonian physics, itself to be transcended in some future day by a new perception.

If we select values such as these we turn to our science and technology of behavior with a very different set of questions. We will want to know such things as these: Can science aid in the discovery of new modes of richly rewarding living? more meaningful and satisfying modes of interpersonal relationships? Can science inform us on how the human race can become a more intelligent participant in its own evolution—its physical, psychological and social evolution? Can science inform us on ways of releasing the creative capacity of individuals, which seem so necessary if we are to survive in this fantastically expanding atomic age? Oppenheimer has pointed out (*14*) that knowledge, which used to double in millennia or centuries, now doubles in a generation or a decade. It appears that we must discover the utmost in release of creativity if we are to be able to adapt effectively. In short, can science discover the methods by which man can most readily become a continually developing and self-transcending process, in his behavior, his thinking, his knowledge? Can science predict and release an essentially "unpredictable" freedom?

It is one of the virtues of science as a method that it is as able to advance and implement goals and purposes of this sort as it is to serve static values, such as states of being well-informed, happy, obedient. Indeed we have some evidence of this.

Small Example

I will perhaps be forgiven if I document some of the possibilities along this line by turning to psychotherapy, the field I know best.

Psychotherapy, as Meerloo (*15*) and others have pointed out, can be one of the most subtle tools for the control of *A* by *B*. The therapist can subtly mold individuals in imitation of himself. He can cause an individual to become a submissive and conforming being. When certain therapeutic principles are used in extreme fashion, we call it brainwashing, an instance of the disintegration of the personality and a reformulation of the person along lines desired by the controlling individual. So the principles of therapy can be used as an effective means of external control of human personality and behavior. Can psychotherapy be anything else?

Here I find the developments going on in client-centered psychotherapy (*16*) an exciting hint of what a behavioral science can do in achieving the kinds of values I have stated. Quite aside from being a somewhat new orientation in psychotherapy, this development has important implications regarding the relation of a behavioral science to the control of human behavior. Let me describe our experience as it relates to the issues of this discussion.

In client-centered therapy, we are deeply engaged in the prediction and influencing of behavior, or even the control of behavior. As therapists, we institute certain attitudinal conditions, and the client has relatively little voice in the establishment of these conditions. We predict that if these conditions are instituted, certain behavioral consequences will ensue in the client. Up to this point this is largely external control, no different from what Skinner has described, and no different from what I have discussed in the preceding sections of this article. But here any similarity ceases.

The conditions we have chosen to establish predict such behavioral consequences as these: that the client will become self-directing, less rigid, more open to the evidence of his senses, better organized and integrated, more similar to the ideal which he has chosen for himself. In other words, we have established by external control conditions which we predict will be followed by internal control by the individual, in pursuit of internally chosen goals. We have set the conditions which predict various classes of behaviors—self-directing behaviors, sensitivity to realities within and without, flexible adaptiveness—which are by their very nature unpredictable in their specifics. Our recent research (*17*) indicates that our predictions are to a significant degree corroborated, and our commitment to the scientific method causes us to believe that more effective means of achieving these goals may be realized.

Research exists in other fields—industry, education, group dynamics —which seems to support our own findings. I believe it may be conservatively stated that scientific progress has been made in identifying those conditions in an interpersonal relationship which, if they exist in *B,* are followed in *A* by greater maturity in behavior, less dependence on others, an increase in expressiveness as a person, an increase in variability, flexibility and effectiveness of adaptation, an increase in self-responsibility and self-direction. And, quite in contrast to the concern expressed by some, we do not find that the creatively adaptive behavior which results from such self-directed variability of expression is a "happy accident" which occurs in "chaos." Rather, the individual who is open to his experience, and self-directing, is harmonious not chaotic, ingenious rather than random, as he orders his responses imaginatively toward the achievement of his own purposes. His creative actions are no more a "happy accident" than was Einstein's development of the theory of relativity.

Thus we find ourselves in fundamental agreement with John Dewey's statement: "Science has made its way by releasing, not by suppressing, the elements of variation, of invention and innovation, of novel creation in individuals" (*18*). Progress in personal life and in group living is, we believe, made in the same way.

POSSIBLE CONCEPT OF THE CONTROL OF HUMAN BEHAVIOR

It is quite clear that the point of view I am expressing is in sharp contrast to the usual conception of the relationship of the behavioral sciences to the control of human behavior. In order to make this contrast even more blunt, I will state this possibility in paragraphs parallel to those used before.

1) It is possible for us to choose to value man as a self-actualizing process of becoming; to value creativity, and the process by which knowledge becomes self-transcending.

2) We can proceed, by the methods of science, to discover the conditions which necessarily precede these processes and, through continuing experimentation, to discover better means of achieving these purposes.

3) It is possible for individuals or groups to set these conditions, with a minimum of power or control. According to present knowledge, the only authority necessary is the authority to establish certain qualities of interpersonal relationship.

4) Exposed to these conditions, present knowledge suggests that individuals become more self-responsible, make progress in self-actualization, become more flexible, and become more creatively adaptive.

5) Thus such an initial choice would inaugurate the beginnings of a social system or subsystem in which values, knowledge, adaptive skills, and even the concept of science would be continually changing and self-transcending. The emphasis would be upon man as a process of becoming.

I believe it is clear that such a view as I have been describing does not lead to any definable utopia. It would be impossible to predict its final outcome. It involves a step-by-step development, based on a continuing subjective choice of purposes, which are implemented by the behavioral sciences. It is in the direction of the "open society," as that term has been defined by Popper (*19*), where individuals carry responsibility for personal decisions. It is at the opposite pole from his concept of the closed society, of which *Walden Two* would be an example.

I trust it is also evident that the whole emphasis is on process, not on end-states of being. I am suggesting that it is by choosing to value certain qualitative elements of the process of becoming that we can find a pathway toward the open society.

THE CHOICE

It is my hope that we have helped to clarify the range of choice which will lie before us and our children in regard to the behavioral sciences. We can choose to use our growing knowledge to enslave people in ways never dreamed of before, depersonalizing them, controlling them by means so carefully selected that they will perhaps never be aware of their loss of personhood. We can choose to utilize our scientific knowledge to make men happy, well-behaved, and productive, as Skinner earlier suggested. Or we can insure that each person learns all the syllabus which we select and set before him, as Skinner now suggests. Or at the other end of the spectrum of choice we can choose to use the behavioral sciences in ways which will free, not control; which will bring about constructive variability, not conformity; which will develop creativity, not contentment; which will facilitate each person in his self-directed process of becoming; which will aid individuals, groups, and even the concept of science to become self-transcending in freshly adaptive ways of meeting life and its problems. The choice is up to us, and, the human race being what it is, we are likely to stumble about, making at times some nearly disastrous value choices and at other times highly constructive ones.

I am aware that to some, this setting forth of a choice is unrealistic, because a choice of values is regarded as not possible. Skinner has stated: "Man's vaunted creative powers . . . his capacity to choose and our right to hold him responsible for his choice—none of these is conspicuous in this new self-portrait (provided by science). Man, we once believed, was free to express himself in art, music, and literature, to inquire into nature, to seek salvation in his own way. He could initiate action and make spontaneous and capricious changes of course. . . .

But science insists that action is initiated by forces impinging upon the individual, and that caprice is only another name for behavior for which we have not yet found a cause" (*12*, pp. 52–53).

I can understand this point of view, but I believe that it avoids looking at the great paradox of behavioral science. Behavior, when it is examined scientifically, is surely best understood as determined by prior causation. This is one great fact of science. But responsible personal choice, which is the most essential element in being a person, which is the core experience in psychotherapy, which exists prior to any scientific endeavor, is an equally prominent fact in our lives. To deny the experience of responsible choice is, to me, as restricted a view as to deny the possibility of a behavioral science. That these two important elements of our experience appear to be in contradiction has perhaps the same significance as the contradiction between the wave theory and the corpuscular theory of light, both of which can be shown to be true, even though incompatible. We cannot profitably deny our subjective life, any more than we can deny the objective description of that life.

In conclusion then, it is my contention that science cannot come into being without a personal choice of the values we wish to achieve. And these values we choose to implement will forever lie outside of the science which implements them; the goals we select, the purposes we wish to follow, must always be outside of the science which achieves them. To me this has the encouraging meaning that the human person, with his capacity of subjective choice, can and will always exist, separate from and prior to any of his scientific undertakings. Unless as individuals and groups we choose to relinquish our capacity of subjective choice, we will always remain persons, not simply pawns of a self-created science.

III [SKINNER]

I cannot quite agree that the practice of science *requires* a prior decision about goals or a prior choice of values. The metallurgist can study the properties of steel and the engineer can design a bridge without raising the question of whether a bridge is to be built. But such questions are certainly frequently raised and tentatively answered. Rogers wants to call the answers "subjective choices of values." To me, such an expression suggests that we have had to abandon more rigorous scientific practices in order to talk about our own behavior. In the experimental analysis of other organisms I would use other terms, and I shall try to do so here. Any list of values is a list of reinforcers—conditioned or otherwise. We are so constituted that under certain circumstances food, water, sexual contact, and so on, will make any behavior which produces them more likely to occur again. Other things may acquire this power. We do not need to say that an organism chooses to eat rather than to starve. If you answer that it is a very different thing when a man chooses to starve, I am only too happy to agree. If it were not so, we should have cleared up the question of choice long ago. An organism can be reinforced by—can be made to "choose"—almost any given state of affairs.

Rogers is concerned with choices that involve multiple and usually conflicting consequences. I have dealt with some of these elsewhere (*20*) in an analysis of self-control. Shall I eat these delicious strawberries today if I will then suffer an annoying rash tomorrow? The decision I am to make used to be assigned to the province of ethics. But we are now studying similar combinations of positive and negative consequences, as well as collateral conditions which affect the result, in the laboratory. Even a pigeon can be taught some measure of self-control! And this work helps us to understand the operation of certain formulas—among them value judgments—which folk-wisdom, religion, and psychotherapy have advanced in the interests of self-discipline. The observable effect of any statement of value is to alter the relative effectiveness of reinforcers. We may no longer enjoy the strawberries for thinking about the rash. If rashes are made sufficiently shameful, illegal, sinful, and maladjusted, or unwise, we may glow with satisfaction as we push the strawberries aside in a grandiose avoidance response which would bring a smile to the lips of Murray Sidman.

People behave in ways which, as we say, conform to ethical, governmental, or religious patterns because they are reinforced for doing so. The resulting behavior may have far-reaching consequences for the survival of the pattern to which it conforms. And whether we like it or not, survival is the ultimate criterion. This is where, it seems to me, science can help—not in choosing a goal, but in enabling us to predict the survival value of cultural practices. Man has too long tried to get the kind of world he wants by glorifying some brand of immediate reinforcement. As science points up more and more of the remoter consequences, he may begin to work to strengthen behavior, not in a slavish devotion to a chosen value, but with respect to the ultimate survival of mankind. Do not ask me why I want mankind to survive. I can tell you why only in the sense in which the physiologist can tell you why I want to breathe. Once the relation between a given step and the survival of my group has been pointed out, I will take that step. And it is the business of science to point out just such relations.

The values I have occasionally recommended (and Rogers has not led me to recant) are transitional. Other things being equal, I am betting on the group whose practices make for healthy, happy, secure, productive, and creative people. And I insist that the values recommended by Rogers are transitional, too, for I can ask him the same kind of question. Man as a process of becoming—*what?* Self-actualization—for what? Inner control is no more a goal than external.

What Rogers seems to me to be proposing, both here and elsewhere (*1*), is this: Let us use our increasing power of control to create individuals who will not need and perhaps will no longer respond to control. Let us solve the problem of our power by renouncing it. At first blush this seems as implausible as a benevolent despot. Yet power has occasionally been foresworn. A nation has burned its Reichstag, rich men have given away their wealth, beautiful women have become ugly hermits in the desert, and psychotherapists have become nondirective. When this happens, I look to other possible reinforcements for a plausible explanation. A people relinquish democratic power when a tyrant promises them the earth. Rich men give away wealth to escape the accusing finger of their fellowmen. A woman destroys her beauty in the hope of salvation. And a psychotherapist relinquishes control because he can thus help his client more effectively.

The solution that Rogers is suggesting is thus understandable. But is he correctly interpreting the result? What evidence is there that a client ever becomes truly *self*-directing? What evidence is there that he ever makes a truly *inner* choice of ideal or goal? Even though the therapist does not do the choosing, even though he encourages "self-actualization" —he is not out of control as long as he holds himself ready to step in when occasion demands—when, for example, the client chooses the goal of becoming a more accomplished liar or murdering his boss. But supposing the therapist does withdraw completely or is no longer necessary —what about all the other forces acting upon the client? Is the self-chosen goal independent of his early ethical and religious training? of the folk-wisdom of his group? of the opinions and attitudes of others who are important to him? Surely not. The therapeutic situation is only a small part of the world of the client. From the therapist's point of view it may appear to be possible to relinquish control. But the control passes, not to a "self," but to forces in other parts of the client's world. The solution of the therapist's problem of power cannot be *our* solution, for we must consider *all* the forces acting upon the individual.

The child who must be prodded and nagged is something less than a fully developed human being. We want to see him hurrying to his appointment, not because each step is taken in response to verbal reminders from his mother, but because certain temporal contingencies, in which dawdling has been punished and hurrying reinforced, have worked a change in his behavior. Call this a state of better organization, a greater sensitivity to reality, or what you will. The plain fact is that the child passes from a temporary verbal control exercised by his parents to control by certain inexorable features of the environment. I should suppose that something of the same sort happens in successful psychotherapy. Rogers seems to me to be saying this: Let us put an end, as quickly as possible, to any pattern of master-and-slave, to any direct obedience to command, to the submissive following of suggestions. Let the individual be free to adjust himself to more rewarding features of the world about him. In the end, let his teachers and counselors "wither away," like the Marxist state. I not only agree with this as a useful ideal, I have constructed a fanciful world to demonstrate its advantages. It saddens me to hear Rogers say that "at a deep philosophic level" *Walden Two* and George Orwell's *1984* "seem indistinguishable." They could scarcely be more unlike—at any level. The book *1984* is a picture of immediate aversive control for vicious selfish purposes. The founder of *Walden Two,* on the other hand, has built a community in which neither he nor any other person exerts any *current* control. His achievement lay in his original *plan,* and when he boasts of this ("It is enough to satisfy the thirstiest tyrant") we do not fear him but only pity him for his weakness.

Another critic of *Walden Two,* Andrew Hacker (*21*), has discussed this point in considering the bearing of mass conditioning upon the liberal notion of autonomous man. In drawing certain parallels between the Grand Inquisition passage in Dostoevsky's *Brothers Karamazov,* Huxley's *Brave New World,* and *Walden Two,* he attempts to set up a distinction to be drawn in any society between conditioners and conditioned. He assumes that "the conditioner can be said to be autonomous in the traditional liberal sense." But then he notes: "Of course the conditioner has been conditioned. But he has not been conditioned by the conscious manipulation of another *person.*" But how does this affect the resulting behavior? Can we not soon forget the origins of the "artificial" diamond which is identical with the real thing? Whether it is an "accidental" cultural pattern, such as is said to have produced the founder of *Walden Two,* or the engineered environment which is about to produce his successors, we are dealing with sets of conditions generating human behavior which will ultimately be measured by their contribution to the strength of the group. We look to the future, not the past, for the test of "goodness" or acceptability.

If we are worthy of our democratic heritage we shall, of course, be ready to resist any tyrannical use of science for immediate or selfish purposes. But if we value the achievements and goals of democracy we must not refuse to apply science to the design and construction of cultural patterns, even though we may then find ourselves in some sense in the position of controllers. Fear of control, generalized beyond any warrant, has led to a misinterpretation of valid practices and the blind rejection of intelligent planning for a better way of life. In terms which I trust Rogers will approve, in conquering this fear we shall become more mature and better organized and shall, thus, more fully actualize ourselves as human beings.

1. Rogers, C. R. *Teachers College Record,* 1956, **57** (316).

2. Hacker, A. *Antioch Rev.,* 1954, **14** (195).

3. Coleman, C. *Bull. Am. Assoc. Univ. Professors,* 1953, **39** (457).

4. Freund, P. A., et al. *Constitutional law: Cases and other problems.* Boston: Little, Brown, 1954, Vol. 1.

4a. Skinner, B. F. *Walden two.* New York: Macmillan, 1948.

5. Krutch, J. W. *The measure of man.* Indianapolis: Bobbs-Merrill, 1953.

6. Viteles, M. *Science,* 1955, **122** (1167).

7. Negley, G., & Patrick, J. M. *The quest for utopia.* New York: Schuman, 1952.

8. Skinner, B. F. *Trans. N. Y. Acad. Sci.,* 1955, **17** (547)

9. Niebuhr, R. *The self and the dramas of history.* New York: Scribner, 1955, p. 47.

10. Oppenheimer, R. *Am. Psychol.* 1956, **11** (127).

11. Vandenberg, S. G. *Ibid.,* 1956, **11** (339).

12. Skinner, B. F. *Am. Scholar,* 1955–1956, **25** (47).

13. Skinner, B. F. *Am. Psychol.* 1956, **11** (221).

14. Oppenheimer, R. *Roosevelt University Occasional Papers,* 1956, **2.**

15. Meerloo, J. A. M. *J. Nervous Mental Disease,* 1955, **122** (353).

16. Rogers, C. R. *Client-centered therapy.* Boston: Houghton-Mifflin, 1951.

17. Rogers, C. R., & Dymond, R. (Eds.) *Psychotherapy and personality change.* Chicago: University of Chicago Press, 1954.

18. Ratner, J. (Ed.) *Intelligence in the modern world: John Dewey's philosophy.* New York: Modern Library, 1939, p. 359.

19. Popper, K. R. *The open society and its enemies.* London: Rutledge and Kegan Paul, 1945.

20. Skinner, B. F. *Science and human behavior.* New York: Macmillan, 1953.

21. Hacker, A. J. *Politics,* 1955, **17** (590).

A Cognitive Field Theory of Learning

Donald Snygg

Most teachers consider psychological theories of learning impractical and use them only when they are needed to justify something the teacher wants to do anyway. This may seem odd to outsiders since teaching is supposedly a profession, that is, an occupation whose members do not conduct themselves by rote and are presumably educated to deal effectively with situations which have never arisen before. Professional work can be done only on the basis of theories of cause and effect which enable the professional worker to predict what will happen in a given case even though circumstances and situation are completely new.

Knowledge of what has happened in one situation cannot, without a theory of why it happened, enable us to predict what will happen in any other situation if it is different in the slightest degree. If we cannot

Reprinted from *Learning and Mental Health in the School,* edited by W. B. Waetjen and R. R. Leeper. Copyright © 1966, pp. 77–96, by the Association for Supervision and Curriculum Development. Used with permission of the Association for Supervision and Curriculum Development and Donald Snygg.

predict the results of our acts we cannot choose between alternative courses of action or plan new ones. Without a scientific theory of learning, teachers and administrators have to meet new problems with inappropriate routines that were devised long ago to meet other problems or to base their decisions on folk beliefs about learning which, although thoroughly disproved in the laboratories, still pass for common sense.

Teachers are not the only people with professional licenses who tend to drop into the ways of routine workers. As a result of the great surge of scientific discovery, engineers and physicians are having more and more difficulty keeping up with basic theory and are able to remain real professionals only by restricting themselves to narrow fields of specialization. These specialties can be made comprehensible by a narrow band of theory so limited that a busy practitioner can keep in touch with the significant research that bears upon it.

If teachers have not been forced so far on this path of specialization, it may be because the results of teaching are much harder to find and evaluate than the results of engineering or even medicine. Since the primary social purpose of education is a more effective adulthood, the really significant results of teaching do not occur until years afterward. By that time the casual connection between the adult behavior and any classroom events has been covered over by thousands of other experiences and is impossible to trace. As a result, educational innovations tend to be accepted or rejected, not in terms of their results, which are largely unknown, but in terms of the degree to which they fit the beliefs about human nature and human purpose which happen to be in vogue at that time.

NEED FOR THEORY

Each of us accepts the validity of methods and devices that fit our view of reality; but methods which do not fit our personal concept of human nature and educational purpose or which we do not feel capable of using are regarded as "impractical theory" and rejected. This makes for a static profession because once an educational practice has come into use it tends to acquire a legitimacy of its own. Teachers who have encountered such a practice from their kindergarten days perceive it as an essential aspect of real teaching. When the practice was new it was accepted because it conformed to the folk belief or the theory of psychology that passed for common sense at the time. Yet once it becomes an accepted part of school practice it no longer needs the sanction of a theory. Instead such a practice comes to serve as a criterion that teachers and parents use for evaluating new educational and psychological theories. Those theories which do not sanction the now hallowed practice are obviously crackbrained, impractical, and for use only in passing examinations and gaining degrees. If this seems exaggerated, consider how the full-arm system of penmanship hangs on in spite of half a century of research on the motor development of children which has negated every assumption on which the full-arm system was based.

If there is now a new interest in theories of learning it is because the tremendous changes in our society have given us the task of preparing children to live in a very different society than we have had in the past. This is a society whose problems we cannot solve and cannot even anticipate. The social and technological changes now sweeping the world are moving so fast that almost any specific fact or procedure taught today will be obsolete before the learner leaves school. As a result, the new subject matter projects take as their objectives the student's discovery of concepts and generalizations and the development of thinking processes, independent learning skills, and creativity. This is not an education solely for an elite class. Within a very few years all routine tasks outside the home will be done by machines, and the adults who have not been helped to attain the conceptual skills and the attitudes of initiative and responsibility required for technical, managerial or professional work will be economically dispossessed, unable to participate in productive work.

We do not know how many people can be brought to the level of intellect, initiative and responsibility that will be required. Nevertheless, the fact that there is already a shortage of professional and technical workers while several million routine workers are unable to find jobs suggests that we must at once begin our search for a solution to this problem.

This new problem requires new methods. The conventional classroom practices were devised at a time when the chief task of the school was the communication of information and the desired outcome was memorization of this information. The fact that the personal qualities required for professional, technical and managerial work are found in many of our graduates does not mean that these qualities are implanted by the schools. The fact that these qualities are seldom found in disadvantaged neighborhoods and are frequently found among children from middle and upper class homes strongly suggests that these qualities are usually learned in the home and not in school. Also, remembering that the general tone and basic methods of instruction were devised long before psychology had become a field of experimental inquiry, when people harbored a great many beliefs about human motivation and learning that have now been disproved or qualified in important ways, it does not seem likely that we can significantly change the product of our schools by just doing more of what we have been doing all along.

It is true that many teachers, unable to see adequate results from their labors, become discouraged time servers, striving only to "make it look good." However, no one who knows teachers can believe that their failure to achieve results which the schools were not designed to achieve is due to any lack in the personal qualities of our teachers. It seems much more likely that we are failing to achieve the new educational objectives of our society because teachers have to base their campaigns, their strategy and their tactics of teaching on inaccurate assumptions about human nature and human learning.

When the free, compulsory public school first assumed the task of teaching unwilling children what they did not want to know, the first psychology laboratory was still far in the future. On a day to day basis, the classroom teacher in the early public schools, while the mold of tradition was being set, seems to have dealt with the new problems, just as most teachers do now, in terms of one or the other of two prescientific "commonsense" hypotheses about learning, neither of which has stood the test of experimental investigation.

INFLUENCE OF FREQUENCY HYPOTHESIS

The first of these we shall call the habit or frequency hypothesis. Most people who have attempted to analyze the learning process have begun by noticing that learning, particularly schoolroom learning, often does not occur without a great deal of practice. Logic does not insist that since A commonly occurs before B it must be the cause of B; yet this seems to be an easy conclusion to draw. I once knew a cat which, after cleaning the fish out of the neighborhood pond, succumbed to this logical fallacy and spent most of the next winter sitting on a toilet bowl waiting for fish to appear. In time he gave up his delusion that water causes fish. Nevertheless, many teachers, in spite of their frequent observation of practice that has not resulted in perfection or even progress, persist in the delusion that practice, if continued long enough, will eventually result in learning. "Practice makes perfect" is part of the culture and when all else fails teachers can salve their consciences and satisfy the public by devoting more time to drill, assigning more problems in the workbook, or by lengthening the school day or the school year. The only cost of this type of educational reform is the additional money spent for paper, pencils, electricity and fuel.

Experimental psychologists, like teachers, are children of their culture. As a rule they have started, like the teachers, with the assumption that frequency, repetition, practice or exercise causes learning—that habits are caused by practicing them. Yet few of them have been able to keep that opinion for long. In 1929 Knight Dunlap demonstrated that one way to *break* habits was to practice them (7; 22). He cured typists of their characteristic errors by requiring them to practice the error. He cured children of thumb sucking by requiring them to suck their thumbs. It is reasonable to believe that many children have been cured of piano playing by the same method; and it is quite likely that we have cured quite a few of arithmetic and reading.

Confronted by this situation and by the further observation that much repetition and practice do not result in improvement, a learning theorist must find a "cause" of learning which will either supplement the frequency hypothesis or replace it completely. Looking again into the cultural fund of "commonsense" he finds that learning is also believed to be promoted by rewards and punishments.

THE REINFORCEMENT MODEL OF LEARNING

Teachers have traditionally used praise and blame, prizes, marks, gold stars, certificates of merit, smiles, frowns, detention, and, until recently, the rod, to promote learning. On the commonsense level almost everyone assumes that acts which are punished are less likely to be repeated, that acts which are rewarded are more likely to be repeated. But what is rewarding? Pleasure? And what is punishment? Pain? Perhaps. Yet what is pleasant to one person may be painful to another, a fact well known to most families that have only one TV set. Some pupils work hard for high marks; other try to avoid them. A good conduct award in the fourth grade may cause more misconduct than it prevents. Experiments show that under conditions of high motivation strong rewards and punishments *interfere* with problem solving (1). In some experiments animals given an electric shock every time they made the *correct response* have learned faster than comparable animals who did not suffer shock (21; 13).

The conventional methods of teaching—repetition, reward and punishment—are far from reliable. Practice does not insure perfection. In some cases repetition leads to learning; in others it merely leads to inattention. Rewards and punishments may promote learning or they may interfere with it. The folk theories of learning are very unreliable guides to educational planning.

It is no wonder that many teachers, disappointed in the results of their attempts at professional planning, lose faith in themselves and fall back on a ritual of routine practices copied from the teachers they respect.

In an effort to build a more reliable model of the learning process, present-day S-R psychologists have dropped the terms "reward" and "punishment" in favor of positive and negative "reinforcement." Although many people assume that "reinforcement" is merely a technical name for "reward" and think of the two as synonymous, the shift from reward to reinforcement is a very significant one. Reward theory assumed that "rewards," acting independently, will strength the pupil's tendency to perform the act which has been rewarded. "Reinforcement" implies a vaguer theory of causation. Reinforcement is merely defined as whatever strengthens the tendency for a particular response to follow a particular stimulus. That is, a "reinforcement" is identified only by its consequences. In effect, the S-R psychologists, having decided that at this time no one has enough information to tell why reinforcement takes place, have decided to quit worrying about it and to go to other problems. "Reinforcement" is not reward. It is simply the name for a hypothetical process and offers no explanation of the process.[1]

This leaves the teacher who wishes to use reinforcement theory in a bad situation. Without a theory of what causes reinforcement he is unable to make any plans for achieving it. The most anyone can do is to give the practice lip service and go on using the old folk theories of repetition, reward and punishment as teachers have always done. As a matter of fact a good many psychologists do this, too, but they have one advantage in the laboratory that the teacher does not have in the classroom. The psychologist knows by experience that starving a rat or pigeon down to 75 percent of normal body weight provides a situation

---

1. To be accurate, not all S-R psychologists accept the concept of reinforcement. Guthrie was able to construct an S-R theory which did not use this concept.

in which the presentation of food very frequently results in reinforcement. So, if he wants to, he can forget that problem and go on to study other aspects of learning. Public sentiment fortunately prevents the application of this empirical discovery to schoolchildren.

Unquestionably the stimulus-response model of learning is by far the easiest model on which to base research. In the past fifty years an overwhelming majority of learning experiments have used the S-R pattern. Indeed this pattern has had such a monopoly on the field that some psychologists call it "learning theory," implying that no other conceptual model is possible. Others concede that other conceptual models for learning are possible and may even be useful but believe that only the S-R can be scientifically legitimate. This, of course, is nonsense.

The only scientific criterion for judging any theory is its usefulness in predicting previously unknown facts and thus making possible new and better practices. By this criterion the S-R model of learning has failed to justify itself. For fifty years it has almost monopolized the facilities of the experimental laboratories and during that time this theory has not led to the invention of a single educational technique which was not already in use and originally derived from the prescientific folk theories of exercise, reward and punishment. When it has been possible to apply S-R theory to educational practice the results have not validated the model. The early teaching machines were expected to open a new era in education by making possible the immediate reinforcement (by showing when the answer was correct) to the student's response (writing an answer to the stimulus question). A number of research studies have found that their subjects learned just as well when they did not write an answer (make a response) to be reinforced at all but simply read the machine tape, as when they read a book (12; 19). Generally these students learned more in a given length of time than the students who followed the standard procedure because they did not have to spend time writing. Other experimenters found that some of the best learners in their experiments were the subjects who made the most mistakes and consequently had had the fewest correct responses reinforced.

The reinforcement S-R model of learning cannot serve the needs of education in this century because it is a model for teaching that which is already known. The task of the teacher using reinforcement theory looks, on the face of it, very simple. His task is to set up a situation in which the student will make the desired response and then, without delay, the teacher must see that something happens which will result in that response being reinforced. This does not look hard to an experimental psychologist who has a supply of feed and a hungry pigeon or rat in a box where it has only two possible choices. This task, however, is probably impossible for a teacher who is in a room with thirty children with widely differing interests, abilities and personal problems. The essential limitation of the model is that the teacher has to decide what words or actions should be reinforced. An act which does not conform to the teacher's idea of what is good, proper and effective, a problem solution which differs from the solution he would make, cannot be reinforced. In such a situation, conventional, routine behavior is going to be reinforced; creative and inventive behavior is not.

If reinforcement theory could be put into educational practice, it would only serve to teach what is already known, to promote conventional, conforming behavior, to prepare pupils to live in a world exactly like the one in which they are educated. In a world changing as rapidly as the world is changing now, in which we cannot teach our children the answers to their future problems because we cannot even anticipate the problems, an education based on reinforcement theory would be an education for obsolescence. If what is desired is a creative, adaptable citizen, able to deal with problems his teachers could not have envisaged and with problems they were unable to solve, another model for learning must be used.

One of the strong reactions against the reinforcement model for learning has come from the people who have been developing the National Science Foundation projects. They have been confronted with the problem of teaching what Bruner (2) has called the structure or logic of a subject matter area. Although the concept of subject matter structure is not new, most teaching in American schools has conformed to the stimulus-response model of Thorndike's early "pre-belonging" theories. Items of information are taught separately and rewarded or, as in Skinner's learning machine, "reinforced" separately. The scientists given responsibility for the NSF projects have insisted that teaching items of information is not the way to teach science. Each area of science, they insist, is made up of a structure of interrelated concepts and conceptual models which gives meaning to the separate facts and thus makes possible the deduction of new ones. Isolated facts, without a theory to unify them, do not tell us what to expect in new situations and consequently do not equip the student for success in any but routine situations where other people have already worked out the answers. If this is true, the first qualification of a teacher should be the ability to practice the science he is teaching. Yet he must also understand a great many things about teaching, including the answers to some questions about how concepts are taught, that people are just beginning to think about.

COGNITIVE FIELD THEORIES OF LEARNING

Psychologically, the concept of subject matter organization fits into a general concept of cognitive organization and motivation which is being developed by a number of psychologists. Ausubel, Combs, Festinger, Heider, Rogers, Snygg, and Taba and many others have contributed to the general theory. At the present time the work of Piaget (15) is most influential in providing a common ground for definition of problems. While the proponents of the cognitive approach differ from one another in minor ways they have, under the influence of Gestalt psychology, Tolman's cognitive behaviorism, Lewin's field theory, and a number of other sources, come to fairly close agreement on their model of learning. However the particular version which follows is that of the author.

It is assumed that an individual's behavior is always appropriate to his phenomenal field, perceptual field, cognitive field, conceptual field or cognitive structure. Snygg and Combs (17) define the phenomenal field as the universe, including himself, as perceived by the individual at the instant of action and postulate that all his behavior is determined by and appropriate to the field at that instant. If his field changed, he would change his behavior to conform to it. The purpose of education is to promote more effective and realistic behavior. This is done by helping the individual to achieve a more fruitful and realistic concept of himself and of the universe.

The term "field," as used by various writers, implies an organized whole which behaves in such a way as to maintain its organization. Piaget, as interpreted by Taba (20), believes that "the individual in 'any cognitive encounter with the environment' of necessity organizes the objects and events into his existing cognitive structure, and invests them with the meaning dictated by that system." He perceives each new phenomenon in terms of an already existing conceptual framework, and new phenomena have meaning only to the extent that they can be fitted into the patterns of concepts and relationship that already exist in his mind. Festinger (9) postulates that individuals will always perceive in such a way as to reduce the dissonance in the cognitive field; Snygg (16) that the immediate purpose of all an individual's behavior, including his behavior as a perceiver, is the maintenance or organization of his individual field.

Generally speaking, a learner will accept into his field anything which fits what he already believes but there are two qualifications: (a) in order to be perceived or assimilated an object or event must be necessary to the field organization; (b) assimilation of an event involves what another person, looking at the event from the point of view of his own perceptual field, would call distortion. Any item's value and meaning are aspects of its function in the perceiver's particular field at that particular time.

If these conclusions are correct, any attempt to make a really significant change in a student's field by verbal means seems foredoomed to failure. Lectures, reading assignments, and class discussions may give students the raw material for filling in gaps in their perceptual worlds and for rationalizing the preconceptions and prejudices they already have. Such methods by themselves, however, are not at all likely to cause a radical change in any student's concept of reality. We can assume that each external event is perceived, if at all, in such a way as to cause the least possible change in the student's field. The words of a lecturer will only rarely be relevant to the private reality and personal problems of the students he addresses and are very easy to ignore.

The usual plan for overriding this implacable mechanism for protecting the student against the intrusion of dissonant perceptions is to disorganize his field by threats of failure and humiliation in the hope that he will try to remove the threat by learning the required material. The results are frequently far from what teachers and parents intend. All teachers are by now aware of the cheating and the defensive changes in self-concept and personal values that may result among "poor" students. More attention should be given to the problem of the "good" student who learns the required material for examination purposes but keeps it from entering and changing his view of reality by dividing his field into two parts, "reality" and "school," the latter having nothing to do with real life. This is the game that has given the word "academic" its connotation of impractical futility. The bright people who have used this defense and made a success of school without changing their concepts of reality feel more competent in "school" than in "real life." Apparently many such persons become teachers. We often see teachers and children playing the school game together, equally unaware that the concepts they discuss have anything to do with life or action.

Unfortunately for our efforts to write examinations that are easy to mark, the ability of a student to write the verbal definition of a concept does not prove that the student has the concept. A few years ago I had in one of my classes a student from India who was eager to see snow. She had read about snow, she had seen pictures of snow crystals, she had seen snow on the tops of distant peaks in northern India, and she had taught Indian children all about snow. Then one morning in early December she walked out of her dormitory to find the air full of fluttering white objects. "Oh!" she exclaimed, "What kind of insects are these?" The verbal definition is the last stage of development of a concept and the concept will be perceived as part of reality only when it has been discovered by the student as part of the reality of his own experience, in his own perceptual field.

Any concept, no matter how well expressed, can only be accepted if it fits the student's own cognitive field. In conventional terminology he is "ready" for such learning but the trouble is that if he is that ready there is not much change in his field. On the other hand, if the fit is imperfect the law of least change operates with distressing results. If the dissonant statement is heard at all, the most economical way to deal with it, that is to keep the change in the student's field at a minimum, is to accept it as a statement of fact which has no relevance to the real life of the listener. Probably most lecture and reading material is disposed of in this way. Unfortunately for the student, this denial of personal meaning insures that the material will not be available when he needs it later. He may, of course, perceive the statement as pertinent to the school sector of his life, particularly the next class meeting. But since the material is perceived as mainly pertinent to the next recitation, it is not available after that date and has to be reinstated for the examination by cramming. After the examination, as we all know, it is lost forever.

In the sense in which I have been using the term, a concept is defined as "a general meaning, an idea, or a property that can be predicated out of two or more individual terms" (8). Whether he can express it verbally or not, an individual cannot be presumed to have a concept unless he is able to discover and identify new items which fit the concept. Tests for concepts, to be valid, must be performance tests which require applications of the concepts in new situations. Since concepts are cognitive, and since "cognitive" is often mistakenly equated with "verbal," it should be pointed out that when people develop concepts the formulation of a verbal definition has to be the last step in the process, and that it is probably not an essential one. A great many people who have developed their own concepts and who use them with precision have never had the need to put them into words and may not even have the ability to do so.

Can anything be taught by verbal means? Yes, if the words can be used to upset the student's perceptual field or if the student can use them to organize it. Learning takes place when the field is so disorganized that a new perception, which would ordinarily be ignored, is sought out as a means of restoring or enhancing the organization. New ideas are accepted only in situations where their rejection would cause even more change than their acceptance. We postpone the perception of discrepancies as long as possible but once their perception is forced upon us we must go on to a new organization and actively seek a means of achieving it. Piaget calls this extension of the field to fit new demands "accommodation." Taba (20) illustrates it by the example of a child who, having thought of measurement as an operation done with a yardstick, is confronted with the problem of measuring a volume of water and has to enlarge his concept of measurement.

A COGNITIVE FIELD MODEL OF LEARNING

As a pattern for promoting learning from this point of view we can use the following model. It is applicable to both learning and problem solving and is a modification in cognitive field terms of one proposed by Cronbach (6).

Step 1. Awareness of a need for greater organization (e.g., hunger, anxiety).

Step 2. Search of the phenomenal field for some means of achieving organization (e.g., food, self-assurance). This or some means of approaching it is differentiated in some degree as $Goal_1$.

Step 3. Simultaneous search of field for means of reaching or achieving the goal. The tentative path is differentiated into sub-paths. *Perception of Problem$_1$.*

Step 4. Act_1 begins, appropriate to this perception.

Step 5. *Perception of Results$_1$.* If the act or series of acts achieves the goal, no significant reorganization or change of the field is necessary and, as a consequence, nothing is learned.

Step 6. If, however, the results are not as expected or hoped, the situation is reexamined. This results in *Perception of Problem$_2$.*

Step 7. This new and more highly differentiated perception of the situation results in new Act_2.

Step 8. *Perception of Results$_2$.* If the new results are those sought, the search-act-evaluation process in the problem area is terminated and the individual shifts his attention to problems elsewhere.

Step 9. If the desired result has not been attained, the search-act-evaluation process goes on until a new perception of the problem makes possible the attainment of the goal or until the learner differentiates another goal as a more practical way of satisfying his need. The new perception of the problem is what has been learned.

It will be noticed that this concept deposes both practice and reinforcement as "causes" of learning. Each repetition of the problem gives the pupil an opportunity to gain a clearer and more accurate perception of the situation but it does not guarantee that he will either wish or be able to take advantage of the opportunity. Practice, in other words, gives an opportunity for learning but does not cause it. "Reinforcement" is not needed to stabilize the successful response. The learner merely stops reinterpreting the situation because further change in that aspect of the field is unnecessary.

The model is as applicable to skill and nonverbal learning as to concept discovery and problem solving. The object of search in motor learning is the differentiation of more effective muscle feelings, visual and motor cues, and rhythm and breathing patterns. As in cognitive learning, the process is one of increasing differentiation of the total situation during which the perceived task is differentiated into more and more subtasks until the cues essential to solution are discovered.

Transfer of learning from one situation to another occurs when

1. The learner perceives the two situations as similar.
2. When he perceives a solution to one problem as applicable to part of another problem.
3. When he acquires new perceptions of himself or of the world at large which are applicable to both or all situations.

Education for the unforeseeable (an awkward problem for association systems) is thus seen as possible. Personality and character training, which by connectionist theories would have to be achieved by a large number of separate learnings, are achieved by helping the individual to perceive himself as an accepted, responsible, valuable member of society and by helping him learn the knowledge and skill adequate for the role.

IMPLICATIONS OF THE COGNITIVE FIELD THEORY

Assuming the validity of the steps in cognitive field theory listed, teachers and curriculum planners can draw the following implications:

1. (*Goals*) The primary function of the teacher is to help the students to discover problems that demand their personal attention. Giving students answers to problems they do not have short-circuits the whole process of learning by making exploration and reality testing by the students unnecessary and the problem (whose solution they are taught) unimportant. Fundamentally, the curriculum aids the students, not by giving him the answers to problems that he does not have, but by helping him to discover new and more fruitful objectives in his personal campaign for feelings of greater worth and value. Students must be protected from ready-made answers which make their own consideration of the problem unnecessary.

This requires a flexible curriculum, in the sense that the goals it presents must be appropriate to the personal value system, the self-concept, and the present understanding and skill of the student if he is to accept them as personal goals, to be pursued seriously and with persistence.

This requires the teacher to think of himself as a learner who needs to explore his students' perceptions of the subject and of themselves so that he can give special treatment to the individual. This requires a classroom setting in which the student is free to explore and express his own perception of the situation without fear of humiliation or reprisal so that the instructor can see the consequences of his own acts (18). Since each individual selects his goals from among those that seem valuable and feasible to him, different students will have very different goals. And in exploring the situations for the means of reaching their different goals they will make very different discoveries.

2. (*Interpretation*) The teacher uses this knowledge to arrange a situation in which the student will have a better opportunity to solve his problem without direct instruction. This may be done by providing the required tools, by providing the necessary experiences and conceptual models, and sometimes by removing extraneous factors from the situation so that the essential aspects can be more easily differentiated.

A curriculum based upon perceptual field principles will have to assume that the teacher is a professional worker in the true sense and is equipped, as routine workers are not, with a background of professional theory which enables him to deal with unique cases and with situations that have never before arisen.

Different students with the same goal will still interpret any situation differently since they approach it with different field organizations. As a result, group discussions are valuable if the members of the group are willing to learn from one another. This applies to the teacher as well as to the students. He must not assume that his interpretation is the only one that is possible or useful. If one of our purposes is to help people become creative and capable, the validity of other ways of solving a problem and, in some cases, of other solutions must be accepted by the teachers.

3. (*Act*) The validity of our concepts and our perceptions can only be tested by acting on them. In experiments on the effect of minimal stimulation, when people were kept lying in the dark, in soundproof rooms, unable to touch or hear anything, they soon began to have hallucinations, to see and hear objects that were not present. The only way to find the extent to which a perception represents reality is to act upon it. It is in this area of reality testing that our schools are most inadequate.

It is essential that the curriculum and the school situation give the student the opportunity to test his perceptions of reality by acting on them. Ideas not put to the test of action are, quite properly, perceived as doubtful, as play money for tender in examinations but not to be trusted in real life where we are playing for keeps. The failure of students to apply their verbal learnings from the classroom to their behavior outside the classroom is due, from the perceptual field point of view, to the fact that these "learnings" have never been successfully validated by use and thus remain merely something to talk about.

A curriculum based on perceptual field principles will provide many opportunities for the student to put his ideas to the test of action so that he will discover and correct his misconceptions as soon as possible and so that he will gain the confidence required to act on his perceptions and concepts and to make them the basis for his further thinking. In a modern physics curriculum the students do not just talk about gravity, they measure it by methods they understand (because they have helped develop them) (18).

4. (*Perception of Results*) A man spearing fish for the first time sees his spear dart harmlessly by the fish and immediately changes his perception of the situation. An act which does not achieve its expected re-

sult automatically causes a change in the behaver's perceptions of the situation *provided* he is able to see the result. If he cannot discover the results of his act he cannot tell whether his interpretation of the situation needs modification or not. An act, without knowledge of its results, cannot benefit learning.

Papers unread, questions not answered, suggestions not made leave the student in the role of a man trying to spear fish in the dark, not knowing where his spear is going nor where the target is. Better provision for the immediate marking of papers, emphasizing what is successful and what is ingenious and promising at least as much as what is poor, and better facilities for self evaluation by students are greatly needed in most schools. Most important is the invention of new opportunities for students to see the results of their work. Teacher evaluations are obscure, based upon other standards and values, and often threatening because their basis is not understood. Poor students easily rationalize them away by telling themselves that the evaluations are by people with peculiar values. This does not hurt the teachers but it does hurt the pupils by removing them from the teacher's sphere of personal influence.

In learning, the important evaluation is the one made by the learner. To make this evaluation as realistic as possible, he should see the results in as realistic a situation as possible and in a social situation where he feels respected and valued so that he will feel less need to protect himself with rationalizations and excuses.

If this view of learning is valid, learning is a process of exploration and experimentation. Making the class period a testing period and the marking of daily recitations inhibit exploration and learning because the student can take no chances by exploring and trying to learn in a marking situation in which the obvious need is the need to please the teacher.

In the teaching of science, laboratory exercises should be genuine experiments with explicit significance for the student. They should be true explorations of unknown territory and at least part of the procedure should be devised by the student. Ingenious writers might be able to apply the general idea to the social sciences. In mathematics the invention of alternative methods should be encouraged and even required. Following in someone else's footsteps does not help us to solve problems. It merely teaches us to follow footsteps.

Both perceptual field and reinforcement theories suggest that immediate knowledge of the results of an act is essential to learning. Field theory suggests that the essential factor is the learner's discovery of the relation between the cause and the result. For this purpose a teacher's evaluation of the results cannot be an adequate substitute for the student's own perception of the consequences. Strictly speaking, the teacher can tell the student only about the teacher's perception of the results and this may not be pertinent to the student's evaluation of the results when the teacher is not present. This brings back, in a new form, the distinction between intrinsic and extrinsic rewards and suggests that the distinction may be more important than we have thought (18).

The objections to the traditional emphasis on evaluation by the teacher may be summarized as follows:

a. Emphasis on the teacher's evaluation leads the student to concentrate more on making a good impression than on finding an effective solution.

b. Since the instructor's criterion for the evaluation of student papers and recitations must be his own perception of the situation, independent, creative and unorthodox thinking is unintentionally discouraged.

c. Since the teacher's cognitive field necessarily differs from that of the student, his suggestions for revision are often unconvincing to the student.

d. Limitations of language and experience make the transmission of individual perceptions and meanings very risky and inadequate.

e. The tradition of verbal examinations, by focusing attention on the verbal interpretation of problems instead of on appropriate action tends to make education a verbal game and to make teachers and students men of words, incapable of action.

All of these considerations point toward a need for greater cooperation between students and teachers in selecting and defining problems, for more situations where individual interpretations can be put to the test of action, and for the provision of facilities, materials and resources to make this possible.

5. (*Reinterpretation*) Generally the change in the learner's perception of a situation is in the direction of increased awareness of details and in breaking the total problem into a number of sub-problems and related steps until he can relate this situation to a model or concept he has already developed. As long as the teacher does not take over and impose his own solution, based on his own perceptions, he may safely call the student's attention to some details in the situation as factors the student might want to consider.

It is essential, however, that the student not be led to feel that the teacher has taken over the problem or that his own work is unnecessary and valueless. Above all, the student should not be led to become dependent on the teacher. The teacher should not interfere to prevent the student from making mistakes.

One of the most striking implications of perceptual field theory is the function this theory assigns to error. From this point of view learning does not take place unless the learner finds that he has made a mistake or would have made a mistake, that is, unless an act enlarges his perception of the situation by giving rise to results he did not anticipate. The optimum situation for learning is not one in which the learner will make no mistakes, as in current reinforcement theory. Rather, optimum learning takes place in a situation which allows the learner to test his ideas under conditions in which the results are immediately apparent.

LEVEL OF DIFFICULTY

One of the most unconventional implications of the perceptual field theory is the push it gives toward more difficult curricula. Contrary to the general opinion among teachers, which postulates that all failure is detrimental because it causes frustration and thus either aggression or withdrawal, and contrary to the opinion of reinforcement theorists, which tends to assume that material should be so easy that all responses to it will be "correct" (so that they can be reinforced), perceptual field theory suggests that *the optimum level of difficulty is one which allows the student to win success after difficulty.*

If our basic goal is indeed a greater feeling of personal worth and value, tasks which require little talent or effort are bound to be unrewarding and boring and to be as unproductive and harmful from an educational point of view as are problems that are completely beyond the current capacity of the student. Most teachers and educators are well aware of the latter danger; fewer seem to have considered the first.

The success or failure of the implementation of current curricular developments into effective practice may well depend upon the degree to which both curriculum planners and learning theorists will translate the implications of the perceptual field theory into a rigorous upgrading and strengthening of the quality of the educational program throughout the entire school span (18).

Although the field approach is just beginning to come into use as a conceptual model for education, it has already exerted a strong influence on our ideas about pupil readiness and the nature of the IQ. Readiness for a particular experience, from this point of view, depends not only on the student's physical maturity but, even more, on the character of his perceptual field which determines his ability to assimilate new stimuli and the meaning he will ascribe to them. "Readiness" is something which can be achieved through educational experiences. Unless physical inadequacies make experiences impossible or meaningless, readiness for intellectual achievements can be promoted by appropriate experiences. And in the case of children living in environments where the appropriate experiences are not available, waiting for readiness is waiting for accidents that are not likely to happen.

It is now clear that a low IQ may be due, among other things, to the failure of the home and neighborhood to provide the preschool child with the incentives and experiences that prepare most middle-class children for involvement in some degree of abstract thinking and intellectual interests (3; 11). During the great IQ controversy of the 1930's the professors' children in the University of Minnesota and the University of California nursery schools showed no significant change in IQ; but in Iowa City, where the nursery school children came from all sections of the community, there was a significant rise.

A home in which children are taught to approach the world as something to be mastered, where they learn to perceive the world as extended in space and time and to govern their actions by what is beyond the horizon and in the remote future is probably doing all that the very best school can do for young children now. The child whose home and neighborhood do not provide the kinds of opportunities for experience that lead him to see himself as an active participant in shaping the future has to get these experiences elsewhere; and unless he gets them before he enters the regular school program the experiences he gets there will be perceived as having no meaning for his own life.

The danger is that the country is embarking on a great program of preschool education for disadvantaged children before we know what opportunities for experience to give or how to give them. The purpose of teaching three-year-olds to read, if this is tried, should not be to hasten their graduation from school. The purpose is to help them to perceive themselves as individuals who can learn and to discover that their thoughts have significance before their homes and their community have taught them otherwise. It is obvious that applying present day first grade methods to three-year-olds will not automatically achieve these ends. In fact such methods may make matters worse by teaching the children at the age of three instead of at the age of six that they are incompetent and that school activities are meaningless.

1. Birch, H. G. The role of motivational factors in insightful problem solving. *Journal of Comparative Psychology,* 1945, **38,** 295–317.

2. Bruner, J. S. *The process of education.* Cambridge: Harvard University Press, 1961.

3. Combs, A. W. Intelligence from a perceptual point of view. *Journal of Abnormal and Social Psychology,* 1952, **47,** 662–673.

4. Combs, A. W. (Ed.) *Perceiving, behaving, becoming.* Washington, D.C.: Association for Supervision and Curriculum Development, 1962.

5. Combs, A. W., & Snygg, D. *Individual behavior.* New York: Harper & Brothers, 1959.

6. Cronbach, L. J. *Educational psychology.* New York: Harcourt, Brace and World, 1954.

7. Dunlap, K. *Habits: Their making and unmaking.* New York: Liveright Publishing Corp., 1932.

8. English, Horace B., & English, Ava C. *A comprehensive dictionary of psychological and psychoanalytical terms.* New York: Longmans, Green & Company, 1958. Used by permission of the publishers, David McKay Company, Inc.

9. Festinger, L. *A theory of cognitive dissonance.* Stanford, Calif.: Stanford University Press, 1957.

10. Harlow, H. F. Mice, monkeys, man and motives. *Psychological Review,* 1953, **60,** 23–32.

11. Hunt, J. McVicker. *Intelligence and experience.* New York: Ronald Press, 1961.

12. Lambert, P. M., Miller, D. M., & Wiley, D. E. Experimental folklore and experimentation: The study of programmed learning in the Wauwatosa public schools. *Journal of Educational Research,* 1962, **55** (9), 485–491.

13. Muenzinger, K. F. Motivation in learning I. Electric shock for correct response in the visual discrimination habit. *Journal of Comparative Psychology,* 1934, **17,** 267–277.

14. Ripple, R. E., & Hodge, F. P. A comparison of the effectiveness of a programmed text with three other methods of presentation. *New directions in educational research.* Albany, N. Y.: Educational Research Association of New York State (N. Y.) Department of Education, 1963, pp. 61–63.

15. Ripple, R. E., & Rockcastle, V. N. (Eds.) *Piaget rediscovered.* Ithaca, N. Y.: School of Education, Cornell University, 1964.

16. Snygg, D. The need for a phenomenological system of psychology. *Psychological Review,* 1941, **48,** 404–424.

17. Snygg, D., & Combs, A. W. *Individual behavior.* New York: Harper & Brothers, 1949.

18. Snygg, D. A learning theory for curricular change. *Using current curriculum developments.* Washington, D. C.: Association for Supervision and Curriculum Development, 1963, pp. 109–115.

19. Stolurow, L. M., & Walker, C. C. A comparison of overt and covert response in programmed learning. *Journal of Educational Research,* 1962, **55,** 421–429.

20. Taba, H., Levine, S., & Freeman, F. E. *Thinking in elementary school children.* (Cooperative Research Project No. 1574, U.S. Office of Education) San Francisco, Calif.: San Francisco State College, 1963.

21. Tolman, E. C., Hall, C. S., & Bretnall, E. P. A disproof of the law of effect. *Journal of Experimental Psychology,* 1932, **15,** 601–614.

22. Wakeham, G. A quantitative experiment on Dr. K. Dunlap's 'revision of the fundamental law of habit formation.' *Journal of Comparative Psychology,* 1930, **10,** 235–236.

23. White, R. W. Motivation reconsidered: The concept of competence. *Psychological Review,* 1959, **66,** 297–333.

Intrinsic and Extrinsic Motivation— A Regrettable Distinction

Donald L. Avila / William Watson Purkey

In educational circles a distinction is usually made between two kinds of motivation. First there is intrinsic motivation, which is an internal, autonomous, energy source, inherent in the organism. Second, there is extrinsic motivation, which is an external energy source, apparently perceived as being similar in structure and function to the intrinsic source, that the teacher is able to draw on through his training and skill.

Little is done about intrinsic motivation aside from defining it. It is something that the student brings to class and is either directed towards

Reprinted from *Psychology in the Schools,* 1966, **3,** 206–208, by permission of the authors and publisher.

the goals of the teacher or is not. The teacher can do little or nothing to tap this source if it is not already predisposed to function in his favor. Therefore, the majority of the educators' time is spent with the second kind of motivation; with discussing and defining ways in which the teacher can *extrinsically* motivate his students.

This form of categorization is perpetrated by the educator because motivation is perceived as being free from the processes of control or manipulation. Since these terms have singularly negative connotations, the teacher feels a need to engage in processes when teaching that have little or no "control" in them. He fears being accused of controlling or manipulating his students, and therefore claims not to control or manipulate, but to extrinsically motivate his students. It is the contention of the writers that this is an unjustifiable fear, that the intrinsic-extrinsic distinction leads to a tremendous amount of waste and failure, and that those individuals who persist in making the distinction are engaging in self-delusion. There is a distinction to be made, but the intrinsic-extrinsic distinction obscures the true nature of motivation, and prevents the teacher from becoming highly skilled in the process that is truly the essence of all human interaction, that is, controlled manipulation.

Let us first examine the nature of motivation. There is only one kind of motivation, and that is the personal, internal motivation that each and every human being has at all times, in all places, and when engaged in any activity. As Combs (1962) has stated, ". . . people are always motivated; in fact, they are never unmotivated. They may not be motivated to do what we would prefer they do, but it can never be truly said that they are unmotivated." Again turning to Combs (1965) we find a succinct statement of the nature of this motivation, which is, ". . . an insatiable need for the maintenance and enhancement of the self; not the physical self—but the phenomenal self, of which the individual is aware, his self concept." For the teacher, this is a given, a basic drive toward self-fulfillment. It may be inherent, or learned, but in either case, it is present by the time the child enters school; it is a built-in advantage, a force that comes from within the individual that, by school age, cannot be appreciably altered. No human being can ever motivate another, no matter what the situation or how strong the desire.

To conjure up an external force that is similar to basic internal motivation is to create figments of the imagination, to confuse issues, and to distract from the real value of the teacher. The teacher is the external force, and a strong force, yet not as a motivator, but as a manipulator of his charges. He does not motivate, but he controls an environment in which he manipulates himself and other classroom variables in such a way that what he is trying to teach appears to be self-enhancing to his students. He casts the situation and himself in such a way that the information and knowledge he is presenting is personally meaningful and enhancing to the student.

All human relationships are controlled and manipulated. None are without these two processes. Human relationships differ only in the degree to which and the manner in which manipulation and control are administered. Each day we give to and withhold from our children love and material goods. In our classrooms we reward and punish our students by sending them first one place and then another, by praising or blaming, by giving good grades and bad. Each day we greet our friends in an accepting or rejecting manner, bring them into or force them out of our confidence. All of these activities are examples of how we manipulate ourselves and control the objects in our environment in an attempt to get others to do what we want, in an attempt to make our personal interactions satisfying to both ourselves and those with whom we interact. It is on the basis of one degree or another of manipulation and control that all human relationships are established, conducted, and maintained.

Acceptance of this position does not mean that one must give up his basic humanistic philosophy. Even the most student-centered teacher or client-centered counselor is engaging in a process of controlled manipulation when he sets up conditions in such a way, and conducts himself in such a manner that he creates a warm, friendly, accepting atmosphere. One can only be free if he is in a system in which those persons in control allow him to behave freely. Freedom for growth is a basic humanistic principle, yet it is actually not a great deal different, nor less controlling than the rule of the benevolent dictator.

However, unwarranted fear, and failure to accept the reality of control and manipulation have often caused teachers to reject useful ideas and techniques and engage in labored discussions that result in no concrete classroom applications; and schools to encourage slovenly educational practices. The fate that has so often been accorded the ideas of the more behavioristically oriented social scientists offers a perfect example of what can result from this unwillingness to accept the inevitability of manipulation and the responsibility of control.

The behaviorist has sincerely devoted the lion's share of his time to studying the nature of human interaction generally, and the learning process specifically. He has been conscientious and scientific in his explorations, and although his efforts have fallen far short of being a hundred per cent fruitful, he has generated many concepts and techniques that are immediately applicable to classroom use. Yet, many teachers have been unwilling to even listen to these principles, let alone attempt to apply them in practice. The typical teacher responds to behavioristic principles with statements such as "Those tricks are only good for cats and dogs. They are too mechanical. I want to motivate my students, not raise pets!" Or, if accepting their applicability to human behavior, responding with "Conditioning may be all right for some things, but it just involves too much control for me. It takes too much of the humanness out of learning." The teacher is suggesting that control and manipulation are processes apart from human interaction, and that he can have nothing in common with the behaviorist because the behaviorist is so frankly attempting to control human behavior. The teacher, being a humanist, has no use for control. And, therein, as this paper attempts to point out, lies the fallacy. B. R. Bugelski (1964) has recently published a textbook that could well serve as a tremendously practical handbook for the teacher, and help to make him much more efficient at his teaching task if he were to make daily use of the principles it enumerates. Yet, few teachers will probably ever read this little book because behavioristic psychology and humanistic education have little in common in the eyes of the teacher educator as well as the practicing teacher. It is hoped that the present discussion has helped to clarify the wastefulness and futility of perceiving such a cleavage, such a difference in purpose between behavioristic and humanistic philosophies. Such perceptions can prevail simply through a failure to distinguish between motivation and manipulation, and a failure to accept the reality of what is truly involved in the process of human interaction.

Humanistic psychologies, such as phenomenology and self-theory, have defined for the teacher the nature of the organism's motivation, namely self-enhancement, and the conditions that are most likely to result in the greatest amount of learning: a warm, friendly, accepting atmosphere that gives each student an opportunity to invest himself into the learning situation. Behavioristic psychologies, such as operant conditioning, suggest many techniques whereby the teacher can control and manipulate the learner and the learning situation so that the learner will perceive both the material being taught and the learning situation as being self-enhancing. Thus, humanism, behaviorism, the student, and the teacher can and should act as a well organized, cooperative, team that is playing the game for the common purpose of making the learning process as meaningful, useful, and successful as possible.

Bugelski, B. R. *The psychology of learning applied to teaching.* New York: Bobbs-Merrill, 1964.

Combs, A. W. (Ed.) Perceiving, behaving, becoming. *Yearbook of the Association for Supervision and Curriculum Development,* 1962.

Combs, A. W. Some basic concepts in perceptual psychology. Paper read at Amer. Personnel Guid. Assoc., Minneapolis, April 1965.

Some Basic Concepts in Perceptual Psychology

Arthur W. Combs

The Committee originally asked me to speak here today as a representative of self psychology. But self psychology as I see it, is only a portion of a larger understanding of human behavior seen from a perceptual orientation. I am, therefore, going to address my remarks to the broader concept of perceptual psychology which I regard as more fundamental than the problem of the self alone.

Perceptual psychology is one expression of the great humanistic movement which seems to me to be going on, not only in psychology, but in all of the social sciences and in human affairs generally. Abe Maslow has called this movement in psychology "Third Force" psychology. Perceptual psychology it seems to me is one of the expressions of that force in operation. It is a humanistic, phenomenological, personalistic, existential view of behavior which sees man engaged in a continuous process of being and becoming.

There are two frames of reference for looking at human behavior available to us. One of these is the external or objective approach familiar to most of us here in this room as the traditional view of American

Speech from APGA Convention, 1965. Used with permission of the author.

psychology. Seen from this frame of reference, behavior is described from the point of view of the outside observer, someone looking on at the process. Its classic expression is to be found in the various forms of stimulus-response psychology which seeks the explanation of behavior in the observable forces exerted upon the individual. The perceptual psychologist takes a different view. He seeks to understand the behavior of people from the point of view of the behaver himself. His is a phenomenological understanding of human behavior, emphasizing the meaning of events to the person.

Perceptual psychology is basically a field theory and its primary principle is this: *All behavior, without exception, is a function of the behaver's perceptual field at the instant of behaving.* I am using the term perception here in its broadest sense as practically synonymous with meaning. Thus, the individual's behavior is seen as the direct consequence, not of the fact or stimulus with which he is confronted, but the meaning of events in his peculiar economy. That people behave according to how things seem to them seems a simple enough proposition. Each of us as he looks at his own behavior can observe that it is true for him. Self evident as this proposition seems at first glance, however, its ramifications for human interaction are tremendous and its implications for a theory of behavior calls for an entire new psychology. It provides us with a new frame of reference for dealing with some of our most difficult problems. Perceptual psychology is not a denial of former psychologies, let me hasten to say. Rather, it provides us with an additional explanation of particular value to practitioners and to those of us who are confronted with the practical problems of dealing with people, not as subjects in an experiment but, as striving, seeking human beings. It does not deny what we have known before. It extends beyond to give us a new string to our bow.

When the perceptual psychologist speaks of the perceptual field he is referring to all those perceptions existing for the individual at the moment of behaving. This includes all aspects of his awareness, not only those perceptions in clear figure which the person may be able to tell us about but, also, those perceptions he has at lower levels of differentiation which he may be incapable of describing. Freud used the terms "conscious" and "unconscious" to describe these levels of awareness. Such designations, however, seem to give the impression of a clear cut dichotomy so the perceptual psychologist prefers to speak of levels of awareness instead. This is a point often misunderstood by some critics of perceptual psychology who have equated "awareness" with "conscious."

They have assumed that the term perception referred only to those events the individual was able to report on demand. Such a point of view would make perceptual psychology extraordinarily naive! To understand the behavior of the individual the perceptual psychologist says, it is necessary for us to understand the field of meaning or perceptions existing for him at the instant of his behavior. This includes *all* perceptions from those in clearest and sharpest figure to those so deeply imbedded in the ground of the field as to be quite unreportable.

If behavior is a function of perception, it follows that to understand behavior it will be necessary to study the factors influencing perception in the individual. Some of the variables affecting perception with which the perceptual psychologist is concerned are familiar to all of us from more orthodox psychologies. Among these are:

1. The Effect of the Physical Organism. Perception depends upon the possession of the necessary equipment to make it possible. One must have eyes to see, ears to hear, olfactory organs to smell, and so on.

2. The Effect of Time. Perception takes time. What is perceived is dependent upon the time of exposure and the length of time one has lived in the world.

3. The Effect of Opportunity or Environment. Perceptions are learned. To perceive one must have had opportunity to experience the events that make them possible. Eskimos do not normally comprehend bananas, nor Hottentots, snow. What meanings exist for the individual are a consequence of his unique experience in the process of his growing up.

These effects of the physical organism, time and opportunity have long been considered in traditional psychology. They are equally important for the perceptual approach. But perceptual psychology adds some additional variables to the picture among the most important of which is the self concept.

4. THE SELF CONCEPT

Of all the perceptions existing in the perceptual or phenomenal field those pertaining to the individual's self play a crucial role. How a person behaves at any moment is always the result of two kinds of perceptions: how he sees the situation he is in and how he sees himself. By the self

concept is meant all those aspects of the perceptual field to which we refer when we say "I" or "me." It is that organization of perceptions about
self or awareness of self which seems to the individual to be who he is.
It is composed of thousands of perceptions about self varying in clarity,
precision and importance in the individual's peculiar economy. Taken
altogether these concepts of self are described by the perceptual psychologist as the self concept.

The more we study the self concept, the more it becomes apparent how
crucial it is to any understanding of behavior. It is at the very center of
the individual's personal organization and the frame of reference for his
every act: The self concept is learned especially from the experience of
the individual with the significant people in his world in the course of
growing up. It is both product and process.

The self concept is the product of past experience but, once established, exerts its influence on the behavior of its possessor ever after. It
is apparent that we have but barely scratched the surface of the full implications of the self concept for every aspect of human existence. Educators, for example, have discovered that faulty self concepts are often
responsible for children's failures in basic school subjects, like reading,
spelling, arithmetic and language. Modern counseling theory holds that
the practice of counseling is primarily a problem in self exploration. Adjustment and maladjustment turn out on examination to be largely questions of healthy or faulty self concepts. The role of the self concept is
equally important in social psychology. Recent work with the mentally
retarded and the culturally deprived, even seems to indicate that the self
concept is basic to intelligence and human capacity.

Since the self concept is learned as a consequence of experience, it can
therefore presumably be taught. The implications of this idea have vast
importance for education, counseling, social work and all of the helping
professions. It provides the basis for a belief that programs aimed at the
defeat of poverty and human degradation have a chance for success.

In recent years the self concept has become one of the most popular
topics for research even for some psychologists who would rather be
caught dead than described as perceptualists. Researches on the self
concept now number in the hundreds. Dozens more are completed every
week. Many of these unfortunately, are mislabled self concept studies
when they are nothing of the kind. Most of them turn out on closer examination to be studies of the self report which is not the same thing at
all. The self concept is what a person perceives himself to be, it is what
he *believes* about himself. The self report, on the other hand, is what a

person is willing, able or can be tricked into *saying* about himself when he is asked to do so. The assumption that these two concepts are synonymous is naive and represents a return to introspection which psychology gave up sixty years ago. The basic research technique of perceptual psychology is inference. Introspection is no more acceptable to perceptual approaches then to more orthodox psychologies.

Despite the confusion currently existing in the research on the self it is apparent that this concept is an extraordinarily useful device for understanding behavior. It makes it possible for us to deal much more effectively with many problems we have not adequately understood before. Among the most exciting aspects of self concept theory, for me, are those having to do with self fulfillment, self realization or actualization. In these ideas we have new definitions of what it means to be well adjusted. These descriptions are not couched in terms of bell shaped curves in which the well adjusted turn out to be average. It describes them in terms of what it means to be truly living to the fullest of one's potentialities. Better still, these concepts do not simply tell us what such fortunate people are like, they point the way to what we must do to get about the business of producing more of them! In this respect they set the goals for counseling, teaching, social action and all of the helping professions, for whatever we decide what man can become, must automatically become the goal of all our institutions.

For example, one of the things we have been finding out about self actualizing people is that they tend to see themselves in essentially positive ways. They believe they are basically liked, wanted, acceptable, able, dignified, worthy and the like. Psychologically sick people on the other hand see themselves as unliked, unwanted, unacceptable, unable, unworthy and so on. It follows if this is true that the helping professions must find ways of helping clients, students, patients or colleagues to feel more positively about themselves. Furthermore, since perceptions are learned from experience, it points the way to what we need to do to help other people to greater health and productivity; clearly, it is necessary to provide them with experiences which will help them feel more positively about self. And the ways to do this are almost self evident. They are suggested by the very descriptions of self actualization:

How can a person feel liked unless somebody likes him?

How can a person feel acceptable unless somewhere he is accepted?

How can a person feel he has dignity unless someone treats him so?

How can a person feel able unless somewhere he has some success?

In the answers to these simple questions lie the guidelines to the condition for teaching, therapy, social action, supervision and the encouragement of growth and development everywhere.

THE PERCEPTUAL VIEW OF MOTIVES

If behavior is seen as a function of the perception of self and the world in perceptual psychology, what, then, provides the motive force? For perceptual psychology this is a given. The characteristic of all things to maintain organization finds its expression in human beings in an insatiable need for the maintenance and enhancement of the self; not the physical self—but the phenomenal self, the self of which the individual is aware, his self concept.

All human beings are seen as continuously engaged in a search for self actualization or self fulfillment, even, sometimes, at the cost of destruction of the physical body itself. The drive for self fulfillment provides the motive power for behavior. It finds its expression through goals which seem to the individual from time to time, to provide the means for actualization. This basic drive for maintenance expressed physically is the drive on which the physician depends to restore his patient to health. Physiologically it has been called the drive to health, the wisdom of the body, etc. Psychologically, it provides the motive power for human growth and development, recovery from psychological illness and the stretch for human achievement.

In the light of this drive the problem of motivation disappears for the perceptual psychologist, for people are always motivated. Indeed, they are never unmotivated! The motive is always there in the individual's search for the maintenance and enhancement of self. He always does what it seems to him he needs to from his point of view. The problem of motivation as we have usually conceived it is an external problem concerned with the question of how to get somebody else to do something *we* would like him to do.

Such a view of motivation as I have been describing leads to quite different approaches to dealing with people than those of traditional S-R psychologies. A stimulus-response psychology calls for methods of changing behavior based upon techniques of force, coercion, reward, punishment or some form of manipulation. The perceptual view of human need places both helper and helpee on the same team. Both are seeking the optimum development of the helpee and the problem is one of facilitation, encouragement and the freeing of forces already in existence to operate at maximum strength. This is a conception of the nature of man basic to some of the most promising conceptions of human interaction, in counseling, education, social work, medicine, nursing and the practice of the clergy. It lends itself to a hopeful view of man concerned with being and becoming and the basic democratic belief that when men are free they can find their own best ways.

In summary, then, the perceptual psychologist attempts to understand behavior from the point of view of the behaver rather than the outsider. He sees the individual behaving in terms of the peculiar field of personal meanings or perceptions existing for him at the moment of acting and motivated by the person's own need for self fulfillment. In the light of this interpretation, human failures are mostly understood as problems in faulty perception of self, others and of the world. The reasons for faulty perceptions may lie in the world but far more often lie in the individual himself. This means that persons engaged in human relations activities, whatever their nature as supervisors, administrators, parents, counselors, teachers, social workers, nurses or whatever are likely to be successful in the degree to which they understand the perceptual worlds of those they seek to work with and become skillful in helping others to change their perceptions of themselves and their surroundings.

There is even evidence lately to suggest that the essence of successful professional work is itself a matter of the use of the self as an effective instrument rather than a question of methods or information.

But whether or not a worker is able to use himself as an instrument well in the helping professions is also a function of the helper's own perceptions.

In a series of researches we have been carrying on at the University of Florida we have even been finding that the success of various kinds of "helpers" is a function of their perceptual organization. Hundreds of previous researches on good teaching and counseling have been unable to find clear cut differences between good practitioners and poor ones either on the basis of the knowldge they possess or the methods they use. Nevertheless in four studies to date, we have been able to show clear cut differences between "good" helpers and "poor" ones in the ways these workers typically perceive themselves, their clients and their purposes. What is more, this difference obtains in all three groups we have so far investigated: teachers, counselors and episcopal priests!

One of the most exciting contributions of perceptual psychology in my experience is its provision of an immediate frame of reference for understanding behavior to add to the historical one we have lived with so long. Let me clarify what I mean.

Stimulus-response psychology originally taught us that human behavior was a consequence of the stimulus and so we were led to look for the causes of behavior in the forces exerted on the individual. Freud and his students added to this concept by expanding the notion of the stimulus to include all those stimuli to which the individual had been subjected in the course of his growing up. This led us to seek for the causes of behavior in the person's past. Accordingly, for several generations now we have been almost exclusively preoccupied with the nature of behavior as seen from this historical frame of reference. Such a point of view about human behavior has been immensely useful to us in providing guidelines for the construction of programs, social action, and a thousand other applications. But, a historic point of view about behavior is essentially descriptive. It tells us how an individual got like this but frequently offers the practitioner very little in the way of clues as to what to do about it. In Freud's own use, of course, it led to a method of psychotherapy which required digging about in the patient's past history in search of an understanding of causes that was often more helpful to the psychologist than to the patient. For several generations we have been so preoccupied with this historical view as to hardly recognize that any other existed. This is particularly true of professional workers charged with the responsibility of helping the adjustment of others. Unhappily, the historic view of causation has often been more useful for diagnosis than for treatment.

In my own practice of psychotherapy, for example, I find that the clients I have who spend long hours exploring their past, are almost exclusively graduate students in psychology! They have thoroughly learned that their behavior is the function of their past so, when they come for help, they engage in its exploration. Sooner or later, however, they arrive at the conclusion "Well now I *know why* I feel like I do" but almost at once this statement is followed by "But darn it all, I still feel that way!"

Perceptual psychology provides us with a much more adequate treatment orientation. In addition to understanding how the individual got the way he is, it provides us with an understanding of the present dynamics from which we may more adequately derive effective methods of teaching, counseling, persuasion, and solutions to human interaction of many sorts. Perceptual psychology provides us with another frame of reference which makes it possible to deal with behavior in the present.

Perceptions exist in the present. If behavior is a function of perception then it should be possible to modify behavior by changing perceptions in the present. Thus, it may be possible to help an individual to better adjustment even if we do not have any knowledge of his past whatever! For many psychologists this is a startling, shocking, almost irresponsible idea. For many non-psychologists, however, it is good news and comes as a great refreshing breeze. It means that teachers, administrators, counselors, social workers and parents who have to deal with human behavior because their roles demand it can hope to do so with some chance of success without the necessity for being skilled psychologists. It means that if such people can become sensitive enough to how their charges are perceiving and feeling they can find effective ways of being helpful. A teacher who understands that a child feels unliked, unwanted, unacceptable and unable can do things to help such a child even without a knowledge of how he got to feel this way. If this seems to anyone to lessen the importance of psychologists it should not. The purpose of psychology is not, after all, to run the world. It is to help provide the understanding so that others whose job it is can learn to do it better.

The immediate frame of reference, of course, is not a new conception in the field of practice, for beginning with Carl Rogers' early work with client-centered therapy and running through all of the new psychotherapies we have seen in the past twenty years, all are predicated on the notion that it is possible to help clients, even without a full knowledge of the past. What perceptual psychology does for us is to provide a theoretical framework which explains why this is so and thus provides us with a valuable new tool for the understanding of behavior to add to those which traditional psychology has provided us in the past.

Many of the principles of perceptual psychology are deceptively simple. They have an "of course" feeling about them and often fit one's own experience so closely as to seem like one has always known them. This is very upsetting to some psychologists who feel it can't be accurate if it is that simple. Yet, it is necessary to remind ourselves that simplicity is the *goal* of science. What could be simpler, for example, than the physical formula $E = mc^2$? Furthermore, the simple and the "obvious" can have vast implications. Take, for example, the simple fact that reality for each individual lies, not in the outside world but, in his own perceptions. This principle is basic to the problems of communication and human misunderstandings everywhere. People just do not behave according to the "facts" as others see them. They behave in terms of what seems so to them. So we pass each other like ships in the night—not only as individuals but as nations as well.

Perceptual psychology is especially valuable as a practitioner's psychology. It is particularly pertinent to the problems of individual behavior with which the teacher, counselor, social worker, supervisor and therapist must deal. It is particularly appropriate to the helping professions and fits the needs of such workers like hand and glove.

As I indicated at the start of this paper I regard perceptual psychology as a basic expression of the great humanistic, phenomenological, existential movement currently sweeping the social sciences. When Donald Snygg and I stumbled on these concepts twenty years ago we were certain a perceptual psychology was inevitable. Since then we have attempted to set down in two editions of *Individual Behavior,* a systematic framework for a comprehensive perceptual psychology. The response to that effort has been deeply gratifying and has strengthened the hope we expressed in the preface of the first edition that, "as fallible human beings we can only hope that this is if not the truth, then very like the truth."

The Involuntary Bet

William H. Ittelson

How and why do we see the people and things around us? Trying to answer this question—technically called the study of perception—may seem at first glance to be a trivial task. But understanding this simple fact, perhaps just because it is one of the most universal and basic of human experiences, is by no means simple. Ask yourself, for example, why the chair across the room looks the way it does. And does it look the same to someone else? If not, how can either of you know what it really is like? Or how can you ever come to any sort of agreement or decision about the chair? It is just such questions as these that psychologists studying perception are trying to answer. And while they may seem

Reprinted from *Vogue*, 1952, **127**, 76–77, by permission of the author and the publisher.

trivial when asked about a chair, their importance is obvious if we ask them of more complicated perceptions, such as those of the men about a conference table in the United Nations.

Of all the work being done in the study of perception today, beyond any doubt the most fascinating is that of a scientist in Hanover, New Hampshire, Adelbert Ames, Junior, who is today actively collaborating with some of the members of the psychology department at Princeton University in designing new experiments and extending our understanding of this important no-man's-land, the psychology of perception. In commenting on Ames's work, Dr. Allan Gregg, vice-president of the Rockefeller Foundation, has said, as quoted in a recent book, *The Rockefeller Foundation,* by R. B. Fosdick, "I think Ames will be rediscovered in future years as often as anyone the Medical Sciences Division has aided."

Ames believes that his experiments, four of which are described on these pages, show that every perception we have, even of the chair across the room, is essentially an "involuntary bet." These bets are based on the probabilities each of us has learned through previous experiences with similar situations. To the extent that several people have had similar experiences, they will tend to make the same bets, to see the same things. If they have had different experiences, they will tend to see things differently. And since every perception is basically a bet, it can, like any bet, be wrong on occasion. The only way we can tell if any particular perception, any one bet, is right or wrong is by acting on it. If we are successful, the bet was "right." If we fail, it was "wrong."

1. The Three Chairs experiment, from the outside, looks like a big, black box, about the size of two large office desks placed one on top of the other. Along one side of this box are three small peepholes through which one can look into the interior of the box. Looking through each of these peepholes, the observer sees what appears to be the same chair, dimly illuminated inside the completely dark box. The chair seems to be made of heavy wires, but otherwise it looks like an ordinary, solid, well-built chair. The seat is flat, the legs and back are straight, and it sits squarely on the floor. After the observer has noted this through each of the peepholes, he walks to the back of the box, which is open so that he can see what is really inside. To his amazement, he discovers that only one of these objects actually is a wire chair. The other two resemble nothing more than weird wire cobwebs. In each case, what the observer sees does not correspond to what is really there. The three-dimensional "chairness" which he experiences does not exist in the physical objects at which he is looking. After finding out what is actually in the box, the observer can go back and look through the peepholes again. *He still sees the same solid wire chairs* (Fig. 1).

Fig. 1   Upper: Chairs as they appeared to the viewer. Lower: As they actually were made.

2. *The Leaf Room* experiment, as its name suggests, consists of a small room, the inside of which is completely covered with leaves. An observer looks into this room carefully, is allowed to examine it and even to walk in it. He then looks at it while wearing a specially designed pair of aniseikonic glasses which have the peculiar property of altering some of the visual indications he is receiving while not affecting others. Now the room assumes weird and fantastic shapes. The leaves and walls change size and shape and appear to move mysteriously under their own power. The observer becomes confused, bewildered. When asked to walk into the room, he may become terrorized and remain frozen to his seat. Even if he does enter the room, he does so hesitatingly. He can not walk steadily. He is unable to touch objects when he reaches for them. He can not very well describe the room because it seems always to be changing.

For most people this experience is quite disturbing and even frightening. It is frequently described as a "nightmare." Sometimes, if the observer looks at an ordinary, familiar room, instead of the "leaf room," the glasses have little or no effect, and the experience is not at all disturbing. Occasionally, an observer seems to enjoy wearing the glasses even in the "leaf room," but this reaction is most often seen in children. For children, wearing the glasses is better than a party. They laugh and squeal as they go through experiences which terrify many adults. They not only do not mind, but they seem actually to delight in having their own world turned topsy-turvy.

It is interesting that in this demonstration, as in everyday life, no matter how confusing the situation may be, no matter how extreme the conflicts, most people manage to make some decision, to arrive at what seems to be the "best bet" under the circumstances (Fig. 2).

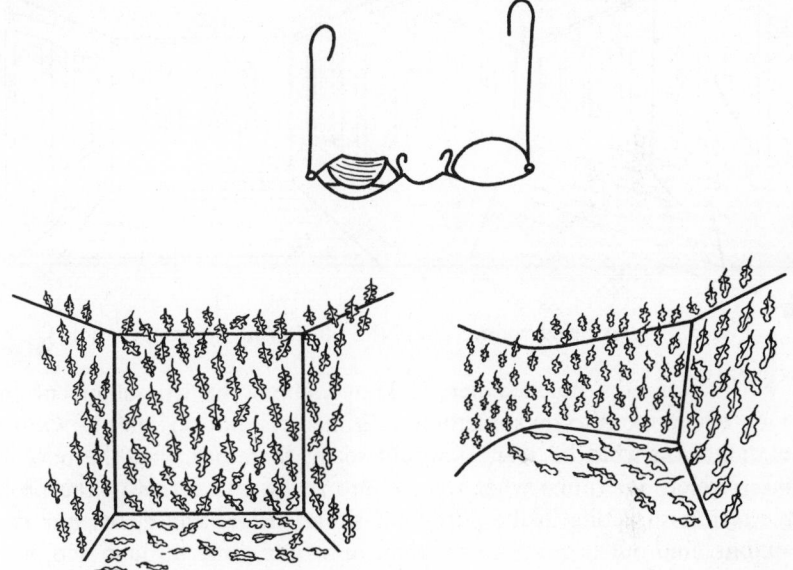

Fig. 2   Leaf room (left), distorted by glasses into nightmare (right).

3. *The Distorted Room* is a model, about the size of a large packing case, of a crazily built room. The floor slopes down, the ceiling slopes up, and back wall slopes away. All the walls are different sizes and shapes. But this peculiar room has one important property—from one *point of view* it looks like an ordinary rectangular room. The observer is shown the room in detail before he looks at it from the viewing position. He examines its construction, shape, and size carefully until he becomes quite familiar with it. No attempt is made to fool him; on the contrary, every effort is made to have him learn all that he can about the room. When

the observer is satisfied that he knows the room thoroughly, he sits at the viewing point. The room now appears to be perfectly rectangular while familiar objects, such as a pair of hands, appear distorted. He experiences a conflict between what he sees and what he knows, accompanied by a sense of confusion and uncertainty. Now the observer is given a pointer and told to hit a spot on one of the side walls as if he were swatting a fly. He confidently swings but misses, wildly smashing the pointer into the back wall (Fig. 3).

Fig. 3   Distorted room (left); the illusion of normalcy (right).

No matter how much a person knows about the true shape of the room, when asked to do something in it, he acts, not on what he *knows,* but rather on what he *sees.* It would seem, therefore, that the bets we make, which determine what we see, are really guesses as to the probable results of acting in the particular situation. We can check our perceptions, find out if our bets are right or wrong, only through action.

In life's constant sequence of checking by acting, the role of failure, of unsuccessful action, is as important as that of success. Success can only confirm what we already know, while failure points out our inadequacies and opens up opportunities for change and development toward greater adequacy. The overprotected child is a familiar example of a person denied this opportunity by never being allowed to experience the consequences of his own actions.

The way a person reacts to a failure is an indication of that person's potentialities for development and growth. In the distorted room, for example, initial failure in "swatting the fly" quickly makes the observer much more able to act in the room than he ever would have been if he just sat and looked at it. But different people react quite differently. Most observers keep on trying after the first failure, some with grim determination, some with nervous embarrassment, and a few with real, wholehearted enjoyment. At the other extreme are those who refuse to try again at all. A few observers have been known to throw the pointer down and stalk from the experimental room in a fury.

4. *The Rotating Trapezoid* consists of a trapezoidal piece of sheet metal or cardboard, with holes cut in it and shadows painted on it to give the appearance of a window. It is mounted on a rod connected to a motor which rotates it continuously about a vertical axis. When an observer views this device, however, he does not see a rotating trapezoid, but instead an oscillating rectangular window, swinging back and forth through an arc of about 100 degrees. A particularly interesting effect can be seen if a solid tube is inserted in the window through one of the openings. Part of the time the tube and the window appear to be swinging in opposite directions so that at one point they seem to hit head on. Different observers see different things when this happens. Some see the tube remain absolutely rigid and appear to cut its way through the window frame. To others, the tube seems to be flexible, so that it appears to stretch out and bend around the window. Here is an important laboratory proof that when different people make different "bets" about the same situation they experience that situation differently. *They literally live in different worlds* (Fig. 4).

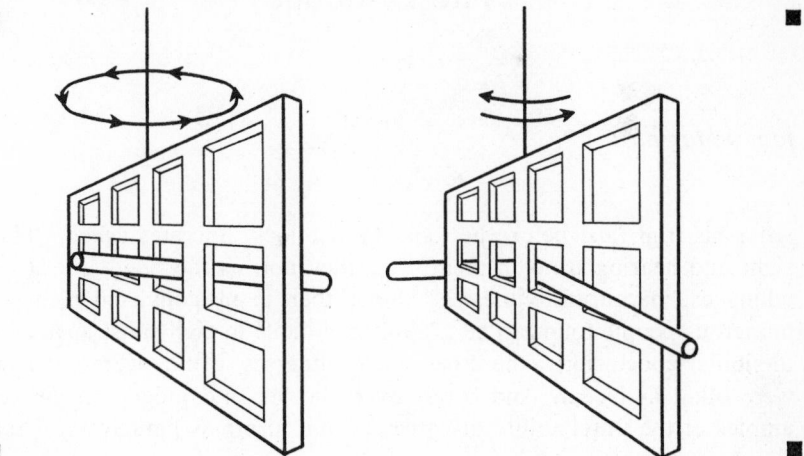

Fig. 4   Actually a revolving object: the illusion (right) an oscillating object.

In one especially interesting experiment using the rotating trapezoid, observers were shown and allowed to feel a steel tube and told that it would be put on the window. They were later shown and handed a rubber tube and told the same thing. Actually a third, wood tube was placed in the window both times. Most observers, however, saw the "steel" tube remain rigid and cut through the window while they saw the "rubber" tube stretch and bend around. Since they had had very little experience in situations like this, the bets they made were quite tentative and easily changed by suggestion or "propaganda."

Such bets are essentially predictions of the results of future actions, based on the probabilities learned from acting in the past. This means that people can pick out of a welter of conflicting possibilities those actions that have the highest probability of being successful. And when we recognize that people never act in a vacuum, that they always act for some purpose of greater or lesser value to them, we can see that the study of perception may eventually help increase our understanding of basic human values.

The Evidence

James Marshall

After his trial, just before he took the hemlock, Socrates asked, "Have sight and hearing truth in them? Are they not, as the poets are always telling us, inaccurate witnesses?" Since then many convicted men, and numerous people found to be at fault and liable in civil suits, have come to similar conclusions: the other side's witnesses, if they were not lying, were blind and deaf. And surely every lawyer and judge can give examples of the unreliability of witnesses and jurors as perceivers of real-

Reprinted from *Psychology Today*, 1969. Copyright © Communications/Research/Machines/Inc.

ity. The psychological sciences have described man's faulty perceptions and erratic memory so that we have a considerable body of empirical evidence supporting Socrates' views.

Nevertheless, the life of our courts, our trial process, is based on the fiction that witnesses see and hear accurately and so testify; and if they do not testify with accuracy on direct examination, cross-examination by counsel will straighten them out. This is another fiction, the idea that "adversary proceedings" can winnow out the truth, when in fact they are directed towards the victory of a cause, not truth, and are geared to developing plausibility, not reality.

Even without the tension and conflict of the adversary proceedings in a courtroom, it is difficult to establish which of conflicting perceptions is the more plausible. This is illustrated in the report of the Warren Commission on the assassination of President Kennedy. There was conflict as to the number of shots fired, the direction from which they were fired, the size of the bag in which Oswald carried the rifle, etc. The commission did not have to come to a decision within a few hours or days. It took months. It had the aid of the FBI, the Secret Service, the Dallas police, photographs and technical laboratories. Nevertheless choices of plausibility had to be made and many people remain unconvinced that the choices were correct.

There are many examples of misperception or distorted perception with which we are all familiar, one or more of which almost certainly occur in automotive accident cases and "blue-collar" criminal cases, such as those involving force, violence, small thefts. If we see a bright and a dull or a large and a small light in the dark, the brighter or larger light will appear nearer than the duller or smaller. Thus, brightness and size are cues to distance and they may also be cues to weight. This may be important in estimating distances at night. Perception of size is relative. An average size person will appear short or tall depending upon whether he is standing with seven-foot-tall basketball players or African pigmies. In other words, our perception of size and distance is relative.

Experiments have shown how inaccurate we are in estimating the speed of a car, particularly when it is coming toward us or going away from us. Color, body style and noise of a car have been found to influence a witness's estimate of speed. Body style and size may also induce bias in some observers. Some police *expect* bright-colored sports models to exceed speed limits.

All these phenomena of perception are related to testimony in court, especially in tort and blue-collar criminal cases, which generally depend upon evidence of spoken words or physical contact. In commercial and corporate litigation, it is more likely that there will be written documentation (a contract, a balance sheet, a record book) or evidence in the form of objects (pictures, bolts of cloth, chemicals) to verify perception and reinforce recollection.

Difficult as accurate perception is in normal situations, inaccuracy is increased in conditions of danger and stress. Danger and stress tend to distort time and distance. We are familiar with the expression that time seems endless when one is in danger. Time expands—distance contracts. Yet in the ordinary motor-vehicle accident case we testify to the distance of one car from another or the speed at which they are going, even though the accident put us in a position of stress. Danger and stress also affect the recalled sequence of events. We must remember that the average motor-vehicle accident takes about 10 seconds. In this short period of time we can scarcely expect that people will be able to estimate accurately the distances, the speed, or the sequence of events.

Stress has a bearing on the *res gestae* rule (the acts, circumstances, and statements that are incidental to the principal facts of a litigated matter and are admissible in evidence in view of their relevant association with the fact). Although hearsay evidence is usually inadmissible, a spontaneous explanation by a participant in a happening will be admitted on the theory that "stress of nervous excitement," as Dean John Henry Wigmore calls it, "will make for a spontaneous and sincere response," i.e., it is not part of a concocted story. The *res gestae* rule assumes that as a matter of fact people will state the truth in stressful circumstances. The opposite is more likely to be correct. People under stress may accurately express their feelings, but those very feelings may reduce the accuracy of the perceptions which they verbalize.

Another exception to the hearsay rule is the admission in evidence of a *dying declaration,* a statement by someone on his death bed who knows he is dying, such as "John Doe shot me." This derives from an assumption that a man will not wish to apply for admittance to heaven and the divine presence with a lie on his lips. However, stress probably will distort the perception of the dying man. Both of these exceptions to the hearsay rule can be questioned because a stressful situation may also affect the witness so as to distort his perception of the dying man's declaration or that of a person involved in a motor accident or assault.

FILLING IN THE BLANKS

What has been said of visual perception is even more likely to be true of aural. Few people hear every word that is said or recall what is said in correct order. What they do is to fill in the blanks in their perception. Their expectations of what would be appropriate to hear are drawn from the bank of their experience. Thucydides, writing his great *History*, refers to the differences in the account of events by eyewitnesses, whether due to imperfect memory or partiality. He admits his own inability to carry in his memory word for word the speeches he heard and repeated. So he wrote, "my habit has been to make the speakers say what was in my opinion demanded of them by the various occasions, of course adhering as closely as possible to the general sense of what they really said." All of us do this. We get the drift of the speaker and these cues give momentum to our memory which carries on the sense of the communication. This is similar to the momentum which causes us to assume that a car will continue at the same speed and in the same direction as we last recalled seeing it move. Such fictions are pragmatic. They are necessary to effective daily living. Obviously, however, they are hazardous bets if the precise words of a conversation or the exact courses of two cars are determining facts in a litigation.

As Hadley Cantril and Charles H. Bumstead have said: "On the basis of the significances we experience, we are constantly guessing that certain things we do will give us the value-qualities of experience we hope for. We try to repeat many types of activities because they show high promise of recapturing or maintaining certain qualities of experience that have already proved satisfying." This accords with theories of homeostasis which hold that people try to maintain internal balances and balances between their inner needs and drives and their perceptions of other people, objects and conditions with whom they have transactions.

RECALL AND INFERENCE

A few years ago, a colleague of mine, Dr. Helge Mannson, and I performed an experiment at New York University. We showed a short motion picture with sound track to law students, police trainees and people who attended a settlement house. The law students were graduate students; the police trainees were all high-school graduates and only a few had attended college; and the settlement-house people, with few exceptions, had not gone beyond elementary school. We found that the higher the educational standing of the viewers, the greater the number of items they correctly recalled from the picture. The higher educated also made a greater number of inferences (or conclusions). The point is that while the more highly educated witness may testify to more items correctly, he may also make a greater number of inferences and that, of course, is the role of the judge or jury, and not the witness. The lower educated, on the other hand, recalled fewer items correctly but the proportion of their inferences to items recalled was even greater than that of the higher educated.

We found also that the quantity of material recalled, the correctness of recall and the proportion of testimony that was inferential were dependent upon the influences of others upon the witness. Thus, a status figure urging our subjects to try to recall the picture correctly affected the amount of recall and the number of inferences. Our law students under influence of a status figure made considerably more inferences than their control group or than the police trainees. The police trainees under influence of their status figure had greater recall than their control group and made no more inferences, i.e., they stuck more closely to the facts than did the law students.

INFLUENCE OF ROLE ON BIAS

Role affects bias. Thus, we found that the role of witness for the defense resulted in less-accurate recall than the role of witness for the prosecution. Albert H. Hastorf and Cantril in an experiment showed how interpretation may be affected by the observer's commitment or loyalty. They played a film before students of Dartmouth and Princeton, showing a football game between the two which had been described as "particularly rough." Ascribing different reasons, the men of each school claimed that the opposing team had been guilty of more infractions of the rules than their team. In litigation, of course, we find that witnesses perceive violations of law or improper behavior by the other side rather than by their side.

In our experiment we also gave our subjects a test for punitiveness. We discovered that the more punitive people in each of our groups had better recall than the less punitive. (On the other hand, I should say that in another experiment we did not find any correlation.) But this discrepancy may not be important for the trial process since we rarely know much about the personality configuration of witnesses in a trial.

The problem of inferences is important. What we seek in testimony is fact, not inferences, not conclusions. Nevertheless, probably all of us in testifying frequently state as fact what is really our inference. We live that way and this is another situation in which we cannot on the witness stand divorce ourselves from our habitual ways of behaving. But the reality is that in all innocence we may be testifying to conclusions, not perceptions.

Groups can influence the perceptions and, consequently, the expectations and actions of their members. In order to maintain his self-image and sense of social power, an individual will tend to conform to the norms of his group if he does not have appropriate norms of his own. In litigation, conformity may not be merely a matter of group loyalty. A witness, even one who is not a party, will tend to have a psychological investment in the success of his side and unconsciously be moved to support that side. There may be a tendency to converge on a common norm when sharing experiences with others. The individual will be in a suggestible relationship to their norms. Thus, when a lawyer interviews witnesses before trial, the mere suggestion that other witnesses have seen things differently will tend to induce a witness to adapt his perception to that of others. This can be done in perfectly good faith by a lawyer trying to find what the real story is or it may be done for the purpose of inducing the prospective witness to conform his testimony to what would be more helpful to the case. A similar process of converging on norms may occur in a trial. But perhaps the most dangerous instance of influencing the perception or recall of witnesses is in identification of an offender. The police and prosecuting attorneys have used many suggestive techniques to get a suspect identified.

HYPNOTIC SUGGESTION

We have to recognize, too, that many persons are highly subject to hypnotic suggestion. This suggestion need not be the result of the practice of hypnotism. The personality of a lawyer interrogating a witness or of a judge interrogating or giving directions to a witness may have hypnotic effect even without the development of a hypnotic trance.

Triers of fact, whether judges or juries, are subject to the same limitations as witnesses. They are in reality witnesses to testimony of the witness. They perceive and recall, make inferences just as witnesses do, basing perception, recall and inferences on prior experience and expectations. Thus, Rita James Simon has shown in her experiment on jury trials where the defense is insanity, that one of the most important elements in a juror's determination is personal experience with other people who have been mentally ill and the resemblance of the defendant to such persons.

In another so far unpublished experiment in which I participated at the University of Michigan with Kent Marquis and Stuart Oskamp, we showed a film and then asked our subjects to write in as great detail as possible what they had seen and heard. The average free-report completeness-index score was low, i.e., 28, but the average accuracy index was extremely high, i.e., 96. This indicates that witnesses do not report much material in free-report testimony but what they do report is almost always correct. (No question of perjury or distortion caused by parties, witnesses or lawyers preparing for trial was involved.)

We then divided our subjects into four groups. The first group was asked broad questions, such as "Describe the setting," or "What did the driver do?" Completeness index jumped from 28 to 48 under this questioning but the accuracy went down from 96 to 90. Another group was asked more specific open-end questions, such as are customarily used in direct examination of witnesses to focus attention on small sets of details about the film. Witnesses were free to answer in their own words. Completeness rose to 56; accuracy fell to 86. The third group was given forced-choice nonbiased questions similar to the multiple-choice tests with which we are all familiar. This line of questioning raised the completeness index to 83; accuracy, however, dropped to 82. Thus, the forced-choice questions produce more testimony without a major sacrifice of accuracy. Finally, we gave forced-choice questions in the form of leading questions, such as those familiarly used in cross-examination. Half of these were in the correct direction and half led towards incorrect answers. Contrary to our expectations the use of these biased questions did not have any large effect on testimony. The completeness index was 84 and the accuracy index about 81 or about the same as in the multiple-choice questions. Thus, it appears the more freedom the witness is given, the greater is the likelihood that he will be accurate, but the less complete will be his testimony.

THE CHANGING OF TESTIMONY

In litigation a witness who changes his testimony is frequently challenged as being incorrect or unreliable. Lawyers will comment on discrepancies and uncertainties and attempt to show that the witness changing his testimony is not credible. We found a trend which indicated that witnesses who, under interrogation, changed the testimony they had given in their free report tended to have more correct recall than those who said they had not changed their testimony or did not wish to do so. We also found that witnesses who had rated themselves as good witnesses tended to be more correct and covered material more completely than those who rated themselves poorly. In other words, people who had self-confidence and positive self-evaluation made the better witnesses. A parallel finding was that if they thought the interrogators regarded them as good witnesses, they tended to believe that they were good witnesses. Morton Deutsch and Leonard Solomon found that they could induce subjects to evaluate their own performances favorably or unfavorably by information that was given to them about their relative performances compared with others.

Another interesting finding was to the effect that those who suspected that the interrogator *wanted* them to give false answers tended to give more accurate answers and omit fewer items than those witnesses who were not suspicious. This corresponds to the experimental results of Nicholas Freyberg, who found that his subjects had greater recall of the arguments of a person pitted against them when they had grounds for suspecting the veracity of the opinions expressed by the other person.

The relationship of experience and expectation to perception has been mentioned. Experience and expectation also pattern the *significances* we attach to our perceptions and, therefore, the inferences or judgments we make. This patterning carries through to the *articulation* of what we have perceived. "No two persons have had the same experience of the Negro, of free enterprise, or even of motherhood," Gardner Murphy wrote. So there must always be some slippage of significance between the articulated testimony of two witnesses and again between witness and triers of fact.

THE CHALLENGES

What I have said suggests several challenges to lawyers and to social scientists. Obviously, we need more empirical knowledge of the trial process. It is evident also that lawyers are rarely capable of the research necessary to obtain such knowledge. This is because lawyers are rarely trained in scientific method and because experiments in the courtroom might well be deemed to deprive a party of due process of law. But, more important, there is great social value in legal stability so that people may expect from the law what they and others like them have experienced. Law must be a stabilizing institution.

Nevertheless, we know that substantive law is continuously changing because of new conditions in the social and economic life of a people. Over the centuries there have been changes, too, in the procedures of the courts. Originally jurors were not impartial persons, but neighbors who knew the facts and the parties. Women were tried for witchcraft. Placed in a pond, fully clothed, they were guilty if they sank. Truth was tested by ordeals of fire and water. Trial by battle was common practice. Only recently has the Supreme Court ruled that every defendant is entitled in a criminal case to representation by an attorney at every stage of the proceeding and the powers of the police to obtain confessions have been restricted.

It is now time for lawyers and social scientists to engage in joint research as to the validity of trial practices; some of them may be valid, others may indicate a need for change. There is no more important enterprise for law schools today. An example of how the courts may modify their practice as the result of empirical research is the action in New Jersey where the court modified its procedure relating to pretrial conference on the basis of empirical research by Professor Maurice Rosenberg in which the court participated. Data from this controlled experiment indicated that pretrial conference increases the likelihood that a case will be well presented at trial and promotes a fairer trial. Further examples of joint research possibilities:

One:

 A. Does the selective process in perception and recall which limits the number of items in any field (in any happening) which are perceived and recalled differ among different socioeducational groups and subcultures of a nation?
 B. Does this selective process differ for witnesses, judges and jurors?
 C. Is it different and, if so, how between participants in and witnesses to a happening?

Two:

To what extent is the apparent greater punitiveness of the police the result of a self-selection process by candidates for police careers, a selective process by those who recruit or choose policemen, or a process of adaptation to the role or career of the police, or all three.

Three:

> A. In order to minimize the effects of recall on the adversary duel in the courtroom, how could trial practice be modified to produce greater objectivity in testimony (for example, comparative study might be made of the Anglo-American and Continental systems of presentation of evidence and their relative effects on judge and jury)?
> B. What legal procedures, other than motor-vehicle accidents, might be withdrawn from the courtroom and handled in a different manner in the interests of effective justice?

But in the meantime, there are changes that can be made in the law. The process of identification of suspects can be altered to give them the most rudimentary protection from the often suggestive and sometimes even hypnotic influence of the police line-up and the prosecutor's office. Why should identification not be done in the presence of a judge? The automotive accident case should rarely, if ever, be tried in court. Since an automotive accident is a risk common to the whole American population it should be covered by insurance and claims should be heard as Workmen's Compensation cases are. For of all evidence, the perception and recall of witnesses in auto accidents are the most unreliable.

Misperception and the Vietnam War

Ralph K. White

I. MISPERCEPTION AS A CAUSE OF TWO WORLD WARS

The fact of continuing war, in a world that desperately wants to avoid it, is a paradox too enormous to be evaded. It is the central problem of

Reprinted from *Journal of Social Issues*, 1966, **22**, 1–19, by permission of the author and publisher.

the human race in the second half of the twentieth century. Few reflective persons anywhere in the world have not had the thought that, in our nuclear age, only a madman could start a war. Yet wars continue.

Naturally, psychologists and psychiatrists have been especially likely to see the problem in psychological terms. We know something about "madmen," since "madness" in all its forms and degrees, including the madness of normal people like ourselves, is in our bailiwick. Many of us have felt especially that *misperception* or cognitive distortion—a variegated psychological process that is accentuated in the psychotic but that pervades normal living as well—is a clue that may help in resolving the paradox. Perhaps it could help to explain how normally sane human beings can unwittingly, without intending the consequences, involve themselves step by step in actions that lead to war.

The following pages consist largely of an exploration of that idea. Psychological research and psychiatric experience are brought in where they seem relevant, but, since history can be described as "psychology teaching by examples," the main emphasis is on recent and contemporary history, psychologically interpreted. There is first a brief examination of the background of World Wars I and II, with an effort to discover and to clarify the role that misperception played in making possible the actions that were most important in bringing about those two wars. There is then a much more detailed examination of the background of the present conflict in Vietnam, again with a primary focus on the possibility of misperception on both sides. There is no assumption that the amount of misperception is the same or even similar on the two sides. The possibility is left open that one side may be much more realistic than the other in perceiving the "actual facts." But a central hypothesis, which the evidence does seem to justify in all three of these conflicts, is that each side is highly unrealistic in perceiving—emphathizing with—what is in the minds of those on the other side. As Cantril might put it, they live in different "reality worlds." On each side men assume that what seems real to them seems real also to the enemy. In many ways both are wrong.

To psychologists this approach is, of course, very familiar. Lippmann, when playing the role of a psychologist, talked about "stereotypes" and "pictures in our heads"; Thomas, about varying "definitions of the situation"; Lewin, about "the psychological environment" and "the life space"; Tolman, about "cognitive maps"; Cantril, about "reality worlds." Freud apparently took something of the sort for granted and proceeded to explore the mechanisms, such as projection, that lead to distortion in men's private worlds. Many are now stressing "empathy," defined as an effort to imagine, realistically, how the world looks to another individual or group. The essential proposition running through all of these is the same: that different individuals and groups perceive the world differently, and that we can scarcely begin to understand their behavior until we have begun to understand how reality as they see it differs from reality as we see it.[1]

In addition to psychologists many other students of international relations have been concerned with the distorted views that one nation may have of another. They have been studied in detail by historians such as Montgelas (1925), Fay (1928), Gooch (1936, 1938) and Albertini (1953), and by political scientists such as North (Holsti and North, 1965) who have explored the thinking of the "other side," the Austrians and Germans, in the events that led to World War I. Emery Reves, in a brilliant chapter (1963, pp. 1–29), has described the reality worlds of the United States, Great Britain, France, Germany and Russia during the inter-war period that led up to and produced World War II. There is a large literature (especially Heiden, 1944) on Hitler's thinking, including his conception of the political world. The differing worlds of the Russians and the Americans since 1945 have been described by historians such as Kennan (1960) as well as by psychologists (Bronfenbrenner, 1961; Osgood, 1962; White, 1965). Felix Greene has sketched his conception of the international reality world of the Chinese Communists in a jolting chapter that should be read by every American who wants to begin to understand the conflict between that country and ourselves (1961), and others such as Barnett (1961), Fairbank (1958,

---

1. The word "perception" has two common uses in psychology: a narrower use in which it means a cognitive response to the immediately presented environment (depth-perception, audio-visual perception, etc.) and a broader use in which it becomes synonymous with all forms of cognition, including even the individual's most basic assumptions about the nature of the world and of man. Throughout this study the word will be used in its broader sense. In other words, it will be used with the same meaning as the more technical word "cognition." It is preferred here to the word "cognition" chiefly because the word "misperception," which will recur continually, is somewhat familiar, while "miscognition" would sound barbarous.

   The word "misconception" is of course more familiar than "misperception," and would be preferable in that respect, but it refers ordinarily to the end-product of a psychological process rather than to the process itself, while the word "misperception" lends itself to use in both senses. In this study we will consider both the process of misperception (i.e., how a person's beliefs come to differ from the evidence available to him) and the products of that process which are commonly called "misconceptions."

1966) and Hinton (1966) have provided much scholarly background for understanding the same conflict.

Burchett, a pro-Communist Australian journalist, on the basis of first-hand contact, has given us an all too uncritically and onesidedly empathic picture of how the Vietnamese conflict looks to the Viet Cong (1965), and a French journalist, Chaffard (1965), also with first-hand contact, has given us a less partisan conception of it. Historians such as Buttinger (1958), Devillers (1962), and Hammer (1954), and many first-hand observers of the contemporary scene such as Fall (1964b), Lansdale (1964), Carver (1964, 1966), Malcolm Browne (1965), Robert Browne (1965), Halberstam (1965), Shaplen (1965) and La-couture (1966) have provided material that is relevant especially to the thinking of anti-Communist Vietnamese and to that of the less articulate inhabitants of Vietnam who may or may not be on one side or the other. In all such concrete efforts to understand the thinking of a group other than our own it is appropriate for the psychologist to play a rather modest role, learning all he can from the historian and the first-hand observer, and applying his "psychological" concepts (derived mainly from a study of other groups in similar conflict situations) only if and when they seem to fit the concrete facts of a particular case.

An enterprise such as this cannot invoke the safeguards and the sanctions of a formal methodology. The value of the discussion depends, to a disconcerting extent, on the writer's efforts to recognize and transcend his own biases. That is too bad, because it goes without saying that every writer does have biases. Though this one has tried to avoid distortion, some of it undoubtedly remains. The reader should therefore be alert to discover—chiefly by comparing this discussion with everything else he knows about the subject—the nature and extent of the distortion.

A. AUSTRIA VS. SERBIA

On the day when Austria-Hungary broke relations with Serbia, setting in motion the escalation that transformed a local dispute into a world war, the perception of the situation in Austrian minds was radically different from the perception of it in the minds of Austria's enemies—a perception which sustained those enemies (ultimately including the United States) through more than four years of one of the bloodiest wars in history. As seen by Austria's enemies, her declaration of war on Serbia was cold-blooded, calculating aggression. In their minds Austria's masters, the militarists who ruled Imperial Germany, had decided to use the essentially unimportant Serbian dispute as a pretext to launch a war that they believed would give them mastery first of Europe and then of the world.

Historical scholarship in the 1920's, however, led to a picture of what happened that apportions war-guilt much more evenly between the two sides, and that includes a more humanly understandable conception of what was in Austrian minds at the time. Historians are now in fair agreement that Austria, not Germany, was the prime mover (Gooch, 1938, p. 445). Germany clearly tried to prevent a major European war. As for the Austrians, from their point of view Serbia was carrying on an intolerable agitation against Austria-Hungary, not stopping even at assassination; it had to be punished, and that was that. Unless Serbia was punished, nationalist agitation throughout the country would get worse, and the very existence of the Austro-Hungarian Empire would be in danger.

To be sure, there were some other thoughts in their minds. One was the terrifying possibility of a bigger war (Gooch, 1938, p. 446). Russia, with her enormous army, might come in. But surely (the Austrians thought) the Czar of Russia, who lived in fear of assassination himself, must realize that the Hapsburg emperor could not tolerate the sort of agitation that had led to the assassination of the Archduke. He must see that Austria-Hungary's very existence as a bastion of civilization and order in Central Europe depended on her taking a firm stand in this new crisis and teaching the conspirators in Belgrade a lesson they could not forget. Also, since the German Kaiser had seen the justice of Austria's position and was standing firmly by her side, the Czar would hardly be so rash as to intervene; he must know that the consequences of a world war would be incalculable. In any case, the risk must be run, because if the Serbian nationalist agitation among the Serbs and Croats who were still under Austrian rule were allowed to continue, it could quickly spread to the other nationalities within the Austro-Hungarian family of nations, and Austria-Hungary herself would disappear as a Great Power—which was, of course, unthinkable.

To the extent that this is a fair picture of what was happening in Austrian minds, it suggests that their reality world was distorted by six forms of misperception:

1. A diabolical enemy-image.
2. A virile self-image.

3. A moral self-image.
4. Selective inattention.
5. Absence of empathy.
6. Military overconfidence.

1/ *The diabolical enemy-image.* In the central focus of Austrian minds was the "criminal" character of the "assassins" who were violating all standards of human decency and endangering the very survival of the beneficent Austro-Hungarian empire. In their black-and-white picture the black was more fully in focus than the white. To them it seemed that such men, and the conspiracy in Belgrade that was responsible for their actions (though this point remained controversial in the minds of detached observers), were so flagrantly evil that all right-minded people even in Russia must be indignant and must see the need to "punish" them.

2/ *The virile self-image.* A preoccupation with prestige and a feeling that humiliation would be intolerable were characteristic not only of the Austrians, in 1914, but also of the other governments involved. In each of the Great Powers there was a fear of "losing our position as a Great Power" and "sinking to the status of a second-class power." In each case, after a "firm stand" had been taken, there was acute consciousness of the danger of backing down, or seeming to back down, and a much less vivid awareness of the pain and death of tens of millions of human beings that might result if one did not compromise. This was true up to the time of the general Russian mobilization, when fear took over as the ruling emotion in Germany, if not in Austria-Hungary, and led directly to a strike-first policy. Up to that time the ruling emotion had been not fear of attack, but fear of humiliation. The chief dimension in which national decision-makers judged themselves, and expected to be judged by others, was not good vs. bad or right vs. wrong but strong vs. weak. The essential goal apparently was to be, and to seem, strong and courageous. The essential thing was to take "a firm stand," a "strong stand," and to do it with such firmness and such obvious lack of fear, on one's own part and on the part of one's allies, that the potential enemy would be sure to back down (cf. Schelling, 1960).

Since this is in the realm of values it is perhaps inappropriate to call it unrealistic in the same sense in which a failure to think about the future is unrealistic. Yet, if at a given time a person or group acts as if prestige-for-its-own-sake were the only goal or the main goal worth striving for, while at other times other goals (such as freedom from pain and death, for oneself or for others) are salient, a question can be raised as to whether there has been selective inattention, not only to certain objective facts but also to certain genuine psychological needs. A compulsive ruling of certain motives out of the field of consciousness, perhaps with a feeling that it would be weak and unmanly to pay attention to them, can be itself a form of unrealism, especially if the main value endangered by the situation is nothing more essential (in the eyes of detached observers) than prestige-for-its-own-sake.

3/ *The moral self-image.* In the crisis of 1914, the Austrians had a black-and-white picture in which only evil was attributed to the Serbian enemy and only good to the Austro-Hungarian self. While their own moral nobility was perhaps less salient in the Austrians' minds than either the diabolical character of the enemy or their own need to take a "firm stand" in the interest of self-preservation, the self that they assumed to be worth preserving was also noble: peace-loving (they never for a moment sought a bigger war, and always feared it), civilized (they were a bastion of civilization in a Central Europe threatened by the barbarian tide of Pan-Slavism), economically rational (their empire was prospering in unity and would suffer economically if broken up), orderly (the Serbian assassins were violating elementary standards of law and order), democratic (theirs was a limited monarchy, and the subject peoples were advancing toward full autonomy as rapidly as possible), etc.

It is not necessary to deny a large kernel of truth in each of these propositions; it is necessary only to notice that the picture was expurgated at one crucial point. It did not include even a candid consideration of the possibility that this noble nation might now be committing aggression. The ultimatum to Serbia included what the Serbs regarded as a virtual demand for submission by Serbia to Austrian authority, and when this was not clearly accepted by Serbia Austria broke relations and began to mobilize for war. In the eyes of most of the rest of the world, this was aggression. It was aggression also by almost any clear definition of the term; for example, if aggression is defined as the use of force or threat of force on another nation's territory and against the wishes of the majority of the politically conscious people of that nation, Austria's action was aggression, however justified it may have been by the Serbian provocation. But the Austrians did not call it that, or seriously think about what to call it. To them it was not aggression at all, but "a firm stand," or "bringing the criminals to justice." Here again there was selective inattention. The charge of aggression was not answered in their minds; it was ignored.

There was also in their minds a curious sort of automatism in the form of a feeling that they could not do otherwise. The initial steps on the path to war were taken with a feeling of necessity; to do otherwise would be "suicide." And once the initial steps were taken, Austrian minds were gripped by what Anatol Rapaport has called "the blindness of involvement" (1960, pp. 259–272). As the Emperor Francis Joseph put it, "We cannot go back now" (Gooch, 1938, p. 437). All moral guilt was thus shifted from the Austrians themselves to a sort of impersonal Fate or Necessity. This was shown most strikingly at two key points: Austria's refusal to reconsider her course of action on July 25, when the conciliatory Serbian reply to the Austrian ultimatum was seen even by the German Kaiser as "doing away with every reason for war" (Montgelas, 1925, p. 137); and her refusal to draw back even when Germany, on July 29, exerted very strong pressure on her to do so. On that day the German Chancellor, Bethmann Hollweg, wired the Austrians: "we cannot allow Vienna to draw us lightly, and without regard to our advice, into a world-wide conflagration" (Montgelas, 1925, p. 148). Berchtold, the Austrian Foreign Minister, had the bit in his teeth, he had put on his blinders, and with a "courageous" unwillingness to consider any alternative course of action he stepped over the brink of the precipice.

(The strong German pressure on Austria to draw back is interesting also as evidence of how mistaken our own diabolical image of Germany was, throughout the First World War. Germany did not try to precipitate a European war; she tried to prevent it.)

4/ *Selective inattention.* Of all the psychological mechanisms involved in misperception of the kinds we have been considering, perhaps the most pervasive is one which in some context may be called "resistance" or "repression" (though the Freudians give a more restricted meaning to each of these terms) and which Sullivan, defining it more broadly, has called "selective inattention." It is involved on both sides of the black-and-white picture, when white or grey elements on the enemy side are glossed over and attention is focused only on the black, and also when black or grey elements on one's own side are glossed over and attention is focused only on the white.

In addition, it should be noted that in nations stumbling toward war there are usually at least three other definable types or aspects of selective inattention: narrow time-perspective, narrow space-perspective, and absence of empathy.

In the minds of the Austrians in 1914 there was vivid and focal awareness of only one aspect of the future as they perceived it: the catastrophic disintegration that they regarded (with much reason) as probable if they could not cope firmly with Serbian nationalism. But this anxiety-filled image was not cognitively well differentiated. It did not distinguish clearly, for example, between what would happen if they merely dealt "firmly" with Serbian and other agitators within their own borders and what would happen if, in the process of "punishing" Serbia, they sent troops beyond their present border into a neighboring country. To most of the rest of the world this distinction seemed the distinction between legitimate maintenance of internal stability and illegitimate aggression that could precipitate world war. But in anxious Austrian minds it was all one thing: a need to punish Serbia, as vigorously as possible, in order to vindicate the image of Austria-Hungary as a virile nation and to stave off destruction.

In addition, there was a failure to pay much attention to any other aspect of the possible future, including what would happen if Russia did intervene, and including the kind of break-up of the Austrian empire that actually did occur as a result of the war that Austria herself had precipitated.

A restriction in their space-perspective was represented by a failure to pay much attention to countries other than the two that were in the main focus of their attention (themselves and Serbia) and the two that were somewhat in the periphery (Russia, whose intervention they feared, and Germany, whose "strong stand" by Austria's side was counted on to deter Russian intervention). Two other countries that were soon to become involved, France and England, were present in their minds but apparently not very seriously considered, and America, which was to join the Allies nearly three years later—partly because of the American impression at the outset that Germany and Austria had committed aggression—was apparently not considered at all.

Still another type of selective inattention, absence of empathy, is of such crucial importance that it deserves a separate section.

5/ *Absence of empathy.* Even in the case of a country that was in the bright central focus of Austrian attention, Serbia itself, the Austrians seemed to fail almost completely to realize how the situation looked from their enemy's point of view. They did not see how, for a Serbian patriot, the Austrian demands would appear as naked aggression, calling for a struggle to the last drop of patriotic Serbian blood. They did not see how Russian pride, smarting after a number of setbacks including the high-handed Austrian annexation of Bosnia six years earlier, would respond to a new arbitrary extension of German-Austrian power in an area in which the Russians felt that their honor and their interest were involved. They failed to see that, while the Russian Czar himself was peacefully inclined and would try to avoid a big war, his close advisers were not necessarily so pacific, and Russia might become entangled in a situation in which its pride and prestige were so deeply involved that war might seem the only alternative to intolerable humiliation (Gooch, 1938, p. 369). They failed to anticipate the pendulum swing of the Kaiser's mood from careless overconfidence to panicky fear (Taylor, 1963, pp. 214, 219, 228) once the Russian general mobilization had started and British entry into the war seemed likely. The Kaiser's desperate feeling after July 29 was expressed by his reference to "a war of extermination" waged against Germany, and his exclamation that "if we are to bleed to death, England shall at least lose India!" (Montgelas & Schucking, 1924, p. 350). They failed to see how the British and French would fear a collapse of the balance of power if they left Russia to fight alone against a smaller but far more efficient German army, or how British public opinion would react if the panicky Germans, anxious to capitalize on their own great asset, the superior efficiency and speed of their fighting force, were to strike at France through Belgium. They failed to realize that America would regard their attack on Serbia as a big country bullying a small one, and would regard Germany's march through Belgium in the same light, with the result that America's sympathies would be engaged immediately on the Allied side, and the way would be prepared for America's ultimate involvement against the German-Austrian alliance. In short, they were so wrapped up in their own anxiety and their own righteous indignation that they had little attention left for considering the reality-world of anyone else.

6/ *Military overconfidence.* It is paradoxical but true that exaggerated fear can be combined with exaggerated military confidence. The Austrians, for example, had what now seems an exaggerated fear of the spreading disaffection of nationalities within their empire that would result if they failed to take a "firm stand" against Serbia. But at the same time, until the Russian mobilization (which quickly created great anxiety in the Germans if not also the Austrians), they had exaggerated confidence that they could "teach Serbia a lesson" and at the same time, with strong German support, keep Russia from intervening. Like the Germans, they pinned their hopes to the possibility of "localizing" the issue, enjoying mastery and venting righteous indignation within a small sphere while remaining safe from the mastery-impulse and the righteous indignation of others in a larger sphere. They were wrong. They misperceived. And the chief way in which reality differed from their perception of reality lay in their selective inattention to the possibility that strong allies of Serbia (Russia, France, Britain, America) might scorn to be intimidated by the Kaiser's appearing at Austria's side "in shining armour." They did not see that their potential enemies, like themselves, might be trying to live up to an indomitable self-image, afraid of showing fear, and therefore "irrationally" ready to fight.

B. HITLER VS. POLAND

The essential facts of Hitler's attack on Poland are familiar enough, and the view of historians as to the origins of World War II has not been subject to a general and radical revision, as has their view of World War I. We can proceed immediately, therefore, to check in this context the six forms of perceptual distortion that emerged from our review of Austrian thinking in 1914. All six were present, in the extreme degree that might be expected from the fact that Hitler, though probably not psychotic, was one of the least rational, least evidence-oriented of men, with unmistakable paranoid tendencies.

1/ The diabolical enemy-image. It is now fairly well established that in Hitler's mind the diabolical character of the enemy, especially the Jewish enemy, was extreme and unmitigated. Post-war studies have confirmed the proposition that his anti-Jewish delusions of persecution were no mere propaganda technique; he seems to have actually believed them. What needs further elaboration is the central role played by these delusions of persecution in his justification of his more outrageous aggressive acts.

He had a real task on his hands in his effort to reconcile these actions with the posture of peacefulness that he had consistently maintained since 1930. He had abandoned his earlier, franker, "war propaganda," represented by certain passages in *Mein Kampf,* and adopted a peace line that was far more acceptable to the German people. It was urgently necessary, therefore, in order to keep the full and willing support of the German people, to present his bloodless conquest of the Czech part of Czechoslovakia, his bloody attack on Poland, and his still more bloody attack on Russia in ways that would at least half-convince the German people that he was no war-mad conqueror but a real man of peace, forced into these actions by the provocation of diabolical opponents. His skill in doing so suggests that he was at least half convinced of it himself.

Three quotations will suggest how he attempted to justify these aggressions. According to him, the march into Prague was legitimate and necessary for several reasons, including the need to remove a threat to German security. The role that had been assigned to Czechoslovakia by its Jewish and democratic masters was

> none other than to prevent consolidation of Central Europe, to provide a bridge to Europe for bolshevik aggression, and, above all, to act as the mercenary of European democracies against Germany. . . . What was expected from this State is shown most clearly by the observation of the French Air Minister, M. Pierre Cot, who calmly stated that the duty of this State in case of any conflict was to be an airdrome for the landing and taking off of bombers from which it would be possible to destroy the most important German industrial centers in a few hours. (Speech to the Reichstag, April 28, 1939; translated in De Sales, 1941.) (Note Hitler's use of the time-honored device of treating arms in the hands of an enemy as equivalent to proof that the enemy has aggressive intentions.)

The attack on Poland was justified, he claimed, not only by the Poles' "increased terror and pressure against our German compatriots" but also by

> the sudden Polish general mobilization, followed by more atrocities . . . I have therefore resolved to speak to Poland in the same language that Poland for months has used toward us. (Speech to the Reichstag, September 1, 1939; 1941, pp. 685, 687)

The attack on Russia was an attempt to break through a ring of encircling enemies. There was

> a new policy of encirclement against Germany, born as it was of hatred. . . . Internally and externally there resulted that plot familiar to

us all between Jews and democrats, Bolshevists and reactionaries, with the sole aim of inhibiting the establishment of the new German people's State, and of plunging the Reich anew into impotence and misery. (Proclamation, June 22, 1941; 1941, pp. 977–8)

2/ *The virile self-image.* Readers of *Mein Kampf* are familiar with Hitler's glorious image of himself and his country, with much more emphasis on strength and courage than on any softer qualities such as peacefulness and good will. While it is true that after coming to power he greatly stressed peacefulness, his emphasis on the hard qualities, strength and courage, continued. And, as a study in how aggressive actions can appear to their perpetrators in an acceptable guise, his great emphasis on the courage theme, during the crises of 1938 and 1939, holds special interest. When a hard action has to be given some label, the label "courage" is far more acceptable than the label "aggression."

In his speech on September 1, 1939—the day he precipitated World War II—he showed extreme adroitness in avoiding even the word "war." He was not attacking Poland, committing aggression, or starting a war. He was "speaking to Poland in the language that Poland for months has used toward us," he was recognizing that "no Great Power can with honor long stand by passively and watch such events," he was showing that his patience and love of peace must not be "mistaken for weakness or even cowardice," he was "meeting bombs with bombs," he was showing a "stout heart," he was "seeing to it that a change is made in the relationship between Germany and Poland that shall insure a peaceful coexistence." The final sentence in his peroration was "If our will is so strong that no hardship and suffering can subdue it, then our will and our German might shall prevail" (1941, pp. 686–690). One can almost feel the lump in the throats of German listeners as they contemplated their own indomitable selves.

3/ *The moral self-image.* A basically mistaken conception of Hitler's propaganda technique is still current in American minds: the assumption that he openly and cynically glorified war, announced his program of world conquest, advocated the "Great Lie" technique, justified oppression of weaker races, etc. This conception can be supported only by selecting extremely atypical quotations and quoting them out of context. Actually, as one might expect of such a thoroughly authoritarian personality, his propaganda after he came to power in 1933 was characterized by an extreme, almost exceptionless adherence (on the verbal level) to conventional standards of morality: peacefulness, respect for the rights of neighbors, truthfulness, etc. (White, 1949). In his words, and perhaps in some sense in his thoughts also, he and Germany were morally spotless. Three quotations will give the flavor:

> I wish to point out first, that I have not conducted any war; second, that for years past I have expressed my abhorrence of war and, it is true, also my abhorrence of warmongers, and third, that I am not aware for what purpose I should wage a war at all. (Speech, April 28, 1939; 1941, pp. 661)

> We have given guarantees for the States in the West, and to all those States bordering on our frontiers, we have given assurances of the inviolability of their territory as far as Germany is concerned. These are no mere words. That is our sacred determination. (Speech, September 26, 1938, at the height of the Munich crisis; 1941, pp. 520)

> I will not war against women and children. I have ordered my air force to restrict itself to attacks on military objectives. (Speech, September 1, 1939, declaring war on Poland; 1941, pp. 688. This is actually the only point in the speech in which he permits himself to use the word "war," and here it is used only negatively, thoroughly embedded in a moral, humane context.)

4/ Selective inattention.   When he made his fateful decision to attack Poland, what was in the focus of Hitler's conscious mind? What was pushed out of the focus but still dynamically important in determining his decision? And what was not dynamically present at all? We can only speculate, of course, using whatever clues his words and his actions give us, but the speculation may be fruitful.

It should be recognized that we are dealing here with a man who had an exceptional capacity for "double-think"—though double-think may be more widespread in the human race than we usually realize. According to Heiden, "On this day (October 26, 1930) Hitler began his peace propaganda which continued uninterrupted for almost ten years. Inexplicable and incredible, it moved men by this very fact, but also by an undeniable breath of passion. With the same passion Hitler had said the exact opposite." (1944, pp. 414) He apparently had a knack of working up a noble passion that he could "sincerely" feel at the time of making a speech, though it would not necessarily remain salient in his mind at a moment of hard decision-making.

Probably, then, when he decided to attack Poland he took more elements of hard reality into account, and was conscious of more long-range plans of conquest, than he proclaimed in his prepared speech to the German people and to the world. His behavior suggests that in the focus of his conscious mind there were at least these thoughts: elation at the immediate prospect of triumphantly crushing Poland and extending the boundaries of the *Reich;* elation at the thought (somewhat anxiously clung to) that, by the great *coup* of the Nazi-Soviet Pact, he and Ribbentrop had successfully divided his enemies and had made it probable that the British and French would either not dare to fight—they had not fought when he marched into Prague—or succumb quickly to his mighty military machine; real anger at the long-standing injustice of Danzig and the Polish Corridor, now about to be eliminated; intense but consciously somewhat artificial anger at Polish "atrocities" and unwillingness to negotiate about the Corridor; pride in Germany's moral grandeur as contrasted with her vindictive, encircling, Jewish-controlled enemies; pride in his personal courage in facing up to dangers which in his more sober moments he recognized as real, though quite unlikely to materialize; clear plans already forming in his mind for capitalizing on this triumph to extend German hegemony throughout Central Europe and the Balkans, with due regard for the appearance of national autonomy in countries such as Hungary and Rumania; vague and wonderful but very private fantasies, which he probably recognized as fantasies that Fate might or might not permit him to fulfill, of total destruction of the Jewish world-octopus and beneficent German hegemony throughout the world. (When he was preparing or delivering a speech and wearing his peaceful, moral, Dr. Jekyll self, Hitler presumably pushed all these morally dubious thoughts out of his mind as completely as possible, and quite possibly he also refrained from verbalizing them or thinking of them clearly at times of hard decision-making. Yet presumably they were more important in the dynamics of his decision-making than he himself realized.)

On the other hand his behavior suggests that certain other things were not in his mind, or not enough in it: the tough nationalism of the Poles, the Yugoslavs, the Russians, the British, and others who stood in his path; the cumulative fear and anger of those who might be so mean-spirited and so influenced by the Jewish press that they would describe his courageous act as "aggression"; the enormous potential military strength of the United States; his own recent promise and "sacred determination" that the territory of all of Germany's neighbors would be "inviolable," and the effect that his violation of that promise might have on others; the word "aggression" as possibly applicable to what he was doing, the word "imperialism" as possibly applicable to the beneficent control of Central Europe that he was immediately contemplating, the word "dictatorship" as possibly applicable to his totalitarian form of government and the word "paranoia" as possibly applicable to his delusions about a Jewish-plutocratic-bolshevist plot against his country.

Among these blind-spots indicated by both his words and his actions, it is possible to discern the same three overlapping categories that emerged in our study of Austrian thinking in 1914: he tended to ignore major future contingencies, realistically considered (as distinguished from grandiose fantasies about the more distant future, fantasies of catastrophe, and immediate practical matters such as the military campaign against Poland); countries such as America that were geographically far from his immediate focus of attention; and the thoughts and feelings of enemies and neutrals. With certain exceptions his time-perspective appears to have been drastically limited, his space-perspective was drastically limited, and he was almost totally devoid of empathy.

As in the case of the Austrians, this last type of selective inattention was so important that it deserves a section of its own.

5/ *Absence of empathy.*   Several of the blindspots that have just been mentioned are at the same time examples of failure of empathy: Hitler's failure to give due weight to the tough, defensive nationalism of peoples such as the Poles, the Yugoslavs and the Russians, who stood in his immediate path; his failure to realize that onlookers such as the French, the British and the Americans would certainly regard his action as naked aggression and as one more violation of his pledged word, with the probable result that they would eventually overcome their extreme distaste for war and that, as his threat grew nearer, their defensive nationalism too would be fully mobilized; his almost total inability to see what was happening in the minds of Jews (instead of seeing their helpless terror he continued to attribute to them a plot to rule the world that must have been, essentially, a projection of his own world-conquering fantasies); an inability to see that others, from their vantage-points, might honestly attribute to him such things as war-making, aggression, imperialism, dictatorship and paranoia.

It may be added that he grossly underestimated, if he perceived it at all, the great change that had occurred in British public opinion and elite opinion after March 1939, when Hitler moved his troops into Prague and took over the purely Czech part of Czechoslovakia. For the British this was the last straw—a final demonstration to all doubters that he was not merely trying to unify Germany (an interpretation they could give to his occupation of the Rhineland, his *Anschluss* with Austria, his taking of the Sudetenland, and even his claim to the Polish Corridor) but that he had embarked upon the conquest of non-German lands, in a career of conquest that could later include Britain itself, and that his word could not be trusted.

Hitler apparently could see none of this. He had his own stereotype of what the British were like: partly proud Nordics like the Germans, and therefore capable of sharing German scorn for the Russians and the inferior peoples of Central Europe; partly calculating imperialists capable of jealousy at Germany's new success, but apparently unwilling to risk war in order to block Germany's ambitions in Central and Eastern Europe—they had not stopped him even when he marched into Prague; partly co-conspirators with the Jews; partly muddle-heads or cowards such as Chamberlain had proved to be at Munich and after Prague.

While there may have been some kernels of truth in this picture, it was probably to a larger extent a projection of his own arrogance and craving for power, and a product of the typical paranoid hypersensitivity to signs of weakness and cowardice in an imagined enemy and potential victim. But, except perhaps for these elements of fear and weakness which Hitler's own basic weakness enabled him to see in others, his picture of the British was external. He did not even try to imagine how their world might look to them, from the inside, on the assumption that they were ordinary peaceloving but proud human beings. He apparently never really asked himself how his own behavior might look from their point of view. As a result, his stereotyped picture was also rigid and static. He could hardly have predicted the great mobilization of pride and of militance that his own behavior evoked in Churchill's Britain, any more than the Japanese militarists could predict the great mobilization of pride and of militance that their attack on Pearl Harbor would evoke in the United States. (In Hitler's speech on September 1 his only reference to Britain, France or the United States was: "When statesmen in the West declare that this affects their interests, I can only regret such a declaration. It cannot for a moment make me hesitate to fulfil my duty.")

6/ *Military overconfidence.* Two extreme examples illustrate Hitler's overconfidence: his assumption that, after the Nazi-Soviet Pact, Britain and France would not dare to fight, and his suicidal attack on Russia.

Although he was presumably not psychotic, he showed to an extreme degree, within the normal range, not only the typical paranoid delusions of persecution but also the typical paranoid delusions of grandeur.

It should not be assumed, however, that military overconfidence is a rare thing, associated mainly with unusual personalities such as Hitler's. In recent history it has appeared over and over again. Both the Russians and the Austrians were militarily overconfident in 1914. The Allied generals continually prophesied an early victory throughout the First World War. During the period 1917–1924, the Communists grossly overestimated their chances of an early worldwide victory. Stalin apparently thought he could defeat Finland easily and quickly. The Japanese militarists who attacked Pearl Harbor could have had little conception of the anger and the ultimate military strength that their action mobilized in the United States. The French doggedly overestimated the feasibility of holding on to both Indochina and Algeria. In the Suez conflict the British, French and Israelis were overconfident that they could win quickly before worldwide opposition could be mobilized. To be sure, there are in recent history some contrary instances of military *under*-confidence. The rule, however, seems to be overconfidence, while under-confidence and strict realism appear to be the exceptions. This is understandable, too, since overconfidence is a form of wishful thinking, and wishful thinking is the rule, not the exception.

Three characteristic forms of military overconfidence can be described. One is common to Austria in 1914 and Hitler in 1939: a failure to take seriously enough the chance that other countries may intervene in support of one's enemy. Austria belittled the chance that Russia, France, Britain or America would intervene in support of Serbia, or be later drawn into the war; Hitler belittled the chance that France, Britain or America would intervene or be later drawn into the war. Similarly the British, French and Israelis were apparently surprised by the speed and strength of opposition to their anti-Egyptian adventure, especially on the part of both the USSR and the United States.

As we have seen, this is related to lack of empathy. It is difficult to realize that one's own behavior, the justification of which seems so obvious to oneself, can appear in the eyes of a neutral or hostile observer as actual aggression. There is also often a failure to realize that, in such a situation, the ally of one's enemy, even if relatively weak, may be too proud to be easily intimidated by one's own or one's allies' threats of intervention. Russia was too proud to be intimidated by the Kaiser's "appearing in shining armour" at the side of Austria; Britain and France were too proud to be intimidated by Hitler's tirades or by the great *coup* of the Nazi-Soviet Pact, even though they felt militarily inferior. This is especially true when the ally of one's enemy feels bound to one's enemy by ties of mutual loyalty or by formal or informal commitments. Russia in 1914 felt in honor bound to protect her Slavic protégé, Serbia; France felt bound by her firm alliance with Russia; Britain felt somewhat bound by her new entente with France. Similarly, though Britain and France had not come to the aid of Czechoslovakia, they became more deeply committed to Poland, and in September, 1939, they felt that if they did not honor their commitments to Poland, Hitler would hardly respect other commitments elsewhere. There is something particularly repulsive to a proud and self-respecting nation in the thought of letting down an ally and violating a commitment because of being intimidated by an enemy when this seems militarily the rational thing to do. Yet the "enemy" often fails to give enough weight to this factor of obligation-plus-pride, assuming that rational calculations of military advantage and fear of war will be enough to keep "outsiders" from intervening. Sometimes they are right and sometimes they are wrong.

Another form of overconfidence was present to a conspicuous degree only in Hitler's case and not in Austria's: underestimation of the difficulty of coping with an aroused people fighting on its own soil against what it regards as foreign invasion. Hitler encountered this on a vast scale in Russia, as Napoleon had done before him. Others who have encountered it have been Napoleon in Spain, the Allied forces that intervened in Russia in 1918–1920, the Italians in Greece, the Germans in Yugoslavia, the Japanese in China, the French in Indochina, the French in Algeria, the Russians in Poland and Hungary, and the Chinese in Tibet.

Here too, a main reason appears to be lack of empathy. The occupying or invading power usually has a case. Characteristically it focuses on the violent acts, often including atrocities, committed by the activists in the local population, and on its own good intentions. But such black-and-white thinking leads, as always, to selective inattention to the human, non-diabolical characteristics of the local patriots, including their conviction that they are defending their homeland against foreign invasion; and this in turn leads to an underestimate of how difficult the activists may be to handle, helped as they often are by many of the non-activist population.

A third form of overconfidence is the tendency to see another nation or group as disunited, with only the evil rulers hostile to oneself, and the mass of the people either neutral or friendly to one's own side. This has been called the "black-top" enemy-image (White, 1965, pp. 249). It is a typical form of the black-and-white picture; as a rule only the leaders at the top of the enemy group are seen as wholly black. The mass of the Serbs and Croats under Austrian rule were not seen by the Austrians as particularly hostile; to them the real enemy consisted of the assassins, the agitators, the nest of conspirators supported by the Serbian government in Belgrade. Similarly, Hitler did not regard the common people of the countries around him as his enemies; it was their Jewish-plutocratic-Bolshevist leaders who were plotting Germany's downfall. The conspiracy theory of history is at the same time a black-top image of the enemy. As such it is similar to many other familiar phenomena: the American public's focus on the Kaiser as the villain of World War I, the complacent employer's conviction that his employees are contented and loyal but misled by union agitators, the Southerner's belief that Negroes in the South would be contented if it were not for "nigger-loving agitators" from the North. It is a wonderfully consoling conception. It simultaneously eliminates the guilt of feeling hostile to a large number of people, creates a positive image of oneself as saving the underdog-masses from their conniving and oppressive leaders, provides a personal, visualizable Devil on whom to concentrate all hostility, and sustains hope that, once the leaders have been firmly dealt with, the battle will be over.

These historical examples of typical, recurrent forms of misperception can sensitize us to possibilities, in our study of perceptions on both sides of the present conflict in Vietnam. Since history seldom comes even close to an exact repetition of itself, all historical analogies should be taken with equal sensitivity to differences between a past situation and a present one. It is always legitimate, however, to formulate them as questions to be asked about the present: Is there now a great absence of empathy on both sides, as there was both in Austrian minds in 1914 and in Hitler's mind in 1939? If so, what thoughts and feelings in the minds of those on one side of the Vietnamese war are typically ignored by most of those on the other side? And so on.

A word is in order also with regard to our own frame of mind as we approach these emotionally explosive questions of fact. The most appropriate frame of mind can perhaps be described as *tough-minded empathy.*

As the examples we have just cited indicate, the effort to empathize is particularly necessary in the case of one's own worst enemy. For the sake of realism in coping with him, if for no other reason, it is important to try to see the enemy's world as he sees it, from the inside, not assuming that even his worst accusations against oneself are necessarily insincere. But at the same time it is advisable to try to combine empathy with tough-mindedness in several ways. There can be full realization that the enemy's leaders are capable of lying, both to oneself and to their own people, for propaganda purposes, and that therefore no one of their public statements can be taken as necessarily sincere—though all are worth listening to. There can be great skepticism as to the validity of everything the enemy believes, even when his belief is regarded as probably sincere. There can be a similarly tough-minded skepticism about the beliefs of one's own group. And there can be a willingness to act with courage and decisiveness on the basis of much less than a totally black-and-white picture. With no illusions as to the possibility of fully achieving such a synthesis, we can aim at empathy without gullibility, without shirking our responsibility to make an independent appraisal of the facts, and without weakness in action even when action has to be based on much less than a perfect case.

The Meaning of Wholeness

Earl C. Kelley

Recently there has been more and more attention given to the psychosomatic nature of the human organism. Even some of those who make their living by ministering to our health have taken it up, at least in some degree. It is now fairly common to have an M.D. make indirect allusions to this fact.

The human organism has two selves, living together in the same body

Reprinted by permission from *ETC: A Review of General Semantics*, Vol. 26, (1); Copyright 1969 by the International Society for General Semantics.

structure. There is the physical self and the psychological self. This is not intended to be a denial of the unity of man, but we have to admit that there are two of them because they feed on different stuffs. The physical self feeds on such things as meat and vegetables; the psychological self feeds on the perceptive stuff of growth, such as what people say, music, sunsets, or, according to one's lot, squalor, degradation. The perceptive stuff of growth cannot be seen, as the physical stuff can. If we could see it, it is possible that we might come to have a whole new set of attitudes toward those less fortunate than we. I say it is just possible, realizing that out attitudes are built on a whole set of circumstances that have nothing to do with compassion or any other of the more human emotions.

At any rate, we have paid far more attention to the physical self than we have to the psychological self. It is hard to say which is the more important because both are essential. The psychological self cannot even exist without a body. I suppose one could cite examples of the physical self existing without much psychological self, but such people are hardly even human, although they are entitled to our compassion, our love, and our best efforts.

The point here is that we have paid too little attention to the psychological self in the past, and while every person must have a body to inhabit, what a person feels is far more important than what he knows. What he knows is important, of course, because that is what he uses to behave with. And the eventual pay-off is in behavior—what a person does. The task of the educator is to pay much attention to the perceptive stuff of growth. This he can do without fear of the neglect of the physical self. The various athletic coaches will see to that.

One of the most important facts about the perceptive stuff of growth is that it is selective, so that the individual sees what he has had experience to see and what is in line with his purposes. The purposive nature of the human individual is described more fully in Chapter 6 of *Education and the Nature of Man*.[1] I will not go into it again in this paper. At any rate, experience alone is not enough to account for what happens. The fact that no two people see the same thing at the same spot in the same way is truly significant. The fact that no two people perceive alike is particularly true in the case of our dealings with other people. It seems to me that other people are the most complex things that we have to view. And this accounts for much of what has seemed to us to be strange

1. Kelley and Rasey (New York: Harper, 1952).

indeed. In the first psychology course I ever took the instructor had an "incident" occur and then asked each of us to write what we thought we had seen. When it came about that none of us had seen the same thing we all laughed merrily and then the teacher proceeded as though it were not so—as though people *do* see the same thing in the same way.

The psychological self has boundaries. These are invisible, as all of the psychological self is. But without boundaries there would be no entity. This self has two overwhelming needs. One is to defend itself; the other is to "keep" other people—to maintain and strengthen its social relationships. How to defend one's self and to do it without alienating other people must surely be the biggest adjustment that the human organism faces. It is simple to defend one's self if that is the only consideration. But everybody has to have other people in order to be provided with the perceptive stuff of growth. Without other people we would become like plants; in fact, there is some evidence that even plants are quite dependent on each other. We are therefore built by the people with whom we come in contact, and we build them. This is an answer to the age-old question, "Am I my brother's keeper?" We had better be; he is the stuff of which we are built, and the quality of life we enjoy depends on him.

It helps me to think of this boundary as a screen. Of course there is no screen, but there seems to be a flow in and out, as there would be if there were a screen. Those things which are perceived to be enhancing are admitted, and those that are seen to be endangering are kept out.

It seems that the outward flow is sometimes kept more open than the inward flow. Fearful people build thick screens. We once had a friend, quite a frequent visitor in our home, who was almost all output and very little intake. She would come in and say, "How are you?" If I were to say I just murdered my wife and her body lay in the next room, this woman would say, "You must hear what has just happened to me!" She never really comprehended that my retirement was approaching and that we would move away, though it was often mentioned in her presence.

If intake and defense were all there was to life, we would not have needed to evolve beyond the oyster. It has a good thick covering and lies at the bottom of the sea, opening up as long as there is food to be had, and closing when it feels endangered. But there is more to life than the oyster knows; and we are not oysters.

Sometimes the flow of the perceptive stuff of growth is cut off altogether in both directions. The people who do this we call catatonic. They just exist. There are infants who just exist too—infants who never cry or smile or babble. We call these autistic, and every large city has a ward in its hospital for them. So far as I know, nobody knows what causes a baby to be autistic, although there has been recent research on them. The research leads to a certain amount of speculation, however; it seems likely that these infants have looked out upon a hostile world and have decided to have none of it. These infants seldom live beyond eighteen months.

Whether infant or adult, and whether complete or incomplete, such people shut off the stuff out of which they are built and become prisoners in their own fortresses.

We need to develop people with open selves, or as nearly open as can be achieved. Thus they will learn more readily. I have found in my teaching that if I could achieve this, learning would be greatly increased. And so, particularly in the later years, I worked more on this than on anything else. If I could bring about confidence and reduce or abolish fear, the learner would become more and more able to take in what there was to take from his environment. In the main, this is where all of to-day's large classes and impersonal relationships break down; this is one of the causes of the present rebellion. I once knew a professor of history who proclaimed that he did not *want* to know his students because he might become fond of them and this would cause a loss of interest in his subject matter. Such attitudes destroy what I hold to be the primary function of the teacher—that of relating to and building people. Of course we have to have something for them to learn, and they will not all learn the same things anyway.

Too often teachers teach in such a way as to make their learners value themselves less and less. This is the wrong way to teach. We need to develop people who will think well of themselves. People who think well of themselves are in turn able to think well of others. This is essential to the complete human being.

We need to develop people who will think well of their teachers. This can be achieved only by having teachers who deserve to be held in confidence and respect. This cannot be achieved by the double-cross, by the surprise test, by asking questions whose answers are to be found only in the footnotes of some textbook, or by any other of the multitudinous methods that have been developed by many teachers. It is not possible for learners to respect a person who is waiting to trick them.

We need people who will see their stake in others, since that is the stuff of which we are built. It is difficult for us to be much better than the stuff of which we are built. This again may be the answer to the age-old question, "Am I my brother's keeper?"

We need people who will see themselves as part of a becoming world, rather than a static world. Thus will not only change be expected, but it will be welcomed. The fact that we do not know what tomorrow will bring should be an exciting thing, a thing that adds interest to life, not something to be dreaded and viewed with apprehension. This view of the universe will add much to the way in which life is held.

We need people who are naturally optimistic. There is no point in being purposive unless we think that the next spot we are in will be better than the one we now occupy. This is essentially what optimism means.

We need people who possess moral courage. I do not mean to limit this to the old set of morals, but to include much more than that. It is a call for people who are nonconformist in the ways that really matter. Thus the moralist can be thwarted in ways that will disturb him most. It is not the little things so many do that are the mark of the real nonconformist. I do not think I need spell these things out in any more detail; let the reader supply the specifics.

We need people who value what a human being is above the outside values so common in our society. This is my concept of what materialism is. What do we care most about? Do we care most about how another human being feels—what is happening to him—or do we care more about a raise in pay, a better automobile, a finer home, a better standing with our neighbors?

It would be easy to say that open selves are produced by having a chance to live the life that is good to live. But this calls for some explanation. The life that is good to live is primarily one in which the individual is loved and is able to feel it. By love I do not mean the sort of love that is accompanied by soft music and moonlight. That is all right too, but the love of an adult for a child is quite another matter. It is more a matter of caring, of concern for the feelings of the child. Nobody can be without this kind of love and grow into anything that is truly human.

The unloved grow into a different kind of people altogether. They do not have the usual capacity for relating to other people. Their handshake is quite noticeably withdrawn. These and many other symptoms reveal the fact that in their infancy and during their childhood they have lacked this most important ingredient.

We have known for a long time that rich environments produce increased intelligence and that poor environments reduce it. By this it is meant that the environment has to be rich not in the material things of life, but rather in the human things. Some of the richest homes from the material point of view are actually the poorest places for children to inhabit, and some of the poorest places materially are filled with love and companionship, the very best places for children to be. We have been slow to recognize this, probably because it has contradicted the precepts so many of us hold dear. The general public has assumed that a wealthy home is a good home, and it has been difficult to persuade people that the opposite may be true.

Each person in our world is different from any other person who has been or will be. This uniqueness is a fact of life which we need to come to value, rather than trying to decry it and counteract it. This fact of life has been provided for by the action of the chromosomes in the cells from which the individual is conceived, and it cannot be altered. There is one partial exception in the case of identical twins, but even here it is impossible to give identical experiences. Even when both are paddled, it makes a great deal of difference which one is paddled first. I have dealt at some length with this in "The Significance of Being Unique," published first in *ETC*. I will not, therefore, devote much space to it now, except to say that if teachers took this into account it would reduce or eliminate the despair that so many teachers feel when, at the end of a course, not everybody knows the same things exactly as the teacher thinks he taught them. Actually, it is because of the very nature of people that they cannot come up with identical answers. Each has to interpret what he sees and hears in the light of his own experience and purpose. Thus differences should be expected and welcomed, rather than decried.

Students need to be involved in what they are doing. This involvement has to be planned for by the teacher or by the students themselves. It will not come about by itself. Of course the student does not have to have his own way about everything, but even if his involvement is actually planned by his fellows, he needs to have a feeling that he had a say in the planning. It makes a great deal of difference whether or not one has been consulted. Few people, and certainly not the ones we can have the most confidence in for the future, do anything with much verve or enthusiasm just because they are told to do it by someone in authority. This is the old teacher-pupil planning about which so much has been said and written, and so little has been done.

In order to live the life that is good to live, one needs to be respected as a person. One can hardly be a whole person unless he is respected by others. The word "respect" is a most interesting one. *Spect* comes from the word which means "to look" and *re* means to repeat, to do again. Thus to be respected means to be looked at again. In order to be looked at again one has to be worth more than a passing glance.

All these factors help to build courage, which is essential to all humanness. For without courage one becomes a mere shadow of a human being. Courage makes it possible to attack many of the problems of life in a truly human and functional way. It makes all the difference between the craven and the bold.

But what do we teachers see as we look out upon the world which we have had a large hand in creating? We see threats taking the place of positive action. We see that we still believe in the theory that "getting tough" will solve problems instead of making them worse and perhaps driving them underground. Or we see students acting as though they were forced to strike and to make demands which, at least to us, seem unreasonable and impossible to comply with. We have left them no choice but to rebel, and, in their frenzy, they make demands which cannot be met. This is the only outlet left to them.

We see fear actually being used as a teaching technique. Fear is an emotion that has no place in the student-teacher relationship. It provokes all kinds of adverse behaviors. It is the cause of many of the evil happenings in our social structure. And to think that we knowingly and deliberately use it!

We see whole people taught piecemeal. Somehow the learner is supposed to put all the pieces together, but he seldom does. The old system of teaching subjects separately, which might have had some validity when schools started centuries ago, still holds us in its grip. The thought of approaching our environment as a whole seems never to have occurred to most educators.

We see many forms of rejection in teaching practice. There are so many ways which even well-meaning teachers have of rejecting people that it is almost impossible to count them. I once had a doctoral student who proposed to do a two-semester-hour study of rejection by visiting schools. In about two weeks he came back and said this was no two-hour study; it was so vast that it would make a doctoral dissertation.

I do not think that we have the right to reject anybody. This does not mean that I would admit anybody to any class regardless of his preparation to do what the class was set up to do. I am thinking mostly of our captive audiences in our elementary and secondary schools. If we are going to require that they be there, it is then also essential that we have something to do which has meaning to them—and that we have the freedom to do it. Rejection leads to alienation from self and others, and it is indeed a poor reason for requiring people to be there.

We will have to give up our faith in violence as a method. Violence never has made anyone better or more educable. Our faith in violence has come full circle now, and we are suffering the consequences.

What we need in this land of ours is better people; and if we are to have better people, the teachers of the nation will have to produce them. The parents and other adults who have influence over our young are products of the old system and have no way of knowing any better. What we need is a revolution among teachers, not in salaries and working conditions, but in attitude and emotion. This would bring about conditions in which our young would have no need for revolt.

The Psychological Basis
of Human Values

Donald Snygg

THE RELATION OF PSYCHOLOGY
TO ECONOMICS

In a rapidly changing society like our own, social and economic situations never repeat themselves exactly. Every situation has something new about it. As a result, no economic, business, or political planning is possible except as the planners have a concept of causation which enables them to make some guess about what people will do under circumstances which have never before arisen. This is true whether we are planning individually as businessmen or consumers or collectively as citizens. The faster the society changes, the more its members have to depend on theory.

One of the major obstacles in the way of getting more dependable concepts for predicting economic behavior is our limited knowledge of psychology. Economic or political behavior is behavior by people. When economists analyze and interpret economic behavior, when they forecast the outcome of this or that economic policy or trend, they are forecasting what people will do. To do this an accurate concept of human nature is essential. Any theories or predictions about what people will do are certain to be inaccurate if they are based on false concepts of the people whose behavior is predicted.

This places economists and other social scientists in an awkward situation. Human beings are complex organisms and there are a great many conflicting theories about them. In choosing among those theories we cannot safely trust our limited personal experience, which may have been with a special kind of people. The social or economic theorist who bases his theories of what people will do on his personal version of human nature is quite likely to get a theory which is applicable only to his own generation of his society or to his own social class. He is in danger of getting a theory which is applicable only to himself.

If he protects himself against this provincialism by basing his economic theories on current psychological concepts, he can still get into difficulties. The conceptual systems of professional psychologists are in the process of development and some of them, including some which psychologists are very hopeful about, are still too specialized to be applicable to the behavior of human beings outside the laboratory. The social scientist who uses a theory of this type without understanding its sources is in danger of building his picture of society on a theory which in its current incomplete form is applicable only to the maze behavior of the white rat.

And no matter which conceptual framework he adopts, he will find many of its concepts unconvincing because they are contrary to what he and his readers have always thought to be common sense.

COMMON–SENSE CONCEPTS OF HUMAN NATURE

One of the main obstacles in the way of our learning more about human nature is the fact that we already "know" so many things about it that are not true. Most people can recognize their ignorance of such subjects as entomology or cultural anthropology or nuclear physics, but few people except professional psychologists feel ignorant about human nature.

Psychology, it is generally believed, is just common sense—what everybody knows. Some may doubt that redheaded people are quick tempered, but it is generally held to be "common sense" that *the* basic human needs are for food, shelter, and clothing; that practice makes perfect; and that the way to cure people of bad habits is to punish them. We delude ourselves, however, when we believe that these generalizations are dependable or that we learned them by experience. "Common sense" about human nature all too often turns out to be an author's epigram or an academic theory, now disproved, which was proposed so long ago that our grandparents heard about it in time to teach it to our parents.

THE FICTION OF ECONOMIC MAN

One of the most prominent of the "common sense" barriers to better understanding of human nature is the widespread belief that economic motives are the only ones that matter in the economic realm. Studies of employee aspirations in American industry do not confirm the idea that pay is the only incentive or even the most important one. Wage incentive systems frequently result in slowdowns by the more efficient workers, who do not wish to outproduce their associates. Among American industrial workers, desire for group membership and approval has usually proved more potent than desire for money when the two are in conflict.

Katona [1] has recently reported that businessmen have a tendency to aim at increased volume rather than increased profits. He believes that economic motives are changing and lists, among others, professional pride and desire for prestige, for power, and for approbation.[2]

1. Katona, G. *Psychological analysis of economic behavior.* New York: McGraw-Hill, 1951.
2. The fiction of complete economic determinism, set up by the early economists as a convenient way of delimiting their field, has been mistaken by a great many people for a demonstrated scientific fact. As such it has had a profound effect on popular thinking about human nature and about our society. At a time when our way of life is under heavy attack, when many of the members of the society have lost faith in its ability to deal with the problems of human need, it is unfortunate that the simplest and most understandable analysis that many educated people are apt to encounter is based on the assumption that our economic system is a mechanism for the satisfaction of greed. Such a picture is not likely to attract converts or to strengthen the loyalty of the present members of the society. Nor does it lead to the effective functioning of the institutions which are caricatured and misunderstood.

COMPETITION AS A MOTIVE OF BEHAVIOR

Another common-sense idea which does not stand up in practice is the idea that people are inevitably competitive. It is quite true that most people measure their achievements by the achievements of their neighbors, and Katona has justifiably concluded that "the more money other people have the more a person wants." [3] As used in many schools and factories, however, competition is a comparatively ineffective way of getting people to work harder. People do not compete actively unless they think they have a chance to win. This causes a large part of any group to withdraw from competition early. These people then exert pressure on the others to drop out of the competition with them. In addition, more people are unwilling to compete when competing means the loss of friends, as it often does. Forced competition, in which people are obliged to compete against their friends, is a threat to the individual and therefore unpleasant. It is not surprising that workers or departments which have been involved in contests frequently drop their output to below normal as soon as the contest is over.[4] As a rule teachers who depend on competition as a means of motivation are able to get the majority of their students to compete only when they "choose up sides" and appeal to group loyalties.

PSYCHOLOGICAL CONCEPTS OF HUMAN NATURE

Although a great deal of progress has been made during the three quarters of a century that psychology has been an experimental science, psychologists are continually reminded of the tentative nature of their generalizations by the fact that competent psychologists may still differ from one another in their preference among the various conceptual frameworks and types of explanation that are used. The truth is that human behavior is so many-sided, so complex, and so variable that there is no single point of view yet discovered by which we can understand it all. The problem is to find a point of view which will enable us to see the whole disorderly mass of phenomena in order and regularity, and, it is hoped, to make it predictable. In looking for a conceptual

3. Katona, *op. cit.*
4. Harrell, T. W. *Industrial psychology.* New York: Rinehart, 1949, p. 280.

system which will make human behavior more understandable, present-day psychologists are following a number of different leads.

THE STIMULUS-RESPONSE APPROACH TO BEHAVIOR

The most obvious approach is to attempt to explain behavior by the known principles of the physical sciences. Such a conceptual system was made quite plausible by the discovery of the reflex arc in 1832. It was discovered that the stimulation of a given nerve always resulted in the contraction of the same muscles, provided the spinal cord had been severed above the point where the nerve entered it. This fixed stimulus-response unit, which could be explained plausibly by several different principles of the physical sciences, was assumed to be the basic unit of behavior.

Following this assumption, the next problem was to discover how these fixed "basic" reflexes combine and interact with one another to produce the more variable and coherent behavior which is characteristic of an undamaged organism, animal or human.

The most important difficulty confronting this concept of behavior is the problem of stimulus selection. There are in any given physical situation great numbers of physical stimuli to which the organism makes no apparent response. A stimulus which sets off a response in one situation or at one time may have no effect at another time or in another situation. Or it may elicit a completely different response. And the stimulus which does elicit the response is not necessarily the strongest one in terms of physical energy.

This variability is ascribed either to changes in the conductivity of the nervous system or to tensions and imbalances which require (drive) the organism to behave so as to relieve them.

This latter concept has diverted the emphasis in physiologically oriented theories of motivation from the external physical stimulus which "triggers" the act to the internal conditions that determine which of the great number of potential factors present in the physical environment will be selected as the objects of the organism's behavior. A number of these conditions, personified as "drives" for food, water, avoidance of injury, rest, elimination, air, and constant body temperature, have been taken over from physiology.

Since the behavior supposedly motivated by these physiological drives or "needs" is essential to the survival of the organism, they are commonly assumed to be the basic drives from which all other "drives" or "needs" are derived. These physiological drives, at least, operate in all living individuals. They are often considered to constitute a single drive for physical survival or for homeostasis, that is, for the maintenance of the organism's physiological balance.

HOMEOSTASIS AS AN EXPLANATION OF BEHAVIOR

This is not a mere change of words. The concept of homeostasis enables us to visualize and use a completely different concept of living organisms from the machine concept of the stimulus-response theorists. It even leads to a different system of ethics.

Thinking in terms of the physics of their own day, the physiologists who a century ago adopted the reflex arc as their conceptual unit of behavior were taking a machine as their model. The motive power of their conceptual man was supplied from the outside in the form of a stimulus, i.e., a spur.

The newer concept of homeostasis, which also originated in physiology, assumes, on the other hand, that the living organism is an organized dynamic field and that, like all organized fields, it must behave so as to maintain its organization. Thus the organized nature of our behavior, the explanation of which has caused the stimulus-response theorists so much trouble, is simply an aspect of our nature as living organisms. An individual's behavior, from this point of view, is both the result of his physical organization and the means by which it is maintained. The physiological evidence in favor of this concept is overwhelming and does not need to be given here. The essential thing is that this point of view leads us to conceive of human beings, not as passive machines which have to be pushed into action, but as living organisms actively exploring their environments for the means of maintaining their own integrity. They actively seek the satisfaction of need and, if we consider them as whole organisms, they have free will. Choices between food and water, for instance, are determined by the physiological state of the organism itself.

All of this, so far, is completely in harmony with the known principles of physics and chemistry and fits into the present framework of the physical sciences.

It is too bad that it is not quite adequate. A large part of human behavior and even some animal behavior cannot be explained by or even reconciled with the purely physiological needs. It is not uncommon for people to eat when they have already eaten more than they need or can comfortably contain. It is not uncommon for them to refuse food when they are famished. People drive too fast for safety, they multilate themselves for beauty, they give their lives as heroes, as martyrs, and as suicides, all activities which are hardly consonant with maintaining the physiological balance. In the wartime experiment [5] on the effects of semistarvation, the thirty-six men who were the subjects lost an average of 25 per cent of their body weight. With it they lost interest in almost everything but food. They dreamed of food; thought constantly about food. Life became, as one expressed it, merely "passing time from one meal to the next." Another reported: "Stayed up till 5:00 A.M. last night studying cookbooks. So absorbing I can't stay away from them."

This extreme preoccupation with food would seem at first glance to be an ideal example of the effect of an urge toward organic homeostasis. But, in spite of the fact that food could easily have been purchased or stolen, only a few of the participants violated their pledge to eat only the prescribed diet. When shopping they did not purchase the food needed by their bodies. Instead they bought cookbooks, cooking utensils, and "bargains." One man hoarded *National Geographic* magazines. Two men stole. But only one stole food. The other stole china cups.

If this is homeostasis, it is not homeostasis in a purely physiological sense.

Even lower animals not infrequently show behavior which is hard to reconcile with a demand for bodily maintenance. The writer once had to remove a white rat from a laboratory activity wheel because of extreme loss of weight. She had been going without food and water in order to keep her cage mates from using the wheel. As soon as she was removed from the cage one of the other animals began behaving in the same way. Homeostasis can explain dominating behavior which results in the individual's getting more food, but when a poorly nourished animal abstains from food and water in order to dominate its cagemates, an explanation of the act as an effort to maintain a constant physiological state seems a little farfetched.

THE CONCEPT OF PSYCHOLOGICAL NEEDS

One way of handling this difficulty is to postulate the existence of additional nonorganic drives or needs, usually called psychological needs. Among the psychological needs proposed by various writers are needs for activity *and* for relaxation, for security *and* for new experience, for

5. Guetzkow, H. S., & Bowman, P. H. *Men and hunger.* Elgin, Ill.: Brethren Publishing House, 1946.

self-assertion *and* for self-abasement, for imitativeness *and* for creative self-expression, for work *and* for leisure, for beauty *and* for practicability, for protection *and* for independence, for emotional security *and* for excitement, for superiority, for dominance, for status, for possession of children, for recognition, for achievement, for affection, for value, for ownership, for knowledge, for power, for prestige, and for "value-in-general."

It should be obvious that this conceptual scheme gets into difficulties since it leads to the postulation of contradictory goals. If we are free to postulate a new psychological need to explain any act otherwise inexplicable, the list will grow and grow. As someone has said, this method could lead to the postulation of a psychological need for pumpkin pie in October.

In spite of the way this theory of mixed physiological-psychological needs frays out into confusion and conflict, it is popular at the present time. For one thing, it provides a convenient formula for explaining anything that anyone has ever done. If none of the many conflicting drives can explain an act, a new drive can easily be added to the list. But it is impossible to predict by this method what an individual is going to do because it offers us no way of knowing which of the many conflicting hypothetical drives will be operating. As a result, applied psychologists, whose planning often requires a fairly accurate prediction of what an individual will do in a particular situation, do not find it helpful.

This puts the psychologist in the same awkward position as the other social scientists. Economists could go about their work with more confidence if the psychologists could give them a reliable psychology to work with; but the psychologists cannot solve their problem of prediction of individual human behavior by the physical-science methods most of them have been taught to prefer. Until the physiologists give them a better base to work on they cannot even begin to attack the problem.

In the meantime we are confronted with pressing problems of education, rehabilitation, and social reconstruction and planning for which a better understanding of human nature is essential. Without it we cannot be sure of our techniques or our goals. It is not safe to try to fit these problems into a theoretical framework which, no matter how bright its prospects for the future, is inadequate for that purpose now. Because they are expected to deal with human beings now and cannot wait for the physiological approaches to be perfected, many educational, clinical, and social psychologists are exploring the possibilities of other points of view.

THE GROUP AS A DETERMINER OF BEHAVIOR

Two different and, to some extent, complementary approaches seem to be developing. The first uses the principle which Professor Emerson has rather happily called social homeostasis. Like physical organisms and other dynamic fields, the social group exists independently of any of its individual parts. It may exist long after all of its individual parts have been replaced; in fact it may continue to exist *because* some of its parts have been sacrificed or discarded. We can predict that so long as the society exists someone will be carrying out the functions required for its existence. As long as the society exists we can be confident that someone is playing these required roles. In an authoritarian society we can expect to find, for instance, leaders, followers, and the scapegoat minority or foreign enemies which are necessary to keep the followers in willing obedience to the leaders. If all of these roles, and many subsidiary ones, were not played the society would collapse.

Another characteristic that human societies and living organisms share with other dynamic fields is that their response to their external environment is selective. The type of response evoked by an environmental change depends upon the nature of the society or the organism; and changes which evoke a violent response from one society will elicit no response from another. A frequently cited example of this selectivity in the social field is Linton's study of the Tanala-Betsileo.[6] These two Madagascar tribes apparently shared the same culture until the Betsileo shifted from dry rice culture to wet rice culture. The wet rice culture has a number of economic advantages since it gives a higher yield, provides for better conservation of the soil, and can be carried out by single families. Since the system does not require frequent removal to new land it has the further advantage of enabling families engaged in wet rice culture to live in better and more permanent homes. Nevertheless, one of the Tanala clans which took up the new method soon abandoned it because it interfered with their religious ceremonies.

This same study furnishes other examples of the way in which societies function as dynamic fields. Because of the interdependent character of the organization in such a field, changes in one part of the field will affect, sometimes drastically, all other parts of the field. Once the Bet-

6. Kardiner, A., & Linton, R. *The individual and his society.* New York: Columbia University Press, 1939. Also in Newcomb, T., & Hartley, E. *Readings in social psychology.* New York: Henry Holt and Company, 1947.

sileo took up wet rice culture a profound change in their society followed. The fact that the land suitable for such cultivation was scattered
and in small plots which could be cultivated more or less permanently
made private ownership of the land desirable. Since the cultivation was
by families rather than by clans (as it had been before), the ownership
was by families. Class distinctions began to appear as a result of differences in family wealth. Slaves acquired economic value. Because the limiting factor in production was water, a strong central power to control
irrigation became essential. The result was that the Betsileo developed a
"rigid caste system with a king at the head, nobles, commoners, and
slaves." In consequence the individual Betsileo has a different style of
behavior and different behavior goals from the individual Tanala.

The recent studies of social class in American communities abound
with examples of the ways in which class membership helps determine the
values, goals, and aspirations of individual Americans. In "Yankee City," [7]
in the early 'thirties, the typical upper-class member believed in heredity
and manners as determinants of worth and status. He wanted money, not
as an end in itself, but as a means of living "properly" in the family
house, surrounded by symbols of the family position in the community,
which it was his goal to maintain. The members of the middle class, on
the other hand, believed in the power of money and education and wanted
them both in order to gain higher status. The typical member of the
25 per cent of the population who constituted the lower-lower class cared
little for education and looked on money as something to be spent for
immediate satisfactions. The different social classes thus seem to obey
different laws of economics. Kinsey [8] has similarly called attention to the
difference in attitude toward sex among the different social classes.

Man is fundamentally a social animal. As an isolated individual he
does not amount to much and he seems to know it. In spite of the accusations often made that the group holds its members back from progress
and self-fulfillment, the truth is that, whatever our role, we can achieve it
only in cooperation with others. Lewin [9] demonstrated that people change
their ways of living faster in groups than they can individually. They also

7. Warner, W. L. *The social system of a modern community.* New Haven: Yale
University Press, 1941.

8. Kinsey, A. C. *Sexual behavior in the human male.* Philadelphia: W. B. Saunders, 1948.

9. Lewin, K. Group decision and social change. In T. Newcomb and E. Hartley
(Eds.) *Readings in social psychology.* New York: Henry Holt and Company,
1947, pp. 314–315.

seem to think more effectively when they do it together. In one experiment [10] Shaw gave three reasoning problems to each of twenty-one individuals and to five groups of four people each. The individuals, working alone, arrived at correct solutions to only 8 per cent of the problems, the groups to 56 per cent. Group membership is important. Sobel,[11] in studying the psychiatric breakdown of army personnel in combat, found that after men had lost interest in defending their country, had forgotten to hate the enemy, were too tired to care about the immediate military objective and too frightened to pretend courage, they were still kept going by their loyalty to their immediate group. The effect of group membership on behavior in schools and factories has already been mentioned. As Murphy [12] puts it, ". . . so that we know his age, sex, subculture, and economic position . . . we can go a long way toward safely describing his personality." If we want to predict what a person will probably do in a given situation, the fastest way is to find what groups he feels part of and what his role is in the groups.

And yet the assumption that an individual behaves as he does because he is a member of a group which requires such behavior leaves a great many questions unanswered. Suppose that a man is a member of many different groups, as most people are nowadays. If the interests of these groups conflict, what will he do? The group-determinant hypothesis cannot tell us.

It is necessary to distinguish, at this point, between the rough hypothesis that the behavior of an individual will be that which is required by his social role and the more sophisticated principle of social homeostasis advanced by Professor Emerson. In a static society [13] like that of the social insects the difference can be ignored. The fact that a society has existed unchanged for a reasonable period of time indicates that it has developed the techniques necessary for its survival. As long as its environment remains unchanged such a society will continue to maintain itself,

10. Shaw, M. E. A comparison of individuals and small groups in the rational solution of complex problems. *Am. Jour. Psychol.,* **XLIV,** 1932, 491–504. Also in Newcomb and Hartley, *ibid.*

11. Sobel, R. Anxiety-depression reactions after prolonged combat experience— The old sergeant syndrome. *Bull. U.S. Army Medical Dept., Combat Psychiatry Supplement,* November, 1949, pp. 137–146.

12. Murphy, G. *Personality.* New York: Harper & Brothers, 1947.

13. A static society can survive only in a static environment. For reasons which will appear later it is unlikely that man will ever have such an environment. (He keeps changing it.)

provided that its members continue to play their required roles.[14] But in human societies, even the most ancient of which are now being forced into constant change by the changes in their social and physical surroundings, the survival of the society is often possible only if the members break out of the traditional pattern and abandon their old roles for new ones.

This places us in an uncomfortable dilemma. If we follow the social-role hypothesis we are unable to explain social change or to predict its course or even its direction because social change requires a change in roles, which the theory does not explain. If we adopt the more subtle and inspiring concept of social homeostasis we cannot explain why some societies and groups fail to make the changes required for successful self-maintenance. Neither concept gives us much help in predicting the behavior of specific persons. Neither one explains why new groups are formed or what happens in situations which the social sanctions do not cover. They do not explain why some people disregard the sanctions of their native society to identify with and accept the sanctions of another.

Effective as they may be for other purposes, it does not seem that any of the psychological approaches we have described so far can give a clear picture of human purpose or human value. The physiological theories seem to imply that a society is good to the extent that it produces and distributes the goods necessary for the physical health of its members; but the fact that "psychological" needs have to be invoked to supplement the purely physiological needs indicates that people need something more than the physical necessities of life. It is hard to say just what this is, because the alleged psychological needs are so diverse and conflicting.

The social-determinant theories of behavior give a picture of value which is even more disconcerting because it seems to disregard completely the fate of the individual human being. The successful society, this approach implies, is the society which survives. Whether or not this society satisfies the need or helps fulfill the destiny of human beings in general or of specific persons in particular is not pertinent to this point of view. It is reasonable to suppose that societies will have better chances for survival if their institutions and customs tend to keep their members alive, maintain their loyalty, and attract new adherents. In other words, the successful society must to some extent satisfy human need. But by itself the group approach, whose basic dynamism is the maintenance and exten-

---

14. In insect societies the role is determined by the physical structure and the individual is physically incapable of changing its role. This is, except for some sex roles, not true of human beings.

sion of the group organization, gives us no inkling about what people need. The basic problem which must be solved before we can understand group dynamics thus turns out to be the problem of basic human values. What is the motivating purpose of human behavior?

THE INDIVIDUAL–FIELD APPROACH

At the present time a number of psychologists [15] appear to be more or less independently converging on a purely psychological theory of behavior which is more capable of dealing with the problems of human purpose and human values than the physiological and group approaches we have already discussed. These people do not form a school or group and do not share a formally organized body of theory, so that what follows is only my personal analysis of the general approach. The basic assumptions appear to be these:

1. The behavior of human beings, although it is often not appropriate to the immediate physical environment, is always appropriate to what is variously called the individual's psychological field, behavioral field, private world, assumptive world, perceptual field, or phenomenal field.

This is the crucial assumption of the approach. Instead of abandoning field dynamics because in the guise of organic homeostasis it is not adequate to explain all behavior, the individual-field psychologists keep the principle and move it to a conceptual causal field where it does work.

In terms of what we know about living organisms some such field is biologically necessary to animals with distance perception. Among those animals which remain small and live in the water or in a host organism, getting their food by drifting into contact with it or having it drift into contact with them, behavior is purely homeostatic. The only part of the

15. I hesitate to name individuals because there are so many, but the following should be listed: in social psychology, G. W. Allport, Cantril, Coutu, Crutchfield, Klee, Krech, Lewin, Murphy, and Sherif; in clinical psychology, Combs, Lecky, Raimy, and Rogers; in education, Hopkins, Kelley, and Woodruff; and in the psychology of economic behavior, Hayes and Katona. The point of view owes much to the work of the Gestalt psychologists, particularly Kohler and Wertheimer; to the writings of L. K. Frank, A. Maslow, and R. H. Wheeler; and to the perceptual studies of Ames, Bruner, Murphy, Postman, and many others. See D. Snygg and A. W. Combs, *Individual Behavior,* New York, Harper & Brothers, 1949.

physical environment which affects the animal or its behavior is that part which is in close contact with its surface. Such an animal lives in a behavioral field one molecule thick, and anything nutritive or noxious within that area is automatically dealt with. The individual has no choice of action and all animals of the species would respond in the same way.

An animal of this kind is unable to perceive food at a distance and move toward it, or to perceive danger at a distance and avoid it. It is completely at the mercy of its environment. If such a species is to survive one of two things has to happen. As one alternative its individual members might develop a high rate of reproduction and enough motility to scatter them so widely that a few, at least, would always be blundering into a favorable environment. Or, after developing motility, the individual organism might increase its chances for survival by developing distance perception [16] so that it could perceive food or danger at a distance and behave accordingly. But this presents a new problem. An animal able to perceive objects at a distance is now exposed to stimuli from a tremendous number of food and danger foci. An organism which responded simultaneously to all of the physical stimuli which bombard it from these sources would tear itself to pieces. In order to maintain its organization it must trim the confusing, stunning, incoherent field with which it is now in contact down to manageable size. It has to pick out that part of the physical field which is most important to the maintenance of its own organization at the moment and deal with that, more or less ignoring the rest.[17] This "cut-down" field is the individual (or psychological) field.[18]

One important feature of the "cut-down" psychological field is that it has a time dimension. It includes a past and a future. For the organism whose behavioral world is limited to its immediate surface nothing exists except what is here and now; but the acquisition of distance perception automatically gives the field a time dimension. Food at a distance is not, for the organism, food now. If it is perceived at all as food it is food-in-the-future. As a result of this development great individual differences and

---

16. This would necessitate a larger organism and therefore a slower rate of reproduction.

17. When a man is being chased by a bull he is not likely to notice the mosquitoes.

18. To realize in a small way how few of the stimuli physically present actually get into the individual's perceptual field, listen for the "s" sounds the next time someone speaks to you. They are so prevalent in English that many foreigners think of English as the "hissing language," but English-speaking people rarely hear them. They are too busy listening for the sense of what is being said.

apparent irrationalities in behavior begin to appear. The degree of choice required by the simplest type of distance perception results in wide differences between the individual fields of different individuals in the same physical situation.[19] And when an organism like man is able to symbolize and introduce into its psychological field objects and concepts not physically present, the range of possible behavior becomes tremendous. The behavior of individuals would be completely unpredictable if it were not for the next principle.

2. The psychological field is an organized dynamic field. The immediate purpose of all of an individual's behavior, including his behavior as a perceiver, is the maintenance of organization in his individual field. If the field organization should disintegrate his physical organization could not be maintained.[20] If he loses faith in his perceptions organized behavior becomes impossible.[21]

The meaning and value of perceived objects and events are determined by the individual's field organization at the time. As examples we can take the different meaning and value to an individual of food before and after a heavy meal.[22] Our perceptions seem to follow dynamic-field principles in

19. The irrationalities are only apparent. Behavior is judged irrational when it is not appropriate to the perceptual field of the observer. The sequence of plays chosen by a quarterback who is trying to coax the defense out of position to set up a breakaway play for a touchdown will appear foolish to a spectator who sees the situation in a shorter time perspective and thinks only in terms of maximum gain on the next down. And the spectator's choices would appear irrational to the quarterback.

20. The nausea of seasickness is a minor example of the breakdown of physical organization which occurs in a disorganized perceptual field. Workers at the Hanover Institute (See H. Cantril, *The "Why" of Man's Experience,* New York, The Macmillan Company, 1950; and E. C. Kelley, *Education for What Is Real,* New York, Harper & Brothers, 1948) report that subjects exposed to perceptual phenomena which they are unable to reconcile with one another frequently become nauseated.

21. Cf. the difficulty of mirror drawing, as a mild example.

22. The economic implications of this illustration are interesting. If the individual is satiated the food has no immediate value to him. In fact it may have a negative value if he has to dispose of it. However, if his field includes a perception of the future as one in which he will want to eat the food or in which he can exchange it for something else which he will want, it will be perceived as having value and he may save it. If he has a pressing immediate problem not relating to food, it is not likely that he will be aware of the food at all. If he has gone through experiences which have caused him to feel that food is always valuable, he may seek it out and eat it or hoard it even if it causes him physical discomfort to do so. Value depends upon the psychological field of the individual, and concepts of "true value" and "fair price" are psychologically unreal.

that events and objects are always interpreted in the way which will require the least change in the field. Suppose, for instance, that a large part of my perceptual field is organized around the belief that a certain man is an enemy. Then on an important occasion he treats me with kindness and generosity. The odds are that I will perceive his behavior as a subtle insult or a deliberate attempt to deceive. If he were unimportant to me, I would be able to change my perception of him as a result of his kind act; but since his supposed enmity plays an important role in my field organization, it will be easier to distort my perception of his act than to change the rest of my field to conform to the act. Many of the demonstrations devised by Ames and his associates at the Hanover Institute illustrate this principle.

3. The perceptual self is the part of the field which is perceived as behaving. As a result it is the focal part of the field. The only aspects of the cosmos which seem important, indeed the only aspects which can enter the field at all, are those which are related to the self. If the principle of field organization is too abstract to be useful, we can paraphrase it by saying that the immediate purpose of all behavior is the maintenance of the behaver's perceptual field, particularly of his perceptual self.

This takes care of the problems of marytrdom and suicide, which are inexplicable by physiological principles and, in the case of suicide in our society where it is socially disapproved, by the concept of group role. It is not the physical self but the self-as-perceived, the perceptual self, which we are trying to preserve. A man who has come to think of himself as selfless and devoted to duty or to others will act so as to maintain that perception of himself, even at the expense of his life. There are strong connotations for character education here. A person who has been taught to perceive himself as an outsider will behave like an outsider, with no feeling of responsibility to the group. A person who has been taught to regard himself as a criminal has to maintain and enhance that concept of himself by believing that "only suckers work."

4. Because human beings are aware of the future, at least of its existence and uncertainties, it is not enough to maintain the perceptual self for the present moment. It has to be maintained in the future, built up and enhanced so that the individual feels secure for the future. And since the future is uncertain and unknown, no enhancement of the individual's experience of personal value,[23] no degree of self-actualization,

---

23. Terminology modified from Cantril, H. *The "why" of man's experience.* New York: Macmillan, 1950.

is enough. Human beings are, by nature, insatiable. This should be an important point for the economists.

The ideal sought is a state in which the individual feels so much in harmony with the universe, so much a part of it, that he does not have to defend himself against any other part.[24]

WAYS OF SATISFYING NEED

Seen in this way, the many conflicting physiological and psychological "needs" which were discussed earlier turn out to be alternative ways of satisfying the individual's basic need for enhancement of his experience of personal worth and value. A more convenient classification of these alternative ways of satisfying need is given below. Since behavior is always determined by the individual field of the behaver, the method used by any individual in any situation will be one which is appropriate to his perceptions of himself and of the external situation at that particular time.[25]

Means of Maintaining and Enhancing the Self

A. Change in body state leading to change in the perceptions of the self.

1. Restoration of the body balance by eating, breathing, elimination, rest, etc.
2. Blocking off organic sensations of fatigue, pain, or tensions indicative of personal inadequacies by the use of alcohol or drugs.
3. Elicitation of an organic mobilization and increase in body strength

---

24. It is significant that this state is said to have been achieved, at least in moments of ecstasy, by some of the saints. It probably involves the perception of the universe as one completely pervaded with infinite love and compassion for all living things. From this point of view the higher religions represent man's greatest insight in their recognition of the ultimate goal of human endeavor and their audacious attempt to move directly toward it.

25. This concept is capable of bringing back the group role in a new form. It is now the individual's concept of what is required to maintain his picture of himself as a member of the group. If he does not perceive himself as a true member of the group his obligations, not being recognized, will have to be enforced, if at all, by police action. In a growing society the members seek and embrace their roles as means of self-enhancement. That is the reason the society is growing. This point of view supports Toynbee's hypothesis that a society whose members have to be held to their posts by coercion is disintegrating.

by entering a dangerous or irritating situation; speeding, gambling,[26] etc.

B. Self-reassurance by demonstration of mastery, control, or superiority.

   1. Over people: Competition leading to victory over worthy opposition.[27] Other demonstrations of superiority by gossip, practical joking, scapegoating, making gifts, etc.

   2. Demonstration of control over material objects.
     a. Creative. Doodling to art.
     b. Destructive. Nailbiting to vandalism.[28]

   3. Accumulation of property, hoarding.

C. Reassurance and enhancement by association and identification with respected individuals and groups. Evidence of respect and love by respected persons. Feeling of identity with a great cause, of being part of a great movement.

D. By change in the nonself part of the field which places the self in a less threatened position.

   1. By change in the physical environment. Travel, moving, redecorating, etc.

   2. By daydreaming or fantasy, including that done by professionals. Radio, television, theater, fiction, etc.[29]

26. Gambling also provides foundations for more convincing daydreams (D2).

27. Even if the individual is defeated he has enhancement through increase in body strength during the competition.

28. Creative activities provide more permanent symbols of self-value than destructive activities, but they usually take longer and require more skill. Destructive acts therefore are more apt to be committed by an immature person or a person under great stress provided that they are not inconsistent with the perceptual self he is trying to enhance.

29. Many activities help to satisfy the need for enhancement in several ways. The most satisfying sex experiences associate means A and C. Cigarette smoking, particularly for smokers who inhale, supplies a tissue irritant which causes a rise in blood pressure and an increase in heartbeat and amount of blood sugar (A2 and A3). The smoker also secures reassurance from manipulating an object and blowing smoke (B2). (Many smokers report that they get less pleasure from smoking in the dark.) He may also use smoking as a way of demonstrating membership in social groups (C) and gain a feeling of value by offering cigarettes and matches to people without them. It is small wonder that so many millions of dollars are year are spent for tobacco.

The Basis of Human Values

Looking at the problem of value from this point of view we can come to the following conclusions:

1. The basic goal of all individuals is for a feeling of increased worth, of greater value.
2. This goal is never completely reached. Given one success, one degree of self-enhancement, human beings will always aspire to more.
3. Satisfaction of the need for greater personal value can be and is sought in a number of alternative ways. Goods and experiences are of value to the individual only as they contribute to the feeling of personal worth.

We are now in a position to make some judgments about values. Since the individual can strive, with some success, for self-enhancement in a number of different ways, no single way is indispensable.[30]

THE SPECIAL STATUS OF ECONOMIC ACTIVITY

Although economic activity is only one of many ways by which the individual strives for an increased feeling of worth, value, and belonging, it is likely to demand a major portion of his time and attention. *Economic activity* takes a great deal of time because it is concerned with the control of "scarce" goods, that is, with materials and services that require conscious effort to get. Many of the scarce materials would be helpful to their possessor even if they were not scarce. Food and clothing, for instance, may be used to maintain or restore the body balance and increase the consumer's perception of body strength. An automobile may be used to increase the driver's feeling of power and value, by helping him to earn his living, or by giving him a chance to exhibit skill and good judgment or daring. But objects or services do not have to be useful in such a direct fashion to be valuable. Scarcity alone can make an object valuable because the mere possession of a scarce object, provided it is sought

30. The only qualification is that if the individual fails to use the methods for seeking enhancement which also result in maintaining the body balance, he will die. As a usual thing he will use such methods because any marked physical disorganization results in such a change in the psychological field (See F. A. Beach, "Body Chemistry and Perception," in R. R. Blake and G. V. Ramsey, *Perception and Approach to Personality*, New York, Ronald Press, 1951) that the individual does act so as to restore the body balance. But this is not always the case.

by others, can be a constant and reassuring symbol of dignity, worth, and power. Air is necessary for self-maintenance but no one will derive the fullest possible satisfaction from air until it is bottled under expensive brand names and sold at such high prices that the consumers (and hoarders) are impressed by their own wealth, extravagance, and good taste. As things stand now we do a great deal of breathing but devote little attention to it. Since air is not scarce, breathing ordinarily presents no problems and therefore no opportunity for self-enhancement by overcoming obstacles.

At a social level in which the minimal physical necessities are so easily obtained that their possession arouses no pride, a great deal of time may be devoted to the economic struggle for such symbols of worth as modern kitchen equipment, antique (or ultramodern) furniture, mink coats, or a private office with its own water cooler, any of which would lose much of their value if they became more plentiful or if people quit competing for them. As long as such objects are scarce, it takes quite a bit of effort and ability or power to get them. As a result they have come to be, in the eyes of many, reassuring symbols of self-worth and status. Such people will sacrifice a great deal to get them. Superficially each individual has a large number of alternative symbolic goals available, but actually he can strive with hope and satisfaction only for the goals which are appropriate to his concept of himself and the situation. Failure to achieve the goals by which he has chosen to measure himself results in humiliation and anguish, which are not lessened by his power to achieve other ends which are not appropriate to his self-concept and are therefore not regarded as enhancing.[31]

The Psychological Function of Trade

This point of view, if it should come to be accepted as common sense, would lead to a better appreciation of the role played by the businessman

31. This gives additional importance to money or liquid assets whose possession appears to give assurance of ability to reach goals the individual has not yet thought of. The accumulation of money can thus become an important goal in itself.

 At the present time, however, the relative importance of this goal is probably declining due to inflation, high income taxes, and the divorce of ownership from control in the large corporations. In this type of organization the distinction between economic and political activities becomes very thin, as the struggle is not only for scarce objects but for scarce titles and positions, an increasing number of which require such special technical skills that their acquisition by outright purchase would be regarded as unethical.

in the production of values. It is sometimes assumed that value is an intrinsic property of the object and that anyone who buys an object for less than that value gets a bargain and anyone who pays more is a loser. This leads to the belief that neither the buyer nor the seller has produced anything. A business transaction, from this point of view, is a contest between two parties each of whom is trying to victimize the other by buying goods for less or selling them for more than their intrinsic worth. From this point of view business is attempted cheating and the model transaction is the purchase of Manhattan Island from the Indians.

From the individual-field point of view, however, both parties to a transaction may, and usually do, profit from it. Objects are valuable to people if they assist them in the satisfaction of their individual need for self-maintenance and enhancement. Since different people strive for satisfaction of this need in different ways, objects and experiences will have different values for different people, and both parties to an exchange which is free from coercion can be expected to profit by it. A model transaction, from this point of view, might be one between a starving man with a keg of water and a man suffering from thirst who has a surplus of food.

THE PROCESS OF CHOICE

This approach also provides a conceptual framework for dealing with the process of choice. Lacking such a framework, economists have had to assume that anyone's choice of goals is perfectly free, limited only by the possibilities of the physical environment. In any actual situation the choice is much more narrowly limited since in order to be chosen an object or experience has to be perceived as a means by which the individual can approach closer to his goal. What will be chosen is thus determined by the nature and organization of the chooser's field at the instant of choice. People in the same physical situation will make different choices because they have different goals, or because they are in different stages of their progress toward their goals, or for a number of other reasons. A person under strong pressure, for instance, is likely to concentrate so strongly on his immediate goal that he will fail to perceive opportunities to by-pass it when they occur. When he feels threatened by intense and immediate loss of self-respect, the future aspects of his private field fade into the background and he acts "without foresight."

There is reason to believe that what people call "foresight" is related to the individual's concept of himself. The person who feels relatively secure in his feelings of personal worth does not need to concentrate so completely on the immediate problem and therefore has a better chance to see it in a broad perspective.

All of this seems to negate another assumption frequently made by economists, which is that the chooser is a completely rational and highly informed being capable of action in his own best interests.[32]

SELF–INTEREST AND ALTRUISM

The fact that man is potentially able to strive for satisfaction of need in many different ways gives us an answer to an important question, which may be stated in two different ways:

"Is man naturally good or evil?" or "Is man essentially altruistic or essentially selfish?"

Since we believe that a man's behavior may be either good or evil, it seems to follow that a good society will help and encourage him to strive for enhancement in ways which further not only his own experience of personal value but the value experiences of others as well. The self-enhancement which accrues from an experience of being needed, from feeling part of a great movement, from contributing to something nobler and more important than our own lives, is just as natural and probably more lasting than the self-enhancement gained through successful aggression. In the long run it is better for the individual himself if he uses the socially desirable ways of seeking enhancement because such methods are not so apt to incite other people to thwart and resist him. There is no necessary conflict between the basic aspirations of the individual and the basic aspirations of others. There is no inevitable conflict between the individual and society.

FAILURE OF IDENTIFICATION WITH OTHERS

Let us consider, however, one way in which man may fall into antihuman behavior. The person who does not feel part of a social group will not

32. Advertisers know better and so do economists, but they have been forced into this position by a dearth of psychological knowledge. Since the psychologists have not furnished the kind of information about people that the economists have needed, the economists have had to go ahead and predict what a simplified hypothetical man would do.

behave as a member of the group. Even though a concept of himself as a just or honorable man may keep him from consciously self-seeking behavior at the expense of the people with whom he does not identify, his feelings and, as a result, his behavior toward them will be essentially selfish. Since the organization of our individual field is largely determined by our own need for a feeling of self-worth, it is easy for such a "good citizen" who does not feel one with his victims to commit great acts of aggression against people "for their own good" or in the name of justice, of patriotism, of economic law, or of preservation of the faith, and to do it in all sincerity and with a great feeling of rectitude. Law and ethics can help prevent injustice that we can recognize, but the best insurance against injustice is complete identification with the potential victim so that injury to the victim is injury to the self. The man who loves his neighbor as himself has not abandoned self-interest. He still seeks for self-maintenance and enhancement, but his self now includes his neighbor.

IDENTIFICATION WITH OTHERS AS THE BASIS OF ETHICS

It is on this base that human ethics seem to have developed best. It is true that on logical grounds it is to almost everyone's advantage to work together on the basis of "You scratch my back and I'll scratch yours." But attempts to explain existing systems of ethics or create new ones on the basis of enlightened self-interest seem to be psychologically unrealistic. For a society to survive it must receive from some of its members sacrifices, sometimes of their lives, for which it cannot compensate them in a material sense. A system of ethics based on *quid pro quo* could in no way command the degree of self-sacrifice required and secured in all societies. This self-sacrifice seems to be a manifestation of identification, love, and faith in something more important than our own lives.

There is a growing feeling among psychologists that self-acceptance is necessary before we can accept or love others. Rogers [33] has concluded on the basis of his clinical experience and research that a person who feels so threatened that he is preoccupied with the necessity for defending

33. Rogers, C. R. *Client-centered therapy*. Boston: Houghton-Mifflin, 1951. See also Maslow, A. H. Self-actualizing people: A study in psychological health. *Personality Symposia,* **39** (1). Values in Personality Research, W. Wolff (ed.) New York: Grune and Stratton, 1950.

himself has little sympathy to give to others. Murphy [34] believes that to love others we have to love (accept) ourselves first.

The degree to which men can attain brotherhood with all men is still unknown. Professor Emerson,[35] looking at the problem against the background of millions of years of biological development, sees it as a goal which is almost assured. From a psychological point of view it does not seem impossible, given enough time. Man is certainly not averse to identifying himself with others. But he tends to identify most completely with comparatively small groups, probably because he can more clearly perceive his value to such a group.

The greatest obstacle in the way of universal brotherhood at the present time is not man's unregenerate selfishness and individualism. It is the fact that to give their lives meaning and dignity the people of the world have identified themselves with a great number of conflicting groups and causes for which many of them are prepared to sacrifice themselves *and others*.

LIMITATIONS OF INDIVIDUAL EXPERIENCE

It is not yet safe to assume that the process of identification with larger and larger groups can go on indefinitely. The individual field is at best only a limited version of reality, and as the group becomes larger and more complex it is more and more difficult for the individual to perceive his value and function in it and consequently to seek identification with it. Education can help; but no matter how highly educated we are, there are physiological and psychological limits to our ability to comprehend and identify with a complex society and many people in our society may already have approached those limits. There is something suspicious about the way one civilization after another gets to the point where there is a high degree of interdependence between people who are not personally acquainted and then goes into a decline.

Even if we should succeed in getting a better conception of our relation to others, the resulting feeling of brotherhood might be disappointingly mild. The "cut-down" nature of the perceptual field makes it impossible for us ever to achieve as warm a feeling of identification with all as we now have with some. The more people we identify with, the less

34. Murphy, G. *Personality*. New York: Harper & Brothers, 1947.
35. Chapter 10.

time and interest we can give to each. It may follow that a man who loves all of mankind equally will not love any one person much.

This brings us to the second source of evil in human nature. It lies in our inability to recognize or accept the limited nature of our perceptual fields. As has been pointed out earlier, the individual's personal field is a limited and often distorted version of reality. Nevertheless, it is the only version he has and he has to trust it. This naïve assurance that our private experience is a valid representation of reality is dangerous. It breeds atrocities. Most of the great enormities of human history have been committed in the name of what the perpetrators believed to be noble causes. They would have been ashamed to commit such atrocities for purely selfish reasons.[36]

There is no reason to suppose that human beings will ever become omniscient, so this source of evil seems certain to remain with us permanently. However, there are reasons for believing that its effects may be alleviated. In a society of people better able to accept themselves and therefore better able to accept others, there would be a greater respect for and acceptance of the corrective insights of others and less disposition to seize on a worthy cause as an excuse for aggression against others.

COMPARISONS BETWEEN SOCIETIES

Since there are many ways in which people can secure some degree of self-actualization, it is reasonable to suppose that there can be many different "good" societies. However, if we judge a society by its contribution to the value experience of individual human beings, a society is good to the extent that it enables its members and neighbors to live with health, security, self-respect, and dignity. It is good to the extent that it enables its members and neighbors to feel adequate to live with reality and, in consequence, to perceive it without distortion. Such a society will institutionalize and encourage techniques of production and cooperation among its members. Each member will have "an opportunity to work, to feel personally successful, and to sacrifice for some cause which to him is important. Each person must have opportunity to feel that his life has

---

36. Compare the mannered observance of the "laws of war" in the admittedly selfish dynastic wars of the eighteenth century with the savagery and ferocity of the religious wars of the sixteenth and seventeenth centuries and the "wars for humanity" of the twentieth.

meaning, importance, and purpose." [37] Such a society will be continually changing. "No successes and no recognition can be enough to give anyone the permanent feeling of adequacy and self-assurance that he needs. Further achievement and growth are always necessary. As a result no society which attempts to remain static can adequately satisfy the needs of its members. A 'good society' must provide its members with opportunities for self-enhancement by pioneering in new fields and at ever more difficult problems." [38]

THE NATURE OF SOCIAL CHANGE

From this point of view there is nothing inevitable about the direction of social change. The Marxist ideas of inevitable communism and the Greek idea of inevitable cycles, both of which seem to have been based on the short-time trends of a single civilization, are equally mistaken. No two societies develop in exactly the same direction because when a "hitch" develops in a society the possibilities for solving it are limited by the character of its individual members and the potentialities of its physical and social environment. These differ in all societies.

In human societies, particularly in civilizations, people are constantly pushing against the frontiers for better ways of satisfying their individual need. Sometimes (frequently in our own society) such a push [39] is so successful that it opens up a whole new field of possibilities and problems

37. Snygg, D. & Combs, A. W. *Individual behavior*. New York: Harper & Brothers, 1949, p. 200.
38. Snygg and Combs, *op. cit*. To the writer the approach which has been described seems to argue against the planned society, particularly if the goal of that society is a static state of perfection. It seems to be a valid corollary of the individual-field approach that planning for other people is ineffective because each has his own individual organization of values and goals which are relatively unrecognized by others. In addition planning by a few for the many is sure to be less realistic than the active explorations of the many because it is based on fewer points of view about nature and about people. Planning by a few in authority is especially dangerous because by reason of their authority and responsibilities they are certain to have developed goals and aspirations not shared by the other members of the society. The result is, all too often, a solution which does not win cooperation and which has to be enforced, if at all, by force, thus splitting the society and destroying its unity.
39. The temper tantrums of a baby and the discovery of nuclear energy both represent such pushes. One difference is that our society has already developed techniques for dealing with temper tantrums.

and creates a crisis because the society has no established practice for dealing with them. In such a situation, with social precedents vague or absent, each member of the society has to make his own decision and in doing so he helps to change his society for the better or for the worse. This is a ticklish moment because there are opportunities for disaster if the attempted solutions are based on false analogies with problems which have already been solved or if they are otherwise based on false concepts of reality. In our own society an increasingly large proportion of our problems have to do with people both in our society and outside of it. In this situation erroneous concepts of human nature are particularly dangerous.

Human Life Goals in the Humanistic Perspective

Charlotte Buhler

INTRODUCTION

With the psychologists' attention having been concentrated for some time entirely on the need aspect of human motivation, the goal aspect has been almost completely neglected. Yet psychologists are beginning to realize the great importance of this aspect, especially within the frame of reference of psychotherapy. "All I hear is questions about goals," a

This paper was read as the Presidential Address at the Fourth Annual Convention of the American Association for Humanistic Psychology in New York, 1966.

Reprinted from *Journal of Humanistic Psychology*, 1967, 36–52, by permission of the author and the publisher.

psychoanalytically-oriented therapist said in a recent discussion in admitting that the handling of goals and values was an unresolved problem.

Research related to goals has been scarce and haphazard. There is no systematic description nor theory of the constituent and contributory *factors* to goalsetting.

From Narziss Ach's studies (1905) on "determining tendencies" at the beginning of this century, over Kurt Lewin's (1926) "aspiration levels," to more recent studies of decision making, of achievement, and of success, we have investigations of special aspects of goalsetting. Developmental aspects of goalsetting were discussed by the author (1962) in a study on "Genetic Aspects of the Self." Goal patterns of healthy, essentially happy, and effective individuals were demonstrated by A. Maslow (1954), while H. Otto (1963) found, on the other hand, that the majority of people who answered his questionnaire on personality strength and personal resources had never given any thought or time to an assessment or evaluation of their potentialities. In accordance with this, I find in my therapy groups that very few of these people chose careers or entered personal relationships under the aspect of their own potentialities or their self-actualization.

Everett Shostrom (1963) found, while standardizing his "Inventory for the Measurement of Self-Actualization," that the most self-actualizing person is the one who "is able to tie the past and the future to the present in meaningful continuity." His study throws some light on the healthy and unhealthy relationships of the individual to time.

But little is known about the continuity of pursuits of those who, in the end, found their lives to be fulfilled as against those who ended in failure. In fact, we know the barest minimum about what people seek in life and what they do with themselves. The whole field is full of speculation.

While this address cannot be the occasion for a systematic investigation of all factors entering goalsetting, I want to point to certain behavioral as well as experiential patterns which in the developmental progression seem to indicate advance in goalsetting. The twelve points which I will discuss are considered very tentative formulations and are not claimed to be final nor necessarily complete. The organizing principle for the twelve points is *developmental;* that is to say, I will enumerate them as I see them coming up in the individual's development.

ACTIVITY

The first behavior contributing to and involving, already from the start, certain characteristics of the individual's goalsetting is the *activity* with which the individual begins his existence even in the prenatal stage.

As Eiduson, Eiduson, & Geller (1962) establish in a careful survey of the most recent literature, the individual starts with a given genetic setup acting in and on a given environment. While this environment's influence becomes immediately a co-determinant of the individual's behavior, there is from the start selectivity in the way the individual responds to all given stimuli.

Some interesting details may be mentioned briefly with respect to the nature of the individual's primary activity.

This primary activity is known to occur in different *levels,* as M. Fries (1953) called it. She distinguished five activity levels, starting from very passive up to overactive behavior. Also some very recent observers, Thomas *et al.* (1963), establish consistency in the infant's activity level.

The activity level seems more or less coordinated with passivity and aggressiveness of approach. This passivity and aggressiveness is seen by L. W. Sontag (1950) as representing the infant's earliest approaches to working out the basic problem of dependency versus independence. This implies a very important assumption: namely, that the natural tendency to be passive or aggressive predisposes the baby, from birth on, to two fundamentally opposed human relationships. They are the *acceptance of dependency* or the *struggle for independence.* Of course, it must be said at once that passivity and aggressiveness could not possibly be the sole determinants of dependent or independent behavior, nor are passivity and aggressiveness themselves completely unalterable. But within limits, Sontag's theory, for which he brings considerable experimental evidence from the Fels Institute's research projects, impresses this writer as sound. Kagan & Moss (1962) pursued this Fels Institute research study on a longitudinal range from infancy into adulthood. They found that the continuity of the previously mentioned traits was later influenced by the individual's sex role standard.

Another characteristic of the infant's primary activity is what the writer (1958) called degrees of curiosity or lack of it, and what Thomas *et al.* (1963) establish as consistently accepting or rejecting responses to new stimuli and experiences. In this we can see roots of later preferences for adventure as against preference for familiar situations. Also creativity and non-creativity—the interest in, or lack of interest in, discovering and doing something new—may have here one of its roots.

SELECTIVE PERCEPTION

The second behavior, contributing also from the start to the individual's later goalsetting, is his selective perception.

Sensory perception, which begins in the intrauterine life, is for quite some time partly vague, partly very specified, and becomes only gradually organized. R. Spitz (1965) has, in continuing our earlier Viennese research, brought systematic evidence for the way in which the awarenes of an object is gradually built up during the first year of life.

All during this process, the infant responds in a very individual way to the world of stimuli that he perceives. His responsiveness is selective from the start, as is now widely acknowledged. Stirnimann (1940) brings comprehensive data proving this selectivity. Tinbergen (1948) speaks of an "innate perceptual pattern." Hilgard (1951) speaks of the pursuit of "innate preferences."

Apart from preferences, there are also such individual features as degrees of sensitivity in response to environmental stimuli. Hypersensitivity is one of the most generally acknowledged inborn characteristics. The vulnerability of the hypersensitive child is one of those conditions which are apt to induce neurotic development.

To what degree and in what way goalsetting is linked up with perception first, and later with imagery or phantasy, is still undecided. Undoubtedly when a person decides to get an orange out of his refrigerator, he must focus his imagination on an object which he knows from his perception.

But when a person has a vague urge for some activity—he may have imagined only vaguely one or another situation—he may fantasize about it, but the main thing in him may be this urge and a variety of feelings. In the creative process, as described by some writers and musicians, there may be a phase in which fleeting images pass through the mind in colors and in a variety of feelings.

There we find a selective imagination brought to life under the directive of an active mind which sets and pursues a goal.

In the two, the ability of *directive activity,* operating in unison with a *selective perception and imagination,* I see the core of the person or the individual's "rudimentary self." With this I mean the beginning of a system of purposeful behavior in the direction of the development of the individual's own potentials.

REACTIONS TO CARE AND CONTACT

A basic goal, from the start, is *psychophysical needs*. However, this satisfaction seems only to be beneficial if brought about in what R. Spitz (1965) called the right "emotional climate." This emotional climate depends on the type of personal care which the mother or her substitute gives to the infant. While subconsciously so, the infant's need seems to be for psychophysical satisfactions received in an atmosphere of love and care. This shows us from the beginning an unconscious intent in the direction of human closeness.

There is more proof of that. We know that as early as from about three to six weeks on, the infant responds with a smile to another person's smile and that it initiates sounds. Piaget (1951) observed, the same as I did, a behavior which must be called "strenuous efforts" at imitating sounds and mouth movements. Here we find rudimentary stages of understanding and of identification.

Thus the earliest tendency to need-satisfaction is, from the start, one in which not only satiation is wanted, but care as well as contact.

WILL, CONSCIENCE, IDENTITY

The fourth behavior contributing to goalsetting becomes conscious in the experiences: *I want.* This getting into conflicts with the experiences, *I must, I should,* results in the two to four-year-old child's first inquiry into *who am I?*—an inquiry which from then on will plague the individual sometimes far into his adulthood or even all through his life.

In his first "I want to" behavior, the child is quite arbitrary regarding his objective. He may say "yes" and "no" in short succession to the same offer or request. He tries out how it feels to make choices and decisions of his own. And he discovers himself, if allowed by his environment, as a person in his own right.

Here, then, is where the autonomous ego is set up, and where the child begins to discover his own self and the possibility of giving himself a direction of his own. Erikson (1959) speaks of the happenings of this period as of the "battle for autonomy."

But clinical studies show more recently how very individually different this period is being experienced. There are some children who, while having tantrums and resisting their environment, do not really set up goals of their own. They just fight submission, but remain in the end just as dependent on their environment as they were before. All they want to do is to be opposite of what their environment wants.

Some of my patients who are now in their thirties or forties, or even older, remember that all they ever wanted was to do the opposite of what was suggested to them. This, then, is the beginning of a completely neurotic self-determination. There are children who are set on neurotic love relationships with a parent and who do not want autonomy but possessive domination.

Besides this neurotic outcome of the battle for autonomy, there are also healthy solutions. Partly depending on the specific environment, partly on the child, the outcome may be a voluntary submission and identification with the adults' goals.

The opposite type, the child with much of a creative potential, begins at this point with his first attempts toward self-realization. The more or less creative child will, in this period, already have ideas of his own of how to set up his identity. This child may feel that she does not want to be like her mother, but like her aunt, whom she admires; or she may want to do things as the neighbor lady does, who can teach her something she wants to learn (Buhler, 1962a).

These tentative early goals show us beginnings of the child's conscious attempts to identify with certain persons and with certain objectives in the humanistic perspective of values.

These first goals may have to do with aptitudes or with moral considerations, "Is he a good boy or is he a bad boy?" asks Peter, two, in talking thoughtfully to himself. "No, he is a bad boy," he concludes with a certain glee. Peter is too young to even speak of himself as "I," yet already conceives of a moral goal for himself. Of course, all this is partly playful, but still it is astonishing how many valid, lasting decisions are being made in this period.

Besides evaluation and identification there is, however, something more to be noted. Vacillating in their directives as these children's self-expressions may be, there is definitely the evidence of a degree of intentionality in them. They are not yet sure what exactly they want or should do with themselves, but they know vaguely there is something to be realized in some distant future.

If we jump from this age to the young adolescents whom Getzels &

Jackson (1962) examined, we find a fully established self-awareness and dependently conforming or independently self-responsible identities. In this excellent study of "Creativity and Intelliegnce," we meet adolescents during their high school years who have very clear ideas about themselves.

There are those like Mary, a high IQ but non-creative girl, who has a positive image of her family and who states in her autobiography that she has "internalized" her mother's ideals and is very close to her (p. 163).

And there are those who, like John, declare, "If I could achieve one thing during my lifetime, I would want it to be 'independence.' "

And his equally original sister, Joan, says, "that, although she thinks of her parents as being pleasant enough, she has no intention of identifying with them. As to her mother, she feels that she need only make an assertive statement on the question of identification: 'When they try to get me to be like my mother, I . . . tell them that I am me.' And that is that" (p. 191).

These identity concepts go along with elaborate self-evaluations. Here we see the beginnings of certain features of long-range goalsetting.

The cases of this study will also serve as examples for the next factor determining goalsetting. That is the factor of potentialities in terms of abilities and aptitudes.

MASTERY

The experience in this area begins with "I can" or "I cannot."

I agree with Lois Murphy (1962) that this "I can" or "I cannot" belongs to the earliest experiences of infancy. This four- to five-month-old baby who swings his rattle under good control, as against that one who hits himself or loses hold of the rattle—this $1\frac{1}{2}$-year-old who successfully puts one block on the other so that it stands, as against that child whose towers always tumble before they are finished—of course these babies do not have a conscious awareness of their being able or unable to master these materials, but semiconsciously they have first realizations of success and of failure. Proofs of this are the happy smiles of the one and the unhappy rages of the other. Observations of the despair and helplessness of these failing children have been made thus far only in an incidental way. They are usually children with birth injuries or childhood schizophrenia, children who are uncoordinated and unintegrated.

Experiences in coping and in mastery contribute essentially to the setting up of a child's personality, as L. Murphy showed (1962) in her extensive observations.

Already, then, the more adaptively and the more creatively coping individual can be distinguished. This difference becomes very pronounced in Getzels & Jackson's studies (1962). And here we already see some distinctive characteristics of life goals.

In these well-known studies of creative versus highly intelligent, non-creative high school students, great pains were taken to establish all relevant variables that could codetermine the subjects' behavior.

The findings show us the creative and the high-achievement though non-creative type associated with different motivational patterns. The non-creative, moving toward conventional standards and conforming with what is expected of them, show themselves in dependency relationships with their environment. The creative group, on the other hand, who move away from models provided by teachers and who seek out careers that do not conform with what is expected of them, show themselves in independence relationships with their environment.

There are further related results regarding the social and moral orientation of these two groups. While both groups participate in activities that are expected and approved by the social order, the adaptive, non-creative group tends more to be what one usually calls socially "adjusted." They are "insiders"; they seem

to prefer social interaction to individual achievement, to seek experiences that are immediately enjoyable as against those that promise more remote gratification, to find more satisfaction in experiencing with others than in asserting their own autonomy, to be willing to sacrifice moral commitment in the interest of interpersonal harmony (p. 159).

The highly creative show the reverse of these trends. They tend to be "outsiders" and stand up individualistically for highly moral principles.

All the described findings are suggestive of different innate tendencies of these two groups. But the possible role of environmental influence is not neglected by Getzels & Jackson ". . . irrespective of the possible role of genetic factors." To quote them further: The findings in this direction are that the high-IQ family "is one in which individual divergence is limited and risks minimized, and the overall impression of the high-creativity family is that it is one in which individual divergence is permitted and risks are accepted" (p. 76).

The cautious conclusion from all these findings would be that in his eventual goal structure and goal development, an individual's inherent tendencies to be more creative and independent or more non-creative and dependent are codetermined by the environment's goals and values. These enhance that "openness to experiences" and that willingness to take risks which were found in the creative child, as they also enhance that orientation toward security and success which are found in the non-creative child.

The question of how the child who is not creative and not so adaptive as the family might expect will fare under these influences has not as yet been established in correspondingly thorough studies.

But from other studies, such as B. Eiduson's (1962) investigation on "Scientists," we gather how extremely complicated the picture becomes, as soon as the dynamics of very different individual lives are compared.

CONSTRUCTIVENESS AND DESTRUCTIVENESS

From the beginning, the infant is under the impact of his environment. Parents, siblings, peers, and other persons contribute essentially to the child's goalsetting by information, guidance, and by all social relationships that are being established. We already mentioned dependency and independence. But apart from these, there is a host of feelings of love and fear, of frustration and hostility, of acceptance, security—or the opposite—of belonging or being a loner and an outsider, of rivalry and jealousy, of submission and domination, of cooperation and opposition, friendships and crushes, and many more.

Apart from the impact which the child receives from his environment, he becomes increasingly aware of how the others—his elders and his peers—are handling themselves and their affairs. He begins to interpret their intents, their selfishness or their kindness. In responding to them and in coping with them, their demands, their rebuffs, their beatings, the eight- to twelve-year child develops ideas, methods, and directions of his own. He becomes an essentially constructive person who handles himself and his social relationships in the direction of goals that benefit him and others, as against the essentially desructive person, who is full of hostilities and whose mind is set on damaging others or even himself.

In introducing the concepts of constructiveness and destructiveness, I want to emphasize that I think of them as complex motivational patterns. Constructiveness is not a simple entity such as activity, but a complex unit, such as achievement. There may be the instinctual element of building in it. But constructiveness and destructiveness, as understood here, are developed under the influence of a person's interaction with his environment. Everybody probably harbors both constructive as well as destructive attitudes. But similar to the achievement attitude, constructiveness or destructiveness may under circumstances be all-pervasive.

Studies on this aspect of constructiveness or destructiveness as basic attitudes to life are not as yet available. Fritz Redl & David Wineman's (1951) studies on "Children Who Hate" come the closest to it in describing and analyzing an all-pervasive destructiveness of a group of preadolescent youngsters.

The definition of the term constructiveness would be that this is the basic orientation of a person who tries to work out things for himself and for others in such a way that there is a beneficial result. Beneficial might be a result that gives pleasure or is helpful or educational or contributory to any kind of growth and development. The opposite orientation of destructiveness is that of persons who harbor much hostility and who try to damage others or themselves. Such damaging might be consciously, or unconsciously, planned and might range from preventing happiness and success of others, or oneself, to actually trying to injure, to ruin, to eliminate people.

Harmful aggression with a destructive intent may be observed even in nursery school children. As a basic attitude of malevolence, it seems to begin to dominate a child from about eight to ten or twelve years on, the age in which some of the conflicts between children and their parents culminate.

In criminal adolescents and adults there is often evidence of a predominant orientation toward destructiveness.

At this point, the two basic goals, to be constructive or to be destructive, can only be introduced as concepts with the hope of later availability of appropriate evidence.

ACHIEVEMENT MOTIVATION

In this period, all foregoing experiences of being able to master things and being successful against failures converge to generate an individual attitude to and concept of achievement. The idea of achievement as a goal has by then become more or less clearly established in the child's mind. Many factors contribute to how it is being conceived by the individual.

In the studies of D. McClelland and his collaborators (1953), the enormous impact of the parental attitude to achievement has not only been established, but also analyzed in its various characteristics.

Achievement styles are established which often remain the same all through life, styles in terms of work habits, of dependence or independence in goalsetting, orientation toward success or failure, and, particularly, attitudes to values and beliefs.

Evidence as accumulated by the McClelland group, by Getzels & Jackson (1962), by Eiduson (1962), by Goertzel & Goertzel (1962), show attitudes to achievement in their consistency and show them almost always linked up with beliefs and values.

BELIEFS AND VALUES

In the eight- to twelve-year-old period, in which a child begins to have some overview over his various personal relationships as well as his competence in life, he consolidates beliefs and values for himself. The constructive or destructive attitudes which he starts building, result from the experiences and evaluations which crystallize now to opinions and convictions. Eight- to twelve-year-old children often debate with others or with themselves issues such as honesty, fairness, popularity, power, being important, being accomplished, and being the best in everything.

In these beliefs and values, the growing child establishes ordering principles for himself. Like some other goal-determining principles which we see at work from the start—namely, need-satisfaction, self-limiting adaptation, creative expansion—the ordering principle is also noticeable from the infant's first attempts at coordination and organization on. I consider all these as basic tendencies and call this last one *tendency to the upholding of the internal order* (C. Buhler, 1959).

LOVE AND OTHER COMMITTING RELATIONSHIPS

We said previously that, from the beginning, the infant's need-satisfaction depends on care given within the framework of a warm, human relationship. Very early in life the infant not only responds to the "emotional climate" which the adult creates, but he also strains himself toward a contact of understanding.

In adolescence, two new goals of human relationships are discovered and aspired. They are intimacy and commitments. Healthy intimacy and commitments may be defined as freely chosen bonds. Their free choice distinguishes them from unfree dependency on the one hand, while on the other hand they represent a voluntary reduction of independence.

Intimacy and commitment in a sex and love-relationship, if shared by both partners, develop it beyond functional enjoyment to something new: namely, the ecstatic experience of a unity. The goal of achieving this is, as everybody knows, one of the, if not *the* most essential, life goals of the maturing person.

Maslow cites it among his peak experiences. Also psychoanalysis recognizes in this a new step in the development of object relations. It is called the development of genitality. "Genitality," says Erikson (1959, p. 96), "is the potential capacity to develop orgastic potency in relation to a loved partner of the opposite sex."

This sex-love unity is probably the most essential of the uniting experiences and goals of the person willing to commit himself, to give and to share. But in the same period, commitments to friends, to groups, to causes, become also freely chosen goals. These commitments bring the beliefs which the eight- to twelve-year-old child began to conceive of, into the sphere of reality.

The development in this whole area is, as we all know, full of problems and perils for the majority of youths. The degree to which they want to allow themselves the pleasure of sexual excitement is one of their problems. The finding of and commitment to a love-partner is a second, the accomplishment of self-dedication through intercourse a third. And the question to what degree these goals may preoccupy them in comparison with achievement goals and with the dedication to groups and causes is perhaps the most difficult to resolve. The pursuit of sexual and other pleasurable excitements easily becomes, for the adolescent, a goal which conflicts with other goals of life, especially achievement goals.

A great deal of conflict concerning the hierarchy of the different values that were developed up to this point is practically unavoidable. A hierarchical order and integration of all the directions which we encountered up to now is a task of younger adulthood, if not of the rest of life.

INTEGRATION

We mentioned the word integration. All during childhood and adolescence, we saw goalsetting being developed in various and increasing directions. In this development, several factors are obviously of decisive influence. The complexity of the process of goalsetting is extraordinary, and the integrative task required is tremendous.

Very little research has been dedicated, up to now, to this whole question of integration. Thomas French (1952) has devoted a comprehensive investigation to this principle of integration. He has particularly dwelt on the factor of hope as an integrating principle. Hope is undoubtedly of fundamental importance in holding a person together and in keeping a person going.

However, before it comes to hope, there are problems regarding the inner organization of our goals. One principle of organizing seems to be given in the individually varying roles of different values and beliefs. G. Allport (1961) also sees a hierarchy of values as the organizing principles of the self. But what determines that hierarchy of values?

In the first instance, we must think of it as changing in time and being determined by age.

A second codeterminant is obviously the genetic factor, about which we know least of all. But, undoubtedly, a person's dispositions—his gifts and aptitudes, as well as his deficiencies—are codetermining the hierarchy of values and with it the structure of his goalsetting.

Thirdly, there is the host of environmental influences.

Emotional dynamics are nowadays the best-known factor of all which influence a person. However, as far as goalsetting is concerned, here, also, only recent clinical studies give us relevant information regarding the environmental impact.

The same is true of socio-cultural influences on goalsetting, a factor which recent social psychological studies have explored (Strodtbeck, 1958).

While we have increasing knowledge of all these factors, little is known regarding the integrating procedure by means of which the individual evaluates and orders all these codeterminants of his goalsetting. While much of this may take place in the unconscious, it still remains a question of how it is done.

How do people choose? Or how does it come about that in one case the impact of a mother's ambition—in another case a cultural prejudice acquired in a group—plays a decisive role in what a person believes and wants? It does not explain anything to say one factor was "stronger." Obviously, it is the individual who reacts more strongly to one or the other factor. And what determines his choices and decisions? A discussion of these factors of goalsetting has been prepared by the author and collaborators (in press).

Little has been done to investigate integration in its early stages. A. Weil (1956), who specialized in the study of childhood schizophrenias, comes to the conclusion that the unevenness of these children's maturational patterning, apart from their peculiarities, is the reason why their development lacks integration at all times. In this, she sees their basic pathology. And, indeed, the inability of integration seems part of the basic pathology of schizophrenia at any age.

But correspondingly, then, is an even and regular maturational progress a guarantee of successful integration?

It seems to me that we know far too little about people's inner organization, about decisions between preferences, about what ultimate needs they have as against more visible or more pressuring ones.

Very few people know themselves in this respect. Most subjects or patients whom I ask: What do you want ultimately? What is ultimately important to you? will give vague answers. "I wish I knew myself," they will say.

DIRECTION, PURPOSE, AND MEANING

The problem of integration entails the factor of direction, purpose, and meaning in a way, because it seems that we integrate ourselves with the view of certain goals in mind. These goals may be closer or farther away, shortsighted or seen under a big perspective; whatever they are, they have an influence on the way an individual organizes his behavior. The integrative process of the person who wants the "here and now" will undoubtedly be different from the one who has a long-range plan. Some concrete answers as to how a great variety of determining factors may be absorbed and integrated into a specific way of life, with specific goals and purposes, result from B. Eiduson's study of *Scientists* (1962).

In this study, the development and personalities of forty scientists were examined by means of tests and interviews. All of these men, says Eiduson,

> whose early determining factors show a great variety, seem to have in common that their excellent intellectual abilities lead them to early concentration on intellectual interests, and they all turn away from their families during adolescence or when starting college (p. 66).

This independence factor which we found associated with creative abilities in earlier studies, also becomes apparent here.

These scientists show, as Eiduson (1962) states in summarizing her findings, "a great diversity of sources that fed the investment in the intellectual" (p. 89). Yet they are all men whose life goals, to an extraordinary degree, are identified with, and related to, their creative research.

From this and other research it appears that the creative person finds it easier to set a direction and goals for himself. Also, they are goals which lead the creative person in a more natural way to transcend himself, which V. Frankl (1966), as well as Maslow (1964), considers a specifically human accomplishment. It becomes increasingly evident that in dedicating himself to a self-transcending goal, a person feels his life to be meaningful, as V. Frankl pointed out. But to be meaningful, and, with this, to fulfill a basic existential human need, this goal must be chosen in accordance with a person's own best potentialities.

This concept of meaningfulness, which has a long history regarding its definition, occupied many thinkers, historically speaking, since Brentano and Husserl, W. Dilthey, E. Spranger, and K. Buhler, my own work—then in existentialistic writings like Paul Tillich's and recently V. Frankl's (1966)—in its application to psychotherapy. This concept seems to refer to the development of an existential quality of life which I think is best defined by two characteristics, one emphasized by K. Buhler (1927), who says, what is meaningful is a contributory constituent to a teleological whole; the other by P. Tillich (1952), whose discourse on the despair of meaningfulness calls for an act of faith by which to accept oneself in a meaningful act.

As for creative work, it also usually enhances a person's enthusiasm for life and his self-esteem. It helps him more quickly to find his identity and to establish himself as a person in his own right.

For all these reasons, the humanistic psychologist is greatly interested in awakening and increasing people's creative potentials. H. Otto (1962) has recently started systematic work with older persons in this direction. And, luckily, schools and parents begin to become aware of the fundamental importance of this factor of creativity, the existence of which, as Guilford (1950) observed, had been almost forgotten in psychology and education.

However, not everybody is primarily creative. What about the direction of those people who are primarily non-creative?

In Getzels & Jackson's previously mentioned studies, it is very apparent how the non-creative youngsters whom they examined and who were essentially healthy, non-neurotic persons, found it easy and natural to fall in with their families' and their teachers' guidance and ideas for their futures. That means they allowed their elders to help them find their direction in life.

A mutually satisfactory development under this kind of influence does, however, not only depend on the willingness and adaptability of the child. It depends perhaps even more on the wisdom and adequate understanding of the grown-up environment.

The questions that pose themselves at this point will be taken up from a different angle when we discuss our last factor.

FULFILLMENT AND FAILURE

What is a human being living toward? The presumable end result has been described in different terms. Some think of no result at all and see only a growth and decline process with a peak somewhere in the earlier part of the middle. Some never see any other goal than the attainment or restoring of equilibrium. Some think of the full development of the self as the ultimate satisfaction. The humanistic psychologists, as you know, usually speak of self-realization as the goal.

I personally considered this concept at about the same time as K. Horney (1950) first introduced it into the literature. In discussing it, I rejected it in favor of the concept of fulfillment. I find that, while a good objective description of a very important aspect of a fulfilled life, self-realization is only one aspect, and, at that, it is one that only relatively few people are fully aware of.

What do people want to get out of their lives? Naïve people, as you know, speak of happiness and various goods that they think will bring it to them. More materialistic and/or ambitious people may speak of the success they want to end up with. But if one talks with older people, as I did in a study I am presently engaged in, one hears quite other things.

If not very analytical, the essentially fulfilled people may say: they had a good life and they would not want it any different or much different if they had to live it all over again.

In the opposite case of complete failure, they may say, "It all came to nothing," or they are tired and glad it is all over. Or as Sonja Kowalewska expressed it in the title of a drama she left after her suicidal death: "As it was and as it could have been."

In the case of a resigned ending, they may say, there were so many disappointments.

All this is to say people have, toward their end, inclusive feelings of fulfillment or failure or a kind of resignation in between. Even people who in earlier years lived with short-range goals or from day to day, seem to have toward the end an inclusive reaction to their life as a whole.

If, in talking with more analytically-minded people, one tries to let them specify the main aspects of their fulfillment or failure feelings, four major considerations could be distinguished.

The first is the aspect of *luck*. Practically always people mention that they had much luck, or lack of luck, in meeting the right persons or getting the right opportunities at the right time. This factor seems to contribute most to happiness or unhappiness, to the feeling of being a fortunate or an unfortunate person. In religious persons, this is an area where they see, most of all, God's hand.

The second may be called the aspect of the realization of *potentialities*. This is usually referred to in terms as these: "I did most of what I wanted to do," or "I did what was right for me," or "I did many things that were wrong for me," or "I could not really make the best out of myself."

The third is the aspect of *accomplishment*. Most people I talked with feel strongly about this aspect. They feel that their life should amount to something; it should have borne fruit; it should represent an accomplishment of some kind. There should be "something to show" for the past life. This factor contributes greatly to their ultimate satisfaction or dissatisfaction with their lives.

Finally, a fourth factor is that of a *moral* evaluation. Often persons emphasized that they had lived *right,* meaning in terms of their moral and/or religious convictions. Many persons mentioned objectives they had lived for in some form of self-dedication, be it the family or social groups, mankind, or progress in some field of endeavor.

The four aspects correspond essentially to the goals of the four tendencies all of which I had assumed to be basic tendencies toward fulfillment.

The most successful lives in terms of fulfillment I found to be those who were rather conscious of their life being something they ought to do something with and they were responsible for—be it in religious terms of relationship to a God, or in existential terms in relationship to the universal order, or simply in ethical terms of non-metaphysical convictions.

Religion, philosophy, and moral convictions are, of course, as we know, not sufficient to help a person live a healthy life and conquer his destructive neurotic tendencies. The essentially fulfilled lives that I studied seem to have been able to be essentially successful in sustaining an individually balanced equilibrium between their basic tendencies to *need-satisfaction, self-limiting adaptation, creative expansion,* and *upholding of the internal order,* and to be constructive under whichever aspect they believed in.

SUMMARY

Human goalsetting is, as you see, a very complex process emerging from a multiplicity of ingredients. I pointed out twelve main developmental advances on different levels and in different areas of personality functioning. Briefly summarized, they are: (1) *Activity* with a more passive or more aggressive approach; (2) selective *Perception;* (3) *Care and Contact;* (4) *Identity* and *Intentionality* beginnings with choice and direction of the person who feels he wants or he must or he should; (5) *Mastery* beginnings based on the experience "I can" or "I cannot," with success and failure, adaptive and creative behavior; (6) *Constructiveness* and *Destructiveness* developed in the dynamic interrelationships with the environment; (7) *Achievement* motivation; (8) *Beliefs and Values* with opinions and convictions; (9) *Love* and other committing relationships; (10) *Integration* of factors; (11) *Direction, Purpose, and Meaning;* (12) *Fulfillment, Resignation, and Failure.*

One of the results of the studies (in preparation) of lives which accomplished essential fulfillment as against lives ending in the resignation of a heap of unordered experiences, many disappointments, or in the despair of failure, is this:

Fulfillment seems to result primarily from a constructive and thoughtful way of living; constructive to the degree that even major tragedies as well as great misfortunes are overcome and used beneficially; thoughtful in the use of even mediocre potentialities for accomplishments and meaningful self-dedication; thoughtful also in attempting to look repeatedly backwards and forward at the whole of one's existence and to assess it in whatever terms one believes in.

Ach, N. *Uber die Willenstätigkeit und das Denken* (About will and thinking). Göttingen: Vandenhock & Ruzprecht, 1905.

Allport, G. *Pattern and growth in personality.* New York: Harper, 1961.

Buhler, C. Earliest trends in goalsetting. *Rev. Psychiat. Infantile,* 1958, **25,** 1–2 and 13–23.

Buhler, C. Theoretical observations about life's basic tendencies. *Amer. J. Psychother.*, 1959, **13** (3), 561–581.

Buhler, C. *Genetic aspects of the self.* New York: Academic Sciences, 1962. (a)

Buhler, C. *Values in psychotherapy.* Glencoe, Ill.: Free Press, 1962. (b)

Buhler, C. *Intentionality and fulfillment.* San Francisco: Jossey-Bass, in press.

Buhler, C., & Massarik, F. (Eds.) *The course of human life. A study of life goals in the humanistic perspective.* New York: Springer, 1968.

Buhler, K. *Die Krise der Psychologie.* Jena: G. Fischer, 1927. (Transl. *The crisis of psychology.* Cambridge: Schekman Publishing Co., in press.)

Eiduson, B. *Scientists.* New York: Basic Books, 1962.

Eiduson, B., Eiduson, S., & Geller, E. Biochemistry, genetics and the nature-nurture problem. *Amer. J. Psychiat.*, 1962, **58.**

Erikson, E. *Identity and the life cycle.* New York: International University Press, 1959.

Frankl, V. Self-transcendence as a human phenomenon. *J. Humanistic Psychol.*, 1966, **6** (2), 97–106.

French, T. *The integration of behavior.* Chicago: University of Chicago Press, 1952, 1954, 1956 (3 vols.).

Fries, M., & Woolf, P. Some hypotheses on the role of the congenital activity type in personality development. *The psychoanalytic study of the child.* New York: International University Press, 1953, Vol. 8.

Getzels, J., & Jackson, P. *Creativity and intelligence, explorations with gifted students.* New York: Wiley, 1962.

Goertzel, V., & Goertzel, M. *Cradles of eminence.* Boston: Little, Brown, 1962.

Guilford, J. P. *Fields of psychology.* New York: Van Nostrand, 1950.

Hilgard, E. The role of learning in perception. In R. R. Blake & G. V. Ramsey (Eds.), *Perception.* New York: Ronald Press, 1951.

Horney, K. *Neurosis and human growth.* New York: W. W. Norton, 1950.

Kagan, J. Acquisition and significance of sex typing and sex role identity. *Child Development Research, Russell-Sage Foundation.* Philadelphia: Wm. F. Fell, 1964.

Kagan, J., & Moss, H. A. *Birth to maturity.* New York: Wiley, 1962.

Lewin, K. Vorsatz, Wille und Bedürfris (Intention, will and need). *Psychol. Forschg.*, 1926, **7**, 330–385.

Maslow, A. *Motivation and personality.* New York: Harper, 1954.

Maslow, A. *Religions, values, and peak-experiences.* Columbus: Ohio State University Press, 1964.

McClelland, D. Atkinson, W. Clark, R., & Lowell, E. *The achievement motive.* New York: Appleton-Century-Crofts, 1953.

Murphy, L. *The widening world of childhood.* New York: Basic Books, 1962.

Otto, H. The personal resource development research—The multiple strength perception effect. *Proceedings of Utah Acad. Sci., Arts, & Letters,* **38,** 1961–1962.

Otto, H. Self-perception of personality strengths by four discrete groups. *J. Human Relations,* 1963, **12** (4).

Piaget, J. *Dreams and imitation in childhood.* New York: W. W. Norton, 1951.

Redl, F., & Wineman, D. *Children who hate, the disorganization and breakdown of behavior controls.* Glencoe, Ill.: Free Press, 1951.

Shostrom, E. Personal orientation inventory. San Diego: Educational and Industrial Test Service, 1963.

Sontag, L. The genetics of differences in psychosomatic patterns in childhood. *Amer. J. Orthopsychiat.,* 1950, **20** (3).

Spitz, R. Genèse des premières relations objectales, *Rev. franç. Psychanal.,* Paris, 1954.

Spitz, R. *The first year of life.* New York: International University Press, 1965.

Stirnimann, F. *Psychologie des neugeborenen Kindes.* Zurich und Leipzig: Rascher Verl., 1940.

Stirnimann, F. Psychologie des neugeborenen Kindes. In E. Schachtel (Ed.), *Metamorphosis.* New York: Basic Books, 1959.

Strodtbeck, F., McClellend, D., et al. *Talent and society.* Princeton: Van Nostrand, 1958.

Thomas, A., et al. *Behavioral individuality in early childhood.* New York: New York University Press, 1963.

Tillich, P. *The courage to be.* New Haven: Yale University Press, 1952.

Tinbergen, N. Social releases and the experimental method required for their study. *Wilson Bull.,* 1948, **60,** 6–51.

Weil, A. Some evidences of deviational development in infancy and early childhood. Vol. 11. *Psychoanalytic study of the child.* New York: International University Press, 1956.

III

The Helping Process

This part of the sourcebook deals with the essence of helping—the process and the helper. The articles presented here have been chosen for the insights they give into the helping process and some of the problems helpers must face in practicing the profession.

The article by C. R. Rogers makes the very important point that all helping relationships are essentially learning situations. This point has also been made by the authors of this sourcebook in another book, *Helping Relationships: Basic Concepts for the Helping Professions,* and they believe that it is an important one. An unwarranted distinction is often made between one kind of helping and another with regard to the type of variables, goals, and processes involved as, for example, between teaching and counseling. Because they are regarded as quite different functions, counselors and teachers often misunderstand each other; as a consequence both tasks may fail. But all helping relationships are learning situations, and this common element must be understood as the basis for the design of effective practice in whatever form the helping process may be used.

A second major theme is presented by Carkhuff and Truax, who point out that it is not the manipulation of methods and techniques that is important for success but the nature of the relationship established. Some studies of therapeutic outcomes have suggested that people who didn't engage in some form of therapy improved quite as well as those who did. Carkhuff and Truax suggest that this discouraging result occurs because researchers only recorded the fact that a therapeutic relationship had taken place, and ignored the much more important question of the character and quality of the relationship. Rogers, Carkhuff, and Truax also discuss some of the interpersonal attitudinal factors which can determine the success or failure of a helping relationship.

Most helping relationships are temporary and terminal. Their purpose is not to support and sustain a person throughout his life, as is a drug such as insulin. Rather, their purpose is to begin a growth process that will assist a person toward eventually solving his own problems successfully without help. In his article "Fostering Self-Direction," Dr. Combs deals with this major goal of all helping processes. He suggests some things helpers must do if they are to contribute to the development of self-sufficient human beings.

Dr. Roethlisberger focuses on the question of communication, the *sine qua non* of any human relationship. His main contention is that communication often fails because most people are poor listeners—a point which he illustrates most effectively in his paper.

The last four papers in Part III are concerned with the process of helping as well as with the helper himself. They ask the reader to analyze his own behavior as a helper. They look at what a helper should be as well as what he should not be.

Dr. Purkey directs his attention to some positive qualities of a good helper. He points out that one of the most important aspects of being a good helper has to do with what one thinks of himself as a person and a professional worker. Dr. Lawton's paper points out some common mistakes a helper can make in attempting to satisfy his own needs. Not unlike Dr. Purkey, he makes it clear that helpers must know themselves as well as their clients lest, unwittingly, they satisfy their own needs while sabotaging their clients.

Dr. Aspy, in a short but poignant paper, brings us sharply face to face with a human failing of which we have all been guilty and which would be a particularly devastating characteristic for helpers to possess. "How did he get there?" is a striking portrait of personal envy.

For some years, Dr. Arthur Combs has supervised a series of studies at the University of Florida designed to discover the personal characteristics of good and poor helpers. In this paper he reports the findings from some of this research. The results of these studies are interesting, but the overall conclusion that Dr. Combs and his colleagues reach is even more so. For many years, programs for training helpers have concentrated on techniques and methods presumed necessary for the development of successful practitioners. Education has been searching for the perfect teaching style, ministers have sought for ideal methods, counseling and therapy for effective techniques, and so on. But the Florida studies suggest that techniques, methods, and styles have very little to do with the success or failure of helpers. It appears that a helper's *basic beliefs and values,* rather than his grand schemes, methods, techniques, or years of training are the real determiners of whether or not he will be effective or ineffective as a helper.

The Interpersonal Relationship in the Facilitation of Learning

Carl R. Rogers

> It is in fact nothing short of a miracle that the modern methods of instruction have not yet entirely strangled the holy curiosity of inquiry; for this delicate little plant, aside from stimulation, stands mainly in need of freedom; without this it goes to wrack and ruin without fail.
>
> ALBERT EINSTEIN

I wish to begin this paper with a statement which may seem surprising to some and perhaps offensive to others. It is simply this: Teaching, in my estimation, is a vastly overrated function.

Having made such a statement, I scurry to the dictionary to see if I really mean what I say. Teaching means "to instruct." Personally I am not much interested in instructing another. "To impart knowledge or skill." My reaction is, why not be more efficient, using a book or programmed learning? "To make to know." Here my hackles rise. I have no wish to *make* anyone know something. "To show, guide, direct." As I see it, too many people have been shown, guided, directed. So I come to the conclusion that I *do* mean what I said. Teaching is, for me, a relatively unimportant and vastly overvalued activity.

But there is more in my attitude than this. I have a negative reaction to teaching. Why? I think it is because it raises all the wrong questions. As soon as we focus on teaching, the question arises, what shall we teach? What, from our superior vantage point, does the other person need to know? This raises the ridiculous question of coverage. What shall the course cover? (Here I am acutely aware of the fact that "to cover" means both "to take in" and "to conceal from view," and I believe that most courses admirably achieve both these aims.) This notion of coverage is based on the assumption that what is taught is what is learned; what is presented is what is assimilated. I know of no assumption so obviously untrue. One does not need research to provide evidence that this is false. One needs only to talk with a few students.

But I ask myself, "Am I so prejudiced against teaching that I find no situation in which it is worthwhile?" I immediately think of my experience in Australia only a few months ago. I became much interested in the Australian aborigine. Here is a group which for more than 20,000 years has managed to live and exist in a desolate environment in which a modern man would perish within a few days. The secret of his survival has been teaching. He has passed on to the young every shred of knowledge about how to find water, about how to track game, about how to kill the kangaroo, about how to find his way through the trackless desert. Such knowledge is conveyed to the young as being *the* way to behave, and any innovation is frowned upon. It is clear that teaching has provided him the way to survive in a hostile and relatively unchanging environment.

Now I am closer to the nub of the question which excites me. Teaching and the imparting of knowledge make sense in an unchanging environment. This is why it has been an unquestioned function for centuries. But if there is one truth about modern man, it is that he lives in an environment which is *continually changing*. The one thing I can be sure of is that the physics which is taught to the present day student will be outdated in a decade. The teaching in psychology will certainly be out of date in 20 years. The so-called "facts of history" depend very largely upon the current mood and temper of the culture. Chemistry, biology, genetics, sociology, are in such flux that a firm statement made today will almost certainly be modified by the time the student gets around to using the knowledge.

We are, in my view, faced with an entirely new situation in education where the goal of education, if we are to survive, is the *facilitation of change and learning*. The only man who is educated is the man who has learned how to learn; the man who has learned how to adapt and change; the man who has realized that no knowledge is secure, that only the process of *seeking* knowledge gives a basis for security. Changingness, a reliance on *process* rather than upon static knowledge, is the only thing that makes any sense as a goal for education in the modern world.

So now with some relief I turn to an activity, a purpose, which really warms me—the *facilitation of learning*. When I have been able to transform a group—and here I mean all the members of a group, myself included—into a community of *learners*, then the excitement has been almost beyond belief. To free curiosity; to permit individuals to go charging off in new directions dictated by their own interests; to unleash curiosity; to open everything to questioning and exploration; to recognize that everything is in process of change—here is an experience I can never forget. I cannot always achieve it in groups with which I am associated but when it is partially or largely achieved then it becomes a never-to-be-forgotten group experience. Out of such a context arise true students, real learners, creative scientists and scholars and practitioners, the kind of individuals who can live in a delicate but ever-changing balance between what is presently known and the flowing, moving, altering, problems and facts of the future.

Here then is a goal to which I can give myself wholeheartedly. I see the facilitation of learning as the aim of education, the way in which we might develop the learning man, the way in which we can learn to live as individuals in process. I see the facilitation of learning as the function which may hold constructive, tentative, changing, process answers to some of the deepest perplexities which beset man today.

But do we know how to achieve this new goal in education, or is it a will-of-the-wisp which sometimes occurs, sometimes fails to occur, and thus offers little real hope? My answer is that we possess a very considerable knowledge of the conditions which encourage self-initiated, significant, experiential, "gut-level" learning by the whole person. We do not frequently see these conditions put into effect because they mean a real revolution in our approach to education and revolutions are not for the timid. But we do find examples of this revolution in action.

We know—and I will briefly describe some of the evidence—that the initiation of such learning rests not upon the teaching skills of the leader, not upon his scholarly knowledge of the field, not upon his curricular planning, not upon his use of audio-visual aids, not upon the programmed learning he utilizes, not upon his lectures and presentations, not upon an abundance of books, though each of these might at one time or another be utilized as an important resource. No, the facilitation of significant learning rests upon certain attitudinal qualities which exist in the personal *relationship* between the facilitator and the learner.

We came upon such findings first in the field of psychotherapy, but increasingly there is evidence which shows that these findings apply in the classroom as well. We find it easier to think that the intensive relationship between therapist and client might possess these qualities, but we are also finding that they may exist in the countless interpersonal interactions (as many as 1,000 per day, as Jackson [1966] has shown) between the teacher and his pupils.

What are these qualities, these attitudes, which facilitate learning? Let me describe them very briefly, drawing illustrations from the teaching field.

REALNESS IN THE FACILITATOR OF LEARNING

Perhaps the most basic of these essential attitudes is realness or genuineness. When the facilitator is a real person, being what he is, entering into a relationship with the learner without presenting a front or a facade, he is much more likely to be effective. This means that the feelings which he is experiencing are available to him, available to his awareness, that he is able to live these feelings, be them, and able to communicate them if appropriate. It means that he comes into a direct personal encounter with the learner, meeting him on a person-to-person basis. It means that he is *being* himself, not denying himself.

Seen from this point of view it is suggested that the teacher can be a real person in his relationship with his students. He can be enthusiastic, he can be bored, he can be interested in students, he can be angry, he can be sensitive and sympathetic. Because he accepts these feelings as his own he has no need to impose them on his students. He can like or dislike a student product without implying that it is objectively good or bad or that the student is good or bad. He is simply expressing a feeling for the product, a feeling which exists within himself. Thus, he is a person to his students, not a faceless embodiment of a curricular requirement nor a sterile tube through which knowledge is passed from one generation to the next.

It is obvious that this attitudinal set, found to be effective in psychotherapy, is sharply in contrast with the tendency of most teachers to show themselves to their pupils simply as roles. It is quite customary for teachers rather consciously to put on the mask, the role, the facade, of being a teacher, and to wear this facade all day removing it only when they have left the school at night.

But not all teachers are like this. Take Sylvia Ashton-Warner, who took resistant, supposedly slow-learning primary school Maori children in New Zealand, and let them develop their own reading vocabulary. Each child could request one word—whatever word he wished—each day, and she would print it on a card and give it to him. "Kiss," "ghost," "bomb," "tiger," "fight," "love," "daddy"—these are samples. Soon they were building sentences, which they could also keep. "He'll get a licking." "Pussy's frightened." The children simply never forgot these self-initiated learnings. Yet it is not my purpose to tell you of her methods. I want instead to give you a glimpse of her attitude, of the passionate realness which must have been as evident to her tiny pupils as to her readers. An editor asked her some questions and she responded: " 'A few cool facts' you asked me for. . . . I don't know that there's a cool fact in me, or anything else cool for that matter, on this particular subject. I've got only hot long facts on the matter of Creative Teaching, scorching both the page and me" (Ashton-Warner, 163, p. 26).

Here is no sterile facade. Here is a vital *person,* with convictions, with feelings. It is her transparent realness which was, I am sure, one of the elements that made her an exciting facilitator of learning. She does not fit into some neat educational formula. She *is,* and students grow by being in contact with someone who really *is.*

Take another very different person, Barbara Shiel, also doing exciting work facilitating learning in sixth graders.[1] She gave them a great deal of responsible freedom, and I will mention some of the reactions of her students later. But here is an example of the way she shared herself with her pupils—not just sharing feelings of sweetness and light, but anger and frustration. She had made art materials freely available, and students often used these in creative ways, but the room frequently looked like a picture of chaos. Here is her report of her feelings and what she did with them.

I find it (still) maddening to live with the mess—with a capital M! No one seems to care except me. Finally, one day I told the children . . . that I am a neat, orderly person by nature and that the mess was driving me to distraction. Did they have a solution? It was suggested they could have

1. For a more extended account of Miss Shiel's initial attempts, see Rogers, 1966a. Her later experience is described in Shiel, 1966.

volunteers to clean up. . . . I said it didn't seem fair to me to have the same people clean up all the time for others—but it *would* solve it for me. "Well, some people *like* to clean," they replied. So that's the way it is (Shiel, 1966).

I hope this example puts some lively meaning into the phrases I used earlier, that the facilitator "is able to live these feelings, be them, and able to communicate them if appropriate." I have chosen an example of negative feelings, because I think it is more difficult for most of us to visualize what this would mean. In this instance, Miss Shiel is taking the risk of being transparent in her angry frustrations about the mess. And what happens? The same thing which, in my experience, nearly always happens. These young people accept and respect her feelings, take them into account, and work out a novel solution which none of us, I believe, would have suggested in advance. Miss Shiel wisely comments, "I used to get upset and feel guilty when I became angry—I finally realized the children could accept *my* feelings, too. And it is important for them to know when they've 'pushed me.' I have limits, too" (Shiel, 1966).

Just to show that positive feelings, when they are real, are equally effective, let me quote briefly a college student's reaction, in a different course. ". . . Your sense of humor in the class was cheering; we all felt relaxed because you showed us your human self, not a mechanical teacher image. I feel as if I have more understanding and faith in my teachers now. . . . I feel closer to the students too." Another says, ". . . You conducted the class on a personal level and therefore in my mind I was able to formulate a picture of you as a person and not as merely a walking textbook." Or another student in the same course,

> . . . It wasn't as if there was a teacher in the class, but rather someone whom we could trust and identify as a "sharer." You were so perceptive and sensitive to our thoughts, and this made it all the more "authentic" for me. It was an "authentic" *experience,* not just a class (Bull, 1966).

I trust I am making it clear that to be real is not always easy, nor is it achieved all at once, but it is basic to the person who wants to become that revolutionary individual, a facilitator of learning.

PRIZING, ACCEPTANCE, TRUST

There is another attitude which stands out in those who are successful in facilitating learning. I have observed this attitude. I have experienced it.

Yet, it is hard to know what term to put to it so I shall use several. I think of it as prizing the learner, prizing his feelings, his opinions, his person. It is a caring for the learner, but a non-possessive caring. It is an acceptance of this other individual as a separate person, having worth in his own right. It is a basic trust—a belief that this other person is somehow fundamentally trustworthy.

Whether we call it prizing, acceptance, trust, or by some other term, it shows up in a variety of observable ways. The facilitator who has a considerable degree of this attitude can be fully acceptant of the fear and hesitation of the student as he approaches a new problem as well as acceptant of the pupil's satisfaction in achievement. Such a teacher can accept the student's occasional apathy, his erratic desires to explore by-roads of knowledge, as well as his disciplined efforts to achieve major goals. He can accept personal feelings which both disturb and promote learning—rivalry with a sibling, hatred of authority, concern about personal adequacy. What we are describing is a prizing of the learner as an imperfect human being with many feelings, many potentialities. The facilitator's prizing or acceptance of the learner is an operational expression of his essential confidence and trust in the capacity of the human organism.

I would like to give some examples of this attitude from the classroom situation. Here any teacher statements would be properly suspect, since many of us would like to feel we hold such attitudes, and might have a biased perception of our qualities. But let me indicate how this attitude of prizing, of accepting, of trusting, appears to the student who is fortunate enough to experience it.

Here is a statement from a college student in a class with Morey Appell.

> Your way of being with us is a revelation to me. In your class I feel important, mature, and capable of doing things on my own. I want to think for myself and this need cannot be accomplished through textbooks and lectures alone, but through living. I think you see me as a person with real feelings and needs, an individual. What I say and do are significant expressions from me, and you recognize this (Appell, 1959).

One of Miss Shiel's sixth graders expresses much more briefly her misspelled appreciation of this attitude, "You are a wounderful teacher period!!!"

College students in a class with Dr. Patricia Bull describe not only these prizing, trusting attitudes, but the effect these have had on their other interactions.

> . . . I feel that I can say things to you that I can't say to other professors . . . Never before have I been so aware of the other students or their personalities. I have never had so much interaction in a college classroom with my classmates. The climate of the classroom has had a very profound effect on me . . . the free atmosphere for discussion affected me . . . the general atmosphere of a particular session affected me. There have been many times when I have carried the discussion out of the class with me and thought about it for a long time.
>
> . . . I still feel close to you, as though there were some tacit understanding between us, almost a conspiracy. This adds to the in-class participation on my part because I feel that at least one person in the group will react, even when I am not sure of the others. It does not matter really whether your reaction is positive or negative, it just *is*. Thank you.
>
> . . . I appreciate the respect and concern you have for others, including myself. . . . As a result of my experience in class, plus the influence of my readings, I sincerely believe that the student-centered teaching method does provide an ideal framework for learning; not just for the accumulation of facts, but more important, for learning about ourselves in relation to others. . . . When I think back to my shallow awareness in September compared to the depth of my insights now, I know that this course has offered me a learning experience of great value which I couldn't have acquired in any other way.
>
> . . . Very few teachers would attempt this method because they would feel that they would lose the students' respect. On the contrary. You gained our respect, through your ability to speak to us on our level, instead of ten miles above us. With the complete lack of communication we see in this school, it was a wonderful experience to see people listening to each other and really communicating on an adult, intelligent level. More classes should afford us this experience (Bull, 1966).

As you might expect, college students are often suspicious that these seeming attitudes are phony. One of Dr. Bull's students writes:

> . . . Rather than observe my classmates for the first few weeks, I concentrated my observations on you, Dr. Bull. I tried to figure out your motivations and purposes. I was convinced that you were a hypocrite. . . . I did change my opinion, however. You are not a hypocrite, by any means. . . . I do wish the course could continue. "Let each become all he is capable of being." . . . Perhaps my most disturbing question, which relates to this course is: When will we stop hiding things from ourselves and our contemporaries? (Bull, 1966).

I am sure these examples are more than enough to show that the facilitator who cares, who prizes, who trusts the learner, creates a climate for learning so different from the ordinary classroom that any resemblance is, as they say, "purely coincidental."

EMPATHIC UNDERSTANDING

A further element which establishes a climate for self-initiated, experiential learning is emphatic understanding. When the teacher has the abilty to understand the student's reactions from the inside, has a sensitive awareness of the way the process of education and learning seems *to the student,* then again the likelihood of significant learning is increased.

This kind of understanding is sharply different from the usual evaluative understanding, which follows the pattern of, "I understand what is wrong with you." When there is a sensitive empathy, however, the reaction in the learner follows something of this pattern, "At last someone understands how it feels and seems to be *me* without wanting to analyze me or judge me. Now I can blossom and grow and learn."

This attitude of standing in the other's shoes, of viewing the world through the student's eyes, is almost unheard of in the classroom. One could listen to thousands of ordinary classroom interactions without coming across one instance of clearly communicated, sensitively accurate, empathic understanding. But it has a tremendously releasing effect when it occurs.

Let me take an illustration from Virginia Axline, dealing with a second grade boy. Jay, age 7, has been aggressive, a trouble maker, slow of speech and learning. Because of his "cussing" he was taken to the principal, who paddled him, unknown to Miss Axline. During a free work period, he fashioned a man of clay, very carefully, down to a hat and a handkerchief in his pocket. "Who is that?" asked Miss Axline. "Dunno," replied Jay. "Maybe it is the principal. He has a handkerchief in his pocket like that." Jay glared at the clay figure. "Yes," he said. Then he began to tear the head off and looked up and smiled. Miss Axline said, "You sometimes feel like twisting his head off, don't you? You get so mad at him." Jay tore off one arm, another, then beat the figure to a pulp with his fists. Another boy, with the perception of the young, explained, "Jay is mad at Mr. X because he licked him this noon." "Then you must feel lots better now," Miss Axline commented. Jay grinned and began to rebuild Mr. X. (Adapted from Axline, 1944.)

The other examples I have cited also indicate how deeply appreciative students feel when they are simply *understood*—not evaluated, not judged, simply understood from their *own* point of view, not the teacher's. If any teacher set herself the task of endeavoring to make one nonevaluative, acceptant, empathic response per day to a pupil's demonstrated or verbalized feeling, I believe he would discover the potency of this currently almost nonexistent kind of understanding.

Let me wind up this portion of my remarks by saying that when a facilitator creates, even to a modest degree, a classroom climate characterized by such realness, prizing, and empathy, he discovers that he has inaugurated an educational revolution. Learning of a different quality, proceeding at a different pace, with a greater degree of pervasiveness, occurs. Feelings—positive and negative, confused—become a part of the classroom experience. Learning becomes life, and a very vital life at that. The student is on his way, sometimes excitedly, sometimes reluctantly, to becoming a learning, changing being.

THE EVIDENCE

Already I can hear the mutterings of some of my so-called "hard-headed" colleagues. "A very pretty picture—very touching. But these are all self reports." (As if there were any other type of expression! But that's another issue.) They ask, "Where is the evidence? How do you know?" I would like to turn to this evidence. It is not overwhelming, but it is consistent. It is not perfect, but it is suggestive.

First of all, in the field of psychotherapy, Barrett-Lennard (1962) developed an instrument whereby he could measure these attitudinal qualities: genuineness or congruence, prizing or positive regard, empathy or understanding. This instrument was given to both client and therapist, so that we have the perception of the relationship both by the therapist and by the client whom he is trying to help. To state some of the findings very briefly it may be said that those clients who eventually showed more therapeutic change as measured by various instruments, perceived *more* of these qualities in their relationship with the therapist than did those who eventually showed less change. It is also significant that this difference in perceived relationships was evident as early as the fifth interview, and predicted later change or lack of change in therapy. Furthermore, it was found that the *client's* perception of the relationship, his experience of it, was a better predictor of ultimate outcome than was the perception of the relationship by the therapist. Barrett-Lennard's original study has been amplified and generally confirmed by other studies.

So we may say, cautiously, and with qualifications which would be too cumbersome for the present paper, that if, in therapy, the client perceives his therapist as real and genuine, as one who likes, prizes, and empathically understands him, self-learning and therapeutic change are facilitated.

Now another thread of evidence, this time related more closely to education. Emmerling (1961) found that when high school teachers were asked to identify the problems they regarded as most urgent, they could be divided into two groups. Those who regarded their most serious problems, for example, as "Helping children think for themselves and be independent"; "Getting students to participate"; "Learning new ways of helping students develop their maximum potential"; "Helping students express individual needs and interests"; fell into what he called the "open" or "positively oriented" group. When Barrett-Lennard's Relationship Inventory was administered to the students of these teachers, it was found that they were perceived as significantly more real, more acceptant, more empathic than the other group of teachers whom I shall now describe.

The second category of teachers were those who tended to see their most urgent problems in negative terms, and in terms of student deficiencies and inabilities. For them the urgent problems were such as these: "Trying to teach children who don't even have the ability to follow directions"; "Teaching children who lack a desire to learn"; "Students who are not able to do the work required for their grade"; "Getting the children to listen." It probably will be no surprise that when the students of these teachers filled out the Relationship Inventory they saw their teachers as exhibiting relatively little of genuineness, of acceptance and trust, or of empathic understanding.

Hence we may say that the teacher whose orientation is toward releasing the student's potential exhibits a high degree of these attitudinal qualities which facilitate learning. The teacher whose orientation is toward the shortcomings of his students exhibits much less of these qualities.

A small pilot study by Bills (1961, 1966) extends the significance of these findings. A group of eight teachers was selected, four of them rated as adequate and effective by their superiors, and also showing this more positive orientation to their problems. The other four were rated as inadequate teachers and also had a more negative orientation to their problems, as described above. The students of these teachers were then asked to fill out the Barrett-Lennard Relationship Inventory, giving their perception of their teacher's relationship to them. This made the students very happy. Those who saw their relationship with the teacher as good were happy to describe this relationship. Those who had an unfavorable relationship were pleased to have, for the first time, an opportunity to specify the ways in which the relationship was unsatisfactory.

The more effective teachers were rated higher in every attitude measured by the Inventory: they were seen as more real, as having a higher level of regard for their students, were less conditional or judgmental in their attitudes, showed more empathic understanding. Without going into the details of the study it may be illuminating to mention that the total scores summing these attitudes vary sharply. For example, the relationships of a group of clients with their therapists, as perceived by the clients, received an average score of 108. The four most adequate high school teachers as seen by their students, received a score of 60. The four less adequate teachers received a score of 34. The lowest rated teacher received an average score of 2 from her students on the Relationship Inventory.

This small study certainly suggests that the teacher regarded as effective displays in her attitutes those qualities I have described as facilitative of learning, while the inadequate teacher shows little of these qualities.

Approaching the problem from a different angle, Schmuck (1963) has shown that in classrooms where pupils perceive their teachers as understanding them, there is likely to be a more diffuse liking structure among the pupils. This means that where the teacher is empathic, there are not a few students strongly liked and a few strongly disliked, but liking and affection are more evenly diffused throughout the group. In a later study he has shown that among students who are highly involved in their classroom peer group, "significant relationships exist between actual liking status on the one hand and utilization of abilities, attitude toward self, and attitude toward school on the other hand" (1966, p. 357–58). This seems to lend confirmation to the other evidence by indicating that in an understanding classroom climate every student tends to feel liked by all the others, to have a more positive attitude toward himself and toward school. If he is highly involved with his peer group (and this appears probable in such a classroom climate), he also tends to utilize his abilities more fully in his school achievement.

But you may still ask, does the student actually *learn* more where these attitudes are present? Here an interesting study of third graders by

Aspy (1965) helps to round out the suggestive evidence. He worked in six third-grade classes. The teachers tape-recorded two full weeks of their interaction with their students in the periods devoted to the teaching of reading. These recordings were done two months apart so as to obtain an adequate sampling of the teacher's interactions with her pupils. Four-minute segments of these recordings were randomly selected for rating. Three raters, working independently and "blind," rated each segment for the degree of congruence or genuineness shown by the teacher, the degree of her prizing or unconditional positive regard, and the degree of her empathic understanding.

The Reading Achievement Tests (Stanford Achievement) were used as the criterion. Again, omitting some of the details of a carefully and rigorously controlled study, it may be said that the children in the three classes with the highest degree of the attitudes described above showed a significantly greater gain in reading achievement than those students in the three classes with a lesser degree of these qualities.

So we may say, with a certain degree of assurance, that the attitudes I have endeavored to describe are not only effective in facilitating a deeper learning and understanding of self in a relationship such as psychotherapy, but that these attitudes characterize teachers who are regarded as effective teachers, and that the students of these teachers learn more, even of a conventional curriculum, than do students of teachers who are lacking in these attitudes.

I am pleased that such evidence is accumulating. It may help to justify the revolution in education for which I am obviously hoping. But the most striking learnings of students exposed to such a climate are by no means restricted to greater achievement in the three R's. The significant learnings are the more personal ones—independence, self-initiated and responsible learning; release of creativity, a tendency to become more of a person. I can only illustrate this by picking, almost at random, statements from students whose teachers have endeavored to create a climate of trust, of prizing, of realness, of understanding, and above all, of freedom.

Again I must quote from Sylvia Ashton-Warner one of the central effects of such a climate.

> . . . The drive is no longer the teacher's, but the children's own. . . . The teacher is at last with the stream and not against it, the stream of children's inexorable creativeness (Ashton-Warner, p. 93).

If you need verification of this, listen to a few of Dr. Bull's sophomore students. The first two are mid-semester comments.

. . . This course is proving to be a vital and profound experience for me. . . . This unique learning situation is giving me a whole new conception of just what learning is. . . . I am experiencing a real growth in this atmosphere of constructive freedom. . . . The whole experience is very challenging. . . .

. . . I feel that the course has been of great value to me. . . . I'm glad to have had this experience because it has made me think. . . . I've never been so personally involved with a course before, especially *outside* the classroom. It's been frustrating, rewarding, enjoyable and tiring!

The other comments are from the end of the course.

. . . This course is not ending with the close of the semester for me, but continuing. . . . I don't know of any greater benefit which can be gained from a course than this desire for further knowledge. . . .

. . . I feel as though this type of class situation has stimulated me more in making me realize where my responsibilities lie, especially as far as doing required work on my own. I no longer feel as though a test date is the criterion for reading a book. I feel as though my future work will be done for what *I* will get out of it, not just for a test mark.

. . . I have enjoyed the experience of being in this course. I guess that any dissatisfaction I feel at this point is a disappointment in myself, for not having taken full advantage of the opportunities the course offered.

. . . I think that now I am acutely aware of the breakdown in communications that does exist in our society from seeing what happened in our class. . . . I've grown immensely. I know that I am a different person than I was when I came into that class. . . . It has done a great deal in helping me understand myself better. . . . Thank you for contributing to my growth.

. . . My idea of education has been to gain information from the teacher by attending lectures. The emphasis and focus were on the teacher. . . . One of the biggest changes that I experienced in this class was my outlook on education. Learning is something more than a grade on a report card. No one can measure what you have learned because it's a personal thing. I was very confused between learning and memorization. I could memorize very well, but I doubt if I ever learned as much as I could have. I believe my attitude toward learning has changed from a grade-centered outlook to a more personal one.

. . . I have learned a lot more about myself and adolescents in general. . . . I also gained more confidence in myself and my study habits by realizing that I could learn by myself without a teacher leading me by the hand. I have also learned a lot by listening to my classmates and evaluating their opinions and thoughts. . . . This course has proved to be a most meaningful and worthwhile experience. . . . (Bull, 1966).

If you wish to know what this type of course seems like to a sixth grader, let me give you a sampling of the reactions of Miss Shiel's youngsters, misspellings and all.

. . . I feel that I am learning self abilty. I am learning not only school work but I am learning that you can learn on your own as well as someone can teach you.

. . . I have a little trouble in Socail Studies finding things to do. I have a hard time working the exact amount of time. Sometimes I talk to much.

. . . My parents don't understand the program. My mother say's it will give me a responsibility and it will let me go at my own speed.

. . . I like this plan because thire is a lot of freedom. I also learn more this way than the other way you don't have to wate for others you can go at your on speed rate it also takes a lot of responsibility (Shiel, 1966).

Or let me take two more, from Dr. Appell's graduate class.

. . . I have been thinking about what happened through this experience. The only conclusion I come to is that if I try to measure what is going on, or what I was at the beginning, I have got to know what I was when I started—and I don't. . . . So many things I did and feel are just lost . . . scrambled up inside. . . . They don't seem to come out in a nice little pattern or organization I can say or write. . . . There are so many things left unsaid. I know I have only scratched the surface, I guess. I can feel so many things almost ready to come out . . . maybe that's enough. *It seems all kinds of things have so much more meaning now than ever before.* . . . This experience has had meaning, has done things to me and I am not sure how much or how far just yet. I think I am going to be a better me in the fall. *That's one thing I think I am sure of* (Appell, 1963).

. . . You follow no plan, yet I'm learning. Since the term began I seem to feel more alive, more real to myself. I enjoy being alone as well as with other people. My relationships with children and other adults are becoming more emotional and involved. Eating an orange last week, I peeled the skin off each separate orange section and liked it better with the transparent shell off. It was jucier and fresher tasting that way. I began to think, that's how I feel sometimes, without a transparent wall around me, really communicating my feelings. I feel that I'm growing, how much, I don't know. I'm thinking, considering, pondering and learning (Appell, 1959).

I can't read these student statements—6th grade, college, graduate level—without my eyes growing moist. Here are teachers, risking themselves, *being* themselves, *trusting* their students, adventuring into the existential unknown, taking the subjective leap. And what happens? Exciting, incredible *human* events. You can sense persons being created, learnings being initiated, future citizens rising to meet the challenge of unknown worlds. If only one teacher out of one hundred dared to risk, dared to be, dared to trust, dared to understand, we would have an infusion of a living spirit into education which would, in my estimation, be priceless.

I have heard scientists at leading schools of science, and scholars in leading universities, arguing that it is absurd to try to encourage all students to be creative—we need hosts of mediocre technicians and workers and if a few creative scientists and artists and leaders emerge, that will be enough. That may be enough for them. It may be enough to suit you. I want to go on record as saying it is *not* enough to suit me. When I realize the incredible potential in the ordinary student, I want to try to release it. We are working hard to release the incredible energy in the atom and the nucleus of the atom. If we do not devote equal energy— yes, and equal money—to the release of the potential of the individual person, then the enormous discrepancy between our level of physical energy resources and human energy resources will doom us to a deserved and universal destruction.

I'm sorry I can't be coolly scientific about this. The issue is too urgent. I can only be passionate in my statement that people count, that interpersonal relationships *are* important, that we know something about releasing human potential, that we could learn much more, and that unless we give strong positive attention to the human interpersonal side of our educational dilemma, our civilization is on its way down the drain. Better courses, better curricula, better coverage, better teaching machines, will never resolve our dilemma in a basic way. Only persons, acting like persons in their relationships with their students can even begin to make a dent on this most urgent problem of modern education.

I cannot, of course, stop here in a professional lecture. An academic lecture should be calm, factual, scholarly, critical, preferably devoid of any personal beliefs, completely devoid of passion. (This is one of the reasons I left university life, but that is a completely different story.) I cannot fully fulfill these requirements for a professional lecture, but let me at least try to state, somewhat more calmly and soberly, what I have said with such feeling and passion.

I have said that it is most unfortunate that educators and the public think about, and focus on, *teaching*. It leads them into a host of questions which are either irrelevant or absurd so far as real education is concerned.

I have said that if we focused on the facilitation of *learning*—how, why, and when the student learns, and how learning seems and feels from the inside, we might be on a much more profitable track.

I have said that we have some knowledge, and could gain more, about the conditions which facilitate learning, and that one of the most important of these conditions is the attitudinal quality of the interpersonal relationship between faciltator and learner. (There are other conditions, too, which I have tried to spell out elsewhere [Rogers, 1966b]).

Those attitudes which appear effective in promoting learning can be described. First of all is a transparent realness in the facilitator, a willingness to be a person, to be and to live the feelings and thoughts of the moment. When this realness includes a prizing, a caring, a trust and respect for the learner, the climate for learning is enhanced. When it includes a sensitive and accurate empathic listening, then indeed a freeing climate, stimulative of self-initiated learning and growth, exists.

I have tried to make plain that individuals who hold such attitudes, and are bold enough to act on them, do not simply modify classroom methods—they revolutionize them. They perform almost none of the functions of teachers. It is no longer accurate to call them teachers. They are catalyzers, facilitators, giving freedom and life and the opportunity to learn, to students.

I have brought in the cumulating research evidence which suggests that individuals who hold such attitudes are regarded as effective in the classroom; that the problems which concern them have to do with the release of potential, not the deficiencies of their students; that they seem to create classroom situations in which there are not admired children and disliked children, but in which affection and liking are a part of the life of every child; that in classrooms approaching such a psychological climate, children learn more of the conventional subjects.

But I have intentionally gone beyond the empirical findings to try to take you into the inner life of the student—elementary, college, and graduate—who is fortunate enough to live and learn in such an interpersonal relationship with a facilitator, in order to let you see what learning feels like when it is free, self-initiated and spontaneous. I have tried to indicate how it even changes the student-student relationship—making it more aware, more caring, more sensitive, as well as increasing the self-related learning of significant material.

Throughout my paper I have tried to indicate that if we are to have citizens who can live constructively in this kaleidoscopically changing world, we can *only* have them if we are willing for them to become self-starting, self-initiating learners. Finally, it has been my purpose to show that this kind of learner develops best, so far as we now know, in a growth-promoting, facilitative, relationship with a *person*.

Appell, M. L. Selected student reactions to student-centered courses. Mimeographed manuscript, 1959.

Appell, M. L. Self-understanding for the guidance counselor. *Personnel and Guidance Journal,* October 1963, **42**(2), 143–148.

Ashton-Warner, S. *Teacher.* New York: Simon and Schuster, 1963.

Aspy, D. N. A study of three facilitative conditions and their relationship to the achievement of third grade students. Unpublished Ed.D. dissertation, University of Kentucky, 1965.

Axline, Virginia M. Morale on the school front. *Journal of Educational Research,* 1944, **38**, 521–533.

Barrett-Lennard, G. T. Dimensions of therapist response as causal factors in therapeutic change. *Psychological Monographs,* **76**, (562), 1962.

Bills, R. E. Personal correspondence, 1961, 1966.

Bull, Patricia. Student reactions, Fall 1965. State University College, Cortland, New York. Mimeographed manuscripts, 1966.

Emmerling, F. C. A study of the relationships between personality characteristics of classroom teachers and pupil perceptions. Unpublished Ph.D. dissertation, Auburn University, Auburn, Ala., 1961.

Jackson, P. W. The student's world. University of Chicago. Mimeographed, 1966.

Rogers, C. R. To facilitate learning. In Malcolm Provus (Ed.), NEA Handbook for Teachers, *Innovations for time to teach.* Washington, D.C.: Department of Classroom Teachers, NEA, 1966a.

Rogers, C. R. The facilitation of significant learning. In L. Siegel (Ed.), *Contemporary theories of instruction.* San Francisco, Calif.: Chandler, 1966b.

Schmuck, R. Some aspects of classroom social climate. *Psychology in the Schools,* 1966, **3**, 59–65.

Schmuck, R. Some relationships of peer liking patterns in the classroom to pupil attitudes and achievement. *The School Review,* 1963, **71**, 337–359.

Shiel, Barbara J. Evaluation: A self-directed curriculum, 1965. Mimeographed, 1966.

Toward Explaining Success and Failure in Interpersonal Learning Experiences

Robert R. Carkhuff / Charles B. Truax

A decade ago Eysenck (1952) and Levitt (1957) drew and substantiated conclusions that the helping professions were not effective in producing improvement in their clients at all developmental levels. A careful review of carefully controlled research exploring the efficacy of various therapeutic, counseling, and guidance activities established no significant average differences in the outcome indices of persons who were treated and persons who were not treated. In spite of the fact that so many have devoted so much in the anticipation of positive change, this challenge has gone unanswered for years. That such a challenge has not been specifically leveled at parents and teachers, coaches, ministers and personnel workers is attributable not to the absence of this same interpersonal phenomenon in those spheres, but rather to the absence of any substantial body of research investigating the outcome criteria of these relationships.

A RESPONSE TO THE CHALLENGE

The findings from a program of intensive research with hospitalized schizophrenics (Rogers, 1962; Truax, 1963; Truax & Carkhuff, 1964) found similarly: no overall *average* differences between patients receiving more traditional forms of counseling and psychotherapy and matched control patients; however, and this is an important "however," the patients receiving counseling and psychotherapy showed significantly greater variability on a variety of change criteria at the conclusion of the thera-

Reprinted from *Personnel and Guidance Journal,* 1966, 723–728, by permission of the authors and the American Personnel and Guidance Association.

peutic process than did the controls. More therapy patients demonstrated positive behavioral change and more demonstrated negative behavioral change than did control patients who received no therapy.

A view of the chronically mentally ill patient as the deteriorated consequence of a progression of particular kinds of relationships dictates that we trace back along his developmental path in an attempt to explicate the interpersonal processes contributing to his negative change— an outcome certainly unintended by the number of people interested in facilitating his positive development and learning. Studies of the effects of counseling and psychotherapy with outpatient, neurotic-type populations have yielded data of startling consistency to that of the research with schizophrenics (Barron & Leary, 1955; Bergin, 1963; Cartwright & Vogel, 1960): (a) there are no overall outcome differences between "traditionally" treated groups and their controls; (b) the patients receiving counseling and psychotherapy show significantly greater variability on change indices at the conclusion of the processes than did the controls. Thus, encounters in counseling and psychotherapy with less disturbed clients may also have a positive or negative outcome on indices of behavioral change. Some clients appear to improve and some appear to deteriorate.

We might have expected similar findings in other studies but most often such analyses were not conducted. Eysenck (1960) based some of his later and stronger conclusions upon such research as the extremely well-designed study of 325 potentially delinquent boys and their controls over approximately a 10-year period (Powers & Witmer, 1961; Teuber & Powers, 1953). Forms of supervised treatment varying from a "big-brother" approach, in which the case-worker *attempted* to be a warm, interested friend who offered the youths a positive model, to the more traditional psychotherapeutic approaches yielded no significant differences.

Even here, while the project was neither designed nor the data analyzed in such a way as to provide the necessary information, one critical, if not systematic, finding emerged: certain caseworkers tended to form less effective relationships with the youths in terms of the intended goals, i.e., keeping the potential delinquents out of court and jail; other caseworkers tended to form more effective relationships in achieving the goals of the project. The inference may be drawn, then, that the variety of therapeutic approaches as implemented by the individual caseworkers might have been facilitative or retarding. Here the evidence, while more sparse, is supportive of the thesis presented. Mink and Isaksen (1959), working with nearly 100 junior high school students who were divided into a group receiving guidance and a group receiving no guidance, found no significant differences in adjustment outcome. Further, the students' actions taken as a result of guidance counseling of both the more traditionally clinical and the nondirective variety did not differ from those not counseled. However, again the variability on the change indices was significantly greater for the counseled group than for the noncounseled group, that is, significantly more improvement as well as regression in social adjustment was in evidence in the treated groups. Thus, the findings seem to support the suggestion that even with shorter-term guidance counseling with a younger, relatively non-pathological population, the interpersonal encounter may have a positive or a negative impact.

In general, then, the relevant findings seem to offer an explanation for the puzzling mass of data already existing concerning the overall lack of efficacy of the "helping" relationship. Together these studies suggest one very consoling and one very distressing message to those of us who have dedicated our lives to "helping" others. First, *we have an impact!* Second, the findings force us to take a long, hard view at this impact for clearly the impact may be in a constructive or deteriorative direction. *Counseling may be "for better or for worse"!*

Thus, at a variety of different developmental stages we find that "helping" relationships may be facilitative or deteriorative. The problem then becomes one of looking at outcome and then tracing back through the process (and this makes out a case for some form of the all-too-often neglected recording of the process) in an attempt to explicate those process variables that facilitate positive movement and those that inhibit this goal or even contribute to individual deterioration. "How can we incorporate the multitude of potentially significant variables into one meaningful system?" becomes a critical question to which we must address ourselves.

SOME DIMENSIONS ARE DISCERNED

In spite of the bewildering array of theories and practice in counseling and psychotherapy, there have been many recurring themes. Psychoanalytic, client-centered, and various eclectic theorists alike have emphasized: (a) the importance of the counselor's ability to sensitively and accurately understand the patient in such a manner as to communicate this deep understanding; (b) the importance of non-possessive warmth and acceptance of the client by the counselor; (c) the necessity for the counselor to be integrated, mature, and genuine within the counseling encounter. These three elements of the counseling relationship are aspects of the counselor's behavior that cut across the more parochial theories of effective "helping" processes and appear to be common elements in a wide variety of interpersonal approaches.

When rating scales of adequate reliability were used with hospitalized schizophrenic patients (Rogers, 1962; Truax, 1961; Truax, 1963; Truax & Carkhuff, 1964) to divide them according to the level of these conditions provided by the therapists of differing orientations, patients receiving high levels of empathy, positive regard and genuineness demonstrated significant process movement and constructive personality and behavioral change. Patients who received low therapeutic conditions did not become engaged in positive therapeutic process movement and actually deteriorated on the outcome criteria. The very significant and exciting counseling outcomes experienced by chronic hospitalized mental patients when they interacted with hospital attendants trained only in operationalizing the dimensions of empathy, positive regard, and genuineness in the counseling encounter (Carkhuff & Truax, 1965 a; b) provide an additional source of supportive evidence. Thus, even in the case of the severely regressed schizophrenic, the presence or absence of certain relationship variables may act to facilitate or retard the learning or relearning process.

Such is also the case with less pathological populations. Working with neurotic-type populations, Bergin and Soloman (1963) at Teachers College found evidence that accurate empathic understanding was significantly related to predominantly psychoanalytically trained therapists' efficacy. An analysis of substantial samples of a number of recorded counseling cases from the University of Chicago and Stanford University indicated that accurate empathy ratings were significantly higher for the more successful than for the less successful cases (Traux, 1963). In addition, the works of Halkides (1958) and Barrett-Lennard (1962) have strongly supported the relevance of the counselor characteristics of empathy, warmth, and genuineness for success with counseling center cases. Further, in the aforementioned Cambridge-Somerville study (Powers & Witmer, 1961; Teuber & Powers, 1953), the results of which were not analyzed very systematically for our present purposes, it was found that ineffectual relationships between the caseworker and the delinquents were characterized by such factors as "mutual misinterpretation" which continued throughout the case. Thus, increasing evidence has established the efficacy of the facilitative conditions for a variety of populations in a variety of different settings such as Wisconsin, New York, Kentucky, Massachusetts, Illinois, and California.

SOME GENERALIZATIONS ARE MADE

The findings that certain counselor-offered conditions are related to the likelihood of progress or retardation has direct relevance to teacher-student and parent-child relationships. If the current evidence is reliable and a lack of such elements as empathy, warmth, and genuineness tends to impede or retard positive movement, while the presence of higher levels of these conditions lead to constructive gain, then the model for interpersonal processes may be a reversible one: the model can be used to predict positive movement and gain as well as to predict negative movement or deterioration. The absence or low levels of facilitative conditions in relationships with parents, teachers, and other significant figures in all likelihood contributes to the development of the difficulty or psychopathology in the first place. It makes sense that counselors offering a continuation of these same conditions will continue to produce further deterioration.

There is today a growing body of literature directly supportive of the presence of related conditions in teacher-student relationships. (Davitz, 1964; Isaacson, McKeachie, & Milholland, 1963; Pace & Stern, 1958; Thistlewaite, 1959). It is significant, for example, that Willis (1961), in *The Guinea Pigs after 20 Years,* points out that the value of the secondary school program most frequently and spontaneously mentioned by graduates 20 years later was the "warmth and human atmosphere" communicated by the school teachers and administrators, i.e., "the friendly relations of the students with each other and with the teachers; the homelike feeling of the school; the school was living as well as learning; there was freedom, but the abuse of freedom was handled in a firm but friendly manner, the classes were small, the atmosphere informal. . . ." The next two categories spontaneously emitted included "learning as a process of discovery (perhaps highly related to the process of exploration and counseling and therapy)" and the genuine concern of the school teachers and administrators for the individuals.

At the primary and preschool level there is additional evidence for the effectiveness of high levels of facilitative conditions and the ineffectiveness resultant from the absence or low levels of these conditions. In a more rigorous study of the school setting, extensive support was found for the role of the teacher's positive regard and warmth for her students in effective positive changes in the preschool adjustment of the children (Truax, 1960). Partial, yet extremely promising, support was discerned for the relationship between the teacher's empathic understanding of her students and the student's improved adjustment. Even on non-adjustment indices the results are very exciting. Christensen (1960), for example, found the warmth of teachers to be significantly related to the vocabulary and arithmetic achievement of primary grade pupils.

The suggestion here is, then, that those teachers who are facilitative, who "hook" the students in a lifelong learning and growing process involving or leading to self-exploration, self-direction and dependence and self-realization, creativity, democratic living, social sensitivity, and the method of intelligence, and the variety of other goals that have been prescribed by and for our educational system, are not unlike the effective counselors, those who provide the highest levels of these facilitative conditions. This is not to negate the critical nature of knowledgeable and "quality" faculty, although only 10 per cent of the former students designated this category as having been particularly meaningful in terms of their constructive development in Willis' work. (In this regard, the finding by Feifel and Eells [1963] that clients tend to focus on the opportunity to talk over problems and emphasized the "human" characteristics of the counselor while the counselor focused upon the successful implementation of his technique is relevant and stimulating.) A "quality faculty" might instead didactically bring to bear in an alterable form that accumulated knowledge that has proved to be of value in the past in a relationship based upon conditions of genuineness, warmth, and understanding, conditions that elicit the value of a potentially heretic present in the form of the student's openness of his current experiencing and their expression.

Similarly, there is a growing body of evidence in the child-rearing province to suggest that the absence or low levels of these facilitative conditions in the parent-child relationship often seems to lead to the development of problems and/or psychopathology as discerned by our present change indices. An inordinate degree of interpersonal conflict, and lack of warmth, for example, has been found in the homes of schizophrenic patients (Frazee, 1953; Lidz, Cornelison, Fleck, & Terry, 1957); the parent-child relationships have been variously described as ingenuine, distant, stereotyped, defensive, and unsatisfying (Baxter, Becker, & Hooks, 1963; Bowen, 1960; Lidz & Lidz, 1949; Wynne, Ryckoff, Day, & Hirsch, 1958) and the entire family has been described as tending to use styles of communication that are unempathic, inefficient, contradictory and conflict arousing (Bateson, Jackson, Haley, & Weakland, 1956; Weakland, 1960). In addition, the backgrounds of children who display a great amount of social maladjustment (Cass, 1953; Montalto, 1952) and overt hostility (Chorost, 1962) are characterized by higher levels of parental authoritarian control and lower levels of parental warmth and awareness of their needs than is the case with children who are better adjusted socially.

TOWARD FAILURE OR FULFILLMENT?

While the present effort is only a beginning attempt to explicate some of the critical dimensions of interpersonal learning processes, it takes a step toward demonstrating that these interrelationships may indeed facilitate or retard functioning in a variety of areas. Let us turn again for a moment to the severely and chronically (perhaps permanently) disturbed patient. He is the negative consequent of a succession of relationships which have in no way facilitated his efforts. At almost each significant encounter (and each encounter may become more significant for the individual moving in a negative direction) he has demonstrated negative outcome.

Thus, our subject is a failure in life. More importantly, perhaps, he may have been failed. He may have been failed by the numerous significant people who have not provided those conditions that would appear to be conducive to his constructive growth. Indeed he has often been provided with the reverse of facilitative conditions—retarding conditions where the persons involved with him have been almost totally unconcerned or have lacked any real comprehensive understanding of him. He has been failed by his parents, his teachers and his counselors. Such failure, especially by teachers and counselors, may be preventable for, unlike the case with parents, we can say something about who they will be and what they will do.

There may, of course, be variations on this theme. While the evolution of the severely disturbed might include a series of failing relationships, less severely disturbed or moderately distressed may be seen as the consequents of some relationships that have been facilitative and some which have been retarding. Thus, the less severely disturbed individual may be seen as the end product of a succession of deteriorative relationships interrupted by possibly one important facilitative relationship. Similarly, the moderately distressed case may be the result of a number of relationships of varying degrees of facilitation or retardation while the healthy case results from a succession of essentially successful relationships, which significantly outweigh the potentially negative direction which might otherwise be dictated by those important figures offering low condition relationships.

It has yet to be systematically determined which of these relationships are of greatest consequence. It may be that early relationships are most significant and give the basic directionality for life. Then again, it may be that with each failing relationship, the next relationship comes to be more critical. By the time, for example, that the hospitalized patient encounters his therapist it may be that there is no "next relationship" to which to look forward. How critical is the therapist standing before him! Not to be understood at this point is to be doomed to eternal confusion.

The task of further discerning, understanding, operationalizing and implementing facilitative conditions in human encounters looms large before us. The knowledge that all interpersonal processes have the potential for constructive or deteriorative consequences impels us onward to this task.

Barrett-Lennard, G. T. Dimensions of therapist response as causal factors in therapeutic change. *Psychol. Monogr.,* 1962, **76**(43) (Whole No. 562).

Barron, F., & Leary, T. Changes in psychoneurotic patients with and without psychotherapy. *J. Consult. Psychol.,* 1955, **19**, 239–245.

Bateson, G., Jackson, D., Haley, J., & Weakland, J. H. Toward a theory of schizophrenia. *Behav. Sci.,* 1956, **1**, 251–264.

Baxter, J. C., Becker, J., & Hooks, W. Defensive style in the families of schizophrenics and controls. *J. Abnorm. Soc. Psychol.,* 1963, **66**, 512–518.

Bergin, A. E., & Soloman, Sandara. Personality and performance correlates of empathic understanding in psychotherapy. Paper read at American Psychological Association, Philadelphia, September 1963.

Bergin, A. E. The effects of psychotherapy: Negative results revisited. *J. Counsel. Psychol.,* 1963, **10**, 244–250.

Bowen, M. A family concept of schizophrenia. In D. Jackson (Ed.), *The etiology of schizophrenia.* New York: Basic Books, 1960, pp. 346–372.

Carkhuff, R. R., & Truax, C. B. Training in counseling and psychotherapy: An evaluation of an integrated didactic and experiential approach. *J. Consult. Psychol.,* 1965, **29**, 333–336. (a)

Carkhuff, R. R., & Truax, C. B. Lay mental health counseling. *J. Consult. Psychol.*, 1965, **29**, 426–431. (b)

Cartwright, Rosalind D., & Vogel, J. L. A comparison of changes in psychoneurotic patients during matched periods of therapy and no therapy. *J. Consult. Psychol.*, 1960, **24**, 121–127.

Cass, Loretta K. Parent-child relationships and delinquency. *J. Abnorm. Soc. Psychol.*, 1953, **47**, 101–104.

Chorost, S. B. Parent child-rearing attitudes and their correlates in adolescent hostility. *Genet. Psychol. Mongr.*, 1962, **66**(1), 49–90.

Christensen, C. M. Relationships between pupil achievement, pupil affect-need, teacher warmth and teacher permissiveness. *J. Educ. Psychol.*, 1960, **51**, 169–174.

Davitz, J. R. *The communication of emotional meaning.* New York: McGraw-Hill, 1964.

Eysenck, H. J. The effects of psychotherapy: An evaluation. *J. Consult. Psychol.*, 1952, **16**, 319–324.

Eysenck, H. J. *The handbook of abnormal psychology.* New York: Basic Books, 1960.

Feifel, H., & Eells, Janet. Patient and therapist assessed the same psychotherapy. *J. Counsel. Psychol.*, 1963, **27**, 310–318.

Frazee, H. E. Children who later become schizophrenic. *Smith Coll. Stud. Soc. Work.*, 1953, **23**, 125–149.

Halkides, Galatia. An investigation of therapeutic success as a function of four variables. Unpublished doctoral dissertation, University of Chicago, 1958.

Isaacson, R. L., McKeachie, W. J., & Milholland, J. E. A correlation of teacher personality variables and student ratings. *J. Educ. Psychol.*, 1963, **54**, 110–117.

Levitt, E. E. The results of psychotherapy with children: An evaluation. *J. Consult. Psychol.*, 1957, **21**, 189–196.

Lidz, T., Cornelison, Alice, Fleck, S., & Terry, Dorothy. The intrafamilial environment of schizophrenic patients: II. Marital schizm and marital skew. *Amer. J. Psychiat.*, 1957, **114**, 214–248.

Lidz, Ruth W., & Lidz, T. The family environment of schizophrenic patients. *Amer. J. Psychiat.*, 1949, **106**, 332–345.

Mink, O. G., & Isaksen, H. L. A comparison of effectiveness of nondirective therapy and clinical counseling in the junior high school. *Sch. Counselor*, 1959, **6**, 12–14.

Montalto, F. D. Maternal behavior and child personality. *J. Proj. Tech.*, 1952, **16**, 151–178.

Pace, C. R., & Stern, G. G. An approach to the measurement of physiological characteristics of college environment. *J. Educ. Psychol.*, 1958, **49**, 269–277.

Powers, E., & Witmer, Helen. *An experiment in the prevention of delinquency.* New York: Columbia University Press, 1961.

Rogers, C. R. The interpersonal relationship: The core of guidance. *Harv. Rev.,* 1962, **32,** 416–429.

Teuber, H. L., & Powers, E. Evaluating therapy in a delinquency prevention program. *Proceedings of the Assoc. of Res. in Nerv. Ment. Dis.,* 1953, **31,** 138–147.

Thistlewaite, D. L. College press and student achievement. *J. Educ. Psychol.,* 1959, **50,** 183–191.

Truax, C. B. Conditions relevant to constructive personality change in preschool children. Unpublished manuscript, University of Iowa, 1960.

Truax, C. B. The process of group psychotherapy: Relationships between hypothesized therapeutic conditions and intrapersonal exploration. *Psychol. Monogr.,* 1961, **75**(7) (Whole No. 511).

Truax, C. B. Effective ingredients in psychotherapy: An approach to unraveling the patient-therapist interaction. *J. Counsel. Psychol.,* 1963, **10,** 256–263.

Truax, C. B., & Carkhuff, R. R. For better or for worse: The process of psychotherapeutic personality change. Chapter in *Recent advances in the study of behavior change.* Montreal, Canada: McGill University Press, 1964.

Weakland, J. H. The "double-bind" hypothesis of schizophrenia and three-party interaction. In D. Jackson (Ed.), *The etiology of schizophrenia.* New York: Basic Books, 1960.

Willis, Margaret. *The guinea pigs after 20 years.* Columbus, Ohio: Ohio State University Press, 1961.

Wynne, L. C., Ryckoff, J. M., Day, Juliana, & Hirsch, S. J. Pseudomutuality in the family relations of schizophrenics. *Psychiatry,* 1958, **21,** 205–220.

Fostering Self-Direction

Arthur W. Combs

Schools which do not produce self-directed citizens have failed everyone —the student, the profession, and the society they are designed to serve. The goals of modern education cannot be achieved without self-direction. We have created a world in which there is no longer a common body of information which everyone must have. The information explosion has blasted for all time the notion that we can feed all students the same diet. Instead, we have to adopt a cafeteria principle in which we help each student select what he most needs to fulfill his potentialities. This calls for student cooperation and acceptance of major responsibility for his own learning.

As Earl Kelley has suggested, the goal of education in the modern world must be the production of increasing uniqueness. This cannot be achieved in autocratic atmospheres where all decisions are made by the teachers and administration while students are reduced to passive followers of the established patterns. Authoritarian schools are as out of date in the world we live in as the horse and buggy. Such schools cannot hope to achieve our purposes. Worse yet, their existence will almost certainly defeat us.

The world we live in demands self-starting, self-directing citizens capable of independent action. The world is changing so fast we cannot hope to teach each person what he will need to know in twenty years. Our only hope to meet the demands of the future is the production of intelligent, independent people. Even our military establishment, historically the most authoritarian of all, has long since discovered that fact. For twenty years the armed forces have been steadily increasing the de-

Reprinted from *Educational Leadership,* 1966, **23**, 373–387, by permission of the author and the publisher.

gree of responsibility and initiative it expects of even its lowest echelons. The modern war machine cannot be run by automatons. It must be run by *thinking* men.

Much of the curriculum of our current schools is predicated on a concept of learning conceived as the acquisition of right answers and many of our practices mirror this belief. Almost anyone can pick them out. Here are a few which occur to me:

> Preoccupation with right answers; insistence upon conformity; cookbook approaches to learning; overconcern for rules and regulations; preoccupation with materials and things instead of people; the solitary approach to learning; the delusion that mistakes are sinful; emphasis on memory rather than learning; emphasis on grades rather than understanding and content details rather than principles.

Meanwhile, psychologists are telling us that learning is a *personal* matter; individual and unique. It is not controlled by the teacher. It can only be accomplished with the cooperation and involvement of the student in the process. Providing students with information is not enough. People rarely misbehave because they do not know any better. The effectiveness of learning must be measured in behavior change: whether students *behave differently* as a consequence of their learning experience. This requires active participation by the student. So learning itself is dependent upon the capacity for self-direction.

TOWARD SELF–DIRECTION

What is needed of us? How can we produce students who are more self-directed?

1. We Need To Believe This Is Important

If we do not think self-direction is important, this will not get done. People are too pressed these days to pay much attention to things that are not important. Everyone does what seems to him to be crucial and urgent. It seems self-evident that independence and self-direction are necessary for our kind of world. Why then has self-direction been given such inadequate attention? It is strange we should have to convince ourselves of its importance.

Unfortunately, because a matter is self-evident is no guarantee that people will really put it into practice. It must somehow be brought into clear figure in the forefront of our striving if it is to affect behavior. Everyone knows it is important to vote, too, yet millions regularly fail to vote. To be effective as an objective, each of us must hold the goal of self-direction clear in our thinking and high in our values whenever we are engaged in planning or teaching of any kind.

This is often not easy to do because self-direction is one of those goals which *everyone* is supposed to be working for. As a result, almost no one regards it as urgent! For each person, his own special duties are so much clearer, so much more pressing and his derelictions so much more glaring if he fails to produce. The goals we hold in common do not redound so immediately to our credit or discredit. They are therefore set aside while we devote our energies to the things that *really* matter to us.

To begin doing something about self-direction we must, therefore, begin by declaring its importance; not as a lofty sentiment, but as an absolute essential. It must be given a place of greater concern than subject matter itself, for a very simple reason: It is far more important than subject matter. Without self-direction no content matters much. It is not enough that it be published in the handbook as a "Goal of Education." Each of us at every level must ask himself: Do I really think self-direction is important and what am I doing about it?

2. TRUST IN THE HUMAN ORGANISM

Many of us grew up in a tradition which conceived of man as basically evil and certain to revert to bestial ways if someone did not control him. Modern psychologists tell us this view is no longer tenable. From everything we can observe in humans and animals the basic striving of the organism is inexorably toward health both physical and mental. It is this growth principle on which doctors and psychotherapists depend to make the person well again. If an organism is free to do so—it can, will, it *must* move in positive ways. The organism is not our enemy. It wants the same things we do, the achievement of adequacy. Yet alas, how few believe this and how timid we are to trust our students with self-direction.

A recent best selling book, *Summerhill,* by A. S. Neill has fascinated many educators. In it Neill describes the absolute trust he placed in the children under his care. Many teachers are shocked by his unorthodox procedures and the extreme behavior of some of the children. But whether one approves of Neill's school or not, the thing which impressed me most was this: Here was a man who dared to trust children far beyond what most of us would be willing to risk. Yet, all the things we are so afraid might happen if we did give them such freedom, never happened! For forty years the school continued to turn out happy, effective citizens as well as, or better than, its competitors. It is time we give up fearing the human organism and learn to trust and use its built-in drives toward self-fulfillment. After all, the organism has had to be pretty tough to survive what we have done to it through the ages.

Responsibility and self-direction are learned. They must be acquired from experiences, from being given opportunities to be self-directing and responsible. You cannot learn to be self-directing if no one permits you to try. Human capacities are strengthened by use but atrophy with disuse. If young people are going to learn self-direction, then it must be through being *given* many opportunities to exercise such self-direction throughout the years they are in school. Someone has observed that our schools are operated on a directly contrary principle. Children are allowed more freedom of choice and self-direction in kindergarten (when they are presumably least able to handle it) and each year thereafter are given less and less, until, by the time they reach college, they are permitted practically no choice at all! This overdraws the case, to be sure, but there is enough truth in the statement to make one uncomfortable. If we are to produce independent, self-starting people we must do a great deal more to produce the kinds of experiences which will lead to these ends.

3. THE EXPERIMENTAL ATTITUDE

If we are going to provide young people with increased opportunity for self-direction, we must do it with our eyes open *expecting* them to make mistakes. This is not easy, for the importance of "being right" is in our blood. Education is built on right answers. Wrong ones are regarded as failures to be avoided like the plague. Unfortunately, such attitudes stand squarely in the way of progress toward self-direction and independence.

People too fearful of mistakes cannot risk trying. Without trying, self-direction, creativity and independence cannot be discovered. To be so afraid of mistakes that we kill the desire to try is a tragedy. Autonomy, independence and creativity are the products of being willing to look and eager to try. If we discourage these elements we do so at our peril. In the world we live in, victory is reserved only for the courageous and inventive. It is possible we may lose the game by making mistakes. We will not even get in the game if we are afraid to try.

Experimentation and innovation must be encouraged everywhere in our schools, in teachers as well as students. Each of us needs to be engaged in a continuous process of trying something new. The kind of experimentation which will make the difference to education in the long run is not that produced by the professional researcher with the aid of giant computers but by the everyday changes in goals and processes brought about by the individual teacher in the classroom.

To achieve this, teachers need to be freed of pressures and details by the administration for the exercise of self-direction and creativity. In addition, each of us must accept the challenge and set about a systematic search for the barriers we place in the path of self-direction for ourselves, our colleagues and our students. This should suggest all kinds of places for experimentation where we can begin the encouragement of self-direction. One of the nice things about self-direction is that it does not have to be taught. It only needs to be encouraged and set free to operate.

4. THE PROVISION OF OPPORTUNITY

The basic principle is clear. To produce more self-directed people it is necessary to give more opportunity to practice self-direction. This means some of us must be willing to give up our traditional prerogatives to make all the decisions. Education must be seen, not as providing right answers, but as confrontation with problems; not imaginary play problems either, but *real* ones in which decisions count.

Experiences calling for decision, independence and self-direction must be the daily diet of children, including such little decisions as what kinds of headings and margins a paper should have and big ones like the courses to be taken next year. They must also include decisions about goals, techniques, time, people, money, meals, rules, and subject matter.

If we are to achieve the objective of greater self-direction, I see no alternative to the fuller acceptance of students into partnership in the educative endeavor. Our modern goal for education, "the optimal development of the individual," cannot be achieved without this. Such an aim requires participation of the student and his wholehearted cooperation in the process. This is not likely to be accomplished unless students have the feeling they matter and their decisions count. Few of us are deeply committed to tasks imposed upon us; and students are not much different. Self-direction is learned from experience. What better, more meaningful experience could be provided than participation in the decisions about one's own life and learning?

The basic belief of democracy is that when people are free they can find their own best ways. Though all of us profess our acceptance of this credo, it is distressing how few of us dare to put it to work. Whatever limits the capacity of our young people to accept both the challenge and the responsibilities of that belief is destructive to all of us. It is time we put this belief to work and to expression in the education of our young as though we really meant it.

Barriers to Communication Between Men

F. J. Roethlisberger

In thinking about the many barriers to personal communication, particularly those that are due to differences of background, experience, and motivation, it seems to me extraordinary that any two persons can ever understand each other. Such reflections provoke the question of how communication is possible when people do not see and assume the same things and share the same values.

On this question there are two schools of thought. One school assumes that communication between A and B, for example, has failed when B does not accept what A has to say as being fact, true, or valid. The goal of communication is to get B to agree with A's opinions, ideas, facts, or information.

The position of the other school of thought is quite different. It assumes that communication has failed when B does not feel free to express his feelings to A because B fears they will not be accepted by A. Communication is facilitated when on the part of A or B or both there is *a willingness to express and accept differences.*

Reprinted by permission from *ETC: A Review of General Semantics,* Vol. 9 (2); Copyright 1952, by the International Society for General Semantics.

As these are quite divergent conceptions, let us explore them further with an example. Bill, an employee, is talking with his boss in the boss's office. The boss says, "I think, Bill, that this is the best way to do your job." Bill says, "Oh yeah!" According to the first school of thought, this reply would be a sign of poor communication. Bill does not understand the best way of doing his work. To improve communication, therefore, it is up to the boss to explain to Bill why his way is the best.

From the point of view of the second school of thought, Bill's reply is neither a sign of good nor bad communication. Bill's response is indeterminate. What Bill means, the boss has an opportunity to find out if he so desires. Let us assume that this is what he chooses to do, i.e., find out what Bill means. So this boss tries to get Bill to talk more about his job while he (the boss) listens.

For purposes of simplification, I shall call the boss representing the first school of thought "Smith" and the boss representing the second school of thought "Jones." In the presence of the so-called same stimulus, each behaves differently. Smith chooses to *explain,* Jones chooses to *listen.* In my experience Jones's response works better than Smith's. It works better because Jones is making a more proper evaluation of what is taking place between him and Bill than Smith is. Let us test this hypothesis by continuing with our example.

THE ASSUMPTIONS, PERCEPTIONS, AND FEELINGS OF SMITH [1]

Smith assumes that he understands what Bill means when Bill says, "Oh yeah!" so there is no need to find out. Smith is sure that Bill does not understand why this is the best way to do his job, so Smith has to tell him. In the process let us assume Smith is logical, lucid, and clear. He presents his facts and evidence well. But, alas, Bill remains unconvinced. What does Smith do? Operating under the assumption that what is taking place between him and Bill is something essentially logical, Smith can draw only one of two conclusions: (1) either he has not been clear enough, or (2) Bill is too damned stupid to understand. So either he has to "spell out" his case in words of fewer and fewer syllables, or give up. Smith is reluctant to do the latter, so he continues to explain. What happens?

---

1. For the concepts I use to present my material I am greatly indebted to some very interesting conversations I had with my friend, Irving Lee.

If Bill still does not accept Smith's explanation of why this is the best way for him to do his job, a pattern of interacting feelings is produced of which Smith is often unaware. The more Smith cannot get Bill to understand him, the more frustrated Smith becomes and the more Bill becomes a threat to his logical capacity. Since Smith sees himself as a fairly reasonable and logical chap, this is a difficult feeling to accept. It is much easier for him to perceive Bill as uncooperative or stupid. This perception, however, will affect what Smith says and does. Under these pressures Bill comes to be evaluated more and more in terms of Smith's values. By this process Smith tends to treat Bill's values as unimportant. He tends to deny Bill's uniqueness and difference. He treats Bill as if he had little capacity for self-direction.

Let us be clear. Smith does not see that he is doing these things. When he is feverishly scratching hieroglyphics on the back of an envelope, trying to explain to Bill why this is the best way to do his job, Smith is trying to be helpful. He is a man of good will and he wants to set Bill straight. This is the way Smith sees himself and his behavior. But it is for this very reason that Bill's "Oh yeahs" are getting under Smith's skin. "How dumb can a guy be?"

Unfortunately, Bill will hear this more than Smith's "good intentions." Bill will feel misunderstood. He will not see Smith as a man of good will trying to be helpful. Rather he will perceive him as a threat to his self-esteem and personal integrity. Against this threat Bill will feel the need to defend himself at all costs. Not being as logically articulate as Smith, Bill expresses this need by saying, "Oh yeah!"

ASSUMPTIONS, PERCEPTIONS, AND FEELINGS OF JONES

Let us leave this sad scene between Smith and Bill, which I fear is going to terminate by Bill either leaving in a huff or being kicked out of Smith's office. Let us turn for a moment to Jones and see what he is assuming, seeing, hearing, feeling, doing, and saying when he interacts with Bill.

Jones, it will be remembered, does not assume that he knows what Bill means when he says, "Oh yeah," so he has to find out. Moreover, he assumes that when Bill said this, he had not exhausted his vocabulary or his feelings. Bill may not necessarily mean one thing; he may mean several different things. So Jones decides to listen.

In this process Jones is not under any illusion that what will take place will be essentially logical. Rather, he is assuming that what will take place will be primarily an interaction of feelings. Therefore, he cannot ignore the feelings of Bill, the effect of Bill's feelings upon him, or the effect of his feelings upon Bill. He cannot ignore his relationship to Bill. He does not assume that Bill's attitude toward him makes no difference to what Bill will hear or accept. Therefore, Jones will be paying strict attention to all of the things Smith has ignored. Jones will be addressing himself to Bill's feelings, his own, and the interactions between them.

Jones will, therefore, realize that he had ruffled Bill's feelings with his comment, "I think, Bill, this is the best way to do your job." So instead of trying to get Bill to understand him, he decides to try to understand Bill. He does this by encouraging Bill to speak. Instead of telling Bill how he should feel or think, he asks Bill such questions as, is this what you feel, is this what you see, in this what you assume? Instead of ignoring Bill's evaluations as irrelevant, not valid, inconsequential, or false, he tries to understand Bill's reality as Bill feels it, perceives it, and assumes it to be. As Bill begins to open up, Jones's curiosity is piqued by this process. Instead of seeing Bill as stupid, he perceives Bill as quite an interesting guy.

This is what Bill hears. Therefore, Bill feels understood and accepted as a person. He becomes less defensive. He is in a better frame of mind to explore and re-examine his own perceptions, feelings, and assumptions. In this process he perceives Jones as a source of help. Bill feels free to express his differences. He feels that Jones has some respect for his capacity for self-direction. These positive feelings toward Jones make Bill more inclined to say, "Well, Jones, I don't quite agree with you that this is the best way to do my job, but I'll tell you what I'll do. I'll try to do it that way for a few days, and then I'll tell you what I think."

CONCLUSIONS

I grant that my two orientations do not work themselves out in practice in quite as simple or neat a fashion as I have been able to work them out on paper. Bill could have responded to Smith in many other ways. He might even have said, "O.K., boss, I agree that your way of doing my job is better." But Smith still would not have known how Bill felt when he made this statement or whether Bill was actually going to do his job differently. Likewise, Bill could have responded to Jones in a way different from my example. In spite of Jones's attitude, Bill might still be reluctant to express himself freely to his boss.

The purpose of my examples has not been to demonstrate the right or wrong way of doing something. My purpose has been to provide something concrete to point to when I make the following generalizations:

1. Smith represents to me a very common pattern of misunderstanding. It does not arise because Smith is not clear enough in expressing himself. It arises because of Smith's misevaluation of what is taking place when two people are talking together.

2. Smith's misevaluation of the process of personal communication consists of certain very common assumptions. Three of these very common assumptions are (a) that what is taking place is something essentially logical; (b) that words in themselves apart from the people involved mean something; (c) that the purpose of the interaction is to get Bill to see things from Smith's point of view.

3. Because of these assumptions, a chain reaction of perception and negative feelings is engendered which blocks communication. By ignoring Bill's feelings and by rationalizing his own, Smith ignores his relationship to Bill as one of the most important determinants of the communication. As a result, Bill hears Smith's *attitude* more clearly than the logical content of Smith's words. Bill feels that his individual uniqueness is being denied. His personal integrity being at stake, he becomes defensive and belligerent. As a result, Smith feels frustrated. He perceives Bill as stupid. As a result he says and does things which only provoke more defensiveness on the part of Bill.

4. In the case of Jones, I have tried to show what might possibly happen if we made a different evaluation of what is taking place when two people are talking together. Jones makes a different set of assumptions. He assumes (a) that what is taking place between him and Bill is an interaction of sentiments; (b) that Bill—not his words in themselves— means something; (c) that the object of the interaction is to give Bill an opportunity to express freely his differences.

5. Because of these assumptions, a psychological chain reaction of reinforcing feelings and perceptions is set up which facilitates communication between him and Bill. When Jones addresses himself to Bill's feelings and perceptions from Bill's point of view, Bill feels understood and accepted as a person; Bill feels free to express his differences. Bill sees Jones as a source of help; Jones sees Bill as an interesting person. Bill in turn becomes more co-operative.

6. If I have identified correctly these very common patterns of personal communication, then some interesting hypotheses can be stated:
   (a) Jones's method works better than Smith's not because of any magic, but because Jones has a better map than Smith of the process of personal communication.
   (b) The practice of Jones's method, however, is not merely an intellectual exercise. It depends upon Jones's capacity and willingness to see and accept points of view different from his own, and to practice this orientation in a face-to-face relationship. This practice in-

      volves an emotional as well as an intellectual achievement. It depends in part upon Jones's awareness of himself; it depends in part upon the practice of a skill.

(c) Although our colleges and universities try to get students to appreciate intellectually points of view different from their own, very little is done to help them to implement this general intellectual appreciation in a simple face-to-face relationship—at the level of a skill. Most universities train their students to be logical, lucid, and clear. Very little is done to help them to listen more skillfully. As a result, our educated world contains too many Smiths and too few Joneses.

(d) The biggest block to personal communication is man's inability to listen intelligently, understandingly, and skillfully to another person. This deficiency in the modern world is widespread and appalling. In our universities, as well as elsewhere, too little is being done about it.

In conclusion, let me apologize for acting toward you like Smith. But who am I to violate a long-standing academic tradition!

The Task of the Teacher

W. W. Purkey

Let people realize clearly that every time they threaten someone or humiliate or hurt unnecessarily or dominate or reject another human being, they become forces for the creation of psychopathology, even if these be small forces. Let them recognize that every man who is kind, helpful, decent, psychologically democratic, affectionate, and warm, is a psychotherapeutic force even though a small one.
ABRAHAM H. MASLOW, *Motivation and Personality*

In this book you have been introduced to a body of theory about the self. We have considered some of the self's major characteristics, analyzed how the self and scholastic success are related, and reviewed

Reprinted from Purkey, W. W., *Self Concept and School Achievement,* 1970, pp. 43–65, by permission of Prentice-Hall, Inc., Englewood Cliffs, N.J.

the creation of the self. Now we turn our attention to the task of the teacher: to help each student gain a positive and realistic image of himself as a learner.

Before we consider the process of building positive and realistic self concepts in students, it is necessary to point out the need to avoid instilling negative ones. The self is remarkably conservative, and once a child has formed a negative image of himself as a learner, the task of the teacher becomes extremely difficult. Therefore, the *prevention of negative self concepts is a vital first step in teaching*. The unfavorable features of some schools, which we discussed in the previous chapter, can be modified by teachers who are aware of the need and who want to make changes.

Several studies have shown that it is possible to develop a curriculum in which the expected academic learning takes place while positive self concepts are being built. Frankel (1964) studied the effects of a special program of advanced summer study on the self-perceptions of academically talented high school students. He concluded that the self concepts of the group showed significant gains after attending the program, particularly in the areas of self-reliance and special talents. In a somewhat similar study of the effects of a pre-kindergarten on the self concept, Crovetto, Fischer, and Boudreaux (1967) developed a modified Head Start curriculum specifically designed to affect the child's self concept in a positive direction. When the experimental group of students was compared with a control group, it was found that the experimental class members showed gains on the *Draw-A-Man Test,* while the control group did not. The experimental curriculum appeared to be effective in helping to develop a more positive self concept in children.

Beneath program arrangements and curricular innovations lies the teacher's personal role. What part do teachers play in the development of the child's self? Can teachers change the child's self-image if they try to do so? If they can, what methods of teaching produce what kinds of self-image? Is it possible to distinguish between teachers in the frequency and kind of comment which they make about the child's self? To answer these questions, Staines (1958) conducted a study involving careful observation, recording, and analyzing of data from teacher-child and child-child interaction in four elementary school classrooms. Data were collected on the educational outcomes of the interaction between personalities in the atmosphere of the classroom, particular attention being given to identifying those teachers who could be reliably distinguished by the frequency of their use of words and kinds of situational management which, in the opinion of competent judges who served as observers, are likely to be positive influences on the self concepts of students.

The investigation showed marked differences between teachers in the frequency of references about the child in their comments, particularly in their positive or negative comments on the child's performance, status, and self-confidence or potency. Also, it was found that it is possible to teach so that, while aiming at the normal results of teaching, specific changes can be made in the child's self-image. Staines concluded that changes in the child's self concept do occur as an outcome of the learning situation, and that the self must be recognized as an important factor in learning. Teaching methods can be adapted so that definite changes of the kind sought for will occur in the self without injury to the academic program in the process.

Teachers want to be significant forces in the lives of their students. As Moustakas (1966) declared, every teacher wants to meet the student on a significant level, every teacher wants to feel that what he does makes a difference. Yet in order to influence students it is necessary to become a *significant other* in their lives. We are seldom changed by people whom we see as insignificant or unimportant. The way the teacher becomes significant seems to rest on two forces: (1) what he believes, and (2) what he does.

WHAT THE TEACHER BELIEVES

> No printed word nor spoken plea
> Can teach young minds what men should be,
> Not all the books on all the shelves
> But what the teachers are themselves.
>
> ANONYMOUS

A basic assumption of the theory of the self concept is that we behave according to our beliefs. If this assumption is true, then it follows that the teacher's beliefs about himself and his students are crucial factors in determining his effectiveness in the classroom. Available evidence (Combs, 1969) indicates that the teacher's attitudes toward himself and others are as important, if not more so, than his techniques, practices, or materials. In fact, there do not seem to be any techniques which are always associated with people who are effective in the helping relationship. Rogers (1965) reported that personality changes in therapy come about not because of such factors as professional qualifications and training, or knowledge or skill, or ideological orientation, but primarily because of the attitudinal characteristics of the relationship. Attitudes play an important role, and so we need to examine the teacher's beliefs about himself and his students in some detail.

WHAT THE TEACHER BELIEVES ABOUT HIMSELF

There seems to be general agreement that the teacher needs to have positive and realistic attitudes about himself and his abilities before he is able to reach out to like and respect others. Numerous studies (Berger, 1953; Fey, 1954; Luft, 1966) have reported that there is a marked relation between the way an individual sees himself and the way he sees others. Those who accept themselves tend to be more accepting of others (Trent, 1957) and perceive others as more accepting (Omwake, 1954). Further, according to Omwake, those who reject themselves hold a correspondingly low opinion of others and perceive others as being self-rejecting. From these studies it seems clear that the teacher needs to see himself in essentially positive ways. The manner in which this can be accomplished needs further investigation, but Jersild and Combs have given us some clues.

Jersild (1952, 1960, 1965) has been a pioneer in emphasizing the importance of the attitudes that teachers hold about themselves. He argues that the self-understanding of teachers is a necessary factor in coping with their feelings and in becoming more effective in the classroom. The personal problems of teachers often interfere with their effectiveness in teaching, and an understanding of the influence of these and other attitudes and emotions is vital in working with students. Jersild has suggested that we need to encourage in-service group counseling situations for teachers, in which their attitudes and feelings can be safely explored with others. This, it is hoped, would result in increased understanding of and sensitivity to oneself, and to more effective teaching in the classroom.

A similar view is reported by Combs and his associates (1963, 1964, 1965, 1969) in their research on the perceptual organization of effective helpers. They found that effective teachers, counselors, and priests could be distinguished from ineffective helpers on the basis of their attitudes about themselves and others. Such findings as these have long-range implications for the professional education of teachers. In fact, the suggestion that teacher preparation should be based on a perceptual, self concept approach has already appeared in Combs' *The Professional Education of Teachers* (1965), and an experimental program of teacher training using the perceptual approach was introduced at the University of Florida in 1969.

The way the evidence points is that each teacher needs to view himself with respect, liking, and acceptance. When teachers have essentially favorable attitudes toward themselves, they are in a much better position to build positive and realistic self concepts in their students.

WHAT THE TEACHER BELIEVES ABOUT STUDENTS

The ways significant others evaluate the student directly affects the student's conception of his academic ability. This in turn establishes limits on his success in school. Teachers, in their capacity of significant others, need to view students in essentially positive ways and hold favorable expectations. This is particularly important at the elementary level, but is vital in all grades. Several studies bear directly on the importance of what the teacher believes about students.

Davidson and Lang (1960) found that the student's perceptions of the teacher's feelings toward him correlated positively with his self-perception. Further, the more positive the children's perceptions of their teacher's feelings, the better their academic achievement and the more desirable their classroom behavior as rated by the teacher. Clarke (1960) reported a positive relationship between a student's academic performance and his perception of the academic expectations of him by significant others.

One of the most comprehensive studies of the self concept of ability and school success was that of Brookover and his associates (1965, 1967) which we considered, in part, earlier. Brookover and his associates conducted a six-year study of the relation between the self concept of academic ability and school achievement among students in one school class while in the seventh through the twelfth grades. A major purpose of the study was to determine whether improved self concept results from the expectations and evaluations held by significant others as perceived by the students. As Brookover, Erickson, and Joiner conclude: "The hypothesis that students' perceptions of the evaluations of their academic ability by others (teachers, parents, and friends) are associated with self concepts of academic ability was confirmed" (1967,

p. 110). The almost unavoidable conclusion is that the teacher's attitudes and opinions regarding his students have a significant influence on their success in school. In other words, when the teacher believes that his students can achieve, the students appear to be more successful; when the teacher believes that the students cannot achieve, then it influences their performance negatively. This self-fulfilling prophecy has been illuminated by the research of Rosenthal and Jacobson (1968a, b).

The basic hypothesis of Rosenthal and Jacobson's research was that students, more often than not, do what is expected of them. To test this hypothesis, the two researchers conducted an experiment in a public elementary school of 650 students. The elementary-school teachers were told that, on the basis of ability tests administered the previous spring, approximately one-fifth of the students could be expected to evidence significant increases in mental ability during the year. The teachers were then given the names of the high-potential students. Although in fact the names had been *chosen at random* by the experimenters, when intelligence tests and other measures were administered some months later, those identified as potential spurters tended to score significantly higher than the children who had not been so identified. Also, Rosenthal and Jacobson found that these children were later described by their teachers as happier, more curious, more interesting, and as having a better chance of future success than other children. The conclusion drawn by Rosenthal and Jacobson is that the teacher, through his facial expressions, postures, and touch, through what, how, and when he spoke, subtly helped the child to learn. This may have been accomplished, according to the researchers, by modifying the child's self concept, his expectations of his own behavior, and his motivations, as well as his cognitive style. They summarized their study by stating that the evidence suggests strongly that "children who are expected by their teachers to gain intellectually in fact do show greater intellectual gains after one year than do children of whom such gains are not expected" (1968b, p. 121). The full educational implications of the self-fulfilling prophecy remain to be explored, but it seems certain that the ways the teacher views the student have a significant influence on the student and his performance.

WHAT THE TEACHER DOES

As we have seen, the key to building positive and realistic self-images in students lies largely in what the teacher *believes* about himself and his students. These beliefs not only determine the teacher's behavior, but are transmitted to the students and influence their performance as well. Yet we cannot ignore what the teacher *does* in the classroom, for the behavior he displays and the experiences he provides, *as perceived by students,* have a strong impact in themselves. In this section we will consider two important aspects of the teacher's role: (1) *the attitudes he conveys;* and (2) *the atmosphere he develops.*

THE ATTITUDE THE TEACHER CONVEYS

It is difficult to overestimate the need for the teacher to be sensitive to the attitudes he expresses toward students. Even though teachers may have the best intentions, they sometimes project distorted images of themselves. What a person believes can be hidden by negative habits picked up long ago. Therefore, teachers need to ask themselves:

Am I projecting an image that tells the student that I am here to build, rather than to destroy, him as a person? (Spaulding, 1963, reported that there is a significant relationship between a student's positive self concept as reported, and the degree to which teachers are calm, accepting, supportive, and facilitative, and a negative relationship between a student's self concept and teachers who are threatening, grim, and sarcastic.)

Do I let the student know that I am aware of and interested in him as a unique person? (Moustakas, 1966, maintains that every child wants to be known as a unique person, and that by holding the student in esteem, the teacher is establishing an environmental climate that facilitates growth.)

Do I convey my expectations and confidence that the student can accomplish work, can learn, and is competent? (Rosenthal and Jacobson, 1968b, have shown that the teacher's expectations have a significant influence on the student's performance.)

Do I provide well-defined standards of values, demands for competence, and guidance toward solutions to problems? (Coopersmith, 1967, has provided evidence that self-reliance is fostered by an environment which is well-structured and reasonably demanding, rather than unlimitedly permissive.)

When working with parents, do I enhance the academic expectations and evaluations which they hold of their children's ability? (Brookover, et al., 1965, has illustrated that this method yields significant results in enhancing self concept and improving academic achievement.)

By my behavior, do I serve as a model of authenticity for the student? (Both Jourard, 1964, and Rogers, 1965, suggest that a most important factor in the helping relationship is the helper serving as a model of genuineness, without "front.")

Do I take every opportunity to establish a high degree of private or semi-private communication with my students? (Spaulding, 1963, found a high relationship between the pupil's self concept and the teacher's behavior when it involved personal and private talks with students.)

The above questions are samples of how the teacher may check himself to see if he is conveying his beliefs in an authentic and meaningful fashion. As Gill reported, teachers' attitudes toward students are vitally important in shaping the self concepts of their students. Gill summarized his study by saying that "teachers should consider self concept as a vital and important aspect of learning and development which the school, through its educational process, should seek to promote and foster in every child" (1969, p. 10).

THE ATMOSPHERE THE TEACHER CREATES

Six factors seem particularly important in creating a classroom atmosphere conducive to developing favorable self-images in students. These are (1) challenge; (2) freedom; (3) respect; (4) warmth; (5) control; and (6) success. A brief discussion of each of these may be helpful.

CHALLENGE

Because of the focus of this book, little has been said about high standards of academic accomplishment. This omission should not be taken to mean that achievement should be minimized. As we have seen, high academic expectations and a high degree of challenge on the part of teachers have a positive and beneficial effect on students. A good way to create challenge is to wait until the chances of success are good, and then say: "This is hard work, but I think that you can do it." The teacher chooses the right moment to put his trust on the line with students. Of course, an important part of challenge is relevance. If the required learning is relevant to the student's world of experience and has some personal meaning to him, then he is likely to work hard—*if* he feels free to try. This brings us to the question of freedom.

FREEDOM

It is difficult for self-esteem to grow in an environment where there is little or no freedom of choice. If the student is to grow and develop as an adequate human being, he needs the opportunity to make meaning-ful decisions for himself. This also means that he must have the freedom to make mistakes, and even to laugh at his inadequacies. Carlton and Moore (1966, 1968) have shown that the freedom of self-directed dramatization improved the reading ability and enhanced the self con-cept of elementary-school youngsters. This general emphasis on freedom has been highlighted by Moustakas, who wrote: "Self values are in jeopardy in any climate where freedom and choice are denied, in a situa-tion where the individual rejects his own senses and substitutes for his own perceptions the standards and expectations of others" (1966, pp. 4f). When the student has a say in his own development and is given personal decisions to make, he develops faith in his own judgments and thoughts.

Closely related to the notion of freedom of choice is the idea of free-dom from threat. Children seem to learn and develop best in an atmo-sphere characterized by much challenge and little threat. Kowitz has noted, for example, that if the child feels evaluation takes place with "vicious assault upon his self concept" (1967, p. 163), there can be little real freedom. In fact, some students fear failure so much that they avoid achievement whenever they can and, when they cannot, do not try to succeed. In this way, they can avoid the task of trying to achieve. A comprehensive study of the person who fears failure is provided by Birney, Burdick, and Teevan (1969).

What this means to the teacher is that students will learn, provided the material appears to be relevant to their lives and provided they have the freedom to explore and to discover its meaning for themselves. We know that exploration is curtailed in an atmosphere in which one must spend most of his time avoiding or reducing the experience of anxiety brought about by threat to the self. Sarason (1961) has reported that a poor performance by anxious subjects occurred only when the task was presented as a threat. When anxious subjects were told that failure was normal and expected, they actually outperformed subjects who were less anxious. The freedom to try without a tiger springing at you if you fail is essential to a healthy atmosphere in the classroom.

In considering the factors of freedom and challenge, the classroom teacher can ask himself:

Do I encourage students to try something new and to join in new activities?

Do I allow students to have a voice in planning, and do I permit them to help make the rules they follow?

Do I permit students to challenge my opinions?

Do I teach in as exciting and interesting a manner as possible?

Do I distinguish between students' classroom mistakes and their personal failure?

Do I avoid unfair and ruthless competition in the classroom?

Questions like these can help the teacher evaluate himself and the classroom climate he creates.

RESPECT

A basic feeling by the teacher for the worth and dignity of students is vital in building self concepts in them. No aspect of education is more important than the feeling on the part of the teacher that the individual student is important, valuable, and *can* learn in school. Sometimes teachers forget the importance of respect and run roughshod over the personal feelings of students. Using both the official and unofficial school practices which we cataloged in Chapter 3, teachers sometimes lower the feelings of worth of many young people. One of my students told me why he could never get along with his previous English teacher. It was because, although his name is Cribbidge, "She always called me cabbage whenever she called roll, and then laughed." The rule seems to be that whenever we treat a student with respect, we add to his self-respect, and whenever we embarrass or humiliate him, we are likely to build disrespect in him both for himself and for others.

If the teacher genuinely values and respects students, it will be reflected in everything he does. Davidson and Lang (1960) found that when students feel that teachers value and respect them, they are likely to value and respect themselves. Moustakas summed it up this way: "By cherishing and holding the child in absolute esteem, the teacher is establishing an environmental climate that facilitates growth and becoming" (1966, p. 13).

The need for respect is particularly important in working with culturally disadvantaged students. These are the children whose behavior makes them most difficult to respect, but who probably need respect the most. Teachers must make an extra effort to communicate to these young people a feeling of trust, positive regard, and respect. Closely related to respect is the concept of warmth.

WARMTH

There is considerable evidence to support the assumption that a psychologically safe and supportive learning situation encourages students to grow academically as well as in feelings of personal worth. Cogan (1958) reported that students with warm, considerate teachers produced unusual amounts of original poetry and art. Christensen (1960) found the warmth of teachers significantly related to their students' vocabulary and achievement in arithmetic. Reed (1962) concluded that teachers characterized as considerate, understanding, and friendly, and with a tolerance for some release of emotional feeling by students, had a favorable influence on their students' interest in science.

Relating more directly to the task of building favorable self concepts, Spaulding's research (1964) supported the findings of previous investigators regarding positive attitudes toward the self. He found significant correlations between the height of the self concept and the degree to which the teachers in his study were calm, accepting, supportive, and facilitative. It is interesting to note that significant negative correlations with the height of pupils' self concepts were found when teachers were dominating, threatening, and sarcastic.

An important part of warmth is commitment. Teaching has been described as a delicate relationship, almost like a marriage, where, in a sense, the teacher and student belong to each other. The student says "There is *my* teacher" and the teacher says "These are *my* students." The process of commitment is illustrated by the story of the chicken and pig who were walking down a country lane: The chicken excitedly told the portly pig of his latest business idea. "We'll prepare and franchise the best tasting ham 'n eggs money can buy, and we'll make a fortune." The pig thought it over for a moment and replied: "It's easy for you to get enthused. For you it's an occupation, but for *me* it means *total* commitment!" Perhaps total commitment is asking too much of teachers, but certainly they need to feel that their work with students is more than an occupation. A warm and supportive educational atmosphere is one in which each student is made to feel that he belongs in school and that teachers care about what happens to him. It is one in which praise is used in preference to punishment, courtesy in preference to sarcasm, and consultation in preference to dictation.

Some practical questions about respect and warmth which the teacher might ask himself are:

Do I learn the name of each student as soon as possible, and do I use that name often?

Do I share my feelings with my students?

Do I practice courtesy with my students?

Do I arrange some time when I can talk quietly alone with each student?

Do I spread my attention around and include each student, keeping special watch for the student who may need extra attention?

Do I notice and comment favorably on the things that are important to students?

Do I show students who return after being absent that I am happy to have them back in class, and that they were missed?

It is in ways such as these that we tell the student that he is important to us.

CONTROL

Coopersmith (1967) has suggested that children who are brought up in a permissive environment tend to develop less self-esteem than those reared in a firmer and more demanding atmosphere. The assumption that clearly established and relatively firm guidance produces more self-esteem in children can also be applied to the classroom. It is important for the teacher to maintain discipline, for the type of control under which a child lives has considerable effect on his self-image. It is yet another way of telling the student that the teacher cares about him and what he does. Classroom control does not require ridicule and embarrassment. The secret seems to be in the leadership qualities of the teacher. When he is prepared for class, keeps on top of the work and avoids the appearance of confusion, explains why some things must be done, and strives for consistency, politeness, and firmness, then classroom control is likely to be maintained. When punishment is unavoidable (and often it *can* be avoided), then it is best to withdraw the student's privileges. Of course, this means that teachers must be sure that there *are* some privileges in school which can be withdrawn. Poor control procedures would include punishing the entire class for the transgressions of a few, using corporal punishment, or using school work as punishment.

In considering classroom control, teachers might ask themselves:

Do I remember to see small disciplinary problems as understandable, and not as personal insults?

Do I avoid having "favorites" and "victims"?

Do I have, and do my students have, a clear idea of what is and what is not acceptable in my class?

Within my limits, is there room for students to be active and natural?

Do I make sure that I am adequately prepared for class each day?

Do I usually make it through the day without punishing students?

Questions such as these help the teacher to estimate his ability to handle students in a way which maintains discipline and, at the same time, builds positive and realistic self concepts in students.

Some teachers believe that warmth and firmness are in opposition to each other, but this is not so. Warmth is more than the obvious display of affection, it is also expressed by firmness which says to the student, "You are important to me and I care about the ways in which you behave."

SUCCESS

Perhaps the single most important step that teachers can take in the classroom is to provide an educational atmosphere of success rather than failure. Reviewing over a dozen experiments, Wylie (1961) made the tentative statement that students are likely to change their self-evaluations after experimentally induced success or failure. This statement has been echoed in more recent studies. Costello (1964) found that over- all, regardless of the task or the ability of the students, praise produces more improvement in performance than blame. Ludwig and Maehr (1967) showed that the approval of significant others caused an increase in self-ratings and an increased preference for activities connected with the criterion task, and that disapproval resulted in a lowered self-rating and a decreased preference for related activities. Moreover, the reaction to the evaluation was followed by a spread of effect, from the areas di- rectly approved by the significant others to related areas of self-regard.

A number of writers have pointed out some of the steps involved in giving honest experiences of success. Page's (1958) research showed that pupils' performance improved significantly when teachers wrote encour- aging comments on their written work. A control group, given conven- tional grades without comment, lost ground. Walsh (1956) explains that it is helpful to show students that they have mastered even the smallest step, rather than vaguely saying "That's nice" about everything.

The sensitive teacher points out areas of accomplishment, rather than focusing on mistakes. Continuing awareness of failure results in lowered expectations, not learning. According to Combs and Snygg (1959) a positive view is learned from the ways people treat the learner. People learn that they are able, not from failure but from success. Questions about success which the teacher might ask himself when he thinks about success experiences for students include:

Do I permit my students some opportunity to make mistakes without penalty?

Do I make generally positive comments on written work?

Do I give extra support and encouragement to slower students?

Do I recognize the successes of students in terms of what they did earlier?

Do I take special opportunities to praise students for their successes?

Do I manufacture honest experiences of success for my students?

Do I set tasks which are, and which appear to the student to be, within his abilities?

What all of this discussion hopes to say to teachers is that a backlog of challenge, freedom, respect, warmth, control, and success develops positive self-images in students and encourages academic achievement. The absence of these factors makes for the person who is crippled psychologically.

THE SENSITIVITY THE TEACHER DEVELOPS

You can know me truly only if I let you, only if I want you to know me. . . . If you want me to reveal myself, just demonstrate your good will—your will to employ your powers for my good, and not for my destruction.

SIDNEY JOURARD, *The Transparent Self*

"Sensitivity" is a term which is used to serve many purposes and to describe various processes. In this book it is defined as the ability to sense what an individual feels about himself and the world. Sensitivity first requires the honest *desire* to become aware of how others are experiencing things. This sounds simple, but the fact is that many people don't take the necessary time and trouble to be sensitive to others. After the desire must come the habit of really listening, and listening for meanings rather than words. For instance, a student might say that he does not wish to try, when he means that it is better not to try than to try and be proved wrong.

Entering a person's private world in order to understand how he is seeing things is difficult, for the individual self can only be approached through the perceptions of some other person, perceptions filled with all sorts of prejudices, aspirations, and anxieties. Fortunately, however, most teachers have a great supply of sensitivity, as do most humans. It's just a matter of applying this sensitivity more deliberately to teaching. To the degree to which a teacher is able to predict how his students are viewing themselves, their subject, and the world, to that degree he is in a position to become a successful teacher.

Throughout this book the idea has been stressed over and over that the teacher must give the self concepts of students far greater emphasis than is presently given. The purpose of this section is to assist teachers to become more competent in assessing the self concepts of the students with whom they work. For a long time, many of us in education and psychology have been saying that theory about the self has a vital role to play in the educative process and that teachers should be made more aware of the importance of how students view themselves. Yet little has been done to equip teachers and counselors with simple clinical techniques and instruments which would enable them to be more sensitive to their students. It would seem that we in education have the responsibility, within the limits of our training, to investigate, to understand, and to utilize the self concept as a means of facilitating scholastic success. What a person says about himself, and the influences we draw from his behavior, are valuable data for teachers. However, these are problems in understanding how students view themselves, as we shall see.

PROBLEMS IN EVALUATING THE SELF

> "First of all," he said, "if you can learn a simple trick, Scout, you'll get along a lot better with all kinds of folks. You never really understand a person until you consider things from his point of view—"
> "Sir?"
> "—until you climb into his skin and walk around in it."
>
> HARPER LEE, *To Kill a Mockingbird*

No one, of course, can ever climb into another's skin, or see this construct we call the self, but we can infer that self in a number of ways. Two of these ways are: (1) "self-report," that which can be inferred from an individual's statements about himself; and (2) "observations," that which can be inferred from the individual's behavior. Before we turn to these methods, however, it is wise to remind ourselves that the self is multidimensional and tremendously complex and that there are two major cautions that we need to be aware of in assessing it: our *limitations* and our *biases*.

Limitations. Ideally, when you desire to assess the self, you need training and supervised experience in measurement, clinical psychology, and personality theory. Even without this preparation, however, it is possible to understand the concept of the self and to be aware of the means of measuring it. Regardless of your training, you should seek out counselors, school psychologists, and other qualified helpers to assist you in your assessments. It would also be helpful to seek out and read some of the References at the end of this book and give you a clearer understanding of the complexity of measuring the self.

Above all, keep in mind your own limitations. This means being aware of the extent of your training and of the possible cost of errors in judgment, being able to tolerate ambiguity, not being too hasty with answers but instead trying to base your inferences on sufficient evidence, and that remembering that the self is many times more difficult to assess than is some tangible object.

Biases. It is helpful to keep in mind that a self must be studied through the perceptions of someone. Even when you try to describe your *own* self, it can only be a rough approximation. As we shall see later, one's observation of oneself is open to distortion, either involuntarily or deliberately. Therefore, in making inferences about the self, it is vital to recognize your own biases and try to take them into account as much as possible. Your task is to gain a clearer understanding of the student's self, not to try to give him yours. To put it another way, you should have a fair understanding of yourself before you attempt to evaluate the self of others.

EVALUATING THE SELF THROUGH SELF-REPORTS

Through the years there has been controversy over the validity and reliability of self-report inventories. One is dealing with validity when he asks the question: *Is the instrument measuring what it claims to measure?* If so, it is a "valid" instrument. One is dealing with reliability when he asks: *How consistent are the findings through various administrations?*

If the findings are consistent through repeated administrations, the instrument is considered "reliable."

Rogers (1951) has taken the position that self-reports are valuable sources of information about the individual. And Allport (1955, 1961) has written that the individual has the right to be believed when he reports his feelings about himself. Both these authorities believe that if we want to know more about a person, we should ask him directly. Sarbin and Rosenberg (1955) concluded from their research that their self-report instrument was useful in getting at meaningful self-attributes quickly and with a minimum of effort. Perhaps this general viewpoint can best be summarized by a statement of Strong and Feder: "[E]very evaluative statement that a person makes concerning himself can be considered a sample of his self concept, from which inferences may then be made about the various properties of that self concept" (1961, p. 170). Numerous other studies have been based on the assumption that evaluative statements made by the individual about himself are vaild and reliable data.

The major critics of self-reporting believe that while the self concept is what an individual believes about himself, the self-report is only what he is willing and able to disclose to someone else. Combs, Courson, and Soper (1963) argue that these are rarely, if ever, identical. They refer to Combs and Soper (1957), who reported that the degree to which the self-report can be relied upon as an accurate indication of the self concept depends upon such factors as: (1) the clarity of the subject's awareness; (2) his command of adequate symbols for expression; (3) social expectancy; (4) the cooperation of the subject; and (5) his freedom from threat.

Three additional variables which might influence self-reports are the *familiarity of the item, response set,* and *social desirability.* Purinton (1965) reported that changes in self-reports with repeated usage could be related to the student's familiarity with the items and would not necessarily reflect a change in his self concept. Shulman (1968) found that there are yea-sayers and nay-sayers who respond in a particular pattern irrespective of the inventory questions. Heilbrun (1965) has maintained that the social desirability of a response has something to do with its probability of endorsement on a self-report test.

Wylie (1961) concluded from her comprehensive review of research on self concept:

> We would like to assume that a subject's self-report responses are determined by his phenomenal field. However, we know that it would be

naive to take this for granted, since it is obvious that such responses may also be influenced by the: (a) subject's intent to select what he wishes to reveal to the examiner, (b) subject's intent to say that he has attitudes or perceptions which he doesn't have, (c) subject's response habits, particularly those involving introspection and the use of language, and (d) host of situational and methodological factors which may not only induce variations of (a), (b), and (c) but may exert other more superficial influences on the responses obtained (1961, p. 24).

Clearly, there are a host of contaminating variables in self-reports. For the teacher, this means that conclusions about self concept based solely on self-reports must be taken with a great deal of salt. However, in spite of their weaknesses and limitations, self-reports do reveal characteristics of the self and are important to teachers. Used sensitively in conjunction with other evidence, self-reports give rich insights into how the child sees himself and his world. A few of the better known self-report inventories are listed below. For a more complete description of these and other self-report inventories, the reader is referred to Purkey (1968).

The Self-esteem Inventory. The SEI was developed by Stanley Coopersmith of the University of California. It was especially constructed for the research reported in *The Antecedents of Self-esteem* (Coopersmith, 1967). All the statements in the scale have been worded for use with children 8 to 10.

The Bledsoe Self Concept Scale. The BSCS, which was designed by Joseph Bledsoe of the University of Georgia, has been used with success from the third through the eighth grades, (Bledsoe, 1967). It consists of a checklist of 30 trait-descriptive adjectives.

The Self-appraisal Scale. Another recent self-report inventory is the SAS, developed by Helen Davidson and Judith Greenberg of the City College of the City University of New York for their research on scholastic achievers from a deprived background (Davidson and Greenberg, 1967.) It consists of 24 items, each of which has been tested for its intelligibility to fifth-grade children.

The How-I-See-Myself-Scale. This popular instrument was developed by Ira Gordon of the University of Florida from 1958 to 1967. It was devised from the categories developed by Jersild (1952), out of the compositions of children. The scale consists of a 40 (elementary form) or 42-item (secondary form) five-point scale. Additional information may be found in Gordon (1966, 1968) and Yeatts (1967).

Q-Sort. Q-sort is not so much an instrument as it is a method. It requires the subject to sort a number of self-reference statements (usually 70 to 150 items) into a series of piles or classes along a continuum of appropriateness of self-description, from those "most like" him to those "least like" him. The number of items sorted into each pile is specified in such a way that the resulting frequency distributions approximates that of a normal distribution. For an extensive reference on this method, see Cummins (1963).

Semantic Differential. The semantic differential technique of measuring the "meaning systems" of individuals was developed by Charles Osgood of the University of Illinois. The method is described in detail in Osgood, Suci, and Tannenbaum (1957). Basically, it involves sets of polar adjectives such as Happy–sad, Hard–soft, and Slow–fast, with five to seven spaces between each set. The concept to be measured is placed at the top of the scale and the subject is to place a check somewhere along the continuum to indicate his attitude. It is a popular and flexible method of measuring the dimensions of one's system of meanings about himself and the world in which he lives.

There are other commercially produced self-report inventories which are designated to be used by individuals with special training in psychometrics. Two of the more popular are the *Tennessee Self Concept Scale* (Fitts, 1964) published by Counselor Recordings and Tests, Box 6184, Acklen Station, Nashville, Tennessee, 37212, and the *California Psychological Inventory* (Gough, 1956) published by Consulting Psychologists Press, Inc., 577 College Ave., Palo Alto, California.

Whether the self-report inventory you use is commercially prepared or locally produced, it is a good idea to remember four rules in giving self-report scales:

1. When working with younger students, items should be read to the students while the children read silently.
2. Stress the fact that there are no *right* or *wrong* answers. The student is to express those ideas he holds true about himself.
3. All self-report inventories should be administered under conditions which are as unthreatening as possible.
4. Maintain the confidentiality of the results.

EVALUATING THE SELF THROUGH OBSERVATIONS

Traditionally, observers of human behavior have been encouraged to be as passive, uninvolved, and detached as possible, in order to facilitate their learning and avoid disrupting the person being observed. The goal was to strive for objective perception of the individual and his behavior and to separate the observer's self from that which is being observed (Carbonara, 1961). In fact, the more like a camera, the more depersonalized and detached the observer became, the better.

A more recent approach to observation is that of Combs (1965a) who believes that observations are unnecessarily frustrating because "of a mistaken belief that observations must be made objectively" (1965a, p. 64). He believes that sensitivity is a matter of commitment, and that the observer should be looking for *reasons* for behavior rather than at behavior itself. He explains (p. 66):

> I have given up asking my students to make coldly factual, detailed observation reports. I now ask them to do what I do myself when I watch a child behaving or a teacher teaching—to get the "feel" of what's going on, to see if they can get inside the skin of the person being observed, to understand how things look from his point of view. I ask them, "What do you think he is trying to do?" "How do you suppose he feels?" "How would you have to feel to behave like that?" "How does he see the other kids?" "What does he feel about the subject?" and so on.

It seems that Combs' approach encourages the teacher's exploration, involvement, and sensitivity to the individual.

For our purposes, we can utilize both approaches. We can be as objective as possible when making observations, and then we can be free to form our more subjective inferences.

Making observations. We can never view ourselves or anyone else with complete objectivity, for the meanings we assign things, people, and events are products of our past experience and the processes of how we view ourselves, as we have seen. Yet teachers need to minimize bias as much as possible. A good way to do this is to understand the process of observation.

In observing a person we usually begin with his appearance. We can become aware of the clothes he wears and the way he wears them. We can consider his height and weight, his posture, his grooming, and his general cleanliness. We can take note of any physical problems and his apparent state of health. Next we can take into account his behavior— his speech, his movements, his facial expressions, his manner, his habits, and his reactions. We can be particularly alert to fleeting clues which tell us how he relates to his peer group and to adults, taking into account the things he seeks out and the things he avoids, the way he reacts to success and to failure, to approval and disapproval, and the ways he spends his spare time. From all these observations we gather the raw material which we may use to draw inferences. Always, we should keep in mind that *his perceptions* of his appearance and behavior are more important to our understanding of him than his appearance and behavior in themselves. Sometimes a student with a seriously negative self concept will look fine.

Often it is possible for us to structure our observations by having the student respond to stimuli like those presented in structured interviews or simple quasi-projective techniques. In the structured interview, questions are carefully organized and may be open-ended. They usually deal with the student's hopes, fears, likes, dislikes, family, and school life, and are posed in an atmosphere of acceptance and permissiveness. Sacks (1966) gives a number of tips on the techniques involved in using such structured interviews.

Simple quasi-projective techniques, which we can think of as the process of drawing inferences from the student's productions, involve having the student evaluate himself by writing an autobiography, complete interest records, participate in play situations, or make up stories or complete sentences. The younger child's drawings can be used as indications of his self (Harris, 1963). Dinkmeyer (1965) provides some useful tips on the inferential aspect of child study.

Before you draw inferences about a student, it will be helpful to ask yourself: "How do I feel about this person?" "What things might distort my perceptions of how this student sees himself and others?" Try to include a number of observations on different days, to avoid misunderstandings based on a person's "off-day." Finally, avoid jumping to conclusions. If a student spends some time alone, it may stem merely from his enjoyment of solitary activities. For a more detailed treatment of methods of observation, Gordon's book (1966) provides a comprehensive treatment.

Drawing inferences. Inference is a valuable scientific tool whose reliability between and within observers has been demonstrated (Courson, 1965). Once appearance and behavior have been carefuly observed, we are prepared to draw some inferences. On the basis of what we've seen, we should ask ourselves: What are some of the beliefs he holds about himself?" "Does he see himself as a student, a leader, an athlete, a popular fellow, a son, or whatever, and in what order?" "Are his beliefs about himself generally positive or negative?" "Which beliefs are more central?" "Which are more value-laden?" "Which beliefs are most likely to resist change?" "What problems does the student have, and what is his most pressing problem *right now?*" It is in the answers we give to questions like these that we find what the individual student is like, how he feels about himself and the world, and why he behaves as he does.

One particular caution should be noted in drawing inferences, and that is the importance of being *conservative* about the use of case histories, cumulative folders, anecdotal reports, information picked up in the teachers' lounge, or any other secondary or indirect information. They involve the perceptions of a third party. While they are sometimes useful, they are also an important source of bias and misunderstanding.

In this final chapter we have seen the importance of what the teacher believes about himself and about his students, and how attitudes toward students are more important than techniques and materials. We've considered some of the things the teacher does: the attitudes he conveys, the atmosphere he creates, and the sensitivity he develops through self-report inventories and observations.

Allport, G. W. *Becoming.* New Haven, Conn.: Yale University Press, 1955.

Berger, E. M. The relation between expressed acceptance of self and expressed acceptance of others. *J. Abn. and Soc. Psychol,* 1953, **47,** 778–782.

Birney, R. C., Burdick, H., & Teevan, R. C. *Fear of failure.* Princeton, N.J.: D. Van Nostrand, 1969.

Bledsoe, J. Self-concept of children and their intelligence, achievement, interests, and anxiety. *Child. Educ.,* 1967, **43,** 436–438.

Brookover, W. B., et al. *Self-concept of ability and school achievement. II: Improving academic achievement through students' self-concept enhancement.* U.S. Office of Education, Cooperative Research Project No. 1636. East Lansing: Office of Research and Publications, Michigan State University, 1965.

Brookover, W. B., Erickson, E. L., & Joiner, L. M. *Self-concept of ability and school achievement. III: Relationship of self-concept to achievement in high school.* U.S. Office of Education, Cooperative Research Project No. 2831. East Lansing: Office of Research and Publications, Michigan State University, 1967.

Carbonara, N. T. *Techniques for observing normal child behavior.* Pittsburgh: University of Pittsburgh Press, 1961.

Carlton, L., & Moore, R. H. The effects of self-directive dramatization on reading achievement and self concept of culturally disadvantaged children. *Reading Teacher,* 1966, **20,** 125–130.

Carlton, L., & Moore, R. H. *Reading, self-directive dramatization and self concept.* Columbus, Ohio: Charles E. Merrill, 1968.

Christensen, C. M. Relationships between pupil achievement, pupil affect-need, teacher warmth, and teacher permissiveness. *J. Educ. Psychol.* 1960, **51,** 169–174.

Clarke, W. E. The relationship between college academic performance and expectancies. Doctoral dissertation, Michigan State University, 1960.

Cogan, M. The behavior of teachers and the productive behavior of their pupils. *J. Exptl. Educ.*, 1958, 27, 89–124.

Cogan, M. *The professional education of teachers: A perceptual view of teacher preparation.* Boston: Allyn & Bacon, 1965. (a)

Cogan, M., Courson, C. C., & Soper, D. W. The measurement of self-concept and self-report. *Educ. and Psychol. Measmt.*, 1963a, **23**, 493–500.

Combs, A. W., & Soper, D. W. The self, its derivate terms, and research. *J. Individual Psychol.*, 1957, **13**, 135–145.

Combs, A. W., & Soper, D. W. The perceptual organization of effective counselors. *J. Counsl. Psychol.*, 1936b, **10**, 222–226.

Combs, A. W., & Snygg, D. *Individual behavior.* 2nd ed. New York: Harper & Row, 1959.

Combs, A. W., et al. *Florida studies in the helping professions.* University of Florida Social Science Monograph No. 37, 1969.

Coopersmith, S. *The antecedents of self-esteem.* San Francisco.: W. H. Freeman, 1967.

Costello, C. G. Ego involvement, success and failure: A review of the literature. In H. J. Eysenck (Ed.), *Experiments in motivation.* New York: Macmillan, 1964, pp. 161–208.

Courson, C. C. The use of inference as a research tool. *Educ. and Psychol. Measmt.*, 1965, **25**, 1029–1038.

Crovetto, A. M., Fischer, L. L., & Boudreax, J. L. *The pre-school child and his self-image.* Division of Instruction and Division of Pupil Personnel, New Orleans Public Schools, 1967.

Cummins, R. E. Some applications of "Q" Methodology to teaching and educational research. *J. Educ. Res.*, 1963, **57**, 94–98.

Davidson, H. H., & Greenberg, J. W. *School achievers from a deprived background* (U.S.O.E. Project No. 2805, Contract No. OE–5–10–132) New York: The City College of the City University of New York, 1967.

Davidson, H. H., & Lang, G. Children's perceptions of their teachers' feelings toward them related to self-perception, school achievement, and behavior. *J. Exptl. Educ.*, 1960, **29**, 107–118.

Dinkmeyer, D. C. *Child development: The emerging self.* Englewood Cliffs, N.J.: Prentice-Hall, 1965.

Fey, W. F. Acceptance of self and others, and its relation to therapy readiness. *J. Clin. Psychol.*, 1954, **10**, 266–269.

Fitts, W. *Tennessee self-concept scale.* Nashville: Counselor Recordings and Tests, 1964.

Frankel, E. Effects of a program of advanced summer study on the self-perceptions of academically talented high school students. *Exceptional Children,* 1964, **30,** 245–249.

Gill, M. P. Pattern of achievement as related to the perceived self. Paper read at the annual meeting of the American Educational Research Association Convention, Los Angeles, February 1969.

Gordon, I. J. *Studying the child in the school.* New York: Wiley, 1966.

Gordon, I. J. *A text manual for the How-I-See-Myself-Scale.* Florida Educational Research and Development Council. Gainesville: University of Florida, 1968.

Gough, J. C. *California psychological inventory.* Palo Alto, Calif.: Consulting Psychologist Press, 1956.

Harris, D. B. *Children's drawings as measures of intellectual maturity.* New York: Harcourt, Brace, 1963.

Heilbrun, A. B., Jr. The social desirability variable: Implications for test reliability and validity. *Educ. and Psychol. Measmt.,* 1965, **25,** 745–756.

Jersild, A. T. *In search of self.* New York: Bureau of Publications, Teachers College, Columbia University, 1952.

Jersild, A. T. *Child psychology.* Englewood Cliffs, N.J.: Prentice-Hall, 1960.

Jersild, A. T. Voice of the self. *NEA J.,* 1965, **54:**23–25.

Jourard, S. M. *The transparent self: Self-disclosure and well-being.* Princeton, N. J.: D. Van Nostrand, 1964.

Kowitz, G. T. Test anxiety and self-concept. *Childhd. Educ.,* 1967, **44,** 162–165.

Ludwig, D. J., & Maehr, M. L. Changes in self-concept and stated behavioral preferences. *Child Developmt.,* 1967, **38,** 453–467.

Luft, J. On nonverbal interaction. *J. Psychol.,* 1966, **63,** 261–268.

Moustakas, C. *The authentic teacher: Sensitivity and awareness in the classroom.* Cambridge, Mass.: Howard A. Doyle Publishing Company, 1966.

Omwake, K. T. The relation between acceptance of self and acceptance of others shown by three personality inventories. *J. Consult. Psychol.,* 1954, **18,** 443 and 446.

Osgood, C. E., Suci, G. J., & Tannenbaum, P. H. *The measurement of meaning.* Urbana: University of Illinois Press, 1957.

Purinton, D. E. The effect of item familiarity on self-concept sorts. *Dissertation Abstr.,* 1965, **26,** 2325.

Purkey, W. W. The search for self: Evaluating student self concepts. *Ibid.* 4 (2), 1968.

Reed, H. B. Implications for science education of a teacher competence research. *Science Educ.,* 1962, **46,** 473–486.

Rogers, C. R. *Client-centered therapy.* Boston: Houghton-Mifflin, 1951.

Rogers, C. R. The therapeutic relationship: Recent theory and research. Reprinted in G. Babladelis and S. Adams (Eds.) *The Shaping of Personality.* Englewood Cliffs, N.J.: Prentice-Hall, 1965, 1967.

Rosenthal, R., & Jacobson, L. 1968a. Teacher expectations for the disadvantaged. *Scientific Amer.,* 1968a, **218,** 19–23.

Rosenthal, R., & Jacobson, L. *Pygmalion in the classroom: Teacher expectation and pupils' intellectual development.* New York: Holt, Rinehart, 1968. (b)

Sacks, B. M. *The student, the interview, and the curriculum.* Boston: Houghton-Mifflin, 1966.

Sarason, I. G. The effects of anxiety and threat on the solution of a difficult task. *J. Abn. and Soc. Psychol.,* 1961, **62,** 165–168.

Sarbin, T. R., & Rosenberg, B. G. Contributions to role-taking theory: IV. Method for obtaining a quantitative estimate of self. *J. Soc. Psychol.,* 1955, **42,** 71–81.

Shulman, L. S. Multiple measurement of self-concept. Paper presented at the meeting of the American Educational Research Association, Chicago, February 1968.

Spaulding, R. L. Achievement, creativity, and self concept correlates of teacher-pupil transactions in elementary schools. U.S. Office of Education, Cooperative Research Report No. 1352. Urbana: University of Illinois, 1963.

Spaulding, R. L. Achievement, creativity, and self concept correlates of teacher-pupil transactions in elementary schools. In C. B. Stendler (Ed.), *Readings in child behavior and development,* 2nd ed. New York: Harcourt, Brace, 1964, pp. 313–318.

Staines, J. W. The self-picture as a factor in the classroom. *British J. Educatl. Psychol.,* 1958, **28,** 97–111.

Strong, D., & Feder, D. Measurement of the self concept: A critique of the literature. *J. Counslg. Psychol.,* 1961, **8,** 223–229.

Trent, R. D. The relationship between expressed self-acceptance and expressed attitudes toward Negro and white in Negro children. *J. Genet. Psychol.,* 1957, **91,** 25–31.

Walsh, A. M. *Self-concepts of bright boys with learning difficulties.* New York: Bureau of Publications, Teachers College, Columbia University, 1956.

Wylie, R. C. *The self-concept: A critical survey of pertinent research literature.* Lincoln: University of Nebraska Press, 1961.

Yeatts, P. P. Developmental changes in the self-concept of children grades 3–12. *Florida Educatl. Res. and Developmt. Council Res. Bull.,* No. 2. Gainesville: University of Florida, 1967.

Neurotic Interaction Between Counselor and Counselee

George Lawton

Marriage counseling is increasingly viewed as a form of short-term psychotherapy (1, 2, 3, 4). Only on rare occasions, however, is it analytically oriented and on even rarer occasions is the analytic approach Freudian in character.

Marriage counseling may deal with the unmarried, the married, and the in-between. It differs from ordinary short-term psychotherapy in that the chief and often the only presenting symptom of the candidate for therapy is some phase of his relationship with the opposite sex or one representative of it. The unmarried candidate is likely to make it the opposite sex in general, and the married candidate one representative in particular.

It has been the writer's experience that the problem of an unmarried adult who has a difficulty with the opposite sex which makes him seek professional help nearly always needs long-term psychotherapy. Since the writer is probably better known as a psychoanalyst than as a marriage counselor, his sampling of both married and unmarried clients is probably somewhat skewed. Within the confines of this nevertheless broad and lengthy experience with this group of unmarried adults we are now discussing, the writer has found a considerable number with strong unconscious homosexual trends, another fairly large group with psychotic patterns in their thinking, and some borderline psychotics. Most of the remainder are severely disturbed neurotics.

The *couple* who applies for pre-marital guidance generally presents relatively simple problems in comparison with the group just mentioned.

Reprinted from *Journal of Counseling Psychology*, 1958, **5**, 28–33, by permission of the American Psychological Association.

These couples more nearly fit the stereotype of premarital counseling as a form of educational guidance regarding mate suitability, preparation for a sexual life, how to draw up a budget, etc.

As for the problems of the married, here we enter upon one of the most difficult and challenging areas in all of psychotherapy. Those with marital problems are generally the most disturbed patients the writer has, and the most difficult to treat. Those with a marital syndrome constitute for the writer's practice the same order of magnitude as schizophrenics, those with psychosomatic problems, homosexuals, alcoholics, and severely disturbed children.

A man or woman whose marriage is in serious trouble is a person in a state of crisis, an emergency perhaps as great as any he can face. He is obsessed with the problem, which he generally defines as due to something his partner is doing, or not doing, of a very drastic kind. He or she wants to talk only about his obsession, namely, how his partner, for some reason, is destroying his every chance for happiness. This is stating the problem in extreme form, but the reality is most often not too far behind. A great number of the cases seen by at least *this* marriage counselor are examples of a (possibly transient) psychosis which may be called *marital paranoia*.

The relationship with individuals of the opposite sex is one of the most important experiences in the life of a patient, but it is equally important to the therapist, who is also a patient only temporarily on the other side of the desk and presumably a little further advanced in understanding and therefore in a position to be helpful to one less advanced.

Since for the writer marriage counseling is a form of psychotherapy, in the discussion that follows, the practitioner will be referred to as a therapist and the person with a problem, a patient. Since the observations made apply to various kinds of psychotherapy, most references from this point onward will not specify "marriage counseling" as such. And, while we speak of neurotic interaction in this symposium, it should be realized that the interaction can also be psychotic on one or both sides, depending on the makeup of the therapist and patient and the type of problem in this area which one or both have still failed to solve.

INTERFERING MOTIVATIONS: COUNTER–IDENTIFCATIONS AND COUNTER–TRANSFERENCES

Neurotic interaction in this paper will be considered under the head of counter-transference and counter-identification phenomena. The therapist acts in a complementary manner to a neurotic or psychotic need of the patient; or the patient's appearance, personality, or problem stirs up in the therapist an old or current problem which has either not been perceived or not been solved. In such a case, the original signal for psychotic or neurotic interaction may unconsciously be sent out by the therapist, and the patient unconsciously responds with the type of behavior which the therapist indicates he (the therapist) needs.

A study of the variety of unconscious motivations which may intrude into the dynamics of the therapeutic relationship is important because they: (a) increase the strain and tension of the therapist's work, (b) complicate the therapeutic relationship unduly, and (c) jeopardize the success of therapy.

THERAPIST INSECURITIES VARIOUSLY EXPRESSED

There are many ways the therapist may unconsciously act on his own insecurities in his interactions with the patient. Out of his fear that he will lose control of the relationship, the therapist may, first of all, *tend to dominate the patient*. He may, for example, determinedly proceed to get the patient to break up a courtship, a marriage, or an extra-marital affair in order to prove his (the therapist's) power. I must put an end to this and fast! the therapist resolves.

A second way a therapist's insecurities may appear is in his competition with other significant authority figures in the life of the patient. He may offer advice in opposition to the minister, physician, spouse, sibling, parent, or friend and see to it that this opposing advice is carried out by the patient in ways of doubtful relevance to the therapy. In extreme cases, this may be a real drive toward omnipotence in the life of the patient: "I, your therapist, am Jehovah. Do unquestioningly what I say and have no other gods before me."

Other therapists evidence their insecurities in a third way: by showering the patient with excessive love and attention. The therapist probably felt himself unloved and neglected by a parent and therefore redresses the old hurt by reliving the roles of parent and child. He now acts both roles at once by making the patient the child he once was and by also becoming his own parent. He is over-parentalizing the patient in return for the patient's grateful affection. Here we find the therapist who goes to extreme lengths to prevent a marriage failure: "This marriage *must* succeed." Glover speaks of "the eagerness of some therapists to give suck."

A fourth form of insecurity expression by a therapist is to function as the child of the patient. He identifies the patient with his own parent. He misses the patient when he is away and welcomes him back with a sigh of pleasure and relief. Parental security is re-established for the child.

Fifthly, the therapist's insecurities may take the channel of the Pygmalion complex. The need to manipulate and to resolve one's own problems in other people's lives leads to the need to make the patient like the therapist.

The therapist, in a sixth fashion, may find his insecurities take the form of resentment of the patient's demands. He may become vindictive toward the patient for his hostility, his negative transference. The resentment may openly emerge in the form of anger toward the patient for his failure to improve or more covertly as despair. Some therapists unconsciously use silence as counter-resistance, counter-attack. They use "controlled apathy" as a punitive measure.

Seventhly, some therapists fear the patient's hostility and try to appease the patient. Such therapists have a need for friendliness, are afraid of their patient's aggression, feel vulnerable to attack and criticism. Whenever a therapist hides behind his beard—that is, uses some ritualistic practice or professional mumbo-jumbo—he should ask himself whether what he is doing is prompted by a desire to cure the patient, or by insecurity.

An eighth form of insecurity expression on the part of the therapist is closely related to the foregoing: his inability to stand the patient's tension and anxiety. Often the patient reminds the therapist too much of his own problems—sexual, marital, illness, death, parent-child interactions. This type of insecurity is apt to result in a glittering pseudo-optimism: "Don't worry; everything will be all right." Such pseudo-optimism creates resistance and counter-resistance to therapy.

SWEET AND AGGRESSIVE THERAPISTS

Two types of counter-transference that deserve our particular attention are (a) the sweet and (b) the aggressive patterns of therapists in their interactions with patients. These patterns (as well as those to be considered later) are also reflective of insecurity feelings of therapists, but are considered under a separate heading merely for convenience.

The sweet therapist has a need to overintellectualize and over-emphasize logic and common sense. The hour is sweetly reasonable, rather than filled with emotions and thoughts that can lead only to storm and trouble, tears and the gnashing of teeth, bloodshed.

The over-emphasis on logic and common sense may represent resistance on the therapist's part to the possibility of the patient's voicing transference feelings which the therapist may find distressing. It may also represent the therapist's resistance to the possibility that he may take the lid off the Pandora box of his counter-transference feelings.

Here belongs the tendency of some therapists to round off each hour with a complete explanation, a summary of important points covered. Is this educational zealousness? Or compulsion? What does the therapist hope to ward off by this ritual of giving a summary at the end of the hour? Persons may become therapists because they seek an intellectual system for their personal problems, but patients don't get cured so cleanly and so sweetly.

Distinguished sharply from the therapist who handles his counter-transference problems in this sweet fashion is the aggressive type of therapist. Some therapists have contempt for their patients. The patient is always wrong; he is an opponent to be outwitted. The therapist says to himself as he faces the patient: "You are going to like what I do or else . . ." The writer knew a therapist who stood up, faced his patients, and thundered angrily and sarcastically at them.

More often, however, aggressions of therapists take somewhat more subtle forms. As expressed earlier, silence may be used punitively. Contempt may slip into the tone of voice, the gesture, the facial expression. Humor is used to "draw blood."

SEDUCTION: A TWO-WAY STREET

Insufficiently analyzed therapists may have difficulty resisting temptations both to seduce and be seduced by their patients. Attempts at the seduction of the therapist by the patient is a form of resistance to therapy, though both patients and therapists may regard it as a means of therapy and proof of it.

Patient seduction may take both verbal and non-verbal forms. Examples of non-verbal seduction devices are glances, gifts, smiles, and payment of bill in advance or over-payments. Verbal wooing devices consist of the outpouring of love and sexual thoughts and feelings and sometimes outright pleas and arguments in favor of sexual response by the therapist. It is here worth noting that the seduction of the therapist may be homosexual as well as heterosexual and that homosexual counter-transference can be a greater source of counter-resistance than heterosexual.

Immature and disturbed therapists may be tempted in the direction of an actively seductive role themselves, for the submissive, child-like patient offers "easy pickings." Some of the verbal wooing devices of a therapist follow: calling the patient by his first name too soon and without ascertaining patient's wishes; using affectionate or meaningful intonation or words; engaging in long, cosy telephone conversations; talking, explaining, interpreting excessively; asking for deep material too soon or too obviously. Non-verbal seduction of the patient by the therapist may take such means as the following: visiting the patient's home at the request of the patient whenever the latter undergoes an emotional emergency of a transference kind; giving affectionate or meaningful glances; putting an affectionate hand on the patient's shoulder or giving a parental pat; allowing the patient to telephone regularly after hours or to see the therapist at ordinarily non-office hour times; charging the patient a fee which the patient feels is lower than called for in a particular situation and letting the patient know this is done because the therapist likes him; and regularly over-running usual and conventional time limits for sessions.

THERAPIST PROJECTIONS

Some therapists see in their work an opportunity to project their personal attitudes. All marital problems are due to the same causes, some marriage counselors believe, and all difficulties are to be solved in the same way. This is the Procrustean school of marriage counseling. Here are some examples:

(a) *The therapist himself is a convert to defeat and self-pity.* He believes privately that the world is a vale of tears and that human beings generally don't or can't get what they want. *He* has not achieved what he hoped for in life, so why should this patient? Let him adjust himself to a world where truth, justice, and love do *not* prevail.

(b) *Then, on the other hand, we find the therapist who believes that life is grand and glorious.* To this therapist, people who have problems do so most unnecessarily: a smile, a cheerful up and at 'em attitude, a hearty, reassuring clap on the back will solve all difficulties. This type of marriage counselor believes that the unhappy, cantankerous husband will change over night if his wife will only make apple pie.

(c) *Some marriage counselors believe that the answer to a sick marriage is inescapably divorce, and others believe that reconciliation is al-*

ways possible. Both are likely to be *projecting their own personal marital attitudes.* The one kind of therapist says to himself: when marriage reaches this point, or when a person has this kind of spouse, divorce *must* be the answer. The other type of therapist is just as incapable of taking an objective view of a particular marriage and will insist on reconciliation in marriages which are obviously distorting the personalities of the participants.

(d) *Some therapists believe that technically satisfactory sexual intercourse is the cure for all emotional problems.* Since most patients, with or without opportunities for satisfactory sexual intercourse, share this point of view, patient and therapist are more in agreement on this attitude than many another. This doctrine starts with the idea that satisfactory sexual intercourse is always good and leads on to the notion that more of it is even better, for you can never have too much of a good thing. Some therapists keep pushing their patients into heterosexual intercourse whether the patient wants it or not, is ready for it or not, is benefited by it or not, or whether it is his problem or not.

(e) *There are therapists at the other end of the sex-projection continuum, however, who over-spiritualize the man-woman relationship.* They are the ones who recommend cold showers and a run around the block for teen-agers with strong sexual urges. Having their own private feud with the sexual impulse, they are glad in a marriage counseling situation to play down the importance of satisfactory sexual experiences and to play up the sublimations.

SUMMARY

We have considered various types of neurotic interations between counselor and counselee which interfere with therapeutic effectiveness. These were dealt with under the general heading of interfering motivations (of the therapist) in the forms of counter-transferences and counter-identifications. For convenience of discussion we sub-divided these interfering motivations into various expressions of therapist insecurities, sweet and aggressive therapists, seductive processes, and therapist projections.

In the light of this discussion, it would seem evident that the psychotherapist who has undergone successful psychoanalysis, or at least psychotherapy, is less likely to get involved in neurotic interactions between himself and his patient. He is also better equipped than the unanalyzed practitioner to deal with neurotic interactions when they do arise. And it is also clearly important that the psychotherapist who is dealing with marital problems should himself have a happy marriage, for such a practitioner is apt to be better equipped to detect and deal with neurotic interactions between himself and his patients.

Our concluding point of emphasis, then, is this: *the most important instrument* in our attempt to understand and treat successfully the problems which a patient may have in relationship to a member of the opposite sex *is our knowledge of our own problems in this area and our ability either to solve or handle these problems in life in general* and in our interactions with patients in particular.

1. Alexander, F. Principles and techniques of briefer psychotherapeutic procedures. *Psychiatric treatment* (Proceedings of the Assn. for research in nerv. & ment. disease), 1953, **21,** 16–20.

2. Ellis, A. A critical evaluation of marriage counseling. *Mar. & Fam. Liv.,* 1956, **18,** 65–71.

3. Harper, R. A. Failure in marriage counseling. *Mar. & Fam. Liv.,* 1955, **17,** 359–362.

4. Laidlaw, R. W. The psychiatrist as marriage counselor. *Am. J. Psychiat.,* 1950, **106,** 732–736.

How Did He Get There?

David N. Aspy

A few days ago several of my friends and I held a reunion, and as usually happens, we began to talk about what our old acquaintances were doing. Since we all were either currently teaching or had been, most of those we discussed were also members of that profession. The conversation was *most* illuminating.

Reprinted from *Peabody Journal of Education,* George Peabody College for Teachers, 1969, **47,** 152–153, by permission of the author and the publisher.

One fellow whose name came up had just returned from Harvard. "You know what he's doing?" someone contributed. "He's in charge of research for a large urban school system!" The shock that ran through the group was obvious on every face. The comments included, "He was the most trifling kid I ever knew," "He has the most 'country' sounding voice I ever heard," and "He's so dumb it hurts." We finally resolved our dissonance by concluding that Harvard was either over-rated or had lowered its academic standards drastically.

Another choice morsel for gossip was tossed out when we discovered that a second "old colleague" was the president of a college! Of course we found ways to downgrade this accomplishment. Our statements were, "They must have been desperate," "I understand he has an awful case of ulcers," and "Some guys are consistently lucky."

After this kind of conversation had run its course, one of our group said, "You know, I wonder how many of our friends are surprised at what we're doing. How many people thought you'd be a college profes-sor? How many thought you'd be a successful businessman? How many thought you'd be a prominent school official? In a way all of us are sur-prises to most people, even ourselves." These observations stopped our conversation by making us think about the course of our own lives.

Our reunion was not unique. Time after time this type of conversa-tion has been repeated, and it seems to stem from some basic concepts deep in most of our beings. Remember, we were all teachers, which means we were engaged in the facilitation of human growth, and yet we were surprised at the development of our former acquaintances. In a sense we were expressing a disbelief in the very process to which we ostensibly were devoting our time and effort. You see, we believed in our own growth, but not in that of others. This is one part of a facilitat-ing life—that of self fulfillment; but a truly facilitative life extends to promoting growth in others, and this we cannot do unless we actually *believe* in it. In other words, we cannot facilitate growth in others until we are convinced that it can be done.

Another revealing aspect of our conversation was reflected by our lack of surprise at others' failures. We expected them! We even pointed out flaws in their personalities which predicted failure. Perhaps the last straw in our negative set was shown in our satisfaction at "being right" in our predictions of failure. In fact, we were more concerned with be-ing right than with the tragedy of some of our friends' lives.

All of the foregoing may make us a little sensitive about expressed cruelty toward others, but there is a potentially constructive element of this kind of experience. At least two major lessons emerge. First, there is a strong possibility that our lack of "positive expectancy" for our former acquaintances retarded their growth. That is, each man is a part of all the people he meets, and, as research indicates, people tend to behave as others expect. Of course, these same acquaintances may have retarded our emergence. The true picture is that we probably retarded each other's growth, but happily most of us found enough constructive people to "make it." Our mutual challenge is to become that kind of facilitative person.

The second lesson is a deeper one and more painful. It is found in the fact that we seemed pleased or relieved that some of our colleagues either had not grown or had actually deteriorated. Of course, we didn't smile on obvious tragedy such as serious illness or death. In fact, we were quite sympathetic with those. The stories which brought pleasure or relief were those about people who were less successful than we. It is as if our hold on our own success was so tenuous that one way to enhance it was by comparing it to that of our colleagues. The subtlety of this fact makes it potent indeed, because it means that we probably functioned in ways which actively promoted the failure of those with whom we were in competition. You see, we were still in a kind of competition with them, because they were our reference points. It was relieving to know that we were not "coming in last" in the race for life.

These lessons are vivid ones when thinking of our relationships with our former colleagues, but they become doubly significant when we bring them into our daily lives. It is imperative that we *see* our students *and* colleagues as well as ourselves as people in the process of actualizing their individual potentials. That is, we must see the human being as a growing organism whose realization can be facilitated or retarded by others' expectations. The evidence indicates that our growth is promoted by those who believe we can grow. This same evidence indicates that when we feel threatened by another person, we actively retard his growth. Thus, when we realize that we hold these attitudes toward some students and colleagues, it is our professional responsibility either to correct these perceptions or to move away from those individuals.

It may be revealing to ask yourself how you see your old colleagues. Examining our own attitudes toward others' success could be an interesting and hopefully a productive process.

An Overview and Next Steps

A. W. Combs

What can we conclude from this series of studies and what directions do they suggest for further research? While these studies leave many questions unanswered and can hardly be regarded as definitive, they nevertheless provide additional support for basic concepts in perceptual theory, shed new light on the nature of the helping professions, and point the way to promising hypotheses for further research.

SUPPORT FOR PERCEPTUAL THEORY

The basic premise of perceptual psychology is that behavior is a function of the perceptual field of the behaver at the instant of action. Most research in human behavior has traditionally been carried on from an external point of view. That is to say, understanding of behavior has been sought from the frame of reference of the outside observer. The thesis of perceptual psychology, on the other hand, is that behavior can also be understood (and sometimes more effectively) when examined from the standpoint, not of the outsider, but of the behaver himself. The results of these studies tend to corroborate that position. They do more. Attempts to distinguish the behavior of professional workers in terms of objective criteria like knowledge possessed, or methods used, or behavior exhibited have generally been disappointing in the past. Several of the studies reported here, however, have demonstrated that significant relationships do, indeed, exist between perception and behavior. Even

Reprinted from Combs, A. W., *Florida Studies in the Helping Professions,* University of Florida Monographs: Social Sciences No. 37, University of Florida Press: Gainesville, 1969, pp. 69–78, by permission of the author and the publisher.

more, they suggest that a perceptual approach to the study of professional workers may provide us with more useful understanding of these persons than has heretofore been possible. Thus, these studies not only support the perceptual hypothesis, but suggest that this approach may be more fruitful in advancing our efforts to understand the helping professions. They seem to place in our hands a new and promising tool for further research.

A major difficulty in perceptual psychology is the problem of measurement. Measurement in more orthodox approaches to psychology can be a pretty straightforward matter of recording observations or counting responses. The study of perception is more difficult since perceptions lie inside people and are not open to direct observation. Because perception can only be approached (at least, at present) by some form of inference, additional problems of reliability of measurement are posed for the researcher using this frame of reference. For some psychologists these problems have seemed so difficult that they have raised serious questions of whether such procedures can be dignified by the term "research" at all. The question requires an answer. The position of the perceptual psychologist is that techniques of inference can, indeed, provide reliable data if the researcher approaches the problem of measurement with the same discipline, care, and rigor demanded of science in any other field of exploration.

In these studies inferences about the perceptual organization of professional workers have been obtained from a wide variety of original sources including observations, interviews, "critical incidents," responses to problem situations, and stories told by the subject. Inferences were obtained by using the observer himself as an instrument of measurement. Observers also demonstrated in these studies that such inferences could be made with highly acceptable degrees of reliability and that such data could be effectively used for the exploration of an important aspect of human behavior.

THE NATURE OF THE HELPING PROFESSIONS

THE COMMON ORIGINS OF THE HELPING PROFESSIONS

The original impetus for these studies grew out of a suspicion that, while the various forms of the helping professions differ with respect to their purposes, clientele, and techniques, nevertheless, they are basically alike in the psychology through which they operate. It seemed to us that the crux of the problem of "helping" lay not in some mysterious special technique. Rather the various helping professions seem really to be expressions of a kind of basic "good" human interrelationship. That is to say, these professions appear to represent the concentration and crystallization of the best we know about human interrelationships for the sake of the person or persons to be helped. The helping professions seem to us not different from life experience but selected from human experience. Within the limited sample represented by these studies, this thesis is given some support.

Ideally, the case for this observation would certainly be stronger had our studies investigated identical criteria with identical techniques in each of the professions we examined. Unfortunately, that is hindsight which suggests the need for further research, to be sure, but does us little good now. From the data we do have, however, there is sufficient evidence to suggest that the perceptual organization of persons who are effective helpers, at least for counselors, elementary teachers, Episcopal priests, and student nurses, have a number of common kinds of perceptions. Our original hunches seem to be supported and we are encouraged to continue exploring in these directions.

THE IMPORTANCE OF PERCEPTUAL ORGANIZATION AS A DISTINGUISHING CHARACTERISTIC

Our early theoretical consideration of these matters led us to the belief that the widespread failure of research efforts to distinguish between effective and ineffective workers in the helping professions was largely due to concentration on symptoms rather than causes. Observed behavior is the end of a process, an expression of it. As such, many diverse behaviors may occur as expressions of a single aspect of individual beliefs or perceptions. Conversely, different perceptual experiences can result in highly similar kinds of behavior. To distinguish clearly between effective and ineffective workers in the helping professions it seemed to us required penetration to the causes of behavior, a hypothesis supported by the observation of other workers that persons are often helped by highly diverse behaviors if the intent of the helper is positive. The accuracy of this reasoning is certainly given support by the findings of these studies. Our studies with elementary teachers, counselors, and Episcopal priests, especially, seem to lend credence to the importance of the perceptual variable in distinguishing between effective and ineffective helpers. The results for our college teachers, when effectiveness is judged by students, at least, also seem to corroborate our hypotheses. The findings of our study with student nurses, however, while not denying our original hypothesis, certainly did not corroborate it.

THE GENERAL FRAME OF REFERENCE OF PROFESSIONAL HELPERS

Three of our studies showing significant differences between effective and ineffective professional workers investigated the frame of reference in which the helper approached his task (Table 1). All these investigated

TABLE 1   FRAME OF REFERENCE CATEGORIES SHOWING SIGNIFICANT DIFFERENCES IN THREE STUDIES

Category	Counselors	Teachers	Priests
People—things	S[a]	S	S
Internal—external	S	S	NM
Perceptual—facts	NM[b]	S	NM
Immediate—historical	NM	S	NM

a. S=Significant difference.
b. NM=Not measured.

the people-things dichotomy, two examined the internal-external approach dimension, and one further examined the perceptual-facts and the immediate-historical dichotomies as well. In view of the fact that the helping professions are designed to help people, it is not surprising to find that workers who tend to be people-oriented are likely to be more effective. The remaining items explored in this category seem to represent a characteristic internal or perceptual approach which effective helpers take toward their students, clients, or parishioners. Such a characteristic frame of reference in the helper would presumably cause him to behave in ways that others would describe as sensitive or empathic, both qualities often described as desirable in counselors, teachers, pastors, and nurses.

THE HELPER'S PERCEPTIONS OF PEOPLE

It is apparent that effective helpers in all four of the professions indicated in Table 2 are characterized by a generally positive view of their subjects and a belief in the capacity of the human organism to save it-

TABLE 2   PERCEPTIONS OF OTHER CATEGORIES SHOWING SIGNIFICANT DIFFERENCES IN FOUR STUDIES

Category	Counselors	Teachers	Priests	Professors[a]
Able—unable	S[b]	S	S	S
Dependable—undependable	S	S	NM	S
Friendly—unfriendly	S	S	NM	NM
Worthy—unworthy	S	S	NM	S
Internally motivated—not	NM[c]	S	NM	S
Helpful—hindering	NM	S	NM	NM

a. Effectiveness determined from student ratings only.
b. S=Significant difference.
c. NM=Not measured.

self. It makes a great deal of difference whether helpers perceive their clients as able or unable. If a counselor, teacher, or priest does not regard his clients as able he can hardly permit them, let them, or trust them to act on their own; to do so would be a violation of responsibility. Apparently, effective helpers tend to see the persons they work with in essentially positive ways as dependable, friendly, and worthy people. This hardly seems like a startling revelation. Indeed, it sounds like little more than good common sense. It is necessary to remind ourselves, however, that these are not factors which helpers *say* about themselves, but characteristic ways of perceiving inferred from their behavior. Effective behavers do not simply verbally ascribe to these qualities; they *behave* in terms of them.

THE HELPER'S PERCEPTIONS OF SELF

Two characteristics stand out in an examination of Table 3. In the first place effective helpers appear to see themselves as one with mankind, as

TABLE 3   PERCEPTIONS OF SELF CATEGORIES SHOWING SIGNIFICANT DIFFERENCES IN FOUR STUDIES

Category	Counselors	Teachers	Priests	Professors[a]
Identified—unidentified	S[b]	S	S	NS[d]
Enough—not enough	S	S	NM	NS
Dependable—undependable	NM[c]	S	NM	NM
Worthy—unworthy	NM	S	NM	NS
Wanted—unwanted	NM	S	NM	S

a. Effectiveness determined from student ratings only.
b. S=Significant difference.
c. NM=Not measured.
d. NS=Not significant.

sharing a common fate. Poor helpers, on the other hand, have a tendency to see themselves as apart from others, as different from them. If the success of helping professions depends upon relationships established between helpers and helpees, as modern theory would seem to suggest, it is easy to see why this characteristic would distinguish between good helpers and poor ones. It is difficult to establish effective relationships with a helper unwilling to get involved.

A second major characteristic of a good helper seems to be the existence of an essentially positive view of self. Such views of self seem to be characteristic also of self-actualizing personalities as reported in the literature. A positive view of self provides the kind of internal security which makes it possible for persons who possess such views of self to behave with much more assurance, dignity, and straightforwardness. With a firm base of operations to work from such persons can be much more daring and creative in respect to their approach to the world and more able to give of themselves to others as well.

THE HELPER'S PERCEPTIONS OF HIS TASK

Effective helpers apparently tend to see their tasks more as freeing than controlling (Table 4). Such a finding certainly gives much support to

TABLE 4   PERCEPTIONS OF PURPOSE CATEGORIES SHOWING SIGNIFICANT
DIFFERENCE IN THREE STUDIES

Category	Counselors	Teachers	Priests
Self revealing—self concealing	S[a]	S	NM
Freeing—controlling	S	S	S
Altruistic—narcissistic	S	NM	NM
Larger—smaller	S	S	NM
Involved—uninvolved	NM[b]	S	S
Process—goals	NM	S	NM

a. S=Significant difference.
b. NM=Not measured.

the growth philosophy underlying most current counseling approaches and to the student-centered concept of teaching advocated by many modern educators. The concern of effective helpers with larger rather than smaller issues also seems to be consistent with the freeing purpose.

The self-revealing characteristic found in the effective helpers seems congruent with the identified-unidentified characteristic of self found in Table 4. Many writers have indicated that self-disclosure is closely related to healthy personality and the capacity to enter into intimate human relationships.

METHODS IN THE HELPING PROFESSIONS

In the original formulation of hypotheses for our studies of the helping professions our seminar listed seven continua which we thought might discriminate between effective and ineffective helpers in connection with the methods they used to carry out their tasks. None of these hypotheses has yet been subjected to test. In our earlier experiments this was because the problem was of less interest to us than hypotheses about the helper's frame of reference, perceptions of self and others, or perception of purposes. Later, we postponed further research on this question because changes in our thinking about the question of methods led us in somewhat different directions.

It will be recalled from our earlier discussion that a review of the literature had shown only very disappointing results with respect to distinguishing between effective and ineffective helpers on the basis of the methods which they used. In our early thinking about this matter it seemed to us we might find more clear-cut differences between effective and ineffective helpers if we looked, not at the methods they used per se, but rather, at the ways in which they were perceiving methods. Accordingly, our early seminar listed eleven continua for examination. As a consequence of our later studies, however, we have come to see the problem as follows. If the self as instrument concept of effective operation in the helping professions is valid, then the search for "right" methods is doomed before it begins. Since helpers as persons are unique, the hope of finding a "common uniqueness," by definition, is a hopeless search. It occurred to us then that perhaps the question of methods in the helping professions is not a matter of adopting the "right" method, but a question of the helper discovering the right method *for him*. That is to say, the crucial question is not "what" method, but the "fit" of the method, its appropriateness to the self of the helper, to his purposes, his subjects, the situation, and so forth. We now believe the important distinction between the good and poor helper with respect to methods is not a matter of his perceptions of methods, per se, but the *authenticity* of whatever methods he uses. There is already some evidence for this in our findings that good helpers are self-revealing, involved, and identified.

We suspect a major problem of poor helpers is the fact that their methods are unauthentic, that is, they tend to be put on, contrived. As such they can only be utilized so long as the helper keeps his mind on them. That, of course, is likely to be disastrous on two counts. In the first place it separates him from his client or student, and the message conveyed is likely to be that he is not "with it," is not really interested, or is a phony. Second, it is almost never possible to maintain attention to the "right" method for very long. As a consequence the poor helper relapses frequently to what he believes or his previous experience has taught him, and so the method he is trying to use fails because of the tenuous, interrupted character of his use of it.

We are about persuaded the question of the helper's perceptions concerning methods are of minor significance. Helpers will find the methods to carry on their tasks effectively if perceptions of self, others, purposes, and the general frame of reference are congruent with that of effective helpers. The validity of this position, of course, remains to be investigated. It is our hope that others will join us in exploring whether or not authenticity is truly the key question with respect to methods.

HOW MANY PERCEPTUAL FACTORS?

In our studies of the perceptual organization of effective helpers we have so far demonstrated that at least twenty-one perceptual characteristics distinguish between good and poor helpers. In our original seminar we listed forty-three hypotheses for exploration. There seems to be no doubt that still others could be added to this list. There is an important question to be answered, however, concerning the number of truly significant variables involved in this matter. All of us engaged in these researches have the very strong feeling that there may, in fact, be comparatively few perceptual criteria related to effective and ineffective operations in the helping professions. In choosing hypotheses from our original list for investigation it became quite clear to us that some of these were duplications. They also seemed to vary considerably in terms of fundamental importance. Even among some of the perceptual characteristics we investigated in the studies reported here, it is apparent from simple observation that items overlap. In addition, in the factor analysis of children's perceptions carried out by Combs and Soper,[1]

1. Combs, A. W., & Soper, D. W. *The relationship of child perceptions to achievement and behavior in the early school years.* Cooperative Research Project No. 814, University of Florida, Gainesville, Florida, 1963.

forty-seven of the forty-nine categories under investigation were reduced to one global factor which these authors called "a feeling of general adequacy." In order to determine the number of truly discreet perceptual characteristics involved in the discrimination of effective and ineffective helpers, we believe a factor analysis study of this matter is called for. Unfortunately, such a study would require a most expensive design and to this point we have not been able to find either the time or finances required to properly carry out such a project. Perhaps, some day, we, or someone else, may.

Ever since the various forms of the helping professions came into being the problem of discriminating between effective and ineffective workers has been a knotty one. We believe these investigations have opened some new avenues for understanding of the matter with broad implications for practical application. To this point we have been primarily interested in exploring these questions for their possible implications in the training of effective persons in the helping professions. This has already borne fruit in suggesting new approaches to the professional education of teachers based upon a perceptual approach to the problem.[2] Benton,[3] Gooding,[4] and Dickman[5] have touched slightly on the implications of their studies for the training of priests, teachers, and nurses. These are matters deserving much more speculation, experiment, and application.

To this point our researchers have been primarily concerned with exploring the perceptual organization of helpers in order to shed light on theoretical questions and to suggest areas of innovation for training more effective helpers in teaching, counseling, nursing, and pastoral care. The measurement techniques we have employed in these studies are at this stage still far less refined than we could wish. In time they will improve and new ones develop as well. If further studies continue the favorable trends we have seen so far, it is likely these measurement tech-

2. Combs, A. W. *The professional education of teachers.* Boston: Allyn and Bacon, 1965.

3. Benton, J. A. Perceptual characteristics of Episcopal pastors. Unpublished doctoral dissertation, University of Florida, 1964.

4. Gooding, C. T. An observational analysis of the perceptual organization of effective teachers. Unpublished doctoral dissertation, University of Florida, 1964.

5. Dickman, J. F. The perceptual organization of person-oriented versus task-oriented student nurses. Unpublished doctoral dissertation, University of Florida, 1967.

niques may also contribute important new approaches to the selection and evaluation of effective helpers.

It is apparent that the studies reported here are little more than pilot studies. Like any research worthy of the name they raise far more questions than they have settled. For those of us involved in these investigations they have been exciting and stimulating explorations in what seem to us to be fruitful new directions.

We believe these studies represent but a small and tentative beginning of research into a most promising new approach to understanding the helping professions. What started as a series of hunches in 1957 has now become a conviction that we are on or close to the right track. If these concepts are not the truth, then we are encouraged by our studies to believe they are very like it. It is our earnest hope that this presentation may encourage others to join us on this path to further discovery.

IV

The Person in the Process

Part IV focuses on the person in the process of being helped. However, since the articles in this section deal with basic principles of human behavior, what is said applies equally as well to the helper. It makes a great deal of difference what helpers believe about the nature of persons and their capacities.

The first two articles are concerned with the basic nature of man. Dr. Kelley's article is so full of insights and implications about the nature of man that it is impossible to sum it up in a few words. Included in his discussion are concerns for the dignity of man and the unity and uniqueness of the organism, themes which he pursued personally and professionally throughout his life. In few other places has the human being been described as beautifully or meaningfully.

No idea in modern humanistic psychology is more important than the self-concept. Its ramifications extend into every aspect of human interaction. C. H. Patterson's article analyzes the core of this vital concept as it is described by Carl Rogers and others.

The remainder of the papers in this volume deal with the potentialities of man. All take the position that the human being is an open, developing system which can be helped to grow and flourish or be hindered and debilitated through the conditions and persons surrounding him.

Ira J. Gordon centers on the flexibility of the organism and discusses the changing conception of children. He points out that beliefs about the human organism have changed from conceiving of development as a pre-set, unfolding process to that of an organism having a tremendous potential for flexibility and development.

Arthur W. Combs continues Ira Gordon's theme, but focuses on the development of intelligence in particular. Dr. Combs suggests that intelligence is a function of a rich, extensive and available field of perceptions and is therefore open to far more modification than we have traditionally believed.

Abraham H. Maslow describes the kind of person we would all like to be and to help others become. He defines the basic characteristics of the self-actualized individual and explains the phenomenon he refers to as "peak experience."

This volume ends with the question of "What Can Man Become?" This is appropriate because it is a positive question and should be the goal of all persons engaged in helping relationships. Dr. Combs gives us some suggestions as to what man might become and presents some ideas about the necessary conditions that must exist before such goals can be met.

Another Look at Individualism

Earl C. Kelley

It is likely that few subjects have been more thoroughly discussed, in conversation and in writing, than individualism. The topic is of great interest to many people. Some see individualism threatened by socialism and communism. Others fear the encroachment of the machine, with its power to force conformity. Still others view with alarm any economic system for fear that it will make robots out of them. Some cherish the notion that they are self-made, like to beat their breasts and proclaim the glories of their achievement.

Discussions of the political, or economic, or religious man depend upon the bias of those doing the discussing. They often become emo-

Reprinted by permission of the author and Wayne State University, Detroit, Mich.

tional, and are loaded with propaganda and indoctrination. They too often depart from the scientific, and known facts about the nature of the human organism are ignored.

It is my purpose here to discuss what the human organism is like, how it is constituted, and how it functions. Conclusions may then be drawn as to how we may live together. This, I believe, is the imperative problem of our time. Since we have moved together we must learn to live together. We have not yet learned, or so it seems to me, how to do this very well.

THE SCIENTIFIC METHOD

Since I propose to use the scientific method in the examination of individualism, a short discussion of this method may be in order. It is precisely at this point that I think other writers in this area have overlooked a possibility. Many people seem to think that the scientific method is something that goes on in laboratories, but does not apply to the ordinary problems of living. Thus, a high school student learns his scientific method in the chemistry and physics classes, and it has nothing to do with his social studies. If this sealing off really worked, it would defeat the purpose of the learning, since few of us spend our lives in laboratories. In fact, the laboratories of our schools may be the poorest places to learn the scientific method. Often learners are told to follow a manual, which is little different from a recipe book. As long as the manual is followed, the experiment turns out to be what the teachers expected.

The scientific method merely means that we look to nature—look to the thing or person—to see what it is like. Then we, having an end in mind, decide what to do to bring about this end. We proceed in the light of what we learn about the person or thing. The teacher, for example, wanting to bring about development and growth in the learner, looks to the learner, to see what he is like, before deciding how to bring this growth about. If he is scientific, he does not look at his textbook and ignore the learner, simply because it is the learner, not the textbook, which he wants to facilitate. The manufacturer, probably through his industrial designer or inventor, always looks to the thing to see what it is like before he decides what to use. He has a conception of what his outcome is to be, but he has to start by looking to nature for the characteristics he wants. If he did not do this, he would not be in business long.

But, one might ask, doesn't everybody do this? In some areas, we always do. The manufacturer's product has to function, or he will not be able to sell it. But in many areas—education, economics, politics—we pay little attention to what the individual is like. And in our daily lives we resort to animism and superstition. Animism is making the inanimate animate. The older practice was to invest with devils the things which behaved in ways which did not suit human purposes. Many of us are convinced of the perversity of inanimate objects. We curse the window which will not open—we blame the hammer when we hit our thumb. A friend of mine, usually scientific, traded his car because he said it was accident-prone.

Galileo's experience with his contemporaries illustrates this point. In his scientific studies, he came to the conclusion that a heavy object and a light one, if dropped at the same time from a height, would reach the ground at the same time. His colleagues said this was obvious nonsense, that as Aristotle has said and as everyone with any sense could plainly see the heavy object would reach the ground first. So Galileo took two balls of different weight and, in the presence of his colleagues, dropped them at the same time. They hit the floor at the same time. In other words he looked to nature—to the balls. His contemporaries then said that the balls were possessed of devils, and that Galileo must be a sorcerer. They animated the balls. They then threw Galileo in jail as a dangerous person. He did not like it there, so he recanted, and they let him out. But a scientific fact had been established, and this did not die. The balls did not recant.

In examining individualism, I propose not to start with economics, or with politics, or religion, but with the nature of the human organism, to see how it is built, and therefore how we may expect it to function. By this method, and I believe, by this method only, can we draw conclusions as to how we may best live together.

EACH PERSON IS UNIQUE

This is the most significant, most important fact about any human being. The fact that each individual is unique means that each person has something, knows something, which nobody else on earth has or knows. It is, of course, not always easy to bring this special contribution out, but it is there if it can be made to function. This difference is what the individual uses, when he makes his own special contribution to any enterprise. This is the way by which an individual achieves significance.

When Thomas Jefferson declared that it was self-evident that all men are created equal, he meant that they were equal politically, before the law, not biologically or psychologically. Little was then known about human biology. If Jefferson had been in possession of present-day research, and had spoken as a biologist, he might have said that "It is self-evident that all men are created unequal." But then as a statesman, he doubtless would have added that "In spite of this fact, all are obviously equal before the law, and are entitled to equal justice."

That all people are different is a fact which everybody accepts in a superficial way. Anybody can see, just by looking at any group of people, that no two are alike. But the depth of this uniqueness is not generally comprehended, and this results in many people behaving as though people were alike. Indeed, in many of our human activities we seem to strive to make people alike. This goes on in all facets of our society—the home, the school, the church, the military.

Often it seems that in spite of superficial knowledge that all people are different, we try to repeal uniqueness, which nature has gone to so much trouble to establish. We seem to cherish likeness, and conformity. A good example of this is what goes on in our schools. I use this example not because the school is the only place in our society where striving for conformity goes on, but because it is well known to most people. For centuries our teachers have striven to bring everyone through their courses knowing the same things. They have frowned upon the learners who let their differences show. They have rewarded the conformers, and punished the ones who resisted conformity, "the trouble makers." One of the worst things a pupil can do is to let his uniqueness show. In other words, the learner must hide that which makes him an individual among others of his kind. Teachers have never yet brought a class through so that they all knew the same things. In the light of what we know about how these individuals are made, we can safely predict that they never will. Yet generation after generation, they keep trying, amazingly unshaken by their perpetual defeat.

But I should not criticize the teachers alone for the wholesale drive toward conformity. Conformity is cherished and uniqueness is frowned upon in industry, in labor unions, in business, in religion; in fact, it is difficult to find a facet of our society where individuality is cherished. I can think of two reasons for mentioning the schools in particular. The first is that any example needs to be as nearly universal in everyone's experience as possible. The second is that teachers are in a somewhat better position to know better than are most other people.

NATURE CHERISHES UNIQUENESS

I have said that nature cherishes uniqueness, and it seems proper that I explain what I mean. I hope that no one will be blocked by my use of the word "nature." This is not the place to go into a discussion of original cause, nor do I consider such a discussion very profitable. I propose to cite some things that have happened, and I hope that if I credit "nature," it will leave an opening for the fundamentalists, the atheists, and all who are between these two extremes. These things did and do occur, and it helps me semantically to say that "nature" did them. They are quite remarkable.

Wherever we look in the world of nature we cannot help being impressed with the fact that nature must abhor likeness. Of all the leaves on all the trees, no two can be found that are exactly alike. Of the billions of blades of grass in the world, it is impossible (or practically so at any rate) to find two that are alike. There are no two scenes which are the same. The straight line, so common in our man-made world, is never found in the natural world.

But these evidences are superficial. They are not really "proof." When we now consider how all higher organisms are made, we will be able to see how uniqueness has been established, and how complicated and difficult this was to bring about.

Since we are concerned with individualism, we are interested in consideration of how *man* is made, not higher plants and animals. In discussing this problem, I shall take up first the physical man or self, and then the psychological self. These two are not a duality. They operate as one, and neither can be well or sick without this being reflected in the other. But they are differently made, and for that reason one has to be described before the other. This is a problem in language, since we have to put one word after another in a linear way, while what we want to describe is usually not linear. This being the case, I shall first describe how the physical self is made and what it feeds on. Then I shall consider the psychological self, how it is made, how it grows, what it feeds on. We can then see how they fit together, pervade the same area, and thus create the individual, making individualism possible.

HOW UNIQUENESS IS ASSURED IN THE PHYSICAL BODY

It is generally accepted now, at least by all scientists, that life on earth began in the form of single cells in water, and that present life in all its many forms developed from these cells. We still have single-celled plants and animals today, but they lead a very limited existence. They absorb food and grow in size until they become cumbersome, and then they simply divide, forming two small cells where there had been one large one. Then these two new cells start to grow, and in time repeat the process. The biologists call the two new cells "daughter cells," although I don't know why, since sex has not yet been invented. This may be one reason why they lead a dull and limited existence. They do not have a "parent problem," since each cell is like the other, and neither can be called the parent of the other.

As long as individual cells continued to reproduce by dividing, it was not possible for them to make any progress. I might suggest that this was true because each cell had to do everything for itself—getting food, digesting, keeping vigil, eliminating, and hence none of these functions could be done very well. And the possibilities presented by the reproductive process which was available (simple division) offered no chance for improving the quality of the breed. I use the word progress here merely in the sense of becoming more complicated, and hence more able to do many different kinds of things. I do not wish to argue the point that we may be worse off now, with the hydrogen bomb hanging over our heads, then we were when life started. We are vastly more complicated and able to introduce novelty into our existence.

The first move in the direction of multi-cellular organisms seems to have come when some of the daughter-cells began to cling together, thus making clumps of undifferentiated cells. They may have been due to incomplete fission (they just stuck together) or it may have been the original "togetherness." Those who consider this last notion to be absurd might read *Cell and Psyche—The Biology of Purpose* by Edmund Sinnott, Chapel Hill, 1950, particularly pages 26–42.

There was not much advantage in "togetherness" as long as each cell had to do everything for itself. Probably the cells in the center of the clump were actually worse off than they had been before, since food and water must have been less available than they were when each cell floated free in the water. At any rate, the cells of the clump began to specialize, so that some cells did all of the digesting, others did all of the alerting, and so on. When cells began to perform special functions for the whole, that was the beginning of organisms. By definition, an independent cell, or a cluster of them, cannot be an organism. It is when parts of the cluster perform special services for the whole that an organism can be said to exist. So when cells in clusters began special services, organisms first came into being and life was on its way to a multitude of complications.

But it was not far on its way. There was as yet no way for very much change to be introduced. The cells still reproduced by simple division. A new organism was started by a piece of the old one breaking off, and starting an independent existence. Perhaps that is where the notion of "a chip off the old block" began. For that was what all young ones were, and they had no choice except to grow into a "reasonable facsimile" of the old block. Some of these plants grew to great size.

After millions of years of this limited existence, a remarkable development took place. Whereas for aeons, the only way to reproduce was division (making two from one) a scheme developed whereby it was possible to make one from two. As long as two were simply parts of the parent, the young could not be any different from the old. But when a way was found to make one from two, the young then being part of two individuals, could not be exactly like either one of them. The young *had* to be somewhat different from either parent; indeed, it had to be different from any other anywhere. This was how uniqueness, so essential to the development of complicated forms of life, especially human life, was brought about. Biologists call this process heterosexual reproduction. Here, in the very early stages of plant and animal life, was the dawn of sex. This phenomenon can be observed under the microscope in biological laboratories by anyone who cares to see it. I first saw it in a slide showing spirogyra, or pond scum. To see this is to make it clear that this process was hard to come by. Here began the groundwork for the "agony and the ecstacy." Since uniqueness, in the physical sense, had been provided for, there was then no end to the possibilities for complications, for progress. We see life now in its myriad forms, all around us. The crowning achievement is man.

I have mentioned that in the very beginning of organism, there had to be cell specialization. This does not seem to be the proper place to describe in detail what happens to the reproductive cells as they have developed for making one out of two instead of two out of one. I might say that the process of cell formation has to be just the opposite from ordinary division, so that when two cells join, one from each parent, the supply of chromosomes (trait carriers) will be back to normal, and not double that number. Anyone who wishes to understand this process better can find a full explanation, with illustrations, in almost any biology textbook. I want to point out merely that the reproductive cells in each organism are so highly specialized that they even divide differently from the others. In a real sense, they are immortal, because they constitute the link between one generation and the next. All of the other cells, which constitute by volume almost the entire organism, are mortal, and carry no bridge to the next generation.

It is in the formation of the reproductive cells (sperm cells in the male, egg cells in the female) that physical uniqueness is guaranteed. This device is such that it is practically impossible, mathematically, for any two organisms to have the same cellular content. This is true in all cases except identical twins, which are rare. And they are alike only in their physical make-up, which is less than half of the story. Perhaps this is why humans almost always produce their young one at a time, rather than in litters. A litter of humans creates quite an uproar. Even in the case of litters, they are usually the product of separate fertilizations, only rarely from a single fusion of egg and sperm. Anyone who wishes to explore further the impossibility of individuals having the same cellular make-up might want to read *What Is Life* by Erwin Schroedinger, Macmillan, 1945.

The reason for giving so much importance to the behavior of the sex cells in heterosexual reproduction is that the cell content of the new individual determines its physical characteristics. This is nature's "invention" to assure that no two individuals shall be exactly alike physically. Where there are differences there may be progress; hence the development of more complicated organisms became possible, and the development of man was made possible. When all offspring are unique, and each is different from its peers and from its parents, some of course will be inferior to the parents, but others will be a step in advance. Change, newness, becomes feasible.

It is still possible, even after millions of years of evolving, for heterosexual reproduction (and thus uniqueness) to be bypassed, and a piece of the parent may grow into an individual like the parent. Regeneration of organs in lower animals, such as tadpoles, or starfish, is readily observed. When an earthworm is cut in two, the part with the head can grow a new tail and become a complete adult.

This process is much more common in plants than in animals. Gardeners purposely graft branches onto roots to avoid the outcomes of uniqueness. When an apple grower, for example, develops a tree which produces beautiful fruit, he knows that he cannot plant the seeds of this tree and hope that the next generation will be the same as the parent. So he may plant the seed to get a root onto which he can graft parts of the parent tree, but he does not take a chance on what this root may produce if left to itself. The new fruit might be better than the parent. But since the parent has been chosen from many, the chances are that it would be of poorer quality.

This grafting process, which is used in the production of many fruits and flowers, is reverting to the method of reproduction which prevailed before the invention of sex, and is done to prevent uniqueness, to short-cut the normal processes of reproduction because whatever the new plant may be like, it is bound to be different.

Of course grafting is not possible in higher animals or in man—their organisms are too complex. And so man's uniqueness, his most valuable possession, is guaranteed. After the fusion of the two sex cells, when the new organism is actually formed, it is fed by its mother on the materials it needs for physical growth. Later on it leaves the mother and learns to feed on all sorts of things. Its choice of what it feeds on is always selective, that is, it eats some things and rejects others, in a highly individualistic manner. The food for the material self is material—meat, potatoes, cabbages, onions—but always somewhat different for different people. Somewhere between sixteen and twenty-five years after its beginning, it stops growing, and uses food for maintenance only for the rest of its life. The mechanism for the stopping of growth is *built in,* and thus the body cannot continue to grow until it becomes cumbersome or grotesque. The wisdom of the body asserts itself. This may not seem important to mention, but psychological growth, I shall show later, does not stop as physical growth does, and this is one of the important facts of life.

And so stands the physical man, uniquely equipped by the make-up of his genes, uniquely grown from what he has to grow on, and his selection of what he will use, and what he will reject.

HOW NATURE GUARANTEES UNIQUENESS IN THE PSYCHOLOGICAL SELF

I have considered it worth while to devote considerable space to the ways by which nature has provided for the individual physical self, so that no two shall be alike. The amazing story of the development of a mechanism whereby one could be made from two, unlike either, instead of two being made from one, is something to contemplate. It is the crucial achievement in the development of complex organisms culminating in man.

But this, long as it may seem to be, is less than half of the story. A fine physical structure is a good thing to have, but with this alone a man would be only a fine animal. What is distinctly human about him depends upon the psychological self which has been developed in him. A man may be a demon or a saint, or perhaps just an animal, with the same physical body, even though nature has made that body unique. What makes a man distinctly human is not his body, although this unique body could not have been evolved without the "invention" of heterosexual reproduction, but his attitudes, habits, beliefs, prejudices. For these control his behavior, what he does with his unique body. These have to be taken into account when we consider individualism.

When we speak of the physical and psychological selves, we must not lose sight of the fact that these two are not separate. They come together at birth, fully integrated, and never become independent of each other. What happens to one also happens to the other. The oneness of the total human organism must not be overlooked. We deal with them separately because we cannot write of both at once, and because they are developed differently, they feed on different kinds of stuff; their uniqueness is guaranteed by two different processes.

When, at the age of nine months, the human infant is born, it is a remarkable organism. It has eyes to see, although it has experienced no light, a stomach to digest, though it has never needed one, and innumerable other provisions of foresight for the individual life to come. Most remarkable of all, perhaps, is that it comes equipped with a part of the brain called the cortex. This cortex is a layer of tissue covering the rest of the brain, an outer layer, as the name cortex implies. This outer layer is to become the facilitating, coordinating organ for the whole.[1] Almost everything that is distinctly human about a person finally resides in this cortex. It is the organ which other living creatures do not possess in sufficient quantity to achieve humanness. The lack of cortex is why horses and dogs, which are among our more intelligent lower animals, have to be trained, while a human can be educated.

This is not to imply that these animals do not have any cortical tissue at all. The beginnings of a cortex can be found in animals as low in the

1. Those interested in a non-technical discussion of the cortex should see Herrick C. Judson, *The evolution of human nature.* Austin, Texas: University of Texas Press, 1956.

evolutionary scales as the amphibians and fishes. It is more pronounced in reptiles. Only in man, however, is it sufficiently developed so that language and other complicated abstract processes are possible.

The newborn babe thus comes equipped with a most remarkable instrument. Its possibilities are practically infinite. Neurologists estimate that even the most brilliant of men uses but a small part of his potential; and so there are no upper limits to human achievement. (Theoretically I suppose there are, but these limits are so far beyond the best of us that for practical purposes there are no limits.)

An important fact, however, is that this distinctly human organ at birth is *undeveloped*. It is a facilitating and coordinating instrument, and it is developed through life itself, for in life there are many facilitating and coordinating functions to perform. Without the cortex, language, with all of its complications, would be impossible. So the cortex is developed, not ready made, and its quality depends upon the quality of the life the individual is privileged or forced to live. In other words, the most distinctly human part of the whole human organism is built by experience. The quality of available experience becomes all-important.

The experiences available to any individual depend upon and are controlled by the process of perception. Perception is what comes into consciousness when outside stimuli impinge upon an organism. These stimuli are received by various organs and interpreted by the brain through the sorting and facilitating function of the cortex. Each time the cortex functions it is also built, so that it becomes what it has experienced.

It is only through the perceptive process that we know anything about what is in our environment; or, that we know anything at all. Perception is not essential to life, because many things, such as trees, live without perceiving. But they are forced to live most limited lives, often to be rooted in the earth, and at the mercy of the elements. When the elements are good to them, they may live for centuries. If the surroundings are hostile, however, they can do nothing about them but to die. Through perception, men and many of the lower animals can do something to order their environments so that hostile surroundings need not destroy them.

And so perception becomes the crucial phenomenon of human life. It is through this process that all learning takes place. The way this process develops the cortex determines the kind of person any newborn individual can become. The psychological self is built by its perceptions.

And this self is what an individual becomes. It has been nearly one hundred years since the formal beginning of the laboratory study of psychology. In that time, not nearly enough attention has been paid to this phenomenon, when we consider that it is the gateway to all knowing and all learning. Some studies have been made, of course, but for the most part perception has been accepted as a "given"—taken for granted. It has been generally believed that the *object* in one's environment was the basis for reality and that the human organism was merely a receiver, and had no choice except to "see things as they are." Being only a receiver reduced man to an unimportant role in the whole process of living. This concept of the status of the individual in the learning-knowing process led to all sorts of demeaning relationships between individuals. The teacher, for example, had only to tell the learner what he wanted the learner to know, and the learner had no choice but to receive it exactly as sent. And of course there was no chance for interpretation. Thus did authoritarianism, with all of its attendant evils, appear to be the logical way of life, especially to the dictator.

Recent research has shown that the receiver notion does not represent what actually happens when stimuli from the outside are received. It will not be possible here to go into detail concerning this research, but only to cite it and explain briefly how it controls the development of the psychological self and guarantees its uniqueness. This research was carried on by Adelbert Ames, Jr., and made possible through the efforts of John Pearson, both of Hanover, N. H. It took place roughly between 1940 and 1955, when Professor Ames died. So it is relatively recent. It is not surprising that these new formulations in perception are not better known when we consider how long it takes new knowledge to affect human behavior.

I will now attempt to state in a few words what the import of Professor Ames's work is, and how it provides the formerly missing block in the understanding of man's uniqueness. This will perforce be most inadequate, but those who find these ideas exciting can read more about them in the books listed below.[2]

The crucial idea, so far as this paper is concerned, developed by Professor Ames in his laboratories is that our perceptions come from us,

2. See Cantril, Hadley *The why of man's experience*. New York: Macmillan, 1950; Cantril, Hadley *The morning notes of Adelbert Ames*. New Brunswick, N.J.: Rutgers University Press, 1960; Kilpatrick, F. P. (Ed.), *Explorations in transactional psychology*. New York: New York University Press, 1961; Kelley, Earl C. *Education for what is real*. New York: Harper & Bros., 1947.

and not from our surroundings. This is the opposite notion of perception so long held by so many. The perceiver decides what a thing is, and where it is. Thus the *individual* becomes the all-important part of the process of perception, rather than the least important. This is not to deny the existence of matter, as some philosophers have done. The object—person or thing—in one's externality starts the process by giving off light or sound stimuli, but the perceiver makes what he can and must of it. No two people make exactly the same of anything; and what any perceiver makes of any person or thing is more or less at variance with the thing itself.

It can now be seen that commonly held notions of the perceptive process are exactly wrong; that the facts now revealed are just the opposite. The perceiver now becomes the crucial part of the transaction, rather than the sender of the stimuli. This fact, when generally held, will be a revolution in man's understanding of himself. It is revolutionary, not evolutionary, because perception takes place in the opposite direction from what has been generally believed.

What one makes of what he sees depends upon what he already is. He decides on the basis of his own past experience. He has to "name" things in the light of what has named them before. His previous expectations and assumptions come into play. Since no two people can have the same experiential background, no two have the equipment through which to come to precisely the same conclusion. As the on-going process of receiving and interpreting goes on, the unique interpretations of the perceiver are built into the structure of the cortex, and the unique psychological self is built. We can see how this could not be if it were true that the human organism is only a receiver.

Here I shall briefly refer to the fact that experience is not enough to account for the selective nature of perception. We do not see everything in our surroundings, although we usually have had experience with each item present at any given time. There are thousands of coincidences in any given scene. But any one individual perceives only a few of them. If he took them all in, his world would be bedlam. So he selects, automatically, a small part of the items to which he will attend. In other words there must be some sort of automatic control over what the psychological self can feed upon.

Since no two people observe the same things in any given scene, although both have had experience with everything in the scene, there must be another factor operating. Ames called this purpose, mostly unconscious purpose because selective perception seems to operate unconsciously and automatically most of the time. It seems that people are unique in this regard as in all others. We can now postulate that the pattern for unique purpose is laid down when the original cells of the individual are formed.

This seems to fit the rest of the pattern. A cell or an organism is an embodiment of energy seeking to spend itself. It is not too much to assume that any embodiment of energy has its own path down which it may best travel. This in part explains behavior in all living things; for it appears that all living tissue is purposive. This idea is appearing in the writings of biologists and those in related areas,[3] although they do not always use the same names.

There are those who are loath to accept this concept of purpose operating in perception because nobody has ever seen it. But of course nobody has ever seen a habit or an attitude except as it is reflected in behavior. Psychologists who resist this notion were raised on the "instinct" concept, which they readily accepted, but later abandoned. As a matter of fact, acceptance of things unseen in the physical world to account for behavior is most respectable. One might raise the question as to whether the electron was discovered or invented. It was of course invented in order to account for the behavior of matter.

The psychological self is built through the perceptive process. This is based on unique experiences and unique purpose, so that the psychological self is unique. The cortex, which in any considerable quantity is the special possession of the human organism, is developed by these perceptions. The psychological self is completely integrated with the physical self. (I am tempted to say it "resides in" the physical self, but this suggests a duality and is a throw-back to outmoded ways of thinking.)

It has been known for a long time, in a superficial way, that no two people see the same things in similar circumstances. In law schools, I am told, it has long been a practice to stage an incident in the class and then ask the students to write what they saw. No two ever saw the same things, and so the law professors used this fact to show the lack of reliability in evidence given by eye-witnesses. The meaning of this for individualism apparently escaped them. This idea of an incident and witness account was used in the first psychology course I ever attended. But then the professor proceeded to teach the course just as though what

---

3. See Sinnott, E. *Cell and Psyche, The Biology of Purpose,* for a somewhat different treatment of the same idea. Those interested in a more extended treatment of purpose see Kelley, Earl C., & Rasey, Marie I. *Education and the Nature of Man,* Harper and Brothers, 1952, Chap. VI.

he had shown through the incident technique was not so. These law and psychology professors were stumbling over one of the most important facts of human life without knowing it. But they have no corner on this. I learned about the behavior of sex cells, observed it in spirogyra with a microscope, before I was twenty-five years old, but the significance of this did not dawn on me for thirty years after that.

THE SELF HAS BOUNDARIES

In order to understand what the individual is, and what individualism means, we need to see that the psychological self has limits or boundaries, so that the individual can be contained and maintained. The skin is the boundary of the physical self, and this of course can be seen and readily accepted. But the psychological self has to "leave off" somewhere too, and it has to be protected just as the skin limits and protects tissue. The boundary to the psychological self seems necessary for it to maintain its integrity, its oneness. Nature has provided for it.

In the very beginning of an individual life, perception is somehow selective. This means that some of the possibilities from the outside are admitted—some excluded. Of course there is nothing physical here for us to see, but I am helped in my thinking about it to imagine an invisible screen, through which some stimuli can enter and some cannot. This screen, this selective device, is essential to individuality, because without it the mass of perceptive material would be overwhelming.

In general, the screen admits that which the individual regards as facilitating, and excludes that which it holds to be endangering. There are many possibilities which are excluded or taken in that are not either facilitating or endangering, but the most significant classification is on this basis.

If I may carry the analogy of the screen a step farther, it is possible to see how, in a hostile environment, it becomes less open as the person sees himself in need of more protection. Hostile, endangering environments tend to thicken and harden the screen, while friendly and helpful surroundings tend to open it up. Thus an individual who sees himself as living in a hostile environment builds his defenses higher and thicker. Under these circumstances it comes about that the screen, or the boundary of the self becomes so impervious that little, in some cases nothing, can get in. We all know people who do not receive any ideas sent to them. Words seem to bounce off them. They have built their defenses so strong that they are actually inaccessible. In some cases, they are able to talk, and do so in volume, but what they say is unrelated to what anyone else has said. It is as though, while others talk, they are preparing what they are going to say. Others cannot seem to get through the boundary either way, and neither listen nor talk. People are then inclined to consider them dull, or boresome, when in fact they are only frightened. Or they have been frightened in the past and have built their defenses to an impractical degree, but no longer feel the fright that rendered them inaccessible.

The boundaries of the psychological self, necessary to the operation of the integrated self, then become barriers rather than boundaries. The self becomes a prisoner within his own wall, and he is thus cut off from communication with other people. This communication is necessary to provide the stuff of growth, and so such people render themselves unable to receive anything to grow on. The imprisoned self starves and practically dies, although the physical structure may continue to live. It is not uncommon, however, for the physical self to become wearied of the untenable condition and also die.

Defenses are necessary, provided they do not become so impervious that they imprison that which they defend. It often happens that defenses are inadequate for the dangers of living. This happens most often to the very young, who have tender psychological selves and inadequate protection. In these cases, which are numerous, the self becomes damaged, and in serious cases crippled. These psychological cripples have to behave as cripples do, and their actions are at wide variance with what is "expected" of them in our culture. From this group society gets its criminals, its deviates, its so-called insane. The person is crippled by conditions over which he has little control, and then because he behaves in a crippled fashion we say he is delinquent, or "insane."

This is not because we are inhuman, or devoid of human compassion. It is because we cannot see the psychological self. Our hearts go out to the physical cripple, and great deference is properly paid to him. If we could see the psychological cripple our blame, hostility, and rejection would be changed to love, and tender nurture. We would not expect him to step lively, and look out for himself. We would cease to subject him to the many forms of rejection which we have devised for those who do not conform.

And so the human individual is built. He has a body like no other. It is a remarkable creation, having built into it many automatic, self-regulating devices. It has enormous recuperative powers, and will stand unconscionable abuse, showing the enormous will to live which we observe in all living things. It feeds on physical things, although these are selectively chosen by each individual and are not the same for any two persons except where there is only one thing to be had. He has a unique psychological self which controls his behavior. This is built out of the perceptive stuff of growth, also selected in keeping with his unique experience and purpose. The food of this self consists of whatever there is around him to select from—squalor, rejection, hostility, love, beauty, sunsets, symphonies. All of these things, physical and perceptual, are what the individual is, and provide the basis for our consideration of individuality.

WHAT, THEN, ABOUT INDIVIDUALISM?

Everything in this paper, up to this point, is, I believe, firmly founded on scientific research. It is based on two enormous pieces of laboratory research. The first part depends upon what the biologists and cytologists have learned about how one body is made out of two, with contributions from both, providing unique physical structures. The second part makes use of what Ames and his associates have discovered about the perceptive process and how it provides for construction of the unique psychological self.

Now I propose to argue beyond the data into meaning. This is admittedly what I see as meaning. It is conceivable that someone else might see something different. We would then be in the hands of the reader, who would have to judge what meanings seemed most logically arrived at. He is always the final arbiter anyway, since he makes what he can out of what he reads, and what is communicated is what he makes of it, not what I think I am communicating.

There is some misunderstanding in some quarters about what scientific data are really for. I have been accused, by critics of some of my previous writings, of "arguing beyond data." This is quite true, but I would like to say that that is precisely what data are good for, and that data have no value by themselves. They only become useful when someone says "What does this mean?" Everybody does this, whether he intends to or not. "Pure" scientists stoutly claim that they uncover the facts, and what the implications of these facts are is none of their business. I doubt that this really happens. How can anyone stop at this point? How, indeed, would the "pure" scientist even be able to tell what data to keep and what to discard? If he decides what to keep, he must make choices in the light of some significance, and by that very act he tampers with his own purity.

Arguing from data to meaning may be said to be the task of the philosopher. A professional philosopher should certainly be aware of what research has to say, as a starting point for discussions. The great risk is not that the philosopher may argue beyond the data, but that he may argue without data, or in disregard of it. Without the basis of some understanding of what research has produced, the philosopher risks slipping into mere babbling.

Since it seems impossible even to select data without some reference to meaning, all scientists become philosophers in some degree. All of the rest of us who learn about data and hold them to be significant become philosophers. And thus the findings of the research workers come into significance in human affairs. It would be pretentious, of course, for all of us who consciously or unconsciously argue meaning from data to class ourselves with the professional philosophers. They are most often historical philosophers. They usually teach as a means of livelihood, and they spend most of their time teaching us what the philosophers who have gone before have postulated. Their scope is mainly from Socrates to Dewey. Since the great men of the past have contributed much, these historical philosophers serve a most important function. We should, however, learn to call their contribution by its right name.

All of this is by way of explaining that I am now going beyond the data to say what I think the cited research means for individualism. Nature's great effort has been to produce uniqueness in all living things of any considerable complexity. The significance of this fact seems to stand out, and to be focal. What does this mean for living together in the compact society in which we now find ourselves?

MAN IS A SOCIAL BEING

This fact can be deduced, first of all, from the way in which the cortex of the brain is developed. The cortex is doubtless the only organ which is distinctly human. In all other ways that I can think of, some animals excel us. Some run faster, some are stronger, some have better eyesight or hearing, and so on. But none has a sizeable cortex, which, when developed, makes possible all of the characteristics which are distinctly human, such as complex language and aesthetics.

This organ has to be developed in social relations with other people. No human ever acquired the distinctive human characteristics without other people. They are a basic requirement for the development of human qualities.

Perhaps this is the meaning of the fact that the human infant is born quite completely helpless, utterly dependent on others, and remains so for considerable time. I know of no other species where this is so true as in the human species. This means that each individual in order to survive is provided with another human being for both physical and psychological nurture. Usually this other person is the mother, but if anything happens to the mother, someone else has to be provided, or the individual dies. Nature seems also to have provided for mother love, which in some cases baffles all human understanding. Maybe this cortical need is why the human young are usually born singly, rather than in litters or clutches. This might be an attempt to force adult attention on the individual.

The implications of this social requirement are many. We can see from this that the quality of the individual depends largely on the quality of the adults he has to develop from. This is not a completely limiting factor, because, once started, the individual may seek other and more promising people for his psychological feeding. But in general, we build and are built by the people around us. And in general, allowing for individual differences, dullness (or brightness) is more on the order of an achievement, rather than a gift.

THE INDIVIDUAL IS DEPENDENT

When we see that the psychological self is built mostly out of the people around it, we can see that the day never comes when the individual can continue to thrive without other people. Growth of self is continuous throughout life, and social contact with other people makes this growth possible. One goes from the complete helplessness of infancy to the competence of adulthood, but he never gets to the point where his self no longer needs to be fed.

There are of course a few instances where individuals isolate themselves from human contacts, but it can be seen that they no longer continue to grow, or, if we can call it growth, they grow in grotesque ways. Very few people achieve complete isolation, even though they try to. For most people, the hunger for others is almost overwhelming. That is why, in our prisons, solitary confinement is the most severe of all punishments, and is used only in especially difficult cases.

It is perhaps more proper to say not that adults are dependent, but that they are interdependent. They must receive from others and cannot thrive without doing so, but they also give. It is an interchange, or a sort of transaction.

We can see that the "self-made" man is a myth. If an individual were really self-made, he never would have got past infancy, except perhaps in a physical sense. There are some infants who withdraw into themselves and never grow and never communicate. They evidently look out upon what appears to them to be a hostile world and draw back within their shells. They are called "autistic" babies. The self-made man would be like this except for other people. We do have some rugged individualists in that they behave in a rugged manner toward most other people, but they have to have other people, though they may only exploit them.

When the rugged individualist, the self-made man, beats his chest and admires his handiwork, little does he know what he would look like if this were really true.

There is always the hazard of having too many people. The individual has to have contact with others, but he also has to have some time by himself, so that he can sort out significances, to derive meaning out of experience through reflection. The meaning derived by the reconstruction of experience is unique to the individual deriving it, and it is therefore individualistic.

It is possible, indeed in these times it often happens, that the individual has so many other people around him, and so little time for reconstruction that there is no chance for any meaning to be derived. This happens where too many people live in the same quarters. It is also true, I believe, in our large schools, where there are too many others to cope with. A large school with four thousand people on the same city block can be the loneliest place in the world. One can observe students attempting to assuage this loneliness by the formation of clubs, cliques, and other small groups to which they may belong. There are however literally hundreds of young people in these schools who do not know how to form these connections, and who are starved for want of human contacts at the very time that they have the most people around them—starving amid plenty.

There is a tendency on the part of some individuals to seek mass situations because they want to escape or withdraw. Reisman has described these people so well in *The Lonely Crowd*. But this is not the normal quest of the healthy individual. It is a withdrawal into anonymity. It is another way of avoiding being a part of what the individual views as a hostile world.

IS THE INDIVIDUAL A CONFORMIST?

He is, part of the time, and in certain situations. In this regard, he has two needs which would be in conflict if he had to satisfy both of them at the same time. These two needs are first, other people, and second, a chance to be himself. Most people do conform most of the time to the customs of the society in which they live. They do this because they want other people to like them and accept them, so that their psychological selves will have something to feed on.

For example, this afternoon I will go from my home to the university to meet students and to teach a class. I will wear a suit, shirt, and tie. These are not the best garb, it seems to me, that could have been invented. But I will wear them because most of my male colleagues and students will be dressed somewhat similarly. Why do I do this when what I wear at home while writing is more comfortable? I do it because I want the acceptance, the love of my colleagues and students. I do not want them to think I am queer, because it is hard enough to break down the barriers between me and my students without that. In short, I conform to the extent of dressing somewhat like others because I want them to like me well enough so that there can be communication between us, and my self can be fed. I do not, however, have to dress this way all of the time. At home I can disregard some of these customs and so I take care of these needs in turn, not both at once.

Now it makes all the difference in the world whether I conform out of my need for others or whether somebody "conforms" me. There is enormous pressure in today's society to make people conform. There is nothing new about this; as far back in human history as we can go there has been effort on the part of those in authority to make everybody alike to suit the authoritarian's purposes. The schools have never given up the idea that they can make people come out all the same. The examples of this effort are many, and run throughout our culture. It is as though they would repeal uniqueness, which nature has gone to so much trouble to establish.

In our schools they have tried ever since they took in different kinds of people to group them so that within any one group they will be all alike, or as nearly so as possible. Part of the rationale for this is that people group themselves anyway, and one can find the bright seeking each other out, and the dumb also seeking their own kind. Whether this happens or not is debatable, but one fact that seems certain is that it is one thing for them to group themselves and quite another to have somebody group them.

To pick up my illustration about dress, it is one thing for me to wear a necktie this afternoon because I think it will make my colleagues and students like me and accept me, and another for the dean or president to decree that no professor would be allowed on campus without a necktie.

The normal individual is a conformist in the degree that he has to be in order to provide for his social need. He is nonconforming in that he is unique, and his uniqueness shows itself in the appropriate situations. I do not include among the "normal" those who use the crowd as a means of withdrawal into anonymity.

THE INDIVIDUAL IS A SPECIALIST

Because the individual is unique, there are some things that he can do better than other things. And he can do these better than other people who are unique in other ways. These special abilities fit together with the specialties of other people, so that no one has to be both a watchmaker and a banker, for example. Occupational satisfaction comes best when the individual finds the specialization which he can do best for the whole society. Society thrives best when individuals can be found in it who can best furnish the special services required for it to thrive. I am fortunate that I do not have to make my own watch or my shoes. The shoe-maker is fortunate that he does not have to write. The capacity to do some things better than others is laid down when the individual is conceived, and is further built by the life he lives after birth.

THE INDIVIDUAL MUST THEREFORE BE COOPERATIVE

Most of us are willing to accept the notion of specialization even without the biological and psychological reasons for it. We are not all so willing to accept the idea that we are cooperative. There is a notion too generally held that cooperation is un-American, and that democracy and cooperation are incompatible.

The opposite of this idea is perhaps the one that I am most anxious to set forth in this paper, because it seems to me that the notion that democracy and cooperation are incompatible is one of the most harmful ones abroad in our land. I have often heard that one cannot be a member of a group without surrendering his individuality. I remember the time that I was director of a workshop of lay citizens. After the workshop was over, one of the citizens said that I must be a communist because I had them working in small groups, and that these groups sat in circles, which suggested one world, and the idea of one world was communistic. This is fantastic enough to have an element of humor in it, but the idea that one cannot work in a group without losing his individuality is not humorous. It is too damaging to be thought funny.

Many people like competition, as long as they are head. But in spite of these notions, this is the most highly specialized and the most cooperative society in the history of mankind. Without the cooperation of many people, our homes would become virtually uninhabitable in a very short time.

The only final good that comes out of working with other people, in a group, for example, comes to the various individuals in it. The group is not an entity. It is ephemeral, an abstraction. It disappears when the meeting is over, and though it may re-form at a later date, it is often different even in personnel. The benefits of the group operation, and they are many, are to the individuals, because they are permanent throughout the lives of the participants.

FREEDOM IS A REQUIREMENT FOR INDIVIDUALISM

By this statement, I mean to say that freedom is not just something good to have, similar to having a new automobile or a fine house. It is essential to the development of a unique personality. No one can become what he might have been without freedom.

While this is not a new idea, we can now understand the basis for it better than was formerly possible. The demand for freedom is not, so far as we know, inherited in the sense of being carried in the genes. But it is inherent in the situation in which the individual finds himself. It seems clear, in the light of what we know about the oneness of matter and energy, that the human organism is an embodiment of energy. Energy seeks to spend itself, and since the individual is unique, there are unique paths down which this energy may be spent. We have called this the purposive nature of the individual. But purpose, or a path down which energy may be spent, has no meaning in the absence of freedom. That is, if someone or something is preventing the individual from doing what seems to fit his special needs, then it does no good to be purposive. Purpose, paths of energy, have no meaning in the absence of freedom. Or, as Plato is alleged to have said, a slave is one who gets his purpose from someone else.

These ideas add in some degree to our understanding of human history. The demand for freedom and democracy did not originate in the American colonies. Nor was it new at the time of Runnymede. It goes back as far as we have records. In considerable degree, the whole history of mankind has been a struggle between those who would oppress and those who would be free. Those who would be free have found many ways to break their chains. In the long run, freedom has always triumphed. Of course the run has not been long enough for some individuals, and they have perished. Some individuals have accepted their roles as slaves. Tyranny, however, never has and, I think, never will succeed eventually. The reason for this is simply that oppression is against the nature of the human organism, and this nature will always assert itself. I must however mention here that a new factor has been added which might alter everything. We have learned now, for the first time, how to destroy all living things on the earth, and of course if this happens it will end this story along with all others.

In stating the individual's requirement for freedom, I do not mean to imply that one is free to do just as he pleases. Nobody has that freedom, or can have it, unless he is willing to go into the wilderness and live entirely on its resources. The moment that anyone joins with one other person, he loses some of his right to do just as he pleases. He has to take the other into account. When we live with many other people, as everyone does in our close-knit society, the freedom to do just as one pleases is long gone.

It is likely that when we give up a low-order of freedom, we achieve a freedom of a higher order. For example, I am not allowed to leave the street in front of my house unpaved, although I have to pay for the paving. No matter how rugged, how self-made I am, I have to pay. But so does everyone else, and so when I drive down the street it is all paved and I don't have to drive through muddy chuck holes left so by other rugged individuals. Also, I am not allowed to drive through a red traffic light, but by surrendering this right, I have a fair degree of safety in urban driving. Freedom within the social scene is the only kind of freedom that is available to us if we are to meet another requirement, to have other people. If a person insists on exercising low-order freedoms which violate the rights and requirements of others, they will isolate him, and thus deprive him of the stuff out of which his psychological self is built.

If freedom is a requirement for the development and maintenance of individualism, what kind of freedom can we have in the close-knit social scene within which most of us live? We must have the chance to make choices in as many areas as possible. We must have a chance to learn how to make choices by making them. Freedom is achieved by learning to exercise it, and this cannot be done in a situation of tyranny.

In this country, we have, in our every-day lives, some opportunities to make choices. I am free to live in this house or move. I can go on a trip, or stay home. There are many such freedoms. Even the man who has to tighten the same nut on an assembly line has part of his day when he can make choices. The more choices that are available to the individual the better.

There are many in our society who lust for power over others, and many who fear freedom. These constitute the conscious and unconscious enemies of freedom. They are the enemies of individualism, because individualism requires freedom.

Those who fear freedom form the larger group. These are found in the home, the church, and most particularly in the schools. Many school teachers and administrators are afraid to take a chance on consulting their young, for fear that they will not come up with the right answers. They fear that unless they sit tight on the lid which contains explosive human energy in great quantity the whole institution of the school will blow up. They fear that nobody will do anything of any value unless they force them to.

I probably dwell on this because I am myself a teacher, and the problems of the school are close to me. The schools, however, are most important if we are to have freedom. They affect the lives of almost everyone who lives in our country. The basic objection which I have concerning our schools is that they do not provide for choices required by free people. The young person of course can do his lessons or not, but this is not a genuine choice, because it is a choice between something or nothing. He cannot explore or initiate, but only follow orders. This produces a society composed of people who are unaccustomed to making choices, and unskilled in it.

The people of such a society are quite easy prey for the demagogues who would deny freedom to others because they want power to oppress.

That, I think, is why we are always living under the threat of some "ism." After World War II we had the threat of communism, which sought to do away with individualism and make everybody belong to the state rather than to himself. The American communists thought that, since they were on the ground floor, they would inherit power when our government was overthrown. This was probably a vain hope, and they would likely have been shot as many other communists have been, but I believe they were motivated mainly by their own lust for power.

Then we had McCarthyism, guilt by association, the ruining of careers of innocent men and women, slander of some of our great democratic leaders, character assassination, and all the rest.

Now we are threatened by another "ism" which could hardly have grown to its present strength in a critical, democracy-loving society. This is John Birchism, coupled with militarism. John Birchism probably would not achieve a great deal of power by itself, but it has invaded the military at least in some degree, and this combination has a potential power much greater than McCarthy ever had. Military coups are common in human history, all the way back to the ancient kinds. They are perhaps the most recurring of all historical events.

These people are being called the "lunatic fringe." This is a dangerous mistake. They are a sizeable part of the American people, uneducated in the ways of freedom and democracy, unaware of the blessings of liberty. As long as we dismiss them as "crackpots" or "lunatic fringe" we imply that they never can amount to much. We might sleep past the point of no return. The people who are easy prey to such "isms" are an indictment against our educational systems, because they have not learned to understand democracy or to appreciate freedom. They are conscious or unconscious enemies of individuality.

We stand before the world as apostles of freedom. We advertise ourselves as the free world. Since freedom is a requirement for the development of individualism, and individualism can thrive only in a democracy, let us insist that freedom be extended to all.

CREATIVENESS IS A CHARACTERISTIC OF INDIVIDUALISM

All free people are creative. This is true because being creative is inherent in the situation, as is the requirement for freedom. The reasoning is as follows: The human organism has a cortex, which distinguishes it from lower organisms. The cortex enables the individual to develop intelligence. Any intelligent creature will do what it can to improve its environment, just to make itself more comfortable, if nothing else. The human being is therefore always in a situation where he needs to contrive in order to modify his environment. He needs to contrive, and he has what it takes to contrive. Man has indeed done much to control the environment under which he lives.

This calls for an explanation of the term creativity. Too often we are prone to think of it as a work of art, such as painting a picture or composing a symphony. These are indeed creative acts, but they are a small part of the creation that is going on all around us. A person is creative whenever he finds himself in a situation which is a dilemma to him, and he invents a new answer to the dilemma. What is invented may not be new to all the world, but it is new to the inventor. It may be entirely new, adding to the store of human knowledge, but usually it is a present answer to an individual problem. We can see then how common creativity is in the lives of people.

In order for an individual to be creative he must have at least some degree of freedom. He has to be in a position to make choices, else he cannot bring about new solutions. It therefore seems to be a fact that freedom and creativity come together. Freedom begets creativity. And creativity is the growing edge of life, the point at which all improvement or progress, all novelty comes into being. Free people create. The millions of slaves who have lived and died have left little to posterity.

Some think of creation as something which took place in the dim past, and has been finished for a long time. When we see the becoming, ongoing nature of life and the universe, we can understand that creation has never been finished, that it never will be. It is now going on, and every free individual is a part of it.

CONCLUSION

When we take another look at individualism from the point of view of man's biological and psychological nature we see that what he has which makes him a person separate from all other persons, is the ways in which he is unique. I am I, and you are you. We cannot change places. I have to go along with me for the rest of my days, and when my time is up, I as an individual will be through. I therefore have to cling to my individuality. It is what I have, by which I may be fulfilled.

There are threats to individualism, some of which have been mentioned. There are those who would enslave, and against these free men must be alert. Under enslavement, it is possible so to control one's perceptions that he becomes what the tyrant wants him to be. We call this conditioning, but it is only possible in great degree among captives. A captive can come to love his chains, and surrender his individuality. We have the threat of the machine, of institutionalization, of "policy." The very nature of industrial society, with its canned entertainment, canned food has a strong tendency to feed us all the same fare, making us all alike. If it were possible to make us all alike, individualism would be gone.

There are some things, however, that authoritarians, with their coercive institutions and their attempts to bring standardization, have not been able to do. They will not be able to do this, as long as people retain a modicum of freedom. The schools, for example, have tried since the beginning of formal education to produce people who all knew the same things and had the same ignorances. They have never succeeded in this, even though they are still trying. The reason that it has not been possible to standardize everybody is that people have uniqueness built in from the very moment of conception. This *is* individualism. Powerful built-in forces thus thwart the authoritarian, the molding institutions, even the machine itself. Without the powerful force of the basic nature of the human organism, I think Orwell's *1984* would have arrived ahead of schedule. I think it will never arrive if we maintain an atmosphere of freedom.

And this is good news. Since human beings are constituted as they are, individualism will not perish from the earth. As John Dewey is reported to have said at the close of a long and complicated lecture, "I think I understand this better now."

Alee, W. C. *Cooperation among animals*. New York: Schumann Co., 1951.
Shows how animals are interdependent and cooperative.

Cantril, Hadley (Ed.), *The morning notes of Adelbert Ames*. New Brunswick, N.J.: Rutgers Press, 1960.
Professor Ames habitually wrote each morning what he had been thinking. Cantril has gathered these notes in this book. Also contains correspondence between Ames and John Dewey.

Cantril, Hadley *The "why" of man's experience*. New York: Macmillan, 1950.
Written as an outcome of spending much time with Professor Ames in his laboratory.

Combs, Arthur, & Snygg, Donald *Individual behavior.* New York: Harper & Bros., 1959.
An excellent treatment of individualism from a psychological and especially a perceptual point of view.

Herrick, C. Judson *The evolution of human nature.* Austin, Texas: University of Texas Press, 1956.
With special reference to the cortex of the brain. The whole book can be read with great profit.

Kelley, Earl C. *Education for what is real.* New York: Harper & Bros., 1947.
The author's attempt to describe what he experienced with Professor Ames and his laboratory with some implications for education.

Kelley, Earl C. *The significance of being unique, ETC.,* A review of general semantics, Spring 1957.
A statement of nature's great effort to establish uniqueness. Probably somewhat repetitive of this essay.

Kelley, Earl C. *Communication and the open self, ETC.,* A review of general semantics, Winter 1954.
How selves are built, and how one's defenses may become his prison.

Kelley, Earl C. The fully functioning self. In A. W. Combs (Ed.), *Perceiving, behaving, becoming,* 1962 Yearbook of Association for Supervision and Curriculum Development, a department of National Education Association.
This book has excellent chapters on the self by Carl Rogers, A. H. Maslow, and Arthur Combs.

Kelley, Earl C., & Rasey, Marie I. *Education and the nature of man.* New York: Harper & Bros., 1952.
Further development of implications for education drawn from the Ames formulations in perception.

Kilpatrick, Franklin P., (Ed.) *Explorations in transactional psychology.* New York: New York University Press, 1961.
A collection of the writings of the editor, and by Ames, Cantril and others assembled in one book. Good description of Ames' laboratory experiments.

Montagu, Ashley. *The origin and nature of social life and the biological basis of cooperation,* Main Currents in Modern Thought, Spring 1949.
Showing that cooperation is not just desirable, but a biological necessity. A mimeographed copy can be obtained by writing the author of this essay.

Reisman, David *The lonely crowd.* New York: Doubleday, 1953.
What happens when fear causes our defenses to become too strong, and how such people seek anonymity in the crowd.

Schroedinger, Erwin *What is life?* New York: Macmillan, 1945.
Of special interest here because a famous physicist writes of the nature of the genes, among other things.

Sinnott, Edmund *Cell and psyche*. Chapel Hill, N.C.: University of North Carolina Press, 1950.
A renowned biologist writes of the purposive nature of all living tissue, from which he draws implications.

The Self in Recent Rogerian Theory

C. H. Patterson

The objective of this paper is to sketch the place of the self in the current client-centered approach to personality. While the self is today becoming of central importance in all theories of personality, it constitutes the core of the Rogerian approach which has, in fact, been designated by some writers (e.g., 9, 15) as "self-theory." Perhaps this is because client-centered theory is based upon the observations of individual clients in therapy.

ROGERS' FORMULATIONS

1947

Rogers' earliest formulation was presented in 1947 (17): "The self is a basic factor in the formation of personality and in the determination of behavior." As the perception of self changes, behavior changes. The person's feeling of adequacy is basic to psychological adjustment. The absence of threat is important for the development of an adequate self-concept and is a condition for changes in the self-concept. The self-concept is, by definition, a phenomenological concept: it is the self as seen by the experiencing person.

Reprinted from *Journal of Individual Psychology,* 1961, 17, 5–11, by permission of the author and the publisher.

1951

In 1951 Rogers (18) amplified and extended his discussion of the self in nineteen propositions. The point of view remained perceptual and phenomenological; there is no reality for the individual other than that given by his perceptions. The self is the central concept of personality and behavior. While the basic drive of the organism is the maintenance and enhancement of the oganism, the psychological self may take precedence over the physiological organism.

Once the self has developed, experiences are perceived and evaluated in terms of their relevance and significance to the self. Behavior is normally consistent with the self-concept, even at the expense of the organism. However, organic experiences or needs which are unsymbolized (because they are unacceptable) may at times lead to behavior inconsistent with the self-concept ("I was not myself"), or to psychological tension and maladjustment. Experiences which are inconsistent with the self-concept may be perceived as threatening, and may be rejected, denied, or distorted; the self-concept is defended.

Psychological adjustment or integration, on the other hand, exists when the self-concept is congruent with all the experiences of the organism. Under conditions of absence of threat to the self, all experiences —including the organismic—may be examined and assimilated into the self-concept, leading to changes in the self-concept. This occurs in therapy.

1959

The most recent and most detailed of Rogers' theoretical discussions, a more systematic and extended formulation of earlier expressions, appeared in mimeographed form in 1955 and in print in 1959 (19). Self-actualization becomes an important aspect of a general actualizing tendency.

The self-concept is defined as "the organized, consistent conceptual Gestalt composed of characteristics of the 'I' or 'me' and the perceptions of the relationships of the 'I' or 'me' to others and to various aspects of life, together with the value attached to these perceptions" (19, p. 200). The ideal self is introduced into the theory and is defined as "the self-concept which the individual would most like to possess, upon which he places the highest value for himself" (19, p. 200).

Several concepts having to do with regard are included. Rogers postulates a basic, though secondary or learned, need for positive regard from others—that is for warmth, liking, respect, sympathy, and acceptance—and a need for positive self-regard, which is related to or dependent upon positive regard from others.

Unconditional self-regard is a state of general positive self-regard, irrespective of conditions. Positive self-regard may be conditional, however, when the individual "values an experience positively or negatively solely because of . . . conditions of worth which he has taken over from others, not because the experience enhances or fails to enhance his organism" (19, p. 209). In this case the individual is vulnerable to threat and anxiety.

The central ideas in Rogers' theory of the self may be stated as follows:

1. The theory of the self, as part of the general personality theory, is phenomenological. The essence of phenomenology is that "man lives essentially in his own personal and subjective world" (19, p. 191).

2. The self becomes differentiated as part of the actualizing tendency, from the environment, through transactions with the environment—particularly the social environment. The process by which this occurs is not detailed by Rogers, but is presumably along the lines described by the sociologists Cooley (8) and Mead (13).[1]

3. The self-concept is the organization of the perceptions of the self. It is the self-concept, rather than any "real" self, which is of significance in personality and behavior. As Combs and Snygg note, the existence of a "real" self is a philosophical question, since it cannot be observed directly (6, p. 123).

4. The self-concept becomes the most significant determinant of response to the environment. It governs the perceptions or meanings attributed to the environment.

5. Whether learned or inherent, a need for positive regard from others develops or emerges with the self-concept. While Rogers leans toward attributing this need to learning, I would include it as an element of the self-actualizing tendency.

6. A need for positive self-regard, or self-esteem, according to Rogers, likewise is learned through internalization or introjection of experiences

---

1. Sociology, I think, anticipated psychology in reacting against behaviorism and recognizing the importance of the self. In the middle thirties, as an undergraduate in sociology at the University of Chicago, I was exposed to the writings of Cooley (8) and Mead (13) on the self. This was where I took on the phenomenological approach. Not until several years later were the self and phenomenology introduced, or rather reintroduced, into psychology. I say reintroduced because James (12) had recognized the importance of the self, and was a phenomenologist as well.

of positive regard by others. But, alternatively, it may be an aspect of the self-actualizing tendency.

7. When positive self-regard depends on evaluations by others, discrepancies may develop between the needs of the organism and the needs of the self-concept for positive self-regard. There is thus incongruence between the self and experience, or psychological maladjustment. Maladjustment is the result of attempting to preserve the existing self-concept from the threat of experiences which are inconsistent with it, leading to selective perception and distortion or denial of experience.

This highly condensed summary does not include the vicissitudes of the self through the processes of disorganization, or the processes of reorganization which take place in therapy.

While a number of persons have contributed to the theory, including Raimy (16), Snygg and Combs (21), and many others who have been associated with Rogers, there has been no other comparable exposition of the theory nor are there any adequately stated alternatives or variations of it. Rogers' terminology differs in some respects from that used by other client-centered writers, but the basic concepts are similar if not identical. For example, some theorists, including myself (14), have used the term self-esteem to refer to what Rogers designates as positive self-regard.

COMPARISON WITH OTHER FORMULATIONS

"ME" VERSUS "I"

Several theorists (2, 4, 13, 22) have emphasized two aspects of the self, essentially distinguishing between the *self as object,* the "me," and the *self as subject,* the "I." The first is often referred to as the *self-concept,* the second as the *ego,* although, as Hall and Lindzey (9, p. 468) point out, there is no general agreement upon terms. James called the "me" the empirical self and the "I" the pure ego—the sense of personal identity or the judging thought. This personal identity, he suggested, may not exist as a fact, "but it would exist as a *feeling* all the same; the consciousness of it would be there, and the psychologist would still have to analyze that" (12, p. 333). The ego would appear to be self-consciousness. Mead's conceptions of the "I" and the "me" appear to be similar, although his discussion is difficult to follow. The "I" appears to be the awareness of the self as of the moment of action (13, pp. 173–178, 192).

These concepts, while preferable to the idea of the "I" as an executive, which lends itself to reification, are vague and difficult to pin down. At least I am not able to differentiate actually, practically, or operationally between the executive aspects of the self, and the self as an object to the self. The self of Snygg and Combs is both an object and doer. Others, including Allport (1) and Sherif and Cantril (20), also appear to adopt this view. Hilgard (10) suggests that the concept of the self as a doer is an error into which psychologists have been led by the common-sense or lay view that behavior seems to be self-determined.

In Rogers' theory the self-concept, although an important determiner of behavior, is not an executive or doer. There is no need for positing such an executive. The organism is by nature continually active, seeking its goal of actualization, and the self as part of the organism is also seeking actualization through its constant activity. The self-concept thus influences the direction of activity, rather than initiating it and directing it entirely. Thus Rogers avoids the problem of reification and the ambiguousness of the concept of the "I" or the ego as an executive. James' sense of personal identity might be considered a part of the self-concept, and the ego or "I" as the awareness of the self-concept. However, I am not sure that this solution is entirely satisfactory.

IDEAL SELF

In his recent formulation of the concept of the ideal self Rogers indicates that the perception of the ideal self becomes more realistic, and the self becomes more congruent with the ideal self, as an outcome of therapy. This suggests that personality disturbance is characterized by an unrealistic self-ideal, and/or incongruence between the self-concept and the self-ideal. This formulation has been the basis of some research by the client-centered school (e.g., 3). But it is not incorporated in Rogers' statement of the theory. The theory apparently does not recognize conflict between the self-concept and the self-ideal as a source of disturbance, but emphasizes the conflict between the self-concept and organismic experiences as its source. This is in contrast to some other theories in which the self-ideal is a central concept and an important factor in psychological adjustment or maladjustment, e.g., Horney (11).

THE SELF

The notion of the self, or the self-structure, is broader than the self-concept. It includes the self-concept and the ideal self. What else it includes, is not clear. Combs and Snygg speak of the phenomenal self, defined as the "organization of all the ways an individual has of seeing himself" (6, p. 126). The self-concept includes "only those perceptions about self which seem most vital or important to the individual himself" (6, p. 127). How these are to be differentiated is not indicated. Rogers considers the self-concept to be in the person's awareness, whereas the self may include aspects not in awareness.

PROBLEMS OF OPERATIONAL DEFINITION

Rogers made an effort to keep his constructs and concepts so that they can be operationally defined. The phenomenological approach, it seems to me, fosters this effort. One is not concerned about the "real" self, the "real" environment, etc., but with the perceptions of particular individuals. The self-concept and the self-ideal are perceptions which can be studied and objectified by instruments such as the Q-sort, or by tests of the "Who am I" variety. The latter, though ideally suited for use with client-centered theory, have not, however, to my knowledge, been used in connection with this theory.

Rogers points out the problem of operationally defining the organismic experiences which, it is assumed, conflict with the self-concept. The aspects of the self other than the self-concept and the self-ideal, are also not operationally defined. Maybe we do not need these concepts. I see no need for unconscious elements of the self, for example. Aspects of the self which are not in awareness but which can be brought into awareness, can be tapped by instructions such as "Sort these statements in terms of your concept of yourself as a father." The self, insofar as it is behaviorally effective, may consist only of the various self-perceptions— thus resolving the problem posed above about the area of the self apart from the self-concept and the self-ideal. The organismic experiences, on the other hand, as an essential aspect of the theory, must be brought within the realm of measurement. The approach of Chodorkoff (5), using Q-sorts of self-referent items by clinicians as an "objective description" of the total experience of the individual, though operational, may be questioned as to its validity.

There is also the problem, pointed out by Combs and Soper (7), that although the self-concept may be operationally defined as the individual's statements about himself, these statements do not necessarily correspond to his perception of himself. His statements may be inaccurate for a number of reasons, including inability or unwillingness to give an accurate report. Yet there is no other approach to determining the self-concept, since by definition it is the perception of the self by the individual, and no one else can report upon it or describe it.

In general, what is needed is a more formal theoretical statement which would lead to testable hypotheses for research, not only with clients in therapy, but in many other situations, with many other kinds of subjects.

SUMMARY

The aspects of Rogers' theory which relate to his central formulation of the self-concept have been summarized. A comparison with the thinking of others regarding the self attempted to clarify some differences and showed other differences in need of resolution. Some problems of operational definition were briefly discussed.

1. Allport, G. W. The ego in contemporary psychology. *Psychol. Rev.,* 1943, **50,** 451–468. Also in *Personality and social encounter: selected essays.* Boston: Beacon Press, 1960, pp. 71–93.

2. Bertocci, P. A. The psychological self, the ego and personality. *Psychol. Rev.,* 1945, **52,** 91–99.

3. Butler, J. M., & Haigh, G. V. Changes in the relation between self-concepts and ideal concepts consequent upon client-centered counseling. In C. R. Rogers & R F. Dymond (Eds.), *Psychotherapy and personality change.* Chicago: University of Chicago Press, 1954, pp. 55–76.

4. Chein, I. The awareness of the self and the structure of the ego. *Psychol. Rev.,* 1944, **51,** 504–514.

5. Chodorkoff, B. Self-perception, perceptual defense, and adjustment. *J. Abnorm. Soc. Psychol.,* 1954, **49,** 508–512.

6. Combs, A. W., & Snygg, D. *Individual behavior,* rev. ed. New York: Harper, 1959.

7. Combs, A. W., & Soper, D. W. The self, its derivative terms, and research. *J. Indiv. Psychol.,* 1957, **13,** 134–145. Also in A. E. Kuenzli (Ed.), *The phenomenological problem.* New York: Harper, 1959, pp. 31–48.

8. Cooley, C. H. *Human nature and the social order.* New York: Scribner's, 1902.

9. Hall, C. S., & Lindzey, G. *Theories of personality.* New York: Wiley, 1957.

10. Hilgard, E. R. Human motives and the concept of the self. *Amer. Psychologist,* 1949, **4,** 374–382. Also in H. Brand (Ed.), *The study of personality.* New York: Wiley, 1954, pp. 347–361.

11. Horney, K. *Neurosis and human growth.* New York: W. W. Norton, 1950.

12. James, W. *The principles of psychology.* Vol. 1. New York: Holt, 1890.

13. Mead, G. H. *Mind, self and society.* Chicago: University of Chicago Press, 1934.

14. Patterson, C. H. *Counseling and psychotherapy: theory and practice,* New York: Harper, 1959.

15. Pepinsky, H. B., & Pepinsky, P. N. *Counseling: theory and practice.* New York: Ronald Press, 1954.

16. Raimy, V. C. Self-reference in counseling interviews. *J. Consult. Psychol.,* 1948, **12,** 153–163. Also in A. E. Kuenzli (Ed.), *The phenomenological problem.* New York: Harper, 1959, pp. 76–95.

17. Rogers, C. R. Some observations on the organization of personality. *Amer. Psychologist,* 1947, **2,** 358–368. Also in A. E. Kuenzli (Ed.), *The phenomenological problem.* New York: Harper, 1959, pp. 49–75.

18. Rogers, C. R. *Client-centered therapy.* Boston: Houghton-Mifflin, 1951.

19. Rogers, C. R. A theory of therapy, personality, and interpersonal relationships, as developed in the client-centered framework. In S. Koch (Ed.), *Psychology: A study of a science.* Vol. 3. New York: McGraw-Hill, 1959, pp. 184–256.

20. Sherif, M., & Cantril, H. *The psychology of ego-involvements.* New York: Wiley, 1947.

21. Snygg, D., & Combs, A. W. *Individual behavior.* New York: Harper, 1949.

22. Symonds, P. M. *The ego and the self.* New York: Appleton-Century-Crofts, 1951.

New Conceptions of Children's Learning and Development

Ira J. Gordon

Changes in our view of the world bring with them changes in our view of the child and of man. When concepts and meanings change, data are reorganized and viewed with new insights. In this age of computers and model building, of technology and automation, ideas developed about machine operations often become models for concepts about man. Ideas from the physical and biological sciences are borrowed, sometimes indiscriminately, by the psychological and social sciences and eventually by education.

We can draw an analogy from the changes in thought about the physical world to the thinking now going on, and still to come, about man. The following diagram is merely a model to depict the movement:

Linear Causation Model Man	*Transactional Model Man*
A mechanistic, fixed, closed system, characterized by	An open-energy, self-organizing system, characterized by
1. development as orderly unfolding	1. development as modifiable in both rate and sequence
a. physical-physiological-genetic	a. genetic-experiential
b. socio-emotional: antecedent-consequent	b. socio-emotional: field, transactional
c. intellectual-fixed	c. intellectual-modifiable
2. potential as fixed, although indeterminable	2. potential as creatable through transaction with environment
3. a telephone-switchboard brain	3. a computer brain

Reprinted from *Learning and Mental Health in the School,* edited by W. B. Waetjen and R. R. Leeper. Copyright © 1966, pp. 49–73, by the Association for Supervision and Curriculum Development. Used with permission of the Association for Supervision and Curriculum Development and Ira Gordon.

Linear Causation (Cont'd)	*Transactional (Cont'd)*
4. steam engine driven motor	4. a nuclear power plant energy system
5. inactivity until engine is stoked	5. continuous internal flow of activity
6. additive collection of past	6. organization into a system
7. uniqueness essentially genetic.	7. uniqueness continuously evolving from organism-environment transactions.

The shift in thought is not complete, either in the minds of some behavioral scientists or those whose task it is to educate the young. There is a cultural lag between the ideas developing among some behavioral scientists and their reception and acceptance by teachers and parents.

In order to discuss readily these two models of man, I have labeled the older model, "Linear Causation," and the newer one, "Transactional." Of course, such labels are never completely accurate, but I hope they will be understood as metaphors. One of the main discontinuities is that the home and school still operate to a great extent on an image of the Linear Causation child while the data supporting the changing view accumulate rapidly. This is to be expected; most of us were reared and educated and formed our behavioral concepts in the "Linear Causation" world. These concepts are still useful as explanations of many events, and tend to keep us from becoming aware of the data which are dissonant. Many Americans would accept the following anthropological descriptive statement as representative of their views:

> The infant as a potential is thought to be a bundle of largely inherited latent traits of emotional expression and abilities for achieving goals which can only be realized gradually as the child develops and which may be influenced by training and growth. Most of the goals available to children and adults in this community are thought to call for particular skills and a particular personality type, both of which must develop naturally or be influenced to develop out of the latent traits in the infant's potential. Children may have a high or low potential for the development of certain skills or personality traits. The combination of both a high potential and the best environmental influences is thought to be essential to the greatest success in achieving the goals. . . . The belief that the potential is in part concealed leads to a great emphasis on techniques for the discovery and disclosure of the child's potential.
>
> The infant is thought of as possessing innate capacities peculiar to himself which will be revealed in the natural course of his development subject to the influences around him. It is thought that the potential can be developed better if it is known or divined in advance. Divining for the potential is highly developed in the community (14).

This reflects the "Linear Causation" model that you can only "bring out" or fail to use whatever are the latent inherited traits of the child; you cannot really change them. It does contain the recognition of a fundamental concept in the new model, the belief in the uniqueness of the individual.

The source of uniqueness, however, shifts from the genes as sole source in the preceding statement to a recognition that uniqueness is a function of organism-environment transactions in the "Transactional" model. This uniqueness runs through all of the characteristics of the model described in the following section.

FROM UNFOLDING MATURATION— MODIFIABLE DEVELOPMENT

The first notion is that development itself—in all of its ramifications—is not fixed. That development is modifiable is an extremely important concept. We learned from Gesell, and we thought that we knew, that the child at six would behave in a "six" way and the child at seven in a "seven" way, and the child at eight in an "eight" way. We also knew there were individual differences in rate, so that a particular youngster might reach the six year old "stage" at five or at seven. Nevertheless, this was the scheme; this was the order this child would go through and one simply waited it out.

Research now indicates that this is not necessarily so. It is not so in a variety of ways. It is not so, obviously, in terms of the ages at which things occur because children are now riding two-wheeled bikes at five when we did not think they could ride two-wheelers until they were twelve.

We know that, with better prenatal care, with control over nutrition, with medical developments leading to immunity from childhood diseases, our youngsters are reaching, in motor development, stages much sooner than they did before. Likewise, physiological maturity is being reached much sooner than before.

The evidence from behavioral biology, from anthropology, from animal psychology and child development points to this new concept. From planaria to man, regardless of species, the data lead to the inference of development as modifiable.

The data will be examined in several analytical ways: by viewing the evidence on infrahuman and human subjects separately, and by organizing the data in areas such as biological (including organic, physiologic, motor development), cognitive (emphasizing new concepts of "intelligence") and social-emotional development.

INFRAHUMAN STUDIES

The lowly rat, long used for learning studies whose findings were therefore often viewed with suspicion by educators, provides us with fascinating information when we either study him in his natural habitat or become more creative in our research approaches. It is clear that the usual laboratory rat, reared in a cage and run through the maze, may be classified in human terms as "culturally deprived."

His cousin, who has roamed free wherever it is that rats roam, can outdistance the laboratory rat in maze learning and complex behavior. The cage is a restrictive environment (2). The series of laboratory researches by Krech and his colleagues has demonstrated that rats reared in environmentally complex environments and subjected to intensive training differ from their littermates in the weight of the cerebral cortex. They differ, also, in the total cholinesterase activity of the brain (cholinesterase being the chemical secretion which seems to facilitate neuron firing in the brain) and in the specific way these secretion levels are distributed in areas of the brain (52).

Further, in investigating whether such differences affected the ability to learn, they found that the timing and extent of experience were important factors. They reported:

> To some degree, the changes induced by an enriched environment can be lost if the animal is placed in an impoverished environment, and to a much greater extent, the originally impoverished animal's brain can be brought to the status of the enriched animal through intensive training on complex problems (30):

Their studies have also shed light on the brain in another way which modifies the older "switchboard" idea in which each part of the brain had a definite, limited function. Experiments with blinded rats, placed in complex environments, showed that these blinded rats could benefit from enriched experience. Even the visual cortex of these rats was modified, "Evidence that the visual cortex participates in non-visual functions" (31). Further, the work of the experimenters led them to test the idea that brain changes were compensatory, that is, the blinded rate overuses other parts of his brain to make up for his deficiency in sight. They conclude, "our present results provide concrete evidence for the often hypothesized possibility of cerebral compensation for blinding" (32).

What does this mean? It suggests that the requirement of usage stimulates structure in the brain, and that all areas of the brain participate, although in differing amounts, in handling the input, coding and response to perceptual-motor stimuli.

When we step up the scale to primates, similar conclusions emerge from the data. Riesen (51) was struck by the fact that visual deficiencies of an organic nature developed in chimpanzees who were reared in darkness. Up to that time, it had been assumed that the optic nerve developed regardless of light stimulation. He concluded that the lack of light affected the normal growth of retina and nerve.

Hunt summarizes some of the other animal studies on deprivation by stating:

> Patterned visual experience appears to be essential for the development of visual perception. . . . Maturation as well as experience plays a role in the acquisition of these visual responses. . . . How permanent and irreversible the effects of visual deprivation are is still unknown as long as no defects within the visual apparatus itself complicates the picture (23).[1]

As in the rat studies, the nature of the organism-environment transaction governs development. The question of irreversibility is a key one, at the human level, for education. Is it ever "too late to learn"?

The above studies clearly show that environment influences organ function and structural development in infrahuman species. It is a long way from infant rats to humans, but the behavioral biologists tell us the path is continuous and not discontinuous. Although we obviously would not conduct similar experiments on human subjects, field studies of children reared under various conditions, to be reviewed in the next section, show similar results. Before going up the phylogenetic scale again, however, animal studies yield significant data and concepts about the modifiability, through experience, of social and emotional development.

Again we begin with the rat. Studies by Levine (33) indicated that rats who were stimulated in infancy were better able to cope with stressful situations later on. Denenberg and his colleagues found that not only did handling and free environmental experience act to reduce emotion-

---

1. Hunt, J. McV. *Intelligence and experience.* Copyright © 1961 The Ronald Press Company.

ality later in life (9) but also that affecting the emotionality of the mother, "resulted in significant emotionality on the part of the offspring in adulthood" (8).

These studies reveal the modifiability of emotional development in rats; the now classic studies of Harlow's monkeys (18) show even more startling evidence in primates. The research on the effects of wire mothers and cloth mothers led him to conclude that warmth, or tactile communication, was more important than feeding as a factor in "mother love." He reached this idea because when the baby monkey was placed in the situation that he perceived as dangerous, he ran to the cloth mother rather than to the wire mother with the bottle on it. Yet Harlow did not stop there. He wrote a followup paper (17), in which he, in effect, said, that when you work with monkeys, you have got to get more monkeys. And, the easiest way to get more monkeys is obviously the way that mankind and the monkey-world have long used. In their attempts to get more monkeys, they found that the monkeys reared on the cloth and the wire monkey mothers did not know how to be monkeys. They did not know what to do except to gaze at each other in amazement. But, Harlow said that they found one male monkey with infinite patience. He finally succeeded with one of the female monkeys, but then they discovered something else. When the new monkey was born, the mother did not know how to be a mother and so she literally beat the baby monkey's head against the floor. The conclusion might be that it takes intermonkey experience early in life and throughout growing up to learn how not only to produce more monkeys but what to do with them after they are born.

Mason's (34) investigation of the social development of monkeys revealed similar findings: Monkeys reared in semi-isolation with limited opportunity for physical contact with other monkeys did not develop adult social behavior.

> Many adult forms of social behavior were absent or appeared in incomplete form. . . . Aggression and adult forms of grooming and sexual behavior were never observed (35).

The evidence from these animal studies is clear: deprivation of experience modifies social, emotional and organic development; complex environments and training lead to anatomic and physiologic superiority as shown by animals reared in natural habitats and the experimental investigation in rats.

HUMAN STUDIES OF MOTOR AND BEHAVIORAL DEVELOPMENT

What about humans? Deprivation studies are available from two field settings, each of which demonstrates the modifiability of development by experience. The "Transactional" view of learning and development requires the conceptualization of the importance of perceptual-motor activity. The more traditional view of learning stressed only the motor aspect—the child had to engage in the direct motor behavior in order to master a motor skill such as learning. The earlier tradition also emphasized the role of maturation as a separate dynamic from learning. Walking, for example, in the new view is learned by either watching people walk (perceptual) or engaging in walking (motor). The child has to have experience in either using his legs and/or seeing people use theirs in order to learn to walk.

The best example of evidence is from some orphanages in Lebanon that were studied by Wayne Dennis. He was able to compare children in an infant's orphanage with those who came to a well-baby clinic in the same community. The social class of both the infant institutional children and those who were with their families was similar. For financial reasons, the infants in the orphanage got very little attention during the first year of life. There was one adult staff member for ten children. They lay swaddled in their cribs which had white covering over the sides to protect the child from drafts and which permitted the child to see only the homogeneous white ceiling and those particular adults who came near only for feeding and necessary care. Light, air, food, sanitation were all better than satisfactory; but attention and stimulation were minimal. Feeding consisted, for example, of getting a bottle propped up on a pillow—not very removed from American middle-class infant feeding. The results showed that from the third to the twelfth month the mean score of these institutional children on the Cattell infant scale was 63 and of the comparison children from the same social class, but not institutionalized, 101. No institutional child between three and twelve months of age had a developmental quotient over 95 (11).

In terms of motor development, the classic chart in human development books shows creeping to crawling to walking. These institutionalized children did not go through creeping to crawling to walking. First of all, sitting alone was greatly retarded and in many cases creeping did not occur. Instead they scooted on their bottoms as their way of navigating. They "scooted" on the crib instead of creeping (10).

In the United States, Provence and Lipton (49) conducted a short-term longitudinal study of institutionalized infants. Their results reveal the wide extent of damage to development due to lack of experience. In the case of physical development, first signs of deprivation occurred in the second month when there was a minimal capacity to make postural adjustments to being held or carried.

They reported delays in the control of the head in the pull-to-sit situation, the development of sitting erect, of moving from sitting position, pulling oneself to a standing position, creeping, walking with support, and in walking alone.

However, the infants did not seem behind in lifting the head and chest from the crib mattress in prone, visual following of an object in this position, and rolling from prone to supine.

Since one of the concepts in the "Transactional" model is the self-stimulability, the competence motivation of the child, what happens to this in deprivation circumstances? The researchers report:

> The behavior of institutionalized infants was impressively different from that of children reared by their mothers in respect to autoerotic activity and those other forms of behavior in which an infant acts to stimulate himself in some way. . . .
> From four to five months on the changes and deviations were dramatic.
> Hand-mouth contacts lessened, thumb sucking disappeared, the mouth took on an appearance of laxity and poor tonus. Toys and other objects were rarely mouthed, sucked, or chewed (50).

Intellectual development as well as physical development is influenced by deprivation. We saw above that exploratory activity is reduced. Even more devastating is what happens to communication, a main source for intellectual development.

> In the last months of the first year the language deficit was even more striking. An occasional mama or dada sound could be evoked after much effort from the adult, but these remained meaningless, nonspecific vocalizations. Altogether there was minimal vocalization of any kind. The repertoire of sounds through which the average baby by this time expresses pleasure, displeasure, anger, eagerness, anticipation, gleefulness, and excitement, or vocalizes something that sounds like a question or interjection was virtually nonexistent. None of the infants had even a single specific word by the end of the first year. Their understanding of the adult's language was also retarded, but less so than was language production (49).

These facts show that experience affects not only the age at which behaviors will occur, but also whether or not they will even occur. And so, experience is a crucial factor for human motor and behavioral development.

STUDIES OF INTELLECTUAL DEVELOPMENT

Intellectual development even more clearly depends upon experience. Only through active transaction with the world is intellectual structure built.

INTELLIGENCE

We are shifting in psychology from a notion that intelligence is fixed and immutable and unchangeable to the notion that we can do something about a youngster's intelligence by the nature of the opportunities for experience that we provide for him. We now believe that intelligence is not a fact, and not a cause of behavior, and not something simply given in the genes. We conceptualize that intelligence is behavior, and behavior comes under environmental control just as much as it comes under biological genetic control. And, therefore, intelligence is changeable.

J. McV. Hunt has forcefully organized and presented data from a variety of sources to demonstrate that "the assumption that intelligence is fixed and that its development is predetermined by the genes is no longer tenable" (24).[2] His review of evidence "came chiefly from three sources: (a) from the studies of identical twins reared apart, (b) from repeated testing of the same children in longitudinal studies, and (c) from studies of the effects of training" (25).[2]

In addition to the research work cited by Hunt, A. W. Combs presented similar beliefs from his theoretical position in 1952, when he defined intelligence as the capacity for effective behavior and stated, "the intelligence of an individual will be dependent upon the richness and variety of perceptions possible to him at a given moment" (6). He said, over a decade ago, "If the conception of intelligence we have been discussing . . . should prove accurate, it seems to me to raise serious questions about some of our common assumptions with respect to intelligence and, at the same time, opens exciting new possibilities for the treatment or education of people we have often assumed to be beyond help" (7).

2. Hunt, J. McV. *Intelligence and experience.* Copyright © 1961 The Ronald Press Company.

Yet we are only beginning to adopt this concept. In 1964, at the Kennedy Foundation dinner, Kirk talked about the crumbling concept of fixed intelligence. His discussion relates to the changed view of the brain. Recently-devised tests and remedial training techniques which he developed show that mentally retarded children may be close to normal in certain functions and severely retarded in other functions. These tests "assess various 'input' or 'output' deficits of the brain, all or any of which could cause low intelligence scores: They focus on the child's ability to interpret and use different kinds of visual, auditory and tactile experience" (1).

The New York City Board of Education discontinued the use of intelligence tests and has enlisted the assistance of the Educational Testing Service in developing better ways to describe the intellectual capacities of children entering first grade. There are three main lines of attack:

> Development of a practical technique with which a teacher can observe and record the ways in which each child displays intelligent behavior, day by day; development of a series of standard performance tasks to elicit intellectual behavior from children whose usual behavior in class provides few clues; development of special and differential test materials which will give each child a chance to demonstrate his verbal and quantitative skills in a context that is familiar to him (13).

For the years between the Iowa studies of the 1930's described by Hunt and the search for new ways to measure intellectual behavior by Educational Testing Service in 1964, the California and Fels longitudinal studies have furnished additional data. Bayley's analysis of the California data on the growth of intelligence points up the transactional, "Einsteinian" position. After stating that intellectual growth results from not only inherent capacities but also from the emotional and material environment, from encouragement and opportunity, she concludes: "I suspect each child is a law unto himself" (3).

Sontag and his colleagues explained the individual changes in IQ over the years by attributing such changes to motivation. We can see this position as again illustrative of the emerging view. As I see their main hypothesis, it was of a cyclical, circular-feedback nature. That is, as the child needed to demonstrate mastery of problems (school-type) and to compete intellectually, he would see school as offering the opportunity. Performance in school would be enhanced, and he would learn to do well the type of work we measure on IQ tests. As he learned to do this successfully, he would have less anxiety and approach such tests as challenges. As he approached these tests with this attitude, and with the learned skills, he would perform at a higher level. And so the cycle would begin again.

Let us take just one of the examples given by Sontag and his colleagues:

> Case E. R. shows a child whose score rose from a base of 118 at 3 years to 129 at 4 years. We attributed this to the fact that he was a slow maturer in motor development. Then, after no consistent change for three years, his scores began an ascent which carried them almost to 180. This boy, while not aggressive, is intensely competitive in school, gets great satisfaction from mastery of such subjects as mathematics and chemistry, and spends his free hours absorbed in a book. He depends relatively little on human relationships, either family or peers, for reassurance (56).

These longitudinal studies not only reveal the unique individual patterns of intellectual growth as measured by the standard IQ test, and the role of experience and personal motivation in performance, but also they explode the idea of a fixed adult ceiling on development of intelligence. Bayley and Oden tested adults on the Concept Mastery test, and concluded that their results disagreed with many of the results of earlier studies of adult intelligence. They attributed this to the test, which was designed to differentiate abilities at the upper level, to the fact that their subjects were well-motivated and highly intelligent, and to the longitudinal design used. They state:

> The implications to be drawn from our data are that this kind of knowledge and ability improves in superior adults, at least between the ages of 20 and 50. This improvement occurs in all levels of occupation represented, but to a greater extent among the middle occupational classes than in the higher classes. Also, within the professional class, the engineers and chemists, whose training was relatively specific and narrow, evidently broaden their abilities with time, so that on this general type of verbal test their scores attain equality with those of the other professions. This broadening tendency may operate generally among intelligent adults in our culture (4).

These data may all be viewed as emphasizing the role of experience, the transactional "Einsteinian" concept in the development of intellectual behavior.

In summary, the current view might be stated as follows:

> First, intelligence is not a single trait carried, like hemophilia, in a single gene. Intelligent behavior has many more aspects than the ability to do

academic classroom work. Although our intelligence tests may measure academic ability with a fair degree of accuracy at a given moment, they are not measuring all the dimensions of intelligent behavior.

Second, the behavior of a person is not the result of an additive process, but develops from an organizing, integrating process in which a self-system is produced which represents a new integration of all organism-environment forces.

The evidences concerning the self-system—a person's organized responses—suggest the following conclusions relative to the roles of heredity and environment in intelligence: (a) there is an organic genetic base for intelligent behavior; (b) the actual measured intelligence of a particular person at a particular time, since performance on a test is behavior, is a result of the complex transactions between the organism and its environment up to that point; and (c) performance, therefore, on an intelligence test can be modified by the exigencies of one's life experiences (15).

The last line perhaps should read, in 1966, "on any task requiring intelligent behavior."

COGNITIVE DEVELOPMENT

The studies of Piaget in Switzerland and of Bruner in the United States are widely known. Piagetian theory may be less well known, especially in its developing concepts about the role of experience, because his experiments do not include the manipulation of instructional variables. Vygotsky, in assessing the role of instruction in the development of thought and language, said, "We have given him (the child) a pennyworth of instruction and he has gained a small fortune in development" (60). The problem in cognitive instruction is *when* and *how* to put the penny in.

Piaget's magnificent studies do not address themselves to these questions. He simply gave children particular tasks to do and recorded how they did these. From this, he developed a sequence of stages. One of the studies he did with five-year-olds was to see whether they could make differentiations between what things float and what things sink and whether they could conceptualize about displacement (26). He showed the child a variety of objects and asked, "Does it sink or does it swim?" The child would place the object in the water and make some sort of judgment. Piaget said that five-year-olds could not figure any of this out, and were completely inconsistent. One time they would say the object would float, the next time they said it would sink. They would say it sinks because it is big and the next time they would say it floats because it is big. If they expected it to sink, they would take their hands and shove the object down and make it do what they wanted it to do. This is an accurate description by Piaget of the natural state of affairs. But, does that mean such a state is fixed?

Ralph Ojemann at the State University of Iowa tested this question experimentally. Ojemann's position, which he has taken for 20 years, is that by what we do in the classroom we can modify children's conceptual development. He and his colleague took a group of Iowa five-year-olds to find out whether there was any way to teach these children concepts of specific gravity. The first question they asked the children was, "Do you think it would be worthwhile trying to find out why things float? Why should anybody spend time worrying about why things float?" The children gave three reasons. They said, "We want to know how things work!" (competence motivation at work). They said, ". . . helps us to know what will happen when things are put into water." For example, what happens when you try to place ice cubes in a full glass of water? And then these children, in their apparently inherent wisdom of Bruner's discovery approach, said, "It might help us to find a way to learn about things."

So, they showed the children a plastic ball about 5″ in diameter, put it in water where it floated. They asked the children, "Why did it float?" Some of the children said, "Because it's light." Some others said, "Because it's made of plastic," (which is a good Piagetian response). Another said, "Because it's soft"; another said, "Because it's big!" Then the children were shown articles of different weights, made of different things, with different qualities of hardness and softness and bigness and littleness. Two of these items, such as a rectangular piece of iron and a metal jar lid, a plastic lid and a dime, a wooden block and an iron piece, a die and a small glass bottle were put in the water simultaneously and the children watched them. The children very soon discovered from their own observation that you could not simply come to the conclusion on the basis of heaviness or plasticity or softness or size; that their previous explanations produced inconsistent results.

The experimenters went one step further and showed the children that when you put something in water, it pushes the water away. The children watched the water level rise when something went in and then the experimenters asked them, "How much water do you think rises?" The youngsters obviously had no idea of this, so they fixed up a beaker with a spout and filled it up to the spout and put a tube of shampoo in it and caught the overflow in a plastic container. They demonstrated with other objects. The youngsters saw that when you put something in water, it pushes the water away. The youngsters measured and weighed the amount of water and the object. The experimenters then tested the children on the Piaget materials and had the youngsters answer the questions: "Will it sink?" "Will it float?" "Why will it sink?" "Why will it float?"

It was quite clear that these youngsters utilized and understood notions of displacement in the answers they gave to the Piaget material. They behaved at age levels far above the predicted age levels from Piaget's norms. More than that, some of the children had gone through three "stages of concept development" and were behaving at the logical stage of the eleven- and twelve-year-old, although they were only five. Ojemann and Pritchett (42) thus demonstrated that one could influence, by a very careful sequence of experiences, the development of an abstract notion.

The work of Vygotsky (59), and his students in the Soviet Union adds to this picture of the role of experience in concept development. Although written over a generation ago, his book was not translated into English until 1962. Based upon studies of "the level of development requisite for learning the basic school subjects—reading and writing, arithmetic, natural science," he reported, "Our investigation shows that the development of the psychological foundations for instruction in basic subjects does not precede instruction, but unfolds in a continuous interaction with the contributions of instruction" (61). Studies of the temporal relation between instruction and development led him to conclude that "the curve of development does not coincide with the curve of school instruction; by and large, instruction precedes development" (62).

The position taken by Vygotsky was one of intellectual structures built upon deliberate instruction, and then the use of these structures by the developing child to increase his ability to deal with more abstract matters. We note again the cyclical operation. Timing, to Vygotsky, was important. Rather than the concept described in the beginning of this chapter of "divining" for potential, or the traditional idea still held by many teachers of an unfolding concept of maturational readiness, Vygotsky claimed that ". . . The only good kind of instruction is that which marches ahead of development and leads it; it must be aimed not so much at the ripe but the ripening functions . . . instruction must be oriented toward the future, not the past. . . . The school years as a whole are the optimum period for instruction in operations that require awareness and deliberate control; instruction in these operations maximally furthers the development of the higher psychological functions while they are maturing" (63).

These ideas sound familiar to students of both John Dewey and Jean Paiget. They stress that development requires active commerce with the world, and they stress the importance of function. They echo Ojemann's concept of guided experience. The transactional position begins with the child—and builds from there. It stresses openness to experience.

The Higher Horizons project, the Great Cities Program, and the nursery school work of Martin Deutsch (12) all support a view of cognitive development as modifiable.

When the data are reviewed, the transactional nature of development becomes clear.

> This research opens up many possibilities for exploring the role of guided experience in concept development. It offers support for the position that what children are does not necessarily control what children may become. It casts suspicion on procedures which utilize only current knowledge of children as the criterion for curriculum development. It emphasizes the vital influence of the transactional field in effecting future self-development. It removes from us the rigid, ontogenetic barrier to understanding behavior (16).

FROM TELEPHONE SWITCHBOARD TO COMPUTER

The studies already referred to, and my interpretation of their meanings, describe what we can see in observable behavior and performance. The question remains: Why does experience play such a crucial role in development? A theoretical position imposes two boundaries upon us. First, it leads us to collect certain kinds of data by studying only certain events in certain ways. Second, it leads us to interpret our findings in keeping with our position. It is only when the data will no longer "fit," or when someone invents a new model or builds a new theory, that we get a reorganization of data and the emergence of new reseach designs.

In this case, the computer model opened the way. When the brain was conceived of as a telephone switchboard, connections between stimulus and response did not alter the system, the connections were specific, and the line could be disconnected when the call was completed. No call could be made unless the wires were in, and there was no concept that making a call did anything fundamental to any of the wires except those involved in the cell. The computer concept, still an analog rather than a "real" representation of the brain, sees the brain as a total active system, with memory drums and feedback mechanism.

The current studies in neurology and physiological psychology by Hebb (20), Miller, Galanter and Pribram (37), Newell, Shaw and Simon (40), all yield data which stress the inherent activity of the brain and its function as an information-processing system. Information received by the brain is stored, not as isolated bits, but as patterns and what Piaget calls "schema," which are analogous to categories, or "concepts." When new sensory inputs reach the brain, they go not only to a particular center, but also the total brain is scanned for similar already-stored data in "memory banks" or memory "tapes." The more information so stored, the more useful the computer becomes. In terms of the living brain, these inputs are organized into patterns or structures.

In an excellent article, written for educators, Pribram challenged the traditional notions of reward and reinforcement and described the brain's operation in terms of the TOTE mechanism:

> . . . the fundamental neural organization in control of the association between stimulus and response can no longer be conceived as a reflex arc. On the basis of many new neurological facts, the suggestion has been made that the reflex arc be replaced by a feedback unit which involves (a) Test of readiness with regard to the input, (b) an Operation that seeks to match the test, (c) a re-Test to see whether match has been accomplished, before (d) Exit from control is effected. This TOTE mechanism is ubiquitous—it is essentially a modified homeostat, a mechanism which can control the very input to which it is sensitive. TOTE's are conceived to be arranged hierarchically into Plans, the antecedents of actions. And structually Plans are nothing more than programs, similar to those that guide the operation of computers—well-worked-out outlines such as those used in programmed texts and teaching machines (47).

Piaget's concepts of *accommodation* and *assimilation* also are useful ways to describe how information is utilized. If the data "match" what is already structured, so the child knows how to behave, he merely assimilates the information, and no learning is required. If, however, the information does not match the already developed structure, but is seen by the child as information that requires processing and new responses from him, then he is required to modify his structure to incorporate the new data. He must, in Piaget's terms, accommodate. It is this accommodation which may be seen as taking place at the time which Vygotsky calls the ripening time. The active child utilizes the instruction or information and increases his competence. The child, in effect, uses information to grow on just as his body uses food.

The concepts of accommodation and assimilation are essential, according to Piaget, in order to explain the development of cognitive structure. He states: "Practically, one would have to rely on three principal factors in order to explain the facts of development: maturation, physical experience, and social interaction. But in this particular case none of these three suffice to furnish us with the desired explanations— not even the three together" (43). After discussing why each of these is insufficient, Piaget attributes the explanation to a fourth factor, *equilibration*. In terms used in the beginning of this chapter, this concept is embodied in the model of an open-energy, self-organizing system, always active with the brain functioning in analogous fashion to the computer. Piaget takes the view that development depends on internal factors (maturation) and external factors (physical or social) equilibrating each other:

> All exchange (mental as well as biological) between the organisms and the milieu (physical and social) is composed of two poles: (a) of the assimilation of the given external to the previous internal structures, and (b) of the accommodation of these structures to the given ones. . . . The mental equilibrium and even the biological one presumes an activity of the subject, or of the organism. It consists in a sort of matching, orientated towards compensation—with even some overcompensation—resulting from strategies of precaution (44).

He concludes:

> Every new problem provokes a disequilibrium (recognizable through types of dominant errors) the solution of which consists in a reequilibration, which brings about a new original synthesis of two systems, up to the point of independence (45).

Motivation is always basic to his concepts of dynamic structure. What is motivating is the push of the child to structure the world. The neurological analog of brain-as-computer and the Piagetian concept of child-as-information-processor can be seen as highly similar. Both models lead away from the drive-reduction notions of motivation, and blend with the construct of the child as active and competence-oriented.

THE CHILD AS ACTIVE AND COMPETENT

THE CHILD AS INTERNALLY ACTIVE

The "Einsteinian" model child is conceived as an active, information-seeking and information-processing system. This activity is inherent in his basic biology. His energy is not limited and rationed and the amount of his energy is not a crucial factor as much as the way the energy is directed. The computer analog is most useful here, since the primary purpose of the computer is the handling of information.

The energy is there, it does not have to be stoked from the outside, but its use by the child is the issue. In the current view, the child does not wait to use this energy in order simply to reduce drive. The drive-reduction principle just does not fit this model, because drive is always present, and often children behave to increase the amount of tension and drive they are experiencing. If a drive-reduction view of motivation is inadequate (22),[3] the current knowledge of the brain as always active (21; 46) leads to a search for the optimum conditions under which this activity is organized for learning and development.

Hebb points out:

> There is no doubt . . . that problem-solving situations have some attraction for the rat, more for Harlow's monkeys, and far more for man. When you stop to think of it, it is nothing short of extraordinary what trouble people will go to in order to get into more trouble at the bridge table, or on the golf course; and the fascination of the murder story, or thriller, and the newspaper accounts of real-life adventure or tragedy, is no less extraordinary. This taste for excitement must not be forgotten when we are dealing with human motivation. It appears that, up to a certain point, threat and puzzle have positive motivating value, beyond that point negative value . . . risk and puzzle can be attractive in themselves, especially for higher animals such as man. If we can accept this, it will no longer be necessary to work out tortuous and improbable ways to explain why human beings work for money, why school children should learn without pain, why a human being in isolation should dislike doing nothing (19).

3. Hunt, J. McV. *Intelligence and experience.* Copyright © 1961 The Ronald Press Company.

THE CHILD AS COMPETENT

The active engagement of the child with his environment, as we have seen, is essential for his maximum development. This active engagement requires perceptual and motor stimulation from the environment, but it also rests on the idea that the child will, when he has not been made apathetic by deprivation, or intensely aroused by threat and frustration, seek out aspects of his environment. It is, in effect, the "full belly and full brain" child (one who has had both biological and intellectual food) who learns the widest range of concepts and develops the more complex cognitive structures.

Two lines of research converge here: one deals with our rediscovery of the competence of the infant, the second is the investigation of competency motivation. The infant as competent should not be read to imply the infant as miniature adult. Nevertheless, some of the earlier notions of neonates as unable to use their senses, as highly unorganized and as inadequate to deal with the world except as a "blob" are under serious attack from a variety of sources. In pediatrics, Smith and his colleagues have shown that "the newborn human, despite significant exceptions, copes with most acquired viral and bacterial infections successfully, associated with the formation of specific antibody. . . . The experimental literature reveals comparable and incontrovertible evidence of neonatal immunological capacity" (55).

Kessen summarized the psychological evidence of the ability of the neonate to make differential responses to a variety of stimuli. He states: *"The young infant is not incompetent,"* or, by Andre Thomas' (58) catching phrase, "The neonate is not a neophyte" (28). He also reinforces the new model of the child by concluding:

> The shift in point-of-view—to set the antitheses sharply—has been from the child who is a passive receptacle, into which learning and maturation pour knowledge and skills and affects until he is full, to the child as a complex, competent organism who, by acting on the environment and being acted on in turn, develops more elaborated and balanced ways of dealing with discrepancy, conflict, and disequilibrium. This shift, I believe, is of incalculable implication and seems to have been accepted to some degree by almost all students of children. Bowlby emphasizes the control by the child in crying and smiling; psychoanalytic theory makes more space for autonomous ego functions; child psychologists dedicated to a learning analysis speak of the child as active; and I suspect Piaget thinks of how he knows it all the time (29).

Competence motivation has been brilliantly summarized by White (64). He coins the word *effectance* to describe the motivation of the child when he is not forced to focus on drive-reduction (hunger, etc.). His view, based upon an intensive review of research, is as follows:

> We are no longer obliged to look for a source of energy external to the nervous system, for a consummatory climax, or for a fixed connection between reinforcement and tension-reduction. Effectance motivation cannot, of course, be conceived as having a source in tissues external to the nervous system. It is in no sense a deficit motive. We must assume it to be neurogenic, its "energies" being simply those of the living cells that make up the nervous system. External stimuli play an important part, but in terms of "energy" this part is secondary, as one can see most clearly when environmental stimulation is actively sought. Putting it picturesquely, we might say that the effectance urge represents what the neuromuscular system wants to do when it is otherwise unoccupied or is gently stimulated by the environment (64).

Why does a child play, for long periods of time, at a single task? We have all seen a youngster so engrossed that the world literally goes on around him. Rather than the old concept of limited attention span for the young child, it is clear that, when the task has meaning to him, he can spend long periods engaged in it. For White, the child does this because he is discovering the nature of the transaction with which he is engaged with the environment. He is finding out what he can do to it, and it to him. White is saying that, given a situation of mild arousal, the child will engage in a wide variety of activities because it is satisfying to him to deal effectively with his environment. He will seek out the more complex tasks over the simpler ones he can already perform.

Simple observation of children on the street or playground shows this: the youngster who has mastered the elements of bike riding tries to do it with "no hands," the prospective little league star chides the novice with the cry that "two hands are for beginners," and the adolescent with the newly acquired driving license is not content merely to drive, but engages in "drag races" and games of "chicken." The adult, in turn, climbs Mount Everest "because it's there."

An experimental investigation by May (36) using nursery school children is but one example of additional evidence. Children given a free choice in the selection of stimuli to play with, overwhelmingly chose the more complex stimuli. Sears and Hilgard, in an excellent review of the role of motivation and learning, conclude:

Even in the laboratory there is a turn away from deprived states to positive motives, such as activity, curiosity and manipulation, to "hope" rather than "fear" as fundamental (53).

Classroom observations abound in data showing children seeking more complex tasks, inventing work to do, extending themselves beyond the subject matter at hand. Teachers have often seen these activities as "discipline problems." They can now be understood as clues that what is being presented to be learned does not necessarily match either the competence motivation of the child or his present structure. He can, in Piaget's terms, assimilate the material when what he is seeking is opportunity to accommodate to new material.

MAN AS A SELF–ORGANIZING SYSTEM

In the preceding description of both the theoretical framework and the research evidence, two continuing concepts emerge: (a) Man is an information-processing, organizing open energy system, in constant transaction with his changing environment. (b) Each individual man, because of his own organism and particular environment, creates his own unique contribution to the environment. Although the process of engaging with the environment is common, the stimuli which become information, and the biochemical organization already present at birth to receive and process these stimuli are specific to each person. In this final section of this chapter, these two concepts will be reviewed.

The computer-brain analog and neurological research theory pointed a way to understanding how the brain does this.

We have described the organism as always active, always engaged, always seeking order or meaning. Pribram indicates how neurological structure lends itself to this concept:

> The suggestion is that reinforcement is the expression of an organism's tendency toward orderliness; that satisfaction results when a degree of orderliness has been achieved. There is good reason to suspect that the central nervous system is so constructed that order is imposed on its inputs if this is at all possible; if it is not, search continues. . . .
>
> The process of satisfaction is to be conceived as intrinsic to the material ordered and intrinsic to the construction of the nervous system. Education so conceived is truly a process of e-ducere, the art of bringing out this tendency to orderliness (48).

This "push for order" can be seen as serving as a basis for concept-building and categorization. The very nature of the child, neurologically, requires of him that he process information in such a way that categories emerge. What particular concepts, and at what levels of abstraction depend, of course, on input. Schooling which utilizes the child's endeavors to structure his world contributes to competence. Schooling which either tries to impose an order when the child cannot grasp it, or presents masses of data expecting the child to order them as the adult does, may lead to mental indigestion and feelings of incompetence. Concepts such as "inquiry training" and "discovery method" utilize the information processing model, and capitalize on this transactional view. Bruner (5), for example, points out that categorizing reduces the complexity of the environment, allows one to see relationships, and cuts down the necessity for constant learning. He emphasizes, in addition, the concept that categorizing is goal-directed. The latter is particularly crucial for application to schooling.

We have stressed the role of perceptual-motor experience in the development of the child. Simon and Newell make explicit, from the computer model, the interaction of these two processes. They see the organism's survival dependent upon the mutual interaction of perceiving the environment and acting in it. The child not only perceives the environment, he processes the information of what happens as he behaves. He stores, then, both external and internal information. He translates his motor behavior into perceptual symbols—and the development of languages is related to this. Words become symbols which represent perceptions of acts and events. In their words, "Language behavior . . . is highly stylized so that to each distinct language 'act' will correspond an easily perceivable and distinguishable perceptual symbol" (54).

In order to master the environment, to know how to deal with the events which surround and impinge upon him, the child thus engages in behavior that leads to concept attainment. These concepts, or networks of inferences about how to deal with one's self and the world, increase his scope and ability. They give him not only competence, but the feeling of competence.

The longitudinal study conducted by Lois Murphy and her colleagues at the Menninger Foundation led them to conclude:

> In everyday parlance, we say that success breeds success. This is more than a matter of modification of structure by function which constantly contributes to the improvement of skill. What we have seen is a combina-

tion of this improvement of skill resulting from the active coping effort; an emergence of belief in or confidence in the worthwhileness of this coping effort which has produced success; the development of a self-image as the child who can master a challenge by his own efforts. That is, triumph or successful results of coping efforts produce motor, affective and cognitive changes which predispose and equip the child for more efforts (38).

Whether or not the child attains both of these is dependent upon the sequences, type and content of experiences provided for him in home, school and community and the unique biochemical organization he brings to these experiences.

THE INDIVIDUAL AS UNIQUE

To quote from Lois Murphy again, ". . . through his coping experiences the child discovers and measures himself, and develops his own perception of who and what he is and in time may become. We can say that the child creates his identity through his efforts in coming to terms with the environment in his own personal way" (39).

The two key phrases above are *creates his identity* and *personal way*.

As mentioned in the opening section of this chapter, individuality was recognized in the traditional "Newtonian" view of the infant. But, this was a "given." Here, individuality is a creation, an emergent. This individuality permeates every dimension which students of human development and behavior have found measurable. Yet, this uniqueness has not been understood and exploited in the educative process. Traditional learning theory has not only ignored it, but also has assumed that the laws of learning apply to all species. It may be both amazing and amusing to educators to note how naive in this area are these learning "experts."

Any parent or teacher recognizes that children are different. However, as Suppes states, "In spite of the obeisance paid to this tenet (of individual differences in rate of learning) in discussions of curriculum, I consider it the most important principle of learning as yet *unaccepted* in the day-to-day practice of subject-matter teaching in the classroom" (57). Even here, only *rate* is being considered, in spite of the considerable evidence of individuality in cognitive style, personality structure, modes of thinking, self-concept, etc.

These concepts will tend to govern our educational system and impose demands upon us to educate our children for such a world. This yearbook, as a whole, addresses itself to the task ahead. I can think of no better chapter ending than this quotation from Earl Kelley:

Perhaps the most all-inclusive thing we can do for individuality is to learn how to live in a changing universe. The fact of change, unless it is indeed a denial of "fact," seems to be one thing we can be sure of. Those who seek an unchanging base on which to stand will always be disappointed and will always be out of tune with the universe. The immutable, if it could be found, or if one thinks he has found it, calls for rigidity and similarity. To some degree, each individual who stands on the immutable blocks the on-going movement of the creative force which he needs, rather, to facilitate. The person who learns to accept change and looks forward to it has the only security available to humans. He does not know what tomorrow will be like. But he knows it will be different from today. He is glad that this is so, he looks forward to this new tomorrow, and in this, he feels secure. In accepting change, he understands that people are unique and learns to cherish their differences (27).

1. *American Psychologist,* April 1964, **19**(4), 293.

2. Barnett, S. *The rat, A study in behavior.* Chicago: Aldine, 1963.

3. Bayley, N. On the growth of intelligence. *American Psychologist,* 1955, **10,** 805–818, 815.

4. Bayley, N., & Oden, M. The maintenance of intellectual ability in gifted adults. *Journal of Gerontology,* 1955, **10:**91–107, 106.

5. Bruner, J., Goodnow, J., & Austin, G. *A study of thinking.* New York: Wiley, 1956.

6. Combs, Arthur W. Intelligence from a perceptual point of view. *Journal of Abnormal and Social Psychology,* 1952, **47,** 662–673, 663.

7. *Ibid.,* p. 671.

8. Denenberg, Victor H., et al. Effects of maternal factors upon growth and behavior of the rat. *Child Development,* March 1962, **33,** 65–71.

9. Denenberg, Victor H., Morton, R., et al. Effects of duration of infantile stimulation upon emotionality. *Canadian Journal of Psychology,* 1962, **16,** 72–76.

10. Dennis, W. Causes of retardation among institutional children: Iran. *Journal of Genetic Psychology,* 1960, **96,** 47–59.

11. Dennis, W., Najarian, P. Infant development under environmental handicap. *Psychological Monographs,* 1957, **71,** 1–13.

12. Deutsch, M. Facilitating development in the pre-school child: Social and psychological perspectives. *Merrill-Palmer Quarterly of Behavior and Development,* 1964, **10,** 249–264.

13. Educational Testing Service *Developments,* May 1964, **12,** 3.

14. Fischer, John L., & Fischer, Ann. The New Englanders of Orchard Town, U.S.A. In B. Whiting, (Ed.) *Six cultures: Studies of child rearing.* New York: Wiley, 1963, pp. 922–923.

15. Gordon, Ira. *Human development.* New York: Harper & Row, 1962. p. 29.

16. *Ibid.,* p. 232.

17. Harlow, H. The hetero-sexual affectional system in monkeys. *American Psychologist,* January 1962, **17,** 1–9.

18. Harlow, H. The nature of love. *American Psychologist,* 1958, **13,** 676–685.

19. Hebb, D. O. Drives and the CNS (Conceptual Nervous System). *Psychological Review,* 1955, **62,** 243–254, 250–251.

20. Hebb, D. O. The motivating effects of exteroceptive stimulation. *American Psychologist,* 1958, **13,** 109–113.

21. Hebb, D. O. op. cit., 1955.

22. Hunt, J. McVicker. *Intelligence and experience.* New York: Ronald Press, 1961.

23. *Ibid.,* pp. 95–97.

24. *Ibid.,* p. 342.

25. *Ibid.,* p. 19.

26. Inhelder, B., & Piaget, J. *The growth of logical thinking.* New York: Basic Books, 1962.

27. Kelley, Earl. The Significance of Being Unique. *ETC* 14:169–84; 1957, p. 184.

28. Kessen, W. Research in the psychological development of infants: An overview. *Merrill-Palmer Quarterly of Behavior and Development,* 1953, **9,** 83–94, 86.

29. *Ibid.,* p. 92.

30. Krech, D., Rosenzweig, M., & Bennett, E. Relations between brain chemistry and problem solving among rats raised in enriched and impoverished environments. *Journal of Comparative and Physiological Psychology,* 1962, **55,** 801–807, 806–807.

31. Krech, D., Rosenzweig, M., & Bennett, E. Effects of complex environment and blindness on rat brain. *Archives of Neurology,* 1963, **8,** 403–412, 412.

32. *Ibid.,* p. 411.

33. Levine, S. The effects of differential infantile stimulation of emotionality at weaning. *Canadian Journal of Psychology,* 1959, **13,** 243–247.

34. Mason, W. Social development of Rhesus monkeys with restricted social experience. *Perceptual and Motor Skills,* 1963, **16,** 263–270.

35. *Ibid.,* pp. 268–269.

36. May, R. Stimulus selection in preschool children under conditions of free choice. *Perceptual and Motor Skills,* 1963, **16,** 203–206.

37. Miller, G. A., Pribram, K., & Galanter, E. *Plans and the structure of behavior.* New York: Holt, Rinehart & Winston, 1960.

38. Murphy, L., et al. *The widening world of childhood.* New York: Basic Books, 1962, p. 366. Copyright © 1962 by Basic Books, Inc., Publishers.

39. *Ibid.,* p. 374.

40. Newell, A., Shaw, J., & Simon, H. Elements of a theory of human problem solving. *Psychological Review,* 1958, **65,** 151–166.

41. Newell, A., & Simon, H. Computer simulation of human thinking. *Science,* 1961, **134,** 2011–2017.

42. Ojemann, R., & Pritchett, K. Piaget and the role of guided experiences in human development. *Perceptual and Motor Skills,* 1963, **17,** 927–940.

43. Piaget, J. The genetic approach to the psychology of thought. *Journal of Educational Psychology,* 1961, **52,** 275–281, 277.

44. *Ibid.,* p. 279.

45. *Ibid.,* p. 281.

46. Pribram, K. Neurological notes on the art of educating. *Theories of Learning and Instruction,* NSSE 63rd Yearbook, Part I. Ernest Hilgard (Ed.). Chicago: University of Chicago Press, 1964.

47. *Ibid.,* pp. 89–90.

48. *Ibid.,* p. 95.

49. Provence, S., & Lipton, R. *Infants in institutions.* New York: International Universities Press, 1962, pp. 118–119.

50. *Ibid.*

51. Riesen, A., et al. Chimpanzee vision after four conditions of light deprivation. *American Psychologist,* 1951, **6,** 282.

52. Rosenzweig, M., et al. Effects of environmental complexity and training on brain chemistry and anatomy: A replication and extension. *Journal of Comparative and Physiological Psychology,* 1962, **55,** 429–437.

53. Sears, P., & Hilgard, E. The teacher's role in the motivation of the learner. *Theories of Learning and Instruction,* NSSE 63rd Yearbook, Part I. Ernest Hilgard (Ed.). Chicago: University of Chicago Press, 1964, p. 207.

54. Simon, H., & Newell, A. Computer simulation of human thinking and problem solving. *Monographs of the SRCD,* 1962, **27,** 137–149, 148.

55. Smith, R., et al. Development of the immune response. *Pediatrics,* 1964, **33,** 163–183, 163–164.

56. Sontag, L., Baker, C., & Nelson, V. Personality as a determinant of performance. *American Journal of Orthopsychiatry,* 1955, **25,** 255–262, 561.

57. Suppes, P. Modern learning theory and the elementary school curriculum. *American Educational Research Journal,* 1964, **1,** 79–94.

58. Thomas, Andre, et al. A longitudinal study of primary reaction patterns in children. *Comprehensive Psychiatry*, 1960, **1**, 103–112.

59. Vygotsky, L. S. *Thought and language.* Cambridge: Massachusetts Institute of Technology Press, 1962. Reprinted from *Thought and Language* by Lev Vygotsky, translated by Eugenia Hanfmann and Gertrude Vakar by permission of The M.I.T. Press, Cambridge, Massachusetts. Copyright © 1962 by The Massachusetts Institute of Technology.

60. *Ibid.,* p. 96.

61. *Ibid.,* pp. 98–101.

62. *Ibid.,* p. 102.

63. *Ibid.,* pp. 104–105.

64. White, R. Motivation reconsidered: The concept of competence. *Psychological Review*, 1959, **66**, 297–323.

Intelligence from a Perceptual Point of View

Arthur W. Combs

There is a growing trend in psychology toward viewing behavior as a function of perception. More and more we have come to understand that the individual's behavior is not so much a function of the physical stimulus as it is a function of his perceptions of the events to which he is exposed. It is the meaning of events to the individual rather than the externally observed nature of events which seems crucial in behavior. As a result, psychologists in increasing numbers are turning their attention to the problems of human perception and are attempting to observe behavior, not from an external point of view, but from the point of view of

Reprinted from *Journal of Abnormal and Social Psychology,* 1952, **47**, 662–673, by permission of the author and the American Psychological Association.

the individual who is behaving. This paper is an attempt to relate this method of observation to the problem of intelligence. The question we wish to explore in this paper is: "What is the nature of intelligence viewed from a perceptual or phenomenological frame of reference?"

INTELLIGENCE AS A PROBLEM OF PERCEPTION

By the term *intelligence* we ordinarily refer to the effectiveness of the individual's behavior. In a personal frame of reference the individual's behavior is described in terms of the perceptions that he can make his own unique perceptive field. This perceptive field has been called by Snygg and Combs *The Phenomenal Field* and has been defined by them as "the universe of experience open to the individual at the moment of his behavior." In other words, the behavior of the individual will be dependent upon the perceptions that the individual makes in his phenomenal field at the moment of action. The effectiveness of his behavior will necessarily be a function of the adequacy of those perceptions.

If an entity in the perceptive field is vague and ill defined, the behavior of the individual will be correspondingly vague and lacking in precision. Until the child has clearly differentiated that 2 plus 2 equals 4, this function is comparatively meaningless and his behavior in arithmetic is correspondingly inaccurate and ineffective. Thus, the precision and effectiveness of the individual's behavior will be dependent upon the scope and clarity of his personal field of awareness. Intelligence, then, from a perceptual point of view becomes a function of the factors which limit the scope and clarity of an individual's phenomenal field.

The perceptions that could be made of any given situation, such as looking at a stone wall, for example, are, theoretically, practically infinite in number and quality. As a matter of fact, however, we are strictly limited in our perceptions of a stone wall to those which we, as human beings, can make. The perceptions possible to us are only those that people can make. We cannot, for instance, perceive the wall as it would appear to a man from Mars, or from the interior of an atom, or as it would appear to a centipede. What is more, we cannot even perceive it as it would appear to all people. Different people will perceive different aspects of the wall differently, even at the same instant. I can only perceive the wall, and hence behave toward it, in terms of the perceptions that I, as an individual, can make regarding it. I may, for instance, perceive it as a fine, sturdy fence enclosing my property, while a stone mason friend might perceive it as having been poorly designed, or as having been built with too little cement in the mortar mixture. The perceptions open to my mason friend are the result of his unique experience. I, not having such experience, am incapable of those perceptions at this moment.

POTENTIAL AND FUNCTIONAL PERCEPTIONS

Before proceeding further with our discussion of the limiting factors in perception, it is necessary for us to pause for a moment to distinguish between potential and functional perceptions. By potential perceptions I mean those perceptions that exist in the individual's unique field of awareness and that, given the right circumstances at any particular moment, *could* occur. The fact that a perception is potentially possible to any individual, by no means, however, means that it will occur at the moment of action. Even those perceptions that I can make potentially may not be active for me at any given moment. Potentially, I might be able, for instance, to perceive the wall that we have just been using as an example as a barrier to be gotten over, as an eyesore to be beautified, as composed of 687 bricks costing me $80.27, or as providing pleasant shade on a hot day. These are all potential perceptions I am capable of making about the wall. They will affect my behavior, however, only when they are active or functioning in my field of perceptions. When I am beating a hasty retreat pursued by a neighbor's angry dog, perceptions about the shade, beauty, or cost of the wall, though potential, are not functional in affecting my behavior. I behave only in terms of my functioning perception of the wall as something to get over—and quickly. The fact that particular perceptions may exist potentially in the phenomenal field of an individual is by no means a guarantee that they may exist functionally at the moment of action.

While the potential intelligence of the individual is of interest in judging his capacities, it is practically always a matter impossible to measure with any degree of accuracy. We can only sample those parts of a phenomenal field that *we* happen to feel are important. Obviously the measurement of a person's potential perceptions in these terms is open to extremely grave sampling error and improves in accuracy only as the individuals tested have common experience in the materials chosen for testing. It seems probable that an intelligence test cannot accurately measure the potential differentiations that the individual can make in his phenomenal field. Rather, what we usually measure are the subject's functional perceptions. That is, we measure what differentiations he can make when confronted with the necessity to do so for one reason or another. We may define these functional perceptions as: those perceptions in the field experienced by the individual at the moment of behaving.

From a perceptual viewpoint, if intelligence is the capacity for effective behavior, *the intelligence of an individual will be dependent upon the richness and variety of perceptions possible to him at a given moment.* To understand and effectively to foster intelligent behavior, it will be necessary for us to be concerned with the limiting factors upon the perceptions of an individual. We need to know not only what the individual *could* perceive, but what he *would* perceive at a given moment of behaving.

SOME LIMITING FACTORS UPON PERCEPTION

PHYSIOLOGIC LIMITATIONS UPON PERCEPTION

Certainly the physical limitations upon the organism affect the differentiations possible in the phenomenal field. Some forms of prenatal anomalies, like mongolism, microcephalia, and similar disorders, indubitably reduce the level of operation at which the individual can function and seriously impair the ability of the organism to make adequate perceptions. Similarly, there seems good reason to believe that some types of mechanical or disease injury to the central nervous system may result in impaired functioning, such as occurs in cerebral palsy, birth injuries, prefrontal lobotomy, the aftermath of such diseases as encephalitis or, even, in common childhood diseases accompanied by prolonged high fever. Various forms of endocrinopathies, particularly cretinism, also appear to have limiting effects upon differentiational capacity for some individuals. Such physical or biological limitations upon the organism have been widely studied but account for only a small proportion of those persons operating at impaired intelligence levels.

Other less dramatic forms of physical handicaps may also have important effects upon the perceptions possible to the individual, however. This is particularly true of individuals suffering impairment of various sense modalities which may inhibit the clarity or even the existence of some perceptions. We need to remind ourselves, however, that such persons may have as rich and varied a perceptive field within their own limitations as we have within ours. Testing persons living in one frame of reference with tests based on those of another can easily lead us astray, a fact well known to the makers of some tests for the handicapped. The limitations imposed upon perception by such physical handicaps as the loss or impairment of locomotion or the use of arms or hands are also important in limiting certain kinds of perceptions. These people experience different, but not necessarily fewer or poorer, perceptions of events than socalled "normals."

Perhaps less well recognized in their effects upon perception are such factors as malnutrition, focal infections, and chronic fatigue, which may reduce both the need for and the ability to make adequate perceptions. It is well known in industrial psychology, for example, that fatigued workers are more likely to have accidents, perhaps because of failure to make the right differentiations at the right time. It is conceivable that persons suffering from chronic fatigue over long periods similarly fail to make differentiations useful to them on later occasions.

Certainly such physical factors as these have important effects upon the ability of the individual to make adequate differentiations in his perceptive field. The more dramatic of these have often been recognized and studied. Others, such as the effects of malnutrition, fatigue, and the like, have been less adequately explored. In spite of the lack of research in respect to some of the physical limitations upon intelligence, far more work has been done in this area, however, than in some of those to be discussed below.

ENVIRONMENT AND OPPORTUNITY AS A LIMITATION UPON PERCEPTION

The differentiations in the phenomenal field that an individual can make will, of course, be affected by the opportunities for perception to which he has been exposed. To appear in the perceptive field an event must have been, in some manner, experienced by the person who perceives it. Environmental effects upon perception appear to be of two types, actual or concrete and symbolic or vicarious.

EXPOSURE TO ACTUAL ENVIRONMENTAL EVENTS

In the first place the perceptions possible to any individual will be limited, in part, by the actual environmental factors to which he has been exposed. Eskimos ordinarily do not comprehend bananas, nor African Bushmen, snow, since neither has had the opportunity to experience these events in their respective environments. It is not necessary to go so far afield for illustration, however. In our own country our experience with the testing of children in various parts of the nation has shown that perceptions are highly limited by the environmental conditions surrounding the individual. Mountain children, for example, often give bizarre responses on intelligence tests. Sherman and Henry found intelligence test results on such children arranged themselves in order of the opportunities provided by their environment.

There are differences also between the perceptions of rural and urban children, children from the North and children from the South, mountain and valley, seaboard and plains. Nor are such differences confined only to children. Adults, too, are limited in their perceptions by environmental factors. During the war I worked for a time in an induction station receiving men from the mountains of Kentucky, West Virginia, and southern Ohio. An intelligence test in use at this station was composed of a series of five pictures with instructions to the subject to cross out that one of each series of five objects that did not belong with the others. One set of five pictures showed four stringed instruments, a guitar, harp, violin, bass fiddle, and a trumpet. Large numbers of these back country men crossed out the harp because they had never seen one or because "all the others are things in our band." We cannot assume that these men were less able to make differentiations or had perceptive fields less rich than their examiner on the basis of these tests. We can only suggest that their perceptions are different from those who made the test. Presumably, had they made the test and administered it to the psychologist, the psychologist would have appeared rather dull!

Exposure to Symbolic or Vicarious Events

Differentiations may occur in the perceptive field upon a symbolic basis as well as from exposure to an actual event. That is, perceptions may occur in the individual's field through indirect exposure to experience as in reading, conversation, movies, and other means of communication. Although I cannot directly perceive that it is dangerous to expose myself to rays from an atomic pile, for example, I can differentiate this notion through what others whom I respect have told me. Ideas and concepts are largely differentiations of this sort, and it is probable that many of our perceptions are acquired through a symbolic rather than an actual exposure. Certainly most of our formal schooling falls in this category which may explain, in part, why so little of it is effective in our behavior.

It will be recognized at once that exposure to events in no sense completely determines the perceptions that the individual will make. Exposure to events is only one of the factors involved in determining whether or not an event will be differentiated. Even with equivalent exposure, the perceptions we make are not alike. Perception is not an all or none proposition but a selective process. The same person in the same situation at different times may perceive quite different aspects of the situation and behave accordingly. The provisions of opportunity to perceive is by no means a guarantee that a particular perception will occur, a phenomenon of which teachers are only too aware. The personal field of the individual is always organized and meaningful and, even with exposure to events, only those aspects that have meaning for the individual in his own unique economy will be differentiated with permanence.

The individual in a particular culture perceives those aspects of his environment that, from his point of view, he needs to perceive to maintain and enhance his self in the world in which he lives. This does not mean he makes fewer perceptions than an individual in another culture; he makes only *different* perceptions. Thus, intelligence tests made in one culture and applied in another do not measure the ability to differentiate, nor do they measure the richness of the individual's field. Perhaps what they really measure is no more than the difference between cultures. American-made intelligence tests applied to other cultures generally show the following arrangement of nationality groups in decreasing order: British Isles, Germany, France, Italy, the Balkans, Asiatic countries. It will be noted that these nationality groups are also roughly arranged in order of the degree of commonality with our own culture.

TIME AS A LIMITATON UPON PERCEPTION

Differentiation requires time. The richness of perception, therefore, will be in part a function of how long the individual has been in touch with experiences. While it is true that a perception is possible only when confronted by an experience, it is also true that this exposure must be long enough to make differentiation possible. This principle is familiar to anyone who has looked at a painting for a period of time. The perceptions which can be made are almost limitless if one looks long enough.

In thinking of the effect of time upon differentiation, it is necessary for us to keep in mind that we are speaking of the duration of the individual's experience with an event and not of the observer's experience. Thus, while it may appear to an outside observer that an individual is confronted by an experience, from the individual's own point of view, he may have no contact with it whatever. A child may sit in school all day, apparently exposed to the curriculum, but may actually be experiencing and perceiving quite different aspects of the situation. Perception is an internal, individual phenomenon and may be quite different from that of another person, even in the same situation.

Most perceptions that the individual makes are functions of previous differentiations he has made in his phenomenal field. For example, before one can perceive the mechanics of multiplication, he must have perceived addition. In the same way, before he can perceive the function of a sand dome on top of the locomotive, he must differentiate the fact that locomotive wheels sometimes slip. Clearly this process of differentiation takes time. It seems axiomatic that to make differentiations an individual must have lived long enough to do so, a fact that we recognize in the construction of intelligence tests calibrated for various age levels, and which teachers recognize in the concept of readiness.

Differentiations in the phenomenal field seem to be occurring continuously as the organism seeks to satisfy its needs in the myriad situations of life. In this sense, intelligence never ceases to develop but is continuously increasing so long as the individual remains alive and operating. That intelligence seems to level off at age sixteen or later is probably a mere artifact of our method of observation. So long as the individual remains in school we have at least a modicum of comparable experience which can be tested in different persons. After the school years, when individuals are free to go their separate ways, this modicum of comparable experience rapidly disappears. The older one gets, the more diverse is his experience. Intelligence tests based upon comparability of experience may thus fail to evaluate properly the effectiveness of adults.

THE INDIVIDUAL'S GOALS AND VALUES AS A LIMITING FACTOR UPON PERCEPTION

Up to this point in our discussion we have been dealing with factors affecting perception that are widely discussed in the literature and for the most part as well understood. In the remainder of this paper let us turn our attention to several factors less well explored as they appear in a phenomenological setting. The first of these has to do with the effects of the individual's own goals and values as a limiting factor on perception.

From a phenomenological view the individual is forever engaged in a ceaseless attempt to achieve satisfaction of his need through the goals and values he has differentiated as leading to that end. These goals and values may be explicit or implicit, simple or complex, but they are always unique to the personality itself. The goals of an individual will vary in another respect as well. The individual's goals and values may be either positive or negative. That is, in the course of his experience, the person may differentiate some things as matters to be sought, while other things may be differentiated as matters to be avoided. What is more, although there is a considerable degree of stability in the major goals and values of a particular individual, there may be great fluctuations on how some goals are perceived from time to time, depending upon the total organization of the perceptual field at any moment.

The goals and values an individual seeks have a most important effect upon the perceptions he can make. Once goals have been established by the individual they continue to affect his every experience. Thus, the person who has differentiated good music as a goal to be sought perceives music more frequently. His entire experience with music is likely to be affected. Certainly his experience will differ markedly from the person who has formulated a goal to avoid music at all costs. In the same way the experiences of children who perceive schooling as something to be sought are vastly different from those of children who try to avoid all aspects of schooling. If the fundamental thesis of this paper is accurate, that intelligence is a function of the variety and richness of the perceptive field, then the individual's goals must have a most important effect upon intelligence. A considerable body of research has been accumulating over the past several years, demonstrating this controlling effect of goals and values on the individual's perceptive experience. Such studies as those of J. M. Levine, R. Levine, Postman, and Bruner are fascinating cases in point.

This effect of goals on perception is by no means limited to the subject whose intelligence we wish to measure. It is equally true of the intelligence test constructor. It leads to the very confusing situation wherein the test constructor with one organization of goals perceives certain experiences to be marks of intelligence for another person who may or may not have similar goals. Indeed, the likelihood is that he, almost certainly, does not have similar goals. Intelligence tests thus become highly selected samplings of perception in terms of what the testers consider important. Low scores do not necessarily mean less rich and varied fields of perception; they may mean only fields of perception more widely divergent from those of the examiner. A young man whom the writer tested at an induction center during the war illustrates the point very well. This young man was a newsboy on the streets of a West Virginia city. Although he had failed repeatedly in grammar school and was generally regarded as "not bright," he appeared on a national radio hook-up as "The Human Adding Machine." He was a wizard at figures. He could multiply correctly such figures as 6235941 × 397 almost as fast as the problem could be written down. He astounded our induction center for half a day with his numerical feats. Yet, on the Binet Test given by the writer he achieved an IQ of less than 60! People in his home town, who bought his papers, amused themselves by giving him problems to figure constantly. When not so occupied this young man entertained himself by adding up the license numbers of cars that passed his corner. He was a specialist in numbers. Apparently as a result of some early success in this field, he had been led to practice numbers constantly, eventually to the exclusion of all else. This was one area in which a poor colored boy could succeed and he made the most of it. His number perceptions were certainly rich and varied but other things were not. Although he was capable of arithmetic feats not achieved by one in millions, he was classified as dull! I do not mean to argue that variety of perception is unimportant in effective behavior. I do mean to suggest the importance of goals in determining perception.

CULTURAL EFFECTS ON GOALS AND PERCEPTIONS

We have stated here that the richness of the individual's perceptive field is in part a function of the goals he has differentiated as important or threatening to him. But, clearly these goals are themselves the results of the individual's experience. The culture one grows up in deeply affects the goals one holds. Cultures both restrict and encourage, approve and disapprove the formulation of goals in the individual. This selective effect of the culture in large measure determines the goals sought and avoided by the individual. These goals in turn must exert important effects upon the perceptions that become part of the individual's perceptive field.

I remember the Kentucky moonshiner to whom I once administered the Wechsler-Bellevue. This man could not tell me "how many pints in a quart" although he had certainly been taught this fact in his early schooling. Knowing that my client did a considerable business in bootleg liquor, I framed the question differently and asked "Well, how do you sell your liquor?" He smiled tolerantly and replied, "Oh Boss, I just sell it by the jug full!" In his community to have done otherwise would have been to risk bankruptcy. In a culture where a jug is standard container for spirits, what need to know about quarts?

It is conceivable that low intelligence may be, at least in part, no more than a function of the goals an individual is striving to reach in achieving his need satisfaction. The well-known phenomenon in which intelligence tests give best results in the school years, when experience and goals have a degree of commonality, and break down badly following those years would seem to corroborate this point. Perhaps by concerning ourselves with human goals we can affect perception, and thus intelligence, much more than we believed possible. Can it be that the child of low apparent intelligence is not so much a problem of an unfortunate heredity as an unfortunate constellation of goals or values? We could do a great deal about intelligence if that were true.

THE SELF–CONCEPT AS A FACTOR LIMITING PERCEPTION

We are just beginning to understand the tremendous effects of the individual's concept of self upon his perceptions and behavior. Lecky, for instance, reports the effect of a change in self-concept in improving the ability of children to spell. Other researches have reported similar effects of the self-concept upon the perceptions which the individual may make. Clinical experience would tend to bear out such observations. Any clinician is familiar with numerous instances in which a child's conception of his abilities severely limited his achievement, even though his real abilities may have been superior to his perception of them. One needs but to go shopping with one's spouse to discover again how one's conception of himself as a male or female affects the things he sees and the things he hears.

Perception is a selective process, and the conception one holds of himself is a vital factor in determining the richness and the variety of perception selected. It makes a great deal of difference, for example, how one perceives the president of our country if one conceives of himself as a Democrat, a Republican, or a Communist. One needs but to observe a group of children to become aware that little boys perceive things quite differently from little girls. Professors do not perceive like truck drivers, although when I have had to ride with professor automobile-drivers, I have often wished they did. Thousands of people in our society avoid perceptions having to do with mathematical functions by their firm concept of themselves as people who "cannot do mathematics." The self-concepts we hold have a very vital effect in selecting the perceptions which become part of our perceptive fields. If the effectiveness of behavior is dependent on our perceptive fields, it follows that the self-concepts we hold must affect the "intelligence" of our behavior.

There is another factor in the effect of the self-concept upon perception that makes it even more important as a selector of experience. That factor is the circular effect of a given concept of self. Let us take, as an example, the child who has developed a concept of himself as "unable to read." Such a child is likely to avoid reading, and thus the very experience which might change his concept of self is bypassed. Worse still, the child who believes himself unable to read, confronted with the necessity for reading, is more likely than not to do badly. The external evaluation of his teachers and fellow pupils, as well as his own observations of his performance, all provide proof to the child of how right he was in the first place! The possession of a particular concept of self tends to produce behavior that corroborates the self-concept with which the behavior originated.

Every clinician has had experience with children of ability who conceive of themselves as unable, unliked, unwanted, or unacceptable and perceive and behave in accordance with their perceptions. And this effect is not limited to children alone. It seems to me one of the great tragedies of our society that millions of people in our society perceiving themselves as able to produce only X amount, behave in these terms. Society, in turn, evaluates them in terms of this behavior and so lends proof to what is already conceived by the individual. Compared to this waste of human potential in our society, our losses in automobile accidents seem like a mere drop in the bucket. It is even conceivable in these terms that we create losses in intelligence. If, in our schools, we teach a child that he is unable and if he believes us and behaves in these terms, we need not be surprised when we test his intelligence to discover that he produces at the level at which we taught him!

It is conceivable that psychology has unwittingly contributed to this situation by the widespread publication of a static conception of intelligence and human capacities. The concept of severe limits upon the capacities of the organism simply corroborates the self-concept of the man in the street and decreases the likelihood of change in his concept of self.

Even more important must be the effect upon our educational system. Teachers who believe in an unchanging character of child capacities provide the attitudes and experiences that produce and maintain a child's conception of self and his abilities. It is notorious that children's grades vary very little from year to year through the course of schooling. This continuous and little-changing evaluation must have important effects on the self-concept of the child. If the school system in which the child lives is thoroughly imbued with the notion that a child's capacities are comparatively fixed, it is even conceivable that the system may in large measure produce a child's intelligence level by the circular effect we have mentioned above.

THREAT AS A FACTOR IN PERCEPTION

The last of the factors I should like to discuss as a possible factor in intelligence is the effect of threat upon the perceptive field. If our fundamental assumption that intelligence is a function of the richness and breadth of the phenomenal field is correct, the effect of threat on this field becomes a most important consideration. Although these effects have been so widely understood by the layman that they have been made a part of his everyday speech, it is interesting that until very recently the phenomenon has been given little attention by psychologists. The perception by the individual of threat to himself seems to have at least two major effects upon the perceptive field.

RESTRICTION OF THE PERCEPTIVE FIELD UNDER THREAT

The first of these effects is the restrictive effect that the perception of threat to self seems to have on the individual's perception. When he feels himself threatened, there appears to be a narrowing of the perceptive field to the object of threat. This has often been described in the psychology of vision as "tunnel vision." The phenomenon is extremely common, and almost everyone has experienced it at some moment of crisis in his lifetime. One hears it described in such comments as "All I could see was the truck coming at us," or, "I was so scared I couldn't think of a thing." There seems reason to believe that this effect is not limited to traumatic experiences alone, but exists in lesser degree in response to milder threats as well. Combs and Taylor, for example, have demonstrated the effect under extremely mild forms of threat.

Such limiting effects on perception must certainly have a bearing upon perceptions available to the individual in his phenomenal field. Subjects who have participated in food deprivation experiments report uniformly that when threatened by hunger, food becomes an obsession. Recently, at the dinner table, I asked my young daughter what she had learned at school that day. "Oh nothing," said she with much feeling, "but was our teacher mad! Wow!" It would appear from her remarks that, feeling threatened by an angry teacher, it was difficult for her to perceive much else. Her perceptions of the day were apparently entirely concerned with the nature of anger. No doubt these are valuable perceptions to possess, but I know of no intelligence test which measures them.

I recall, too, the behavior of two little girls whose mother was taken to a mental hospital at the beginning of the summer. The matter was kept a deep secret from these two children for fear they "would not understand." The children spent most of the summer with the writer's daughter in an incessant game of "hospital." From morning to night this game went on outside our living-room window. Apparently, this preoccupation was the direct outcome of the threat they felt in the loss of their mother, for with the mother's return the game ceased as suddenly as it had begun. To the best of my knowledge it has not occurred since. Under threat there seem to be severe limits imposed upon the breadth and character of perception.

Defense of the Perceptive Field Under Threat

There is a second effect of threat upon the individual's perceptions. This effect has to do with the defense reactions induced in the individual on perceiving himself to be threatened. The perception of threat not only narrows the field and reduces the possibility of wide perceptions, but causes the individual to protect and cling to the perceptions he already holds. Thus, the possibility of perceptual changes is reduced, and the opportunities for new perceptions or learning are decreased. Under threat, behavior becomes rigid. The fluidity and adaptation which we generally associate with intelligent behavior is vastly decreased. A number of interesting experiments in the past few years have demonstrated this phenomenon. Cowen, for example, illustrated this effect in problem solving.

Our own experiment previously mentioned also demonstrated this effect with even very mild forms of threat. This rigidity or resistance of perception to change under threat is well known to the layman and is well illustrated in some of the sayings of our culture. Such aphorisms as

"Nobody ever wins an argument" or "You can lead a horse to water but you cannot make him drink" seem to be illustrations of a vague understanding of the phenomenon in the public mind. It is surprising that this principle has been so long overlooked.

I think it will be generally agreed that intelligent behavior is quite the antithesis of rigidity. In the terms we have used in this article, intelligent behavior is a function of the variety and richness of perception in the phenomenal field. Whatever produces narrowness and rigidity of perception becomes an important factor in limiting intelligence. If this reasoning is accurate, or even partly so, one is led to wonder about the effects of long-continued threat upon the development of intelligence. What of the child who has suffered serious threats to himself for long periods of his life, as in the case of the delinquent, for example? Or what of the child who has been seriously deprived of affection and warmth from those who surround him over a period of years? Is it possible that we have created low intelligence in such children? Axline has reported a number of cases in which intelligence scores improved considerably under therapy. We have observed similar changes in our own clinical practice.

It may be argued that, although threat seems to reduce perception, some people under threat apparently produce more effectively. I think, however, it is necessary for us to distinguish between "threat" and "challenge." In threat, the individual perceives himself in jeopardy and feels, in addition, a degree of inadequacy to deal effectively with the threat perceived. In challenge, the individual perceives himself threatened but feels at the same time a degree of adequacy to deal with the threat. It would appear that whether an event is perceived as threatening or challenging is a function of the individual's feeling of competence to deal with it. If this analysis is correct, it would explain why a situation that appears threatening to a person, from the viewpoint of an outside observer, might one time produce rigidity and another highly effective behavior. This description of events seems characteristic of the history of civilization as well as of individuals, if Toynbee's explanation can be given credence. He points out that the most productive (more intelligent?) societies are those in which the society faces some crisis within its capacities to cope with the situation (challenge), while societies without crisis or in which the crisis is overwhelming produce very little or collapse entirely.

SOME IMPLICATIONS OF THIS CONCEPTION
OF INTELLIGENT BEHAVIOR

If the conception of intelligence we have been discussing in this paper should prove accurate, it seems to me to raise serious questions about some of our common assumptions with respect to intelligence and, at the same time, opens some exciting new possibilities for the treatment or education of persons we have often assumed to be beyond help. It implies that our conception of the limiting factors of intelligence may have been too narrow. It would suggest perhaps that our very point of view with respect to intelligence may have resulted in our own tunnel vision, such that we have not been able to perceive other factors given little attention to this point. Perhaps we have been too impressed with the limitations upon growth and development which we observe in physical maturation. We may, for instance, have jumped too quickly to the assumption that intelligent behavior was limited as severely as physical growth and that we have explored to exhaustion other factors that may limit intelligence.

I am not suggesting that physiologic limits do not exist in respect to intelligence. I am suggesting that we may have conceded too early that we had approached those limits. There is no doubt that we can demonstrate in some cases, such as mongolism, cretinism, and the like, that physical factors severely limit intelligence. But these cases are comparatively few compared to the so-called "familial" cases of low intelligence that we often assume are hereditary in origin. What evidence do we really possess that would lead us to the position that an individual of "normal" physical condition and vigor may be limited in his capacity for effective behavior by some physical condition? We assume there must be such factors operating because we cannot explain his handicap otherwise. That biological science has not yet been able to demonstrate such physical bases has not deterred us in this. On the contrary, we have simply deplored the lack of sufficient advance in that discipline to demonstrate our conclusion! I should like to suggest that this may not be their failure but ours. Until it can be definitely established that limitations exist as biological functions, our task as psychologists is to assume that they may just as well be social or psychological in character and to work just as hard exploring the matter in our discipline as we expect the biologist to work in his.

Let us, for example, explore to the very fullest the possibility that in those cases where we cannot demonstrate biologic impairment, the limitations upon intelligence may be psychological. If it turns out not to be true, we shall find out in time. I do not believe we can afford to limit the places where we look by the preperceptions we have about the matter. Our responsibility here is too great. Education, to name but the most obvious of our social institutions, has in large measure predicated its goals and methods on a concept of humanity with certain static limitations on intelligence. If these limitations are not static, it is up to us as psychologists to find out. The task of the scientist is to question, not to be content with answers. We cannot afford to accept an undemonstrated point of view that prevents us from asking questions.

SOME IMPLICATIONS FOR INTELLIGENCE TESTING

If the concepts of intelligence we have been discussing prove accurate, another area of psychological thought toward which we must cast a quizzical eye is the area of intelligence testing. This is particularly important at a time when our culture has come to accept these instruments as trustingly as the family doctor's prescription. If our approach to intelligent behavior as a function of the variety and richness of the perceptual field is a valid consideration, we need to ask regarding these tests at least the following questions:

1. Is our sampling of the perceptive field truly adequate? If I lived for years in a prison cell, I presume I should become expert in perceptions about that cell. Unfortunately, they would be of little value outside the prison walls, but can it truthfully be said that my perceptions are less rich or varied, or only that they are less rich and varied about things I have not had opportunity to experience? Is the delinquent, with rich and varied perceptions on how to elude the police, less intelligent or has he simply not perceived things society wishes he had?

2. Since perceptions are always closely affected by need, by whose need shall we sample perceptions—yours, mine, society's, the subject's own? I suspect that in terms of his own needs and perceptions the subject might be deemed quite brilliant, though he might or might not appear so from the point of view of society. For the most part our tests are based on the assumption that academic, upper middle-class, intellectual perceptions are important. But are they? Can we assume that the expert machinist, who can perceive things "out of this world" for most of the rest of us about a piece of stock on his lathe, is less intelligent than a diplomat

who perceives many things about foreign affairs? Can we be so sure of our values as to call one bright and the other dull? Can we blame the machinist for his lack of perception about foreign affairs without asking the diplomat to be equally skilled in the machinist's field of perceptions?

3. Finally, if perceptions are affected by the factors we have discussed in this paper, is it fair to sample intelligence irrespective of the control of such factors? Shall we, for example, examine the child who has lacked opportunity to perceive, has possessed a concept of self or been so threatened over a long period of time so as to have been unable to perceive what we wish to sample without consideration of those factors? Shall we overlook such factors and be satisfied that the perceptions important to us are not there, or shall we seek for ways to make it possible for the child to have them? Shall we assume that our failure to discover a particular perception present in the field is, *ipso facto,* evidence of lack of capacity; or seek to discover why it is not? On the positive side of the picture, if the concepts we have here been discussing are sound, there is reason to believe that intelligence may be far less immutable than we have thought. It may be that we can do far more than we have dreamed we could. Perhaps we may even be able to create intelligence!

IMPLICATIONS FOR CONSTRUCTIVE ACTION

Who can say, for example, what results we might be able to achieve by a systematic effort to remove or decrease the effectiveness of the limitations on perception discussed in this paper? It is fascinating to speculate on the possibilities one might try in constructing a situation for a child, or adult, consciously designed to minimize the limitations imposed on perception by physical condition, environment, goals, the individual's self-concept, and the effects of perceived personal threat.

If the position we have taken is accurate, it would suggest that there is much we can do (*a*) to free individuals from the restraints upon perception and (*b*) to provide the opportunities for perception to occur.

1. First and most obviously, we should be able to discover and make available to far more people the means to achieve better physical condition. We have already done a good deal in this area but much needs yet to be done. Who can say, for instance, what completely adequate medical care for all our people might mean a generation hence?

2. If this discussion has merit, there lies the possibility of providing experiences for people that will make adequate perceptions possible. We

have tried to do this in our schools, but have not always accomplished it. We have succeeded very well in gathering information and in making it available to students. We have not succeeded too well in making such information meaningful. Can it be that the decreases in school success with advance through the school years is more a function of lack of meaning for students than lack of intelligence? Is it enough to assume that experience provided by us to the student is truly provided when he is free to experience it? Has the child in school, who is so worried about his relationship with his peers that he cannot perceive what his book is saying, truly been provided opportunity to perceive?

In our training of children of "low intelligence," we often provide situations wherein they are carefully taught to perform repeatedly a simple act. Is it possible that in so doing we may be further narrowing their fields of perception and building self-concepts that produce even narrower perceptive fields?

What kinds of environments could we construct that might more effectively result in increased perception? Such experiments as Lippitt and White have carried on with democratic and autocratic environments suggest some possibilities, but we need to know much more. Perhaps we could learn to build such environments from observing with greater care and understanding the methods of good teachers.

3. Who can say what possible effects might occur from a systematic release of the individual's perceptions by the satisfaction of his most pressing needs or goals? We college professors insist we can produce more, which is another way of saying perceive more, when we have the leisure time to do so, when we are freed from the necessity of spending our time satisfying our needs for sheer existence. Can this be less true of others? It is possible that the child with needs of love, affection, status, prestige, or a girl friend might also be freed to perceive more widely and richly, if we could but find ways of helping him satisfy his needs. Ordinarily, we pay a good deal of attention to the physical needs of a child, understanding that with these needs unfulfilled, he makes a poor student. Is there any good reason to suppose his psychological needs are less pressing or less important in freeing him to perceive widely and accurately? We spend much time and energy trying to find ways of "motivating" people or blaming them for not being motivated to do what we need them to do. We assume that if permitted to seek their own needs, people will not satisfy ours. Perhaps we should get further by helping them satisfy their needs; they might then be free to satisfy ours.

4. Most of our educational methods are directed at the provision of perceptions for the student. He is lectured, required, shown, exhorted, and

coerced to perceive what someone thinks he should. It seems possible that with equal energy devoted to the matter of creating needs, goals, and values in students, rich and varied perceptions might be more efficiently produced.

What effects might we be able to produce by providing experiences that build adequate concepts of self in children and adults? What differences in the richness and variety of perception might result from a generation of people with "I can" rather than "I can't" conceptions of themselves? What possibilities of increased perceptions and hence increased intelligence might accrue to such a program? Clinical experience has demonstrated frequently how a changed perception of self as a more adequate personality can free children for improved school performance, for example.

What would happen if we were consciously and carefully to set about the task of providing experiences that would lead people to conceptions of themselves as adequate, worthy, self-respecting people? If freedom to perceive is a function of adequate perceptions of self, it should not surprise us that the child who perceives himself as unwanted, unacceptable, unable, or unliked behaves in rigid fashion. It should be possible, too, to reverse this process and produce more adequate perceptions by systematic efforts at producing more adequate definitions of self. The possibilities seem tremendous but we have scarcely scratched the surface of this problem.

Finally, if threat to the individual has as important effects as seem indicated in this discussion, the removal of threat would seem a most important factor to consider in the release of the individual to perceive more adequately. The work of Rogers and his students in client-centered therapy has already illustrated to some degree what possibilities freeing the individual to perceive more adequately may accomplish through the provision of a permissive nonthreatening relationship between counselor and client. We have already mentioned the effects Axline has reported following a permissive, nonthreatening form of play therapy.

Such effects do not seem limited to the therapeutic situation, however. A number of workers have applied this principle of permissiveness to the classroom situation with equally gratifying results. Experiments in student-centered teaching at Syracuse have led many of us to believe in the tremendous educational possibilities in the removal of threat.

This paper has asked many questions. Indeed, it has asked far more questions than it has presumed to answer. That, it seems to me, is the function of theory. The picture of intelligence presented here as it seems from a phenomenological viewpoint may be accurate or false or, more likely, partly true and partly false. Only time and the industry of many observers can check its adequacy or inadequacy. It seems to me to pose problems that are both exciting and challenging. If it proves as stimulating to the reader as it has to the author, I shall rest content that a theory has achieved its purpose.

The Creative Attitude

Abraham H. Maslow

My feeling is that the concept of creativeness and the concept of the heathy, self-actualizing, fully-human person seem to be coming closer and closer together, and may perhaps turn out to be the same thing.

Another conclusion I seem to be impelled toward, even though I am not quite sure of my facts, is that creative art education, or better said, Education-Through-Art, may be especially important not so much for turning out artists or art products, as for turning out better people. If we have clearly in mind the educational goals for human beings that I will be hinting at, if we hope for our children that they will become full human beings, and that they will move towards actualizing the potentialities that they have, then, as nearly as I can make out, the only kind of education in existence today that has any faint inkling of such goals is art education. So I am thinking of education through art not because it turns out pictures but because I think it may be possible that, clearly understood, it may become the paradigm for all other education. That is, instead of being regarded as the frill, the expendable kind of thing which it now is, if we take it seriously enough and work at it hard enough and if it turns out to be what some of us suspect it can be, then we may one

Reprinted from *The Structurist*, 1963, (3), pp. 4–10, by permission of the author and the publisher.

day teach arithmetic and reading and writing on this paradigm. So far as I am concerned, I am talking about all education. This is why I am interested in education through art—simply because it seems to be good education in potential.

Another reason for my interest in art education, creativeness, psychological health, etc., is that I have a very strong feeling of a change of pace in history. It seems to me that we are at a point in history unlike anything that has ever been before. Life moves far more rapidly now than it ever did before. Think, for instance, of the huge acceleration in the rate of growth of facts, of knowledge, of techniques, of inventions, of advances in technology. It seems very obvious to me that this requires a change in our attitude toward the human being, and toward his relationships to the world. To put it bluntly, we need a different kind of human being. I feel I must take far more seriously today than I did twenty years ago, the Heraclitus, the Whitehead, the Bergson kind of emphasis on the world as a flux, a movement, a process, not a static thing. If this is so and it is obviously much more so than it was in 1900 or even in 1930—if this is so, then we need a different kind of human being to be able to live in a world which changes perpetually, which doesn't stand still. I may go so far as to say for the educational enterprise: what's the use of teaching facts? Facts become obsolete so darned fast! What's the use of teaching techniques? The techniques become obsolete so fast! Even the engineering schools are torn by this realization. M.I.T. for instance, no longer teaches engineering *only* as the acquisition of a series of skills, because practically all the skills that the professors of engineering learned when they were in school have now become obsolete. It's no use today learning to make buggy whips. What some professors have done at M.I.T., I understand, is to give up the teaching of the tried and true methods of the past, in favor of trying to create a new kind of human being who is comfortable with change, who enjoys change, who is able to improvise, who is able to face with confidence, strength and courage a situation of which he has absolutely no forewarning.

Even today as I read the morning newspaper before coming here, *everything* seems to be changing; international law is changing, politics are changing; the whole international scene is changing. People talk with each other in the United Nations from across different centuries. One man speaks in terms of the international law of the nineteenth century. Another one answers him in terms of something else entirely, from a different platform in a different world. Things have changed that fast.

To come back to my title, what I'm talking about is the job of trying to make ourselves over into people who don't need to staticize the world, who don't need to freeze it and to make it stable, who don't need to do what their daddies did, who are able confidently to face tomorrow not knowing what's going to come, not knowing what will happen, with confidence enough in ourselves that we will be able to improvise in that situation which has never existed before. This means a new type of human being. Heraclitian you might call him. The society which can turn out such people will survive; the societies that *cannot* turn out such people will die.

You'll notice that I stress a great deal improvising and inspiration, rather than approaching creativeness from the vantage point of the finished work of art, of the great creative work. As a matter of fact, I won't even approach it today from the point of view of completed products at all. Why is this? Because we're pretty clearly aware now from our psychological analysis of the process of creativeness and of creative individuals, that we must make the distinction between primary creativeness and a secondary creativeness. The primary creativeness or the inspirational phase of creativeness must be separated from the working out and the development of the inspiration. This is because the latter phase stresses not only creativeness, but also relies very much on just plain hard work, on the discipline of the artist who may spend half a lifetime learning his tools, his skills, and his materials, until he becomes finally ready for a full expression of what he sees. I am very certain that many, many people have waked up in the middle of the night with a flash of inspiration about some novel they would like to write, or a play or a poem or whatever and that most of these inspirations never came to anything. Inspirations are a dime a dozen. The difference between the inspiration and the final product, for example, Tolstoy's "War and Peace," is an awful lot of hard work, an awful lot of discipline, an awful lot of training, an awful lot of finger exercises and practices and rehearsals and throwing away first drafts and so on. Now the virtues which go with the secondary kind of creativeness, the creativeness which results in the actual products, in the great paintings, the great novels, in the bridges, the new inventions and so on, rest as heavily upon other virtues—stubbornness and patience and hard work and so on, as they do upon the creativeness of the personality. Therefore, in order to keep the field of operation clean, you might say, it seems necessary to me to focus upon improvising, on this first flash and, for the moment, not to worry about what becomes of it, recognizing that many of them do get lost. Partly for this reason, among the best subjects to study for this inspirational phase of creativeness are young children whose inventiveness and creativeness very frequently cannot be defined in terms of product. When a little boy discovers the decimal system for himself this can be a high moment of inspiration, and a high creative moment, and should not be waved aside because of some priori definition which says creativeness ought to be socially useful or it ought to be novel, or nobody should have thought of it before, etc.

For this same reason I have decided for myself not to take scientific creativeness as a paradigm, but rather to use other examples. Much of the research that's going on now deals with the creative scientists, with people who have proven themselves to be creative, Nobel prize winners, great inventors, and so on. The trouble is, if you know a lot of scientists, that you soon learn that something is wrong with this criterion because scientists as a group are not nearly as creative generally as you would expect. This includes people who have discovered, who have created actually, who have published things which were advances in human knowledge. Actually, this is not too difficult to understand. This finding tells us something about the nature of science rather than about the nature of creativeness. If I wanted to be mischievous about it, I could go so far as to define science as a technique whereby non-creative people can create. This is by no means making fun of scientists. It's a wonderful thing it seems to me, for limited human beings, that they can be pressed into the service of great things even though they themselves are not great people. Science is a technique, social and institutionalized, whereby even unintelligent people can be useful in the advance of knowledge. That is as extreme and dramatic as I can make it. Since any particular scientist rests so much in the arms of history, stands on so many shoulders of so many predecessors, he is so much a part of a huge basketball team, of a big collection of people, that his own shortcomings may not appear. He becomes worthy of reference, worthy of great respect through his participation in a great and respect-worthy enterprise. Therefore, when he discovers something, I have learned to understand this as a product of a social institution, of a collaboration. If he didn't discover it, somebody else would have pretty soon. Therefore, it seems to me that selecting our scientists, even though they have created, is not the best way to study the theory of creativeness.

I will make one last point before I get to my paper proper. I believe also that we cannot study creativeness in an ultimate sense until we realize that practically all the definitions that we have been using of creativeness, and most of the examples of creativeness that we use are essentially male or masculine definitions and male or masculine products. We've left out of consideration almost entirely the creativeness of women by the simple semantic technique of defining only male products as creative and overlooking entirely the creativeness of women. I have learned recently (through my studies of peak experiences) to look to women and to feminine creativeness as a good field of operation for research, because it gets less involved in products, less involved in achievement, more involved with the process itself, with the going-on process rather than with the climax in obvious triumph and success.

This is the background of the particular problem I'd like to talk about today.

II

The puzzle that I'm now trying to unravel is suggested by the observation that the creative person, in the inspirational phase of the creative furore, loses his past and his future and lives only in the moment. He is all there, totally immersed, fascinated and absorbed in the present, in the current situation, in the here-now, with the matter-in-hand. Or to use a perfect phrase from *The Spinster* by Sylvia Ashton-Warner, the teacher absorbed with a new method of teaching reading to her children says "I am utterly lost in the present."

This ability to become "lost in the present" seems to be a sine qua non for creativeness of any kind. But also certain *prerequisites* of creativeness—in whatever realm—somehow have something to do with this ability to become timeless, selfless, outside of space, of society, of history.

It has begun to appear strongly that this phenomenon is a diluted, more secular, more frequent version of the mystical experience that has been described so often as to have become what Huxley called *The Perennial Philosophy*. In various cultures and in various eras, it takes on somewhat different coloration—and yet its essence is always recognizable—it is the same.

It is always described as a loss of self or of ego, or sometimes as a transcendence of self. There is a fusion with the reality being observed (with the matter-in-hand, I shall say more neutrally), a oneness where there was a twoness, an integration of some sort of the self with the non-self. There is universally reported a seeing of formerly hidden truth, a revelation in the strict sense, a stripping away of veils, and finally, almost always, the whole experience is experienced as bliss, ecstasy, rapture, exaltation.

Little wonder that this shaking experience has so often been considered to be superhuman, supernatural, so much greater and grander than anything conceivable as human that it could only be attributed to transhuman sources. And such "revelations" often serve as basis, sometimes the *sole* basis, for the various "revealed" religions.

And yet even this most remarkable of all experiences has now been brought into the realm of human experience and cognition. My researches on what I call peak experiences (3,4), and Marghanita Laski's on what she calls ecstasies (1), done quite independently of each other, show that these experiences are quite naturalistic, quite easily investigated and, what is to the point right now, that they have much to teach us about creativeness as well as other aspects of the full functioning of human beings when they are most fully realizing themselves, most mature and evolved, most healthy, when, in a word, they are most fully human.

One main characteristic of the peak-experience is just this total fascination with the matter-in-hand, this getting lost in the present, this detachment from time and place. And it seems to me now that much of what we have learned from the study of these peak-experiences can be transferred quite directly to the enriched understanding of the here-now experience of the creative attitude.

It is not necessary for us to confine ourselves to these uncommon and rather extreme experiences, even though it now seems clear that practically all people can report moments of rapture if they dig around long enough in their memories, and if the interview situation is just right. We can also refer to the simplest version of the peak-experience, namely fascination, concentration or absorption in *anything* which is interesting enough to hold this attention completely. And I mean not only great symphonies or tragedies; the job can be done by a gripping movie or detective story, or simply becoming absorbed with one's work. There are certain advantages in starting from such universal and familiar experiences which we all have, so that we can get a direct feeling or intuition or empathy, that is, a direct experiential knowledge of a modest, moderate version of the fancier "high" experiences. For one thing we can avoid the flossy, high-flying, extremely metaphorical vocabulary that is so common in this realm.

Well then, what are some of the things that happen in these moments?

GIVING UP THE PAST

The best way to view a present problem is to give it all you've got, to study *it* and its nature, to perceive *within* it the intrinsic interrelationships, to discover (rather than to invent) the answer to the problem within the problem itself. This is also the best way to look at a painting or to listen to a patient in therapy.

The other way is merely a matter of shuffling over past experiences, past habits, past knowledge to find out in what respects this current situation is similar to some situation in the past, i.e., to classify it, and then to use *now* the solution that once worked for the similar problem in the past. This can be likened to the work of a filing clerk. I have called it "rubricizing" (2). And it works well enough to the extent that the present *is* like the past.

But obviously it *doesn't* work in so far as the matter-in-hand is different from the past. The file clerk approach fails then. This person confronting an unknown painting hurriedly runs back through his knowledge of art history to remember how he is supposed to react. Meanwhile of course he is hardly looking at the painting. All he needs is the name or the style or the content to enable him to do his quick calculations. He then enjoys it if he is supposed to, and doesn't if he is *not* supposed to.

In such a person, the past is an inert, undigested foreign body which the person carries about like keys in his pocket. It is not yet the person himself.

More accurately said: The past is active and alive only in so far as it has re-created the person, and has been digested into the present person. It is not or should not be something *other* than the person, something alien to it. It has now become Person, (and has lost its own identity as something different and other) just as past steaks that I have eaten are now me, *not* steaks. The digested past (assimilated by intussusception) is different from the undigested past. It is Lewin's "ahistorical past."

GIVING UP THE FUTURE

Often we use the present not for its own sake but in order to prepare for the future. Think how often in a conversation we put on a listening face as the other person talks, secretly however preparing what we are going to say, rehearsing, planning a counter-attack perhaps. Think how different your attitude would be right now if you knew you were to comment on my remarks in five minutes. Think how hard it would be then to be a good, total listener.

If we are totally listening or totally looking, we have thereby given up this kind of "preparing for the future." We don't treat the present as merely a means to some future end (thereby devaluating the present). And obviously, this kind of forgetting the future is a prerequisite to total involvement with the present. Just as obviously, a good way to "forget" the future is not to be apprehensive about it.

Of course, this is only one sense of the concept "future." The future which is within us, part of our present selves, is another story altogether (3, pp. 14–15).

INNOCENCE

This amounts to a kind of "innocence" of perceiving and behaving. Something of the sort has often been attributed to highly creative people. They are variously described as being naked in the situation, guileless, without *a priori* expectations, without "shoulds" or "oughts," without fashions, fads, dogmas, habits or other pictures-in-the-head of what is proper, normal, "right," as being ready to receive whatever happens to be the case without surprise, shock, indignation or denial.

Children are more able to be receptive in this undemanding way. So are wise old people. And it appears now that we *all* may be more innocent in this style when we become "here-now."

NARROWING OF CONSCIOUSNESS

We have now become much less conscious of everything other than the matter-in-hand (less distractible). *Very* important here is our lessened awareness of other people, of their ties to us and ours to them, of obligations, duties, fears, hopes, etc. We become much more free of other people, which in turn, means that we become much more ourselves, our Real Selves (Horney), our authentic selves, our real identity.

This is so because *the* greatest cause of our alienation from our real selves is our neurotic involvements with other people, the historical hangovers from childhood, the irrational transferences, in which past and present are confused, and in which the adult acts like a child. (By the way, it's all right for the *child* to act like a child. His dependencies on other people can be very real. *But,* after all, he *is* supposed to outgrow them. To be afraid of what daddy will say or do is certainly out-of-place if daddy has been dead for twenty years.)

In a word, we become more free of the influence of other people in such moments. So, in so far as these influences have affected our behavior, they no longer do so.

This means dropping masks, dropping our efforts to influence, to impress, to please, to be lovable, to win applause. It could be said so: if we have no audience to play to, we cease to be actors. With no need to act we can devote ourselves, self-forgetfully, to the problem.

LOSS OF EGO: SELF–FORGETFULNESS, LOSS OF SELF–CONSCIOUSNESS

When you are totally absorbed in non-self, you tend to become less conscious of yourself, less self-aware. You are less apt to be observing yourself like a spectator or a critic. To use the language of psychodynamics, you become less dissociated than usual into a self-observing ego and an experiencing ego; i.e., you come much closer to being *all* experiencing ego. (You tend to lose the shyness and bashfulness of the adolescent, the painful awareness of being looked at, etc.) This in turn means more unifying, more oneness and integration of the person.

It also means less criticizing and editing, less evaluating, less selecting and rejecting, less judging and weighing, less splitting and analyzing of the experience.

This kind of self-forgetfulness is one of the paths to finding one's true identity, one's real self, one's authentic nature, one's deepest nature. It is almost always felt as pleasant and desirable. We needn't go so far as the Buddhists and Eastern thinkers do in talking about the "accursed ego"; and yet there *is* something in what they say.

INHIBITING FORCE OF CONSCIOUSNESS (OF SELF)

In some senses consciousness (especially of self) is inhibiting in some ways and at some times. It is sometimes the locus of doubts, conflicts, fears, etc. It is sometimes harmful to full-functioning creativeness. It is sometimes an inhibitor of spontaneity and of expressiveness (*But* the observing ego is necessary for therapy).

(And yet it is also true that some kind of self-awareness, self-observation, self-criticism; i.e., the self-observing ego *is* necessary for "secondary creativeness." To use psychotherapy as an example, the task of self-improvement is partly a consequence of criticizing the experiences that one has allowed to come into consciousness. Schizophrenic people experience many insights and yet don't make therapeutic use of them because they are too much "totally experiencing" and not enough "self-observing-and-criticizing." In creative work, likewise, the labor of disciplined construction succeeds upon the phase of "inspiration.")

FEARS DISAPPEAR

This means that our fears and anxieties also tend to disappear. So also our depressions, conflicts, ambivalence, our worries, our problems, even our physical pains. Even—for the moment—our psychoses and our neuroses (that is, if they are not so extreme as to prevent us from becoming deeply interested and immersed in the matter-in-hand).

For the time being, we are courageous and confident, unafraid, unanxious, unneurotic, not sick.

LESSENING OF DEFENSES AND INHIBITIONS

Our inhibitions also tend to disappear. So also our guardedness, our (Freudian) defenses, and controls (brakes) on our impulses as well as the defenses against danger and threat.

STRENGTH AND COURAGE

The creative attitude requires both courage and strength and most studies of creative people have reported one or another version of courage: popularity becomes a minor consideration, stubbornness, independence, self-sufficiency, a kind of arrogance, strength of character, ego-strength, etc. Fear and weakness cast out creativeness or at least make it less likely.

It seems to me that this aspect of creativeness becomes somewhat more understandable when it is seen as a part of the syndrome of here-now self-forgetfulness and other-forgetfulness. Such a state intrinsically implies less fear, less inhibition, less need for defense and self-protection, less guardedness, less need for artificiality, less fear of ridicule, of humiliation and of failure. All these characteristics are *part of* self-forget-fulness and audience-forgetfulness. Absorption casts out fear.

Or we can say in a more positive way, that becoming more courageous makes it easier to let oneself be attracted by mystery, by the unfamiliar, by the novel, by the ambiguous and contradictory, by the unusual and un-expected, etc., instead of becoming suspicious, fearful, guarded, or having to throw into action our anxiety-allaying mechanisms and defenses.

ACCEPTANCE: THE POSITIVE ATTITUDE

In moments of here-now immersion and self-forgetfulness we are apt to become more "positive" and less negative in still another way, namely, in giving up criticism (editing, picking and choosing, correcting, skepti-cism, improving, doubting, rejecting, judging, evaluating). This is like saying that we accept. We don't reject or disapprove or selectively pick and choose.

No blocks against the matter-in-hand means that we let it flow in upon us. We let it wreak its will upon us. We let it have its way. We let it be itself. Perhaps we can even approve of its being itself.

This makes it easier to be Taoistic in the sense of humility, non-interference, receptivity.

TRUST VS. TRYING, CONTROLLING, STRIVING

All of the foregoing happenings imply a kind of trust in the self and a trust in the world which permits the temporary giving up of straining and striving, of volition and control, of conscious coping and effort. To permit oneself to be determined by the intrinsic nature of the matter-in-hand here-now necessarily implies relaxation, waiting, receiving. The common effort to master, to dominate, and to control are antithetical to a true coming-to-terms with or a true perceiving of the materials, (or the problem, or the person, etc.). Especially is this true with respect to the future. We *must* trust our ability to improvise when confronted with novelty in the future. Phrased in this way, we can see more clearly that trust involves self-confidence, courage, lack of fear of the world. It is also clear that this kind of trust in ourselves-facing-the-unknown-future is a condition of being able to turn totally, nakedly, and wholeheartedly to the present.

(Some clinical examples may help. Giving birth, urination, defecation, sleeping, floating in the water, sexual surrender are all instances in which straining, trying, controlling, have to be given up in favor of relaxed, trusting, confident letting things happen.)

TAOISTIC RECEPTIVITY

Both Taoism and receptivity mean many things, all of them important, but also subtle and difficult to convey except in figures of speech. All of the subtle and delicate Taoistic attributes of the creative attitude which follow have been described again and again by the many writers on creativeness, now in one way, now in another. However, everyone agrees that in the primary or inspirational phase of creativeness, some degree of receptivity or non-interference or "let-be" is descriptively characteristic and also theoretically and dynamically necessary. Our question now is how does this receptivity or "letting things happen" relate to the syndrome of here-now immersion and self-forgetfulness?

For one thing, using the artist's respect for his materials as a paradigm, we may speak of this respectful attention to the matter-in-hand as a kind of courtesy or deference (without intrusion of the controlling will) which is akin to "taking it seriously." This amounts to treating it as an end, something *per se,* with its own right to be, rather than as a means to some end other than itself; i.e., as a tool for some extrinsic purpose. This respectful treatment of its being implies that it is respectworthy.

This courtesy or respectfulness can apply equally to the problem, to the materials, to the situation, or to the person. It is what one writer (Follett) has called deference (yielding, surrender) to the authority of the facts, to the law of the situation. I can go over from a bare *permitting* "it" to be itself, to a loving, caring, approving, joyful, *eagerness* that it be itself, as with one's child or sweetheart or tree or poem or pet animal.

Some such attitude is a *priori* necessary for perceiving or understanding the full concrete richness of the matter-in-hand, in *its* own nature and in *its* own style, without our help, without our imposing ourselves upon it, in about the same way that we must hush and be still if we wish to hear the whisper from the other.

This cognition of the Being of the other (B-cognition) has been fully described in (2, 3, 5).

INTEGRATION OF THE B–COGNIZER (VS. DISSOCIATION)

Creating tends to be the act of a whole man (ordinarily); he is then *most* integrated, unified, all of a piece, one-pointed, totally organized in the service of the fascinating matter-in-hand. Creativeness is therefore systemic; i.e., a whole—or Gestalt—quality of the whole person; it is not added-to the organism like a coat of paint, or like an invasion of bacteria. It is the opposite of dissociation. Here-now-allness is less dissociated (split) and more one.

PERMISSION TO DIP INTO PRIMARY PROCESS

Part of the process of integration of the person is the recovery of aspects of the unconscious and preconscious, particularly of the primary process (or poetic, metaphoric, mystic, primitive, archaic, childlike).

Our conscious intellect is too exclusively analytic, rational, numerical, atomistic, conceptual and so it misses a great deal of reality, especially within our selves.

ESTHETIC PERCEIVING RATHER THAN ABSTRACTING

Abstracting is more active and interfering (less Taoistic); more selecting-rejecting than the esthetic (Northrop) attitude of savoring, enjoying, appreciating, caring, in a non-interfering, non-intruding, non-cotrolling way.

The end-product of abstracting is the mathematical equation, the chemical formula, the map, the diagram, the blueprint, the cartoon, the concept, the abstracting sketch, the model, the theoretical system, all of which move further and further from raw reality ("the map is *not* the territory"). The end-product of esthetic perceiving, of non-abstracting is the total inventory of the percept, in which everything in it is apt to be equally savored, and in which evaluations of more important and less important tend to be given up. Here greater richness of the percept is sought for rather than greater simplifying and skeletonizing.

For many confused scientists and philosophers, the equation, the concept, or the blueprint have become more real than the phenomenological reality itself. Fortunately now that we can understand the interplay and mutual enrichment of the concrete and the abstract, it is no longer necessary to devalue one or the other. For the moment we intellectuals in the West who have heavily and exclusively overvalued abstractness in our picture of reality, even to the point of synonymizing them, had better redress the balance by stressing concrete, esthetic, phenomenological, non-abstracting, perceiving of *all* the aspects and details of phenomena, of the full richness of reality, including the useless portions of it.

FULLEST SPONTANEITY

If we are fully concentrated on the matter-in-hand, fascinated with it for its own sake, having no other goals or purposes in mind, then it is easier to be fully spontaneous, fully-functioning, letting our capacities flow forth easily from within, of themselves, without effort, without conscious volition or control, in an instinct-like automatic, thoughtless way; i.e., the fullest least obstructed, most organized action.

The one main determinant of their organization and adaptation to the matter in hand, is then most apt to be the intrinsic nature of the matter in hand. Our capacities then adapt to the situation most perfectly, quickly, effortlessly, and change flexibly as the situation changes; e.g., a painter continuously adapts himself to the demands of his developing painting; as a wrestler adapts himself to his opponent; as a pair of fine dancers mutually adapt to each other; as water flows into cracks and contours.

FULLEST EXPRESSIVENESS (OF UNIQUENESS)

Full spontaneity is a guarantee of honest expression of the nature and the style of the freely, functioning organism, and of its uniqueness. Both words, spontaneity and expressiveness, imply honesty, naturalness, truthfulness, lack of guile, non-imitativeness, etc., because they also imply a non-instrumental nature of the behavior, a lack of willful "trying," a lack of effortful striving or straining, a lack of interference with the flow of the impulses and the free "radioactive" expression of the deep person.

The only determinants now are the intrinsic nature of the matter-in-hand, the intrinsic nature of the person and the intrinsic necessities of their fluctuating adaptation to each other to form a fusion, a unit; e.g., a fine basketball team, or a string quartet. Nothing outside this fusion situation is relevant. The situation is not a means to any extrinsic end; it is an end in itself.

FUSION OF THE PERSON WITH THE WORLD

We wind up with the fusion between the person and his world which has so often been reported as an observable fact in creativeness, and which we may now reasonably consider to be a *sine qua non*. I think that this spider web of inter-relationships that I have been teasing apart and discussing can help us to understand this fusion better as a natural event, rather than as something mysterious, arcane, esoteric. I think it can even be researched if we understand it to be an isomorphism, a molding of each to each other, a better and better fitting together or complementarity, a melting into one.

It has helped me to understand what Hokusai meant when he said "If you want to draw a bird, you must become a bird."

1. Laski, M. *Ecstasy*. London: Cresset Press, 1961.
2. Maslow, A. H. *Motivation and personality*. New York: Harper, 1954.
3. Maslow, A. H. *Toward a psychology of being*. New York: Van Nostrand, 1962.
4. Maslow, A. H. Lessons from the peak-experiences. *Journal of Humanistic Psychology*, 1962, **2**, 9–18.
5. Maslow, A. H. Notes on a psychology of being. *Journal of Humanistic Psychology*, 1962, to be published.
6. Maslow, A. H. Emotional blocks to creativity. *Journal of Individuaᶦ Psychology*, 1958, **14**, 51–56.
7. May, R. (Ed.) *Existential psychology*. New York: Random House, 1961.

What Can Man Become?

Arthur W. Combs

In his inaugural address President Kennedy said to us, "Ask not what your country can do for you. Ask, rather, what you can do for your country?"

Reprinted from *California Journal for Instructional Improvement*, 1961, **4**, 15–23, by permission of the author and the publisher.

This eloquent plea was immediately met with an answering cry from millions of Americans. "Tell us what we can do," we cried. We long for a goal to live for and die for. We long for goals that will define for us where we should stand, what we should work for, what we can commit our lives and fortunes to. These are not idle questions. They are deeply serious ones, for upon our answers to these questions will rest the outcome of the great ideological struggle in which we are now engaged. In such a struggle it is the beliefs, convictions, values we hold that will determine whether we win or lose. We simply cannot sit down at the same table to bargain with adversaries who have already decided before they begin, that they are willing to die for their beliefs unless we have an equally firm commitment. A man without conviction, engaged in discussion with one whose convictions are practically a religion, is a sitting duck to be changed. This is one of the things we learned from our research on the "brain-washed" soldiers who returned from Korea.

Well, what is our commitment? What do we stand for? Freedom, we have said, is our goal. For our forefathers this was easy to define. It was freedom from the tyranny of the British kings, freedom from religious persecution, freedom from want, freedom for the slaves. Even in our own times when we have been attacked we have risen magnificently to defend ourselves against outside aggressors. But what shall be our goals in times of peace and plenty or when outside forces do not press upon us? Goals for the have-nots are self-evident. Goals for those whose basic needs are satisfied are more difficult to define and less pressing to pursue.

REDEFINING FREEDOM IN TERMS OF BECOMING

We all recognize that meaning and character come from striving. We are most alive when happily engaged in the pursuit of a goal. Freedom, we have said, is our goal—but freedom for what? What does freedom mean in a nation of incredible wealth? It is apparent we need a redefinition of freedom translatable into action, not in a time of crisis alone, but applicable as well in times of peace and security.

We have stated our fundamental belief in democracy in these terms: "When men are free, they can find their own best ways." But what is a free man? A man with a full belly? A man without problems? A man with no pressures? Free to do as he pleases? When such things are achieved, a man is still no more than a vegetable. It is not enough to be free to *be*. We need freedom to *become*.

But what can man become? What is the ultimate in human freedom? What does it mean for a man to achieve the fullest possible fulfillment of his potentialities? This is a question which a number of psychologists, sociologists, educators, and humanitarians have been asking for a generation. What does it mean to be a fully-functioning person, operating at the highest peak of his potentialities? What does it mean to be self-actualizing, self-realizing, a truly adequate person in the fullest possible sense of the word?

It would be hard to overestimate the importance of this search. For whatever we decide is a fully functioning, self-actualizing human being must, automatically, become the goal for all of us engaged in the helping relationships. These are the kinds of people we are trying to produce. It is to produce such people that our public schools exist, and the descriptions of these people provide us with the criteria in terms of which we can measure our success or failure.

As a result of the thinking and study of scholars and researchers, little by little, the picture begins to unfold. We begin to get some inkling of what the fully functioning person is like. This is no average man they are describing. Who, after all, wants to be average? This is a Free man with a capital F. This is a goal for us to shoot for, a picture of what can be and might be. Here is a concept of a free man that lifts our sights to what, perhaps, one day man may become.

What is more, a study of the characteristics emerging from the studies provides us with a blueprint for education practice. I believe the work of these people in defining the nature of self-actualization is certainly among the most exciting steps forward in our generation. For me, it has provided new meaning in life. It provides new goals and direction for me, not just in times of crisis, but in the quiet hours between, and in my professional work as well.

I cannot discuss all of the characteristics of these fully functioning, self-actualizing people which have now been described. In the time we have here together, let me describe only two or three of these characteristics and go on to discuss what these characteristics seem to me to mean for education. Each of the characteristics of these people could be spelled out in many aspects of curriculum in terms of what we need to do to produce that kind of characteristic. In fact, this is what the 1962 ASCD Yearbook attempts to do and I recommend it to your attention when it appears.

SELF–ACTUALIZING PEOPLE SEE THEMSELVES
IN POSITIVE WAYS

Highly free people, the studies seem to show, see themselves as liked, wanted, acceptable, able, dignified, and worthy. Feeling this way about themselves, moreover, they are likely to have a deep feeling of personal security which makes it much easier to confront the emergencies of life with far less fear and trembling tnan the rest of us. They feel about themselves that they are people of dignity and worth and they *behave* as though they were. Indeed, it is in this factor of how the individual sees himself that we are likely to find the most outstanding differences between well-adjusted and poorly adjusted people. It is not the people who feel about themselves that they are liked and wanted and acceptable and able and so on who fill our jails and mental hospitals. Rather, it is those who feel themselves deeply inadequate, unliked, unwanted, unacceptable, unable, and the like.

This characteristic of fully functioning personalities, it seems to me, has at least four distinctly important implications for us in education.

In the first place, it seems to me, it means *we must regard the individual's self as a recognized part of the curriculum.* People learn who they are and what they are from the ways in which they are treated by those who surround them in the process of their growing up. What we do in class, therefore, affects the individual's ways of seeing himself whether we are aware of our impact or not. We *teach* children who they are and what they are by the kinds of experiences we provide. Many school deficiencies we now know are the result of a child's *belief* that he cannot read, write, or do math. A child may be taught that he cannot read from the impatience and frustration among those who sought to teach him.

We cannot rule the self out of the classroom, even if we wanted to. A child does not park himself at the door. The self is the dearest thing he owns, and he cannot be induced to part with it for any reason. Even a poor, ragged, and unhappy self must be dragged along wherever he goes. It is, after all, the only one he owns. The self, we now know, determines even what we see and what we hear. Right now in this audience as you listen to me speak, you are judging, determining, deciding about what I am saying, and you will carry away from here only that which, for one reason or another, has basically affected your very personal self.

For some time now it has been a part of our education in philosophy that we need to be concerned about the learner as well as the subject.

Consequently, we have emphasized the importance of the child in the process and have developed a so-called, child-centered school. Indeed, we have sometimes carried this so far that the general public has sometimes become concerned lest we get so involved in understanding the child that we forget to teach him something!

Sometimes this has been expressed in the question, "Are you educating for intellect or educating for adjustment?" Such a dichotomy is, of course, ridiculous. Surely, we are not seeking to produce either smart psychotics, on the one hand, nor well-adjusted dopes, on the other! The fact of the matter is, we simply cannot separate what an individual learns from the nature of the individual himself. Indeed, we do not have to. This is nicely demonstrated in a recent experiment by Staines in New Zealand.

As you know, at the end of the fourth year under the British system children take an examination which determines the direction of their educational program from that point on. Staines studied two groups of fourth-grade children preparing for these examinations. One group was taught by a teacher who paid no attention to the self-concepts of the children. The other class was taught by a teacher who was simply aware of and thinking about the self-concepts of the children, although he did nothing specifically planned to make changes in these matters. At the end of the year the two groups of children did about equally well on the academic aspects of the examination they took.

The adjustment level of the children in the two grades, however, was quite different. Adjustment levels in the classes taught by the teacher who was interested in the youngsters' self-concepts rose, while the adjustment level of the youngsters taught by the teacher who had ignored this factor actually decreased. Being concerned about the child's self-concept does not mean in any sense of the word that it is necessary for us to teach him any less.

Learning, itself, is a highly personal matter. Whether or not any given piece of information will be really learned by a youngster, we now know, is dependent upon whether or not he has discovered the personal meaning of that bit of information for him. It is the personal feeling I have about information, the personal commitment I have with respect to it that determines whether or not I behave differently as a result of having that information. Learning is not the cold, antiseptic examination of facts we once considered it. This is perhaps nowhere better illustrated than in the matter of dietetics. Dietitians have at their fingertips vast stores of information about what people *ought* to eat. Even you and I who are far less well informed know a good deal about what we ought to eat—but don't eat that! We go right on eating what we *want* to eat and *like* to eat, in spite of our information about the matter, until one day we cannot get into our favorite dress or a son says, "Gee, Mom, you're getting fat" or when, perhaps, like me, you visit your doctor for your annual check-up and, poking his finger in your stomach, he says, "Blubber! Sheer blubber!" Then, suddenly the information you have had all along takes on a new meaning and may even, just possibly, begin to affect your behavior.

Learning only happens to people. To ignore the presence of the person in the process simply runs the risk of failing to accomplish anything of very much importance. We cannot afford to ignore this important aspect of our problem. To do so runs the risk of making ourselves ineffective. The self is a part of the learning process and to ignore it is about as silly as saying, "I know my car needs a carburetor to run, but I think I'll run mine without one!"

Since the self is what matters to each of us, if we cast this out of school, we run the serious danger of teaching children that school is only about things that don't matter. If we are totally preoccupied with teaching subject matter, we may miss entirely the child to whom we are trying to teach it. We are all familiar with the examination time "boners." These represent the way the things we taught were seen by those whom we tried to teach.

Secondly, it seems to me, *the need for people who see themselves positively means that whatever diminishes the child's self has no place in education.* Humiliation, degradation, and failure are destructive to the self. It is commonly assumed in some places that shame and guilt are good for people, but this is rarely true, for the people who feel these things the most are the people who need them least.

Whatever makes the self smaller and meaner is not just bad for mental health. It undermines confidence and produces fear and withdrawal. It cuts down freedom of movement, the possibilities of intelligent behavior. What diminishes the self is stupefying and stultifying. Such people are a drag on the rest of us. Even worse are those who see themselves in negative terms as unliked, unwanted, unacceptable, unable, undignified, unworthy, and so on. These are the dangerous people of our society.

A positive self calls for success experience for everyone. People learn they *can* by succeeding, not by failing. There is a general feeling abroad in some places that failure is good for people, but nothing could be further from the truth. Self-actualizing people see themselves in positive ways, and you do not get this from having failures. If we teach a child he is a failure, we have no one to blame but ourselves if he comes to believe us and after that behaves so.

I do not believe it is an accident that for most children, after the third grade, there is very little variation in their grades for the rest of the time they are in school. It is as though, by the time a child reaches the third grade, he has discovered what his quota is, and after that he lives up to it. One learns he is *able* only from his successes. Even the "self-made man" who beats his chest and says, "What a fine fellow I am! I came up the hard way. Kids ought to have it hard," got this way precisely because he did *not* fail. He is a walking example of the man who did not fail.

But failure and success are feelings. They have to do with how the person to whom something happens sees the situation, not how it seems to those who look on from the outside. Success or failure does not happen unless the individual thinks it so. If a child believes he has failed, it doesn't make much difference whether other people think so or not. The important thing is what *he* believes, not what someone else does.

The provision of success for all students obviously calls for widespread curricula changes. Some sixty years ago we decided to educate everyone in this country, but we are still a long ways from discovering how to carry that out. We are still spending vast amounts of money, time, and energy trying to find ways to treat everyone alike. This, despite the fact that the most outstanding thing we know about human beings is that they are almost infinitely different. We are still providing many children with experiences of failure and self-reduction, not because we want to but because we seek to force them into a common mold which they do not fit.

We must provide for individual differences. We have talked now for a generation or more about individual differences, but we have made only a little progress in this direction. We see little in our elementary schools, practically none in our secondary schools, and in our colleges we are not even sure it is a good idea in the first place. Despite all our talk about individual differences we still continue to insist upon group goals and standards, to organize our schools around age groups with thirty students to a class. Many teachers are fearful and insecure when they leave the familiar territory of the textbook or traditional methods and the familiar lock-step of lecture, recitation, and grades. Even our beautiful new buildings are often no more than a dull series of similar boxes, light and airy and cheerful to be sure, but still designed for fixed-size groups.

What would it mean, I ask myself, if we were to organize in such a fashion as to *really* give each child an experience of success? We have talked about it, discussed it, even advocated it on occasion, but mostly we have been too timid and fearful to put it into effect.

The plain fact of the matter is we often impose failure on students by the kind of structure upon which we insist. Many a child in our large modern high school gets lost in the shuffle. What high school teacher can know all 300 students drifting through his class in the course of the day? Adolescence is lonely enough without further subjecting the child to this kind of experience.

We have decided that rich curricula require schools of large size. But people can and do get lost in large schools, and we run the risk of losing on the bananas what we made on the oranges. I recall the snow sculpture standing on the lawn of one of our dormitories at Syracuse University some years ago, a kind of cartoon in 3-D. It had a freshmen student jauntily walking into the University on one side and walking out the other side was, not a student, but an IBM card fully equipped with diploma and all his holes in the right places!

Surely it must be possible to organize our schools in such a way that somebody, somewhere in a junior or senior high school, is in contact with a child for a sufficiently long time to really get to know him. Guidance counselors who see him only an hour or two each semester are no solution. There is no substitute for the classroom teacher. The guidance function cannot be turned over to specialists. One good reason for this is the fact that adolescents simply do not take their problems to strangers. Adolescence is a deeply sensitive time of life, and the persons such children seek out for help are those with whom they have a continuing contact and that usually means a teacher, not a specialist. Some of the world's best guidance is done by coaches, advisers of the HiY, and even by the detention room keeper. The responsibility for knowing and understanding a child cannot be sloughed off. It remains the primary responsibility of the classroom teacher.

We must apply our criteria for self-actualization to every educational experience. Truly free, self-actualizing, fully-functioning people, we are told, are people who see themselves as liked, wanted, acceptable, able, dignified, worthy, and so on. Seeing oneself like this, however, is something one learns as a result of his experience during the years of his growing up. People *learn* that they are liked, wanted, acceptable, able from the things that happen to them and from the important people in their lives. In these statements we find the criteria for what we need to do in order to produce freer, more fully functioning people for our society. Let us apply these criteria to every aspect of educational experience. Let us ask about this school, this program, this policy, this method, this action, plan, or curriculum—does this help our students to feel more liked, wanted, acceptable, able, dignified, worthy, important, and so on? I have tried this with my own classes at the University with fascinating results. It has led me in some cases to reject time-honored methods and procedures. In others, it corroborated things I have known and believed for a long time. But perhaps best of all, it has led me in new directions, to new techniques, new principles. It has not always been easy, for sometimes I have had to give up cherished beliefs, to tread on unfamiliar paths with fear and trembling. Sometimes, even, I have gotten into trouble. I can only conclude, however, that despite the difficulties and tribulations the experimenting has been eminently worthwhile, and certainly never dull!

It is necessary for us to learn how things seem to our pupils. To produce the kinds of people the experts tell us we need and to do the kinds of things we have been talking about here require that we learn to understand how things look from the point of view of our students. Since students behave just as we do, according to how things seem to them, it follows that it is necessary for us to learn how things seem to our pupils. This, however, is not easy for two reasons: We have been taught for so long the importance of being objective, "of getting the facts," that for many of us it is a difficult thing to give up this scientific way of looking. On the other hand, how things seem to each of us seems so right and so *so* that it is a very difficult thing to understand that it may not be. Indeed the way things seem to us seems so certain that when other people do not see them the way we do we jump to either one of two conclusions: Either they must be very stupid or they are simply being perverse. Phyllis McGinley once expressed it very nicely when she said,

I think we must give up the fiction
That we can argue any view
For what in me is pure conviction
Is simply prejudice in you!

We need to develop a sensitivity to how things seem to the people with whom we are working. For a long time we have advocated in teacher-training institutions the idea that teachers need to understand the child. What has often happened, however, is that we have confused understanding *about* a child with understanding the child *himself*. Even when I know a great deal about human growth and development I may fail to understand a given child. When I have made a careful study of him, when I have interviewed his parents, searched his school records, looked over his health and physical records, tested and examined him fore and aft, I still may not understand him. I do not really understand him until I have learned to see how he sees himself and how he sees the world in which he lives. All this information about him will be of limited value until I have come to understand the way he sees things in his private world of meaning and feeling. There is a world of difference between understanding a *person* and understanding *about* him.

The kind of understanding we are talking about here is not a *knowledge about*, but a *sensitivity* to people. It is a kind of empathy, the ability to put oneself in another's shoes, to feel and see as he does. All of us have this ability to some extent, but good teachers have a lot of it.

In some research we have been carrying on at the University of Florida we find that we cannot tell the difference between good teachers and poor teachers on the basis of the methods they use. One of the differences that does seem to exist, however, between good and poor ones has to do with this question of sensitivity. Good teachers seem to be much more sensitive to how things seem to the people with whom they are working. In fact, this sensitivity seems so important that apparently intelligent people who have it can do pretty well at teaching without any instruction in methods whatever. With such sensitivity they find their own methods. On the other hand, equally intelligent people with much instruction in methods may do very badly because they are unable to assess the effect of their methods upon the people they are trying to teach.

SELF–ACTUALIZING PEOPLE ARE OPEN TO THEIR EXPERIENCE

Let us turn now to a second characteristic of these highly self-actualizing, fully functioning personalities. All such people seem to be characterized by a high degree of openness to their experience. That is to say, they are people who are able to look at themselves and the world about them openly and without fear. They are able to see themselves accurately and realistically. Psychologists have sometimes called this the capacity for "acceptance" by which they seem to mean the ability to confront evidence.

Highly self-actualizing people seem to have such a degree of trust in themselves that they are able to look at any and all data without the necessity for defending themselves or distorting events in ways they would like them to be. They are able to accept the facts about the world and about themselves, and because they are able to do this, they are people with a high degree of autonomy. They are free wheelers able to move off in new directions, and this of course is what is meant by creativity. Believing and trusting in themselves, they are able to move out in new directions. What is more, because they are more open to data they are much more likely to have right answers than other people and consequently are much more likely to behave intelligently and efficiently than are the rest of us.

Self-actualizers enjoy exploring; then enjoy discovering. They are not thrown by their experience or defensive against it. They are able to accept what is and to deal with it effectively. Please note that acceptance in the sense we are using it here means the willingness to confront data. It does not mean that acceptance and resignation are synonymous. Because an individual is willing to say, "Yes, it is true I am a stinker," does not mean that he is necessarily resigned to that fact!

This capacity for acceptance, trust in oneself, and openness to experience points to at least three important principles for us in educational practice.

The kind of openness to experience we have been talking about calls for rich opportunities for individuals to explore and test themselves. Such openness comes from opportunities to permit oneself to get involved in events. Like learning to swim, one needs sufficient help to be sure that he does not drown. On the other hand, one can *never* learn to swim if he never goes near the water. Such openness to experience comes about as a consequence of being sufficiently secure where one is that he is able to branch out into new events with courage and determination. This is the road to creativity, so needed in this generation.

One cannot be creative, however, without opportunities to get into difficulties. Indeed, it has been said that the characteristic of genius is the enjoyment of getting into difficulties for the sheer pleasure of getting out of them. Creativity calls for breaking with tradition, going out in the blue, trying one's wings, breaking out of the established ruts. Creativity is bound to be accompanied with a high amount of disorder. A creative class will not be a quiet one, and a rigidly ordered class will not be a creative one. An overemphasis upon order, procedure, custom, tradition, the "right" may actually destroy the kind of openness we are talking about.

This is a strange profession we are in. It is a profession built upon right answers. We pay off on right answers and discourage wrong ones at every level of the teaching profession. Now it is certainly a good thing to be right, but if we are so preoccupied with "being right" that we have no room for people to make mistakes, we may rob them of their most important learning experience. People learn from their mistakes. Some of the most important learnings that most of us have ever had probably came about as a consequence of our mistakes, much more than those instances where we were right.

The fear of making mistakes is almost a disease of our profession. However, an overemphasis on the importance of being right and insistence upon perfection may boomerang to discourage people from trying at all. We need a great deal more freedom to look, to try, to experiment, to explore, to talk about, to discuss. We need to open up our curricula to things we do not grade for. This was beautifully stated by a little boy in the fifth grade who wrote to his teacher after they had had a discussion about love in his classroom: "I was very surprised when we talked in our class about love yesterday. I learned a lot of things and I found out about how lots of others feel. But I was surely surprised because I never knew you could talk about things in school that you didn't get grades for."

The kind of openness called for by the experts requires of us that we help young people to cut loose from dependency far earlier than they do. One of the criticisms we hear most often these days about our public schools is that we are producing a generation of irresponsibles. Like many of the criticisms leveled against us, I do not believe it is by any means as serious as that. I do believe, however, there is a germ of truth to be given some real consideration. The continued extension of childhood, characteristic of every phase of our modern life, tends to keep young people dependent far longer than they need be. Most of this dependency comes about as a consequence of our fear that young people may make mistakes if we set them free. The kind of openness characteristic of self-actualization, however, does not come about as a consequence of increased dependency. Quite the contrary, it comes about as a consequence of responsibility.

There are some who feel the setting up of a separate society by our adolescents is a consequence of this fear. The word "teenager" is practically a cuss word in our society. We simply do not like teenagers. They are permitted no real worthwhile place. We have built a world where there is little or no opportunity for them to have any feeling that they belong or are part of the larger society in which they live. They have little or no voice in what happens to them. They long for a feeling of importance and meaning, something to commit themselves to.

But the usual adult approach to these young people is to build them a new playground or Teen-Town where they are told to "go and play" some more. The plain fact of the matter is they are often an embarrassment to us. Consequently, we treat them as outsiders. It should not surprise us then if they build their own society. Look around you, and you will see that that is precisely what they have done—with their own language, their own customs, traditions, codes of values, even their own music, ways of dress, and symbols of status and prestige. They have done this because we have made no real place for them in our society.

This kind of separation of young people from their culture has the potentiality for great danger. They are people who do not feel they belong, do not feel under any necessity to pay their dues or look out for the members. Membership in a society is not felt by those who are cast out from it. Feelings of belonging and responsibility come about only as a consequence of feeling a part of and being given responsibility for other people.

Responsibility and independence, we need to remind ourselves, are not learned from having these things withheld. Take the case of the teacher who believes her class, for example. The teacher leaves her class telling the group, "I am going down to the office for a few minutes. I want you to be good kids until I get back." She goes to the office and returns to find the room in bedlam. Seeing this, she enters the room and says to her youngsters, "I will never leave you alone again!" If she means this, she has thereby robbed these youngsters of their only opportunity to learn how to behave when the teacher is not there. You cannot learn how to behave when the teacher is not there if the teacher never leaves you!

We do the same thing in the high school with student government. We are so afraid the youngsters might make a wrong decision that we do not let them make any. Whenever they make a decision, we veto that, and it doesn't take long before they get the idea that student government is only a game. Having come to this conclusion, they then tend to treat it like a game, and this infuriates us. We then cry out in despair, "See there, they do not even treat their government as anything but a game!" Perhaps, if they treat it like a game, we have no one to blame but ourselves for teaching them that that is what it is. In order to try one's wings there must be freedom of movement and opportunity to look and explore. If the fears of adults prevent this exploration, we have no one but ourselves to blame.

Let us not be misled by the cries of the young people themselves in this connection. I have often had teachers say to me, "But I want to give them responsibility and they don't want to take it!" This, of course, is often true, but should not discourage us from giving youngsters responsibility. It is only another indication that they are fearful of it because they had so little successful experience with it. The youngster who has not had much responsibility is quite likely to be frightened by having a large dose given to him before he is ready to assimilate it.

The rules of readiness that apply to everything else we know in education apply to learning about responsibility as well. Opportunities have to be paced to capacities. Readiness and capacity, however, are achieved from experience. You cannot expect a child to read if you never let him try, and you cannot expect him to be responsible without some successful experience with it. This is beautifully illustrated in the two old sayings: "If you want something done, get a busy man to do it" and "The rich get richer and the poor get poorer."

WHEN MEN ARE FREE, THEY FIND THEIR OWN WAYS

It is a basic principle of democracy that "when men are free, they can find their own best ways." Modern psychology tells us that in each of us there is a deep and never-ending drive to become the very most we can. Despite the assurances of the psychologists about man's basic nature and the beliefs we ourselves so glibly state about the nature of democracy, nevertheless, most of us still approach children with serious doubts and misgivings. We don't *really* believe they can find their own best ways if we provide the proper conditions.

Recently I have been reading A. S. Neill's fascinating book, *Summerhill*. This is a description of a school in England run by a headmaster who believes in giving children freedom, even to the extent of deciding for themselves whether they will go to class at all. (They do!) The lengths he has gone to in giving personal responsibility are fascinating, even shocking, to many people. Certainly he goes far beyond what I have been willing to do in my teaching. The fascinating thing is this: He has been doing this for forty years *and it works!* Here is a living demonstration that individual freedom can work, that we do not need to be afraid as we have been, that maybe, if we can really have the courage to try, it will work out all right.

In recent years I have been trying to place more responsibility and trust in my students. One thing I have done is to use a method of grading that places most of the responsibility for planning, study, and evaluation on the student. This has been much criticized by my colleagues, but the results it gets in more and better work, in individual commitment, in increased freedom for the student, in more reading and thought and effort are well worth the price. Besides, as one of my students expressed it, "Well, Dr. Combs, sure, some students take advantage of your method of grading, but then the old method took advantage of the student!"

The production of openness and responsibility in students requires courage and trust on the part of teachers. If we ourselves are afraid to try and let others try, if we are so fearful they may make mistakes, we may rob them of their most priceless opportunities to learn and will defeat ourselves as well. We need to remind ourselves of Roosevelt's "The only thing we have to fear is fear itself."

WHEN AN INDIVIDUAL FINDS INNER SECURITY, HE CAN BECOME OPEN TO HIS EXPERIENCE

The kind of openness characteristic of the truly adequate, full functioning personality the experts are describing for us comes about as a consequence of the individual's own feeling of security in himself. It is a product of his feeling that he is important, that he counts, that he is a part of the situation and the world in which he is moving. This feeling is created by the kind of atmosphere in which he lives and works. It is encouraged by atmospheres we are able to create in the classroom and the halls and laboratories that help young people to develop a feeling of trust in themselves.

What causes a person to feel outside undermines and destroys his feelings of trust. Differences must be respected and encouraged, not merely tolerated. As Earl Kelley has told us, the goal of education must be the increasing uniqueness of people, not increasing likeness. It is the flowering of individuality we seek, not the production of automatons. This means differences of all kinds must be encouraged, appreciated, valued. Segregation is not only socially undesirable; it is demoralizing and diminishing as well. We need to remind ourselves there is segregation on a thousand other bases than segregation of white and Negro that can equally as well get in our way. There is segregation, too, on the basis of age, social status, athletic prowess, dress, language, and religion, to name but a few.

The kind of openness we seek in the free personality requires a trust in self, and this means, to me, we need to change the situations we sometimes find in our teaching where the impression is given the student that all the answers worth having lie "out there." I believe it is necessary for us to recognize that the only important answers are those which the individual has within himself, for these are the only ones that will ever show up in his behavior. Consequently, the classroom must be a place where children explore "what I believe, what I think, what seems to me to be so" as well as what other people think and believe and hold to be true.

Since most human behavior is the product of beliefs, values, and convictions, it is these values that must make up a larger and larger part of our educational experience. We have been in the grip of a concept of teaching that worships objectivity for a long time now. Objectivity is of value to be sure, but objectivity requires looking at events with cold and dispassionate regard. People simply do not behave objectively. They behave in terms of their feelings, attitudes, and convictions even about the most scientific matters. I can be objective about your child; I cannot be objective about my own! The things that affect my behavior most importantly and most closely are those things in the realm of values and beliefs. An education system which does not permit me to explore these or which regards these vital aspects of life as unimportant or inadmissible to the classroom runs the risk of making itself an esthetic exercise valuable to only a few, having little to do with life, and making little impact upon the generations it hopes to affect.